Microsoft® Windows™ Guide to Programming

New for Version 3

Written, edited, and produced by
Microsoft Corporation

Distributed by Microsoft Press

MICROSOFT®
WINDOWS™
PROGRAMMER'S
REFERENCE
LIBRARY

PUBLISHED BY
Microsoft Press
A Division of Microsoft Corporation
One Microsoft Way, Redmond, Washington 98052-6399

Library of Congress Cataloging-in-Publication Data

Microsoft Windows : a guide to programming / Microsoft Corporation.
p. cm. -- (Microsoft Windows programmer's reference library)
Includes index.
ISBN 1-55615-308-2
1. Microsoft Windows (Computer programs) I. Microsoft.
II. Series.
QA76.76.W56M53 1990
005.4'3--dc20 90-6035
CIP

Printed and bound in the United States of America.

2 3 4 5 6 7 8 9 FGFG 4 3 2 1 0

Distributed to the book trade in Canada by General Publishing Company, Ltd.
Distributed to the book trade outside the United States and Canada
by Penguin Books Ltd.
Penguin Books Ltd., Harmondsworth, Middlesex, England
Penguin Books Australia Ltd., Ringwood, Victoria, Australia
Penguin Books N.Z. Lyd., 182-190 Wairau Road, Auckland 10, New Zealand

Document No. SY03146-300-R00-1089

Foreword

The *Microsoft Windows Programmer's Reference Library* is the core documentation for Windows programmers that Microsoft provides with the Microsoft® Windows™ Software Development Kit (SDK). The information in these books is the most accurate and up-to-date information on Windows programming available anywhere. The information represents everything Microsoft knows about programming Windows version 3.0 with Microsoft C (the recommended Windows programming language) and the tools we provide in the SDK.

Certain example programs and tools referred to in this book are available only in the Microsoft Windows SDK or Microsoft C 6.0 Professional Development System. However, if you are not currently programming for Windows, these volumes will still provide an excellent overview of the services that Microsoft Windows and the SDK provide to programmers—*Microsoft Windows: A Guide to Programming* and *Microsoft Windows Programming Tools* in particular—and an introduction to graphical user interface (GUI) programming. It is our hope that once you have "kicked the tires" of the Windows SDK by reading these books, you'll be thoroughly convinced—and already prepared—to begin Windows programming the Microsoft way.

Then as you continue to explore the Windows programming environment, *Microsoft Windows Programmer's Reference* will answer many of your programming questions. The book provides information on each Windows application programming interface (API) and describes its calls and services. For many Windows programmers, this book is the most frequently "thumbed," dog-eared, and marked-up volume in the set.

The Microsoft Windows Software Development Kit is available from your Microsoft product dealer. For further information on the Windows SDK or to obtain the name of your nearest Microsoft dealer, call the Microsoft Information Center at 1-800-426-9400.

The Windows Software Development Kit

The Windows high-level application programming interface consists of the functions, messages, data structures, data types, and files you need to develop applications that unleash the full capabilities of personal computers using Intel® 286 and 386™ processors. The API's device independence ensures compatibility with a broad array of displays, printers, and other devices, allowing you to concentrate on your applications and their features and implementation. Development tasks are handled automatically, and advanced tools enable you to design icons, dialog boxes, fonts, menus, and other interface elements.

Here are some of the new or improved features:

- Improved and comprehensive *Guide to Programming*, *Advanced Interface Design Guide*, *Reference*, and *Tools* manuals.
- More source-code examples for hands-on learning.
- Improved tools for editing visual resources.
- New online help-engine facility so you can include a Help system with your applications.
- The Microsoft CodeView® for Windows debugger—the powerful yet easy-to-use source-code debugger for any Windows application.
- New code-execution profiler and segment-swapping analysis facility.

Take advantage of the success of the Microsoft Windows environment—use the Microsoft Windows Software Development Kit to develop powerful, feature-rich graphical applications.

Other Recommended Reading

The following books are recommended for efficient Windows programming and are available from Microsoft Press™:

- *Programming Windows*. Charles Petzold. 862 pages, softcover. An updated second edition will be available in October 1990.
- *Windows: Programmer's Problem Solver*. Richard Wilton. 400 pages, softcover. Available November 1990.
- *Microsoft C Run-Time Library Reference*. Covers version 6. Microsoft Corporation. 852 pages, softcover.

Table of Contents

Introduction

PART 1 Introduction to Writing Windows Applications

Chapter 1 An Overview of the Windows Environment

Chapter 2 A Generic Windows Application

PART 2 Programming Windows Applications

Chapter 3 Output to a Window

Chapter 4 Keyboard and Mouse Input

Chapter 12 Printing

Chapter 13 The Clipboard

PART 3 Advanced Programming Topics

Chapter 14 C and Assembly Language

Chapter 17 Print Settings

Chapter 18 Fonts

Chapter 19 Color Palettes

Chapter 20 Dynamic-Link Libraries

Chapter 22 Dynamic Data Exchange

Tables

Introduction

This introduction provides some background information that you should review before you use this guide.

This introduction covers the following topics:

- Things you should know before you start
- The purpose and contents of this guide
- Tools you'll need to create Windows applications
- Using the sample applications described in this guide
- Notational conventions used throughout this guide
- The manuals that come with the Microsoft® Windows™ Software Development Kit (SDK)

What Should You Know Before You Start?

To start using this guide, you will need the following:

- Experience using Windows and an understanding of the Windows user interface.

  Before starting any Windows application development, you should install Windows version 3.0 on your computer and learn how to use it. Be sure to learn the names, purposes, and operation of the various parts of a Windows application (such as windows, dialog boxes, menus, controls, and scroll bars). Because your own Windows applications will incorporate these features, it is very important for you to understand them so that you can implement them properly.

- An understanding of the Windows user-interface style guidelines.

  One goal of Microsoft Windows is to provide a common user interface for all applications. This ultimately helps the user by reducing the effort required to learn the user interface of a Windows application; it helps you by clarifying the choices you have to make when designing a user interface. To achieve this goal, however, you must base your application's user interface design on the recommended application style guidelines described in the *System Application Architecture, Common User Access: Advanced Interface Design Guide*.

- Experience writing C-language programs and using the standard C run-time functions.

The C programming language is the preferred development language for Windows applications. Many of the programming features of Windows were designed with the C programmer in mind. (Windows applications can also be developed in Pascal and assembly language, but these languages present additional challenges that you typically bypass when writing applications in the C language.)

About This Guide

This guide is intended to help the experienced C programmer make the transition to writing applications that use the Microsoft Windows version 3.0 application program interface. It explains how to use Windows functions, messages, and data structures to carry out useful tasks common to all Windows applications, and illustrates these explanations with sample applications that you can compile and run with Windows version 3.0.

This guide consists of three parts, each of which contain several chapters.

Part 1, "Introduction to Writing Windows Applications," gives an overview of the Windows environment, and provides an in-depth look at a sample Windows application. Part 1 consists of the following chapters:

- Chapter 1, "An Overview of the Windows Environment," compares Windows to the standard C environment, provides a brief overview of Windows, and describes the Windows programming model and the Windows application-development process.
- Chapter 2, "A Generic Windows Application," shows how to create a simple Windows application called Generic. You'll then use this application as a basis for subsequent examples in this learning guide.

Part 2, "Programming Windows Applications," explains basic Windows programming tasks, such as creating menus, printing, and using the clipboard. Each chapter covers a specific topic, and provides a sample application that illustrates that topic. Part 2 consists of the following chapters:

- Chapter 3, "Output to a Window," introduces the graphics device interface (GDI) and shows how to use GDI tools to create your own output.
- Chapter 4, "Keyboard and Mouse Input," shows how to process input from the mouse and keyboard.
- Chapter 5, "Icons," shows how to create and display icons for your applications.
- Chapter 6, "The Cursor, the Mouse, and the Keyboard," explains the purpose of the cursor, the mouse, and the keyboard, and shows how to use them in your applications.

- Chapter 7, "Menus," shows how to create menus for your applications and how to process input from menus.
- Chapter 8, "Controls," explains how to create and use controls, such as push buttons and list boxes.
- Chapter 9, "Dialog Boxes," explains how to create and use dialog boxes, and how to fill them with controls.
- Chapter 10, "File Input and Output," explains the **OpenFile** function, as well as rules about disk files.
- Chapter 11, "Bitmaps," shows how to create and display bitmaps.
- Chapter 12, "Printing," shows how to use a printer with Windows.
- Chapter 13, "The Clipboard," explains the clipboard and shows how to use it in your applications.

Part 3, "Advanced Programming Topics," introduces and explains some advanced topics, such as memory management and Dynamic Data Exchange. Each chapter covers a specific topic. Part 3 consists of the following chapters:

- Chapter 14, "C and Assembly Language," gives some guidelines for writing C-language and assembly-language Windows applications.
- Chapter 15, "Memory Management," shows how to allocate global and local memory.
- Chapter 16, "More Memory Management," provides a more in-depth look at how your application can efficiently manage memory. This chapter also explains how Windows manages memory under different memory configurations.
- Chapter 17, "Print Settings," explains how to tailor printer settings (such as page size and orientation) to your application's needs.
- Chapter 18, "Fonts," shows how to create and load fonts, and how to use them in the **TextOut** function.
- Chapter 19, "Color Palettes," shows how to use Windows color palettes to make the most effective use of color in your application.
- Chapter 20, "Dynamic-Link Libraries," explains how to create and use Windows dynamic-link libraries.
- Chapter 21, "Multiple Document Interface," explains how to create an application that uses the Windows multiple document interface (MDI) to let users work with more than one document at a time.
- Chapter 22, "Dynamic Data Exchange," explains how to pass data from one application to another using the message-based Dynamic Data Exchange protocol.

What Tools Do You Need?

To build most Windows version 3.0 applications, you'll need the following tools:

- Microsoft C Optimizing Compiler: **CL**
- Microsoft Segmented-Executable Linker: **LINK**
- Microsoft Windows Resource Compiler: **RC**
- Microsoft Windows SDKPaint: **SDKPAINT**
- Microsoft Windows Dialog Editor: **DIALOG**

To build Windows libraries and font resource files, you need the following additional tools:

- Microsoft Macro Assembler: **MASM**
- Microsoft Windows Font Editor: **FONTEDIT**

The following tools may also be useful in building and debugging Windows applications:

- Microsoft Program Maintenance Utility: **MAKE**
- Microsoft Symbolic Debugger: **SYMDEB**
- Microsoft CodeView® for Windows: **CVW**
- Microsoft Windows Profiler: **PROFILER**
- Microsoft Windows Swap: **SWAP**
- Microsoft Windows Heap Walker: **HEAPWALK**
- Microsoft Windows Spy: **SPY**

Most of these tools are provided in the Microsoft Windows Software Development Kit version 3.0. The C Compiler, the linker, the Macro Assembler, and the Program Maintenance Utility are not. All are described more fully in *Tools*.

For a list of Windows 3.0 software and hardware requirements, see the *Installation and Update Guide*.

Using the Sample Applications

The sample applications in this guide are written in the C programming language and conform to the user-interface style recommended by Microsoft for Windows applications.

The source files for all sample applications are on the Sample Source Code disk that comes with the SDK. It's a good idea to review the sample application sources while reading the corresponding descriptions in this guide. For your convenience, the subdirectories containing the sample sources are named by chapter. You can also use the sources as a basis for your own applications.

Special Terms

This guide is written for you, the Windows application developer. The word "you" can refer either to you as a developer, or, sometimes, to your application. For example:

> "You create icons, cursors, and bitmaps using the SDKPaint editor."
>
> "You can display text using the **TextOut** function."
>
> "Your application will receive a WM_PAINT message when it needs to refresh its client area."

Throughout this document, the term "user" refers not to you, the application developer, but to the person who will eventually use the applications you write. For example:

> "When the user selects the About menu item, your application displays the About dialog box."
>
> "You can display a checkmark next to a menu item to indicate that the user has selected that item."

Document Conventions

Throughout this manual, the term "DOS" refers to both MS-DOS® and PC-DOS, except when noting features that are unique to one or the other.

The following document conventions are used throughout this manual:

Convention	Description of Convention
Bold text	Bold letters indicate a specific term or punctuation mark intended to be used literally: language key words or functions (such as **EXETYPE** or **CreateWindow**), DOS commands, and command-line options (such as **/Zi**). You must type these terms and punctuation marks exactly as shown. However, the use of uppercase or lowercase letters is not always significant. For instance, you can invoke the linker by typing either **LINK**, **link**, or **Link** at the DOS prompt.
( )	In syntax statements, parentheses enclose one or more parameters that you pass to a function.
Italic text	Italic text indicates a placeholder; you are expected to provide the actual value. For example, the following syntax for the **SetCursorPos** function indicates that you must substitute values for the *X* and *Y* coordinates, separated by a comma: **SetCursorPos**(*X*, *Y*)
`Monospaced type`	Code examples are displayed in a nonproportional typeface.

`BEGIN`
.
.
.
`END`
	A vertical ellipsis in a program example indicates that a portion of the program is omitted.

Convention	Description of Convention
. . .	An ellipsis following an item indicates that more items having the same form may appear. In the following example, the horizontal ellipsis indicates that you can specify more than one *breakaddress* for the **g** command: **g** [[=*startaddress*]] [[*breakaddress*]]...
[[ ]]	Double brackets enclose optional fields or parameters in command lines and syntax statements. In the following example, *option* and *executable-file* are optional parameters of the **RC** command: **RC** [[*option*]] *filename* [[*executable-file*]]
|	A vertical bar indicates that you may enter one of the entries shown on either side of the bar. The following command-line syntax illustrates the use of a vertical bar: **DB** [[*address* | *range*]] The bar indicates that following the **DB** (Dump Bytes) command, you can specify either an *address* or a *range*.
" "	Quotation marks set off terms defined in the text.
{ }	Curly braces indicate that you must specify one of the enclosed items.
SMALL CAPITAL LETTERS	Small capital letters indicate the names of keys and key sequences, such as: ALT + SPACEBAR

Microsoft Windows Software Development Kit Documentation Set

Throughout this documentation set "SDK" refers specifically to the Microsoft Windows Software Development Kit and its contents. The SDK includes the following manuals:

Title	Contents
Installation and Update Guide	Provides an orientation to the SDK, explains how to install the SDK software, and highlights the changes for version 3.0.
Guide to Programming	Explains how to write Windows applications, and provides sample applications that you can use as templates for writing your own programs. The *Guide to Programming* also addresses some advanced Windows programming topics.
Tools	Explains how to use the software-development tools you'll need to build Windows applications, such as debuggers and specialized SDK editors.
Reference	Is a comprehensive guide to all the details of the Microsoft Windows application program interface (API). The *Reference* lists in alphabetical order all the current functions, messages, and data structures of the API, and provides extensive overviews on how to use the API.
System Application Architecture, Common User Access: Advanced Interface Design Guide	Provides guidelines and recommendations for writing programs that appear and act consistently with other Microsoft Windows applications.

Part 1

Introduction to Writing Windows Applications

Although they are usually written in the C language, Windows applications are, in many ways, very different from standard C programs. This is because, to run successfully in the Windows environment, an application must cooperate with Windows and other applications; it must yield control to Windows whenever possible, and must share system resources with Windows and other applications.

Part 1 introduces the Windows environment, and compares it to the environment in which standard C programs normally run. It also explains the basic structure of a Windows application, and describes a simple application that illustrates this structure.

After reading the chapters in Part 1, you should have a basic understanding of the Windows environment and the structure of a typical Windows application.

CHAPTERS

Chapter 1 An Overview of the Windows Environment

Microsoft Windows version 3.0 has many features that the standard DOS environment does not. Because of this, Windows applications are in some ways more complex than standard DOS programs.

This chapter covers the following topics:

- A comparison of Windows applications and standard DOS applications
- Features that the Windows environment offers, and the impact these features have on the way you develop and write applications
- The Windows programming model
- The process you use to develop Windows applications

1.1 Microsoft Windows and DOS: a Comparison

Microsoft Windows has many features that the standard DOS environment does not. For this reason, Windows applications may, at first, seem more complex than standard DOS programs. This is understandable when you consider some of the additional features that Windows offers. These include:

- A graphical user interface featuring windows, menus, dialog boxes, and controls for applications
- Queued input
- Device-independent graphics
- Multitasking
- Data interchange between applications

When writing applications for the DOS environment, most C programmers use the standard C run-time library to carry out a program's input, output, memory management, and other activities. The C run-time library assumes a standard operating environment consisting of a character-based terminal for user input and output, and exclusive access to system memory as well as to the input and output devices of the computer. In Windows, these assumptions are no longer valid. Windows applications share the computer's resources, including the CPU, with other applications. Windows applications interact with the user through a graphics-based display, a keyboard, and a mouse.

The following sections describe some of the major differences between standard DOS applications and Windows applications.

1.1.1 The User Interface

One of the principal design goals of Windows is to provide visual access to most, if not all, applications at the same time. In a multitasking environment, it is important to give all applications some portion of the screen; this ensures that the user can interact with all applications. Some systems do this by giving one program full use of the screen while other programs wait in the background. In Windows, every application has access to some part of the screen at all times.

An application shares the display with other applications by using a "window" for interaction with the user. Technically, a window is little more than a rectangular portion of the system display that the system grants use of to an application. In reality, a window is a combination of useful visual devices, such as menus, controls, and scroll bars, that the user uses to direct the actions of the application.

In the standard DOS environment, the system automatically prepares the system display for your application. Typically, it does so by passing a file handle to the application. You can then use that file handle to send output to the system display using conventional C run-time routines or DOS system calls. In Windows, you must create your own window before performing any output or receiving any input. Once you create a window, Windows provides a great deal of information about what the user is doing with the window. Windows automatically performs many of the tasks the user requests, such as moving and sizing the window.

Another advantage to developing in the Windows environment is that, in contrast to a standard C program, which has access to a single screen "surface," a Windows application can create and use any number of overlapping windows to display information in any number of ways. Windows manages the screen for you, controls the placement and display of windows, and ensures that no two applications attempt to access the same part of the system display at the same time.

1.1.2 Queued Input

One of the biggest differences between Windows applications and standard C programs is the way they receive user input.

In the DOS environment, a program reads from the keyboard by making an explicit call to a function, such as **getchar**. The function typically waits until the user presses a key before returning the character code to the program. In contrast, in the Windows environment, Windows receives all input from the keyboard, mouse, and timer, and places the input in the appropriate application's "message queue." When the application is ready to retrieve input, it simply reads the next input message from its message queue.

In the standard DOS environment, input is typically in the form of 8-bit characters from the keyboard. The standard input functions, **getchar** and **fscanf**, read characters from the keyboard and return ASCII or other codes corresponding to the keys pressed. A program can also intercept interrupts from input devices such as the mouse and timer to use information from those devices as input.

In Windows, an application receives input in the form of "input messages" that Windows sends it. A Windows input message contains information that far exceeds the type of input information available in the standard DOS environment. It specifies the system time, the position of the mouse, the state of the keyboard, the scan code of the key (if a key is pressed), the mouse button pressed, as well as the device generating the message. For example, there are two keyboard messages, WM_KEYDOWN and WM_KEYUP, that correspond to the press and release of a specific key. With each keyboard message, Windows provides a device-independent virtual-key code that identifies the key, the device-dependent scan code generated by the keyboard, as well as the status of other keys on the keyboard, such as SHIFT, CONTROL, and NUMLOCK. Keyboard, mouse, and timer messages all have the same format and are all processed in the same manner.

1.1.3 Device-Independent Graphics

In Windows, you have access to a rich set of device-independent graphics operations. This means your application can easily draw lines, rectangles, circles, and complex regions. Because Windows provides device independence, you can use the same functions to draw a circle on a dot-matrix printer or a high-resolution graphics display.

Windows requires "device drivers" to convert graphics output requests to output for a printer, plotter, display, or other output device. A device driver is a special executable library that an application can load and connect to a specific output device and port. A "device context" represents the device driver, the output device, and perhaps the communications port. Your application carries out graphics operations within the "context" of a specific device.

1.1.4 Multitasking

Windows is a multitasking system: more than one application can run at a time. In the standard DOS environment, there are no particular provisions for multitasking. Programs written for the DOS environment typically assume that they have exclusive control of all resources in the computer, including the input and output devices, memory, the system display, and even the CPU itself. In Windows, however, applications must share these valuable resources with all other applications that are currently running. For this reason, Windows carefully controls these resources, and requires Windows applications to use a specific program interface that guarantees Windows' control of those resources.

For example, in the standard DOS environment, a program has access to all of memory that has not been taken up by the system, by the program, or by terminate-but-stay-resident (TSR) programs. This means that programs are free to use all of available memory for whatever they like and may access memory by whatever method they like.

In Windows, memory is a shared resource. Since more than one application can be running at the same time, each application must cooperatively share memory to avoid exhausting the resource. Applications may allocate what they need from system memory. Windows provides two sources of memory: global memory, for large allocations, and local memory, for small allocations. To make the most efficient use of memory, Windows often moves or even discards memory blocks. This means you cannot assume that objects to which you have assigned a memory location remain where you put them. If there are several applications running, Windows may move and discard memory blocks often.

Another example of a shared resource is the system display. In the standard DOS environment, the system typically grants your application exclusive use of the system display. This means you can use the display in any manner you like, from changing the color of text and background, to changing the video mode from text to graphics. In Windows, your application must share the system display with other applications, so it must not take control of the display.

1.2 The Windows Programming Model

Most Windows applications use the following elements to interact with the user:

- Windows
- Menus
- Dialog boxes
- The message loop

The rest of this section describes these elements in detail.

1.2.1 Windows

A window is the primary input and output device of any Windows application. It is an application's only access to the system display. A window is a combination of a title bar, a menu bar, scroll bars, borders, and other features that occupy a rectangle on the system display. You specify the features you want for a window when you create the window. Windows then draws and manages the window. Figure 1.1 shows the main features of a window:

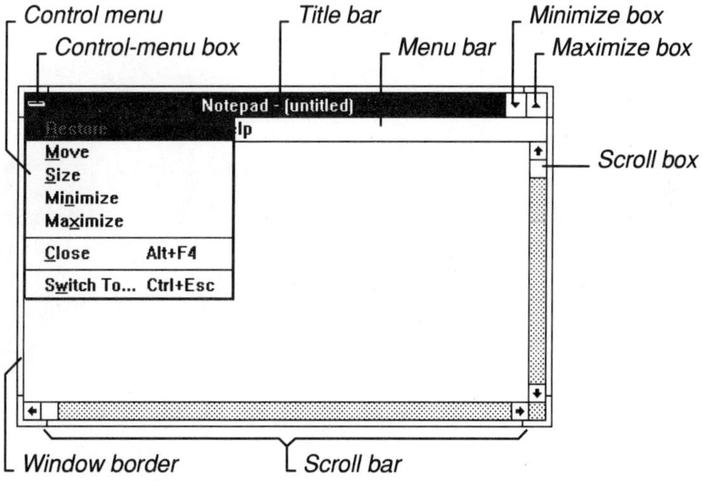

Figure 1.1 Window Features

Although an application creates a window and technically has exclusive rights to it, the management of the window is actually a collaborative effort between the application and Windows. Windows maintains the position and appearance of the window, manages standard window features such as the border, scroll bars, and title, and carries out many tasks initiated by the user that directly affect the window. The application maintains everything else about the window. In particular, the application is responsible for maintaining the "client area" of the window (the portion within the window borders). The application has complete control over the appearance of its window's client area.

To manage this collaborative effort, Windows advises each window of changes that might affect it. Because of this, every window must have a corresponding "window function." The window function receives window-management messages that it must respond to appropriately. Window-management messages either specify actions for the function to carry out, or are requests for information from the function.

1.2.2 Menus

Menus are the principal means of user input in a Windows application. A menu is a list of commands that the user can view and choose from. When you create an application, you supply the menu and command names. Windows displays and manages the menus for you, and sends a message to the window function when the user makes a choice. The message is the application's signal to carry out the command.

1.2.3 Dialog Boxes

A dialog box is a temporary window that you can display to let the user supply more information for a command. A dialog box contains one or more "controls." A control is a small window that has a very simple input or output function. For example, an "edit control" is a simple window that lets the user enter and edit text. The controls in a dialog box let the user supply filenames, choose options, and otherwise direct the action of the command.

1.2.4 The Message Loop

Since your application receives input through an application queue, the chief feature of any Windows application is the "message loop." The message loop retrieves input messages from the application queue and dispatches them to the appropriate windows.

Figure 1.2 shows how Windows and an application collaborate to process keyboard input messages. Windows receives keyboard input when the user presses and releases a key. Windows copies the keyboard messages from the system queue to the application queue. The message loop retrieves the keyboard messages, translates them into an ANSI character message, WM_CHAR, and dispatches the WM_CHAR message, as well as the keyboard messages, to the appropriate window function. The window function then uses the **TextOut** function to display the character in the client area of the window.

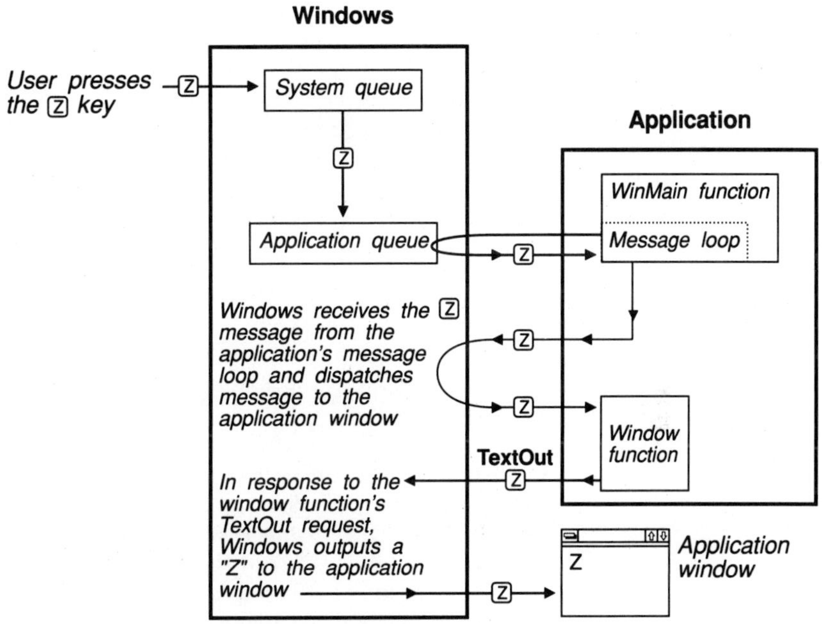

Figure 1.2 Processing Keyboard Input

Windows can receive and distribute input messages for several applications at once. As shown in Figure 1.3, Windows collects all input, in the form of messages, in its system queue. It then copies each input message to the appropriate application queue. The message loop in each application retrieves messages and dispatches them, through Windows, to each application's appropriate window function.

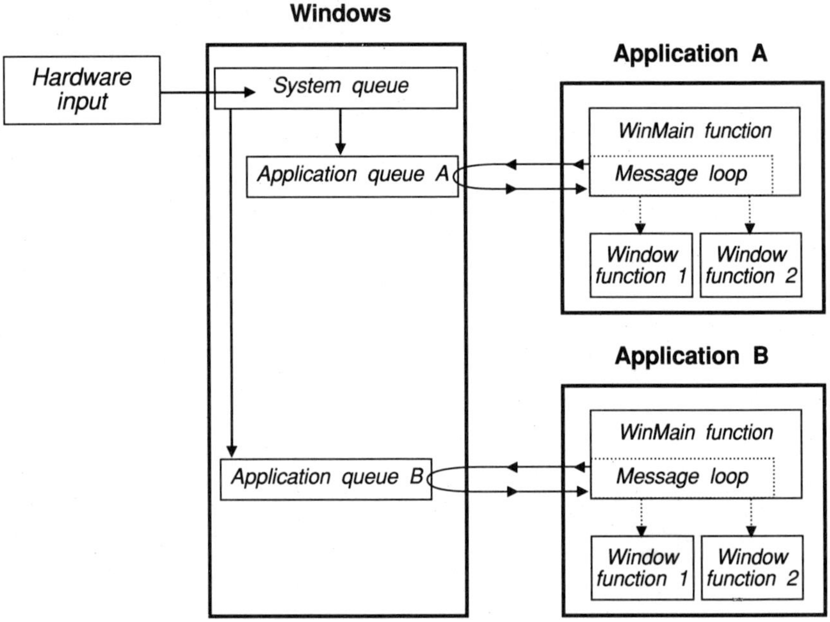

Figure 1.3 Processing Input for Two Applications

In contrast to keyboard input messages, which the application must retrieve from its message queue, Windows sends window-management messages directly to the appropriate window function. Figure 1.4 shows how Windows sends window-management messages directly to a window function. After Windows carries out a request to destroy a window, it sends a WM_DESTROY message directly to the window function, bypassing the application queue. The window function must then signal the main function that the window is destroyed and the application should terminate. It does this by copying a WM_QUIT message into the application queue by using the **PostQuitMessage** function.

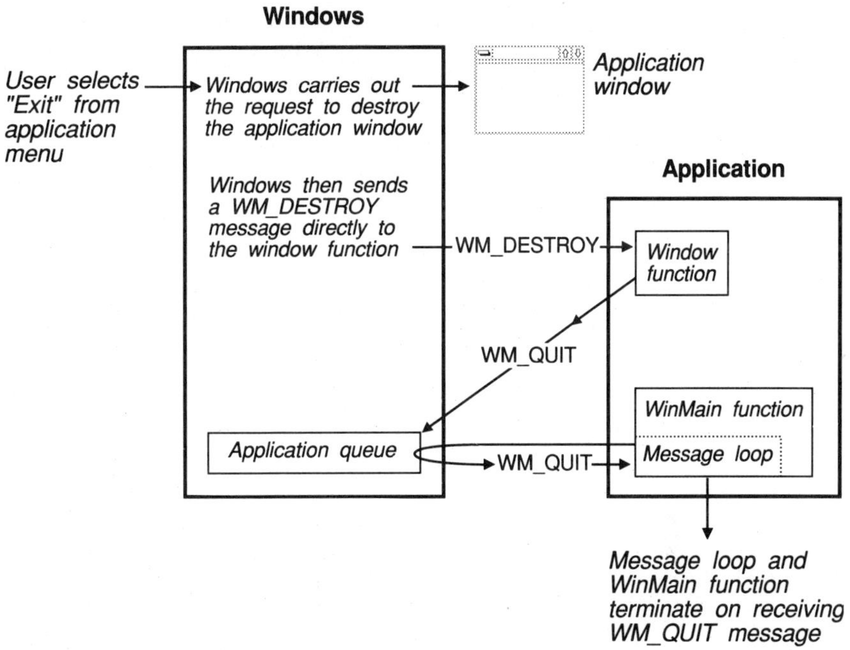

Figure 1.4 Processing Window-Management Messages

When the message loop retrieves the WM_QUIT message, the loop terminates and the main function exits.

1.3 The Windows Libraries

Windows functions, like C run-time functions, are defined in libraries. The Windows libraries, unlike C run-time libraries, are special dynamic-link libraries (DLLs) that the system links with your application when it loads your application. DLLs are an important feature of Windows because they minimize the amount of code each application requires.

Windows consists of the following three main libraries:

Library	Description
User	Provides window management. This library manages the overall Windows environment, as well as your application's windows.
Kernel	Provides system services, such as multitasking, memory management, and resource management.
GDI	Provides the graphics device interface.

1.4 Building a Windows Application

To build a Windows application, follow these steps:

1. Create C-language or assembly-language source files that contain the WinMain function, window functions, and other application code.
2. Use the resource editors (SDKPaint, the Dialog Editor, and the Font Editor) to create any cursor, icon, bitmap, dialog, and font resources the application will need.
3. Create a resource script (.RC) file that defines all the application's resources. The resource script file lists and names the resources you created in the preceding step. It also defines menus, dialog boxes, and other resources.
4. Create the module-definition (.DEF) file, which defines the attributes of the application modules, such as segment attributes, stack size, and heap size.
5. Compile and link all C-language sources; assemble all assembly-language sources.
6. Use the Resource Compiler to compile the resource script file and add it to the executable file.

Figure 1.5 shows the steps required to build a Windows application.

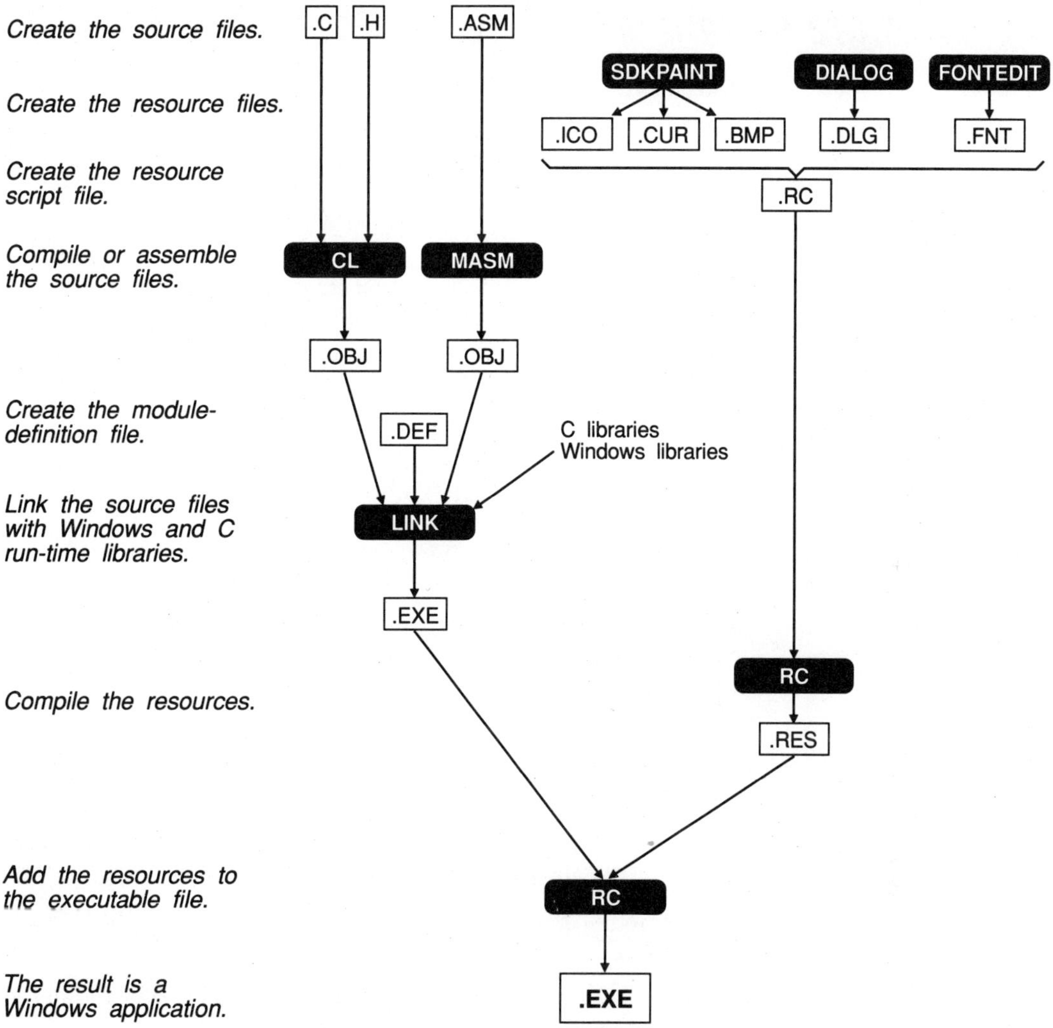

Figure 1.5 Building a Windows Application L02_05

1.5 Software Development Tools

To create a Windows application, you use many new development tools, as well as some familiar tools with new options. This section briefly describes the tools you will use.

1.5.1 C Compiler

To compile Windows applications, you use the Microsoft C Compiler, just as you do for standard C programs. You can use many of the same **CL** command-line options you use for standard C programs. However, Windows also requires two special options: **–Gw** and **–Zp**. The **–Gw** option adds the Windows prolog and epilog code to each function; this code is required for the application to run in the Windows environment. The **–Zp** option packs structures, ensuring that the structures used in your application are the same size as the corresponding structures used by Windows. The following shows a typical **CL** command for compiling a small-model Windows application:

```
CL -c -AS -Gsw -Os -Zdp TEST.C
```

The **–c** option instructs the compiler to perform only the C compilation, but not the linking. The **–c** option is necessary if you wish to compile multiple C source files separately.

1.5.2 The Linker

You use the linker supplied with the Microsoft C Compiler (**LINK**) to produce Windows-format executable files. Unlike normal C applications, Windows applications require a module-definition (.DEF) file. This file:

- Defines a name for the application.
- Marks the application as a Windows application.
- Specifies certain attributes of the application, such as whether a data segment is moveable in memory.
- Lists and names any callback functions in the application.

The following is an example of a module-definition file:

```
NAME    Generic       ; application's module name

DESCRIPTION 'Sample Microsoft Windows Application'

EXETYPE WINDOWS       ; Required for all Windows applications
```

```
STUB    'WINSTUB.EXE' ; The "stub" displays an error message if
                      ; application is run without Windows

CODE    PRELOAD MOVEABLE      ; code can be moved in memory

;DATA must be MULTIPLE if program can be invoked more than once

DATA    MOVEABLE MULTIPLE

HEAPSIZE  1024
STACKSIZE 5120  ; recommended minimum for Windows applications

; All functions that will be called by any Windows routine
; MUST be exported.

 EXPORTS
    MainWndProc    @1  ; name of window-processing function
    AboutDlgProc   @2  ; name of About processing function
```

To link a Windows application, you specify the name of the object files created by the compiler, the name of the Windows import library, the name of the module-definition file, and other options and files. The following example is a typical **LINK** command:

```
LINK /NOD GENERIC, , , SLIBCEW LIBW, GENERIC.DEF
```

For more information on **LINK** and the module-definition file, see *Tools*.

1.5.3 The SDK Resource Editors

You use the Windows resource editors to create application resources such as cursors, icons, and bitmaps. You must then list these resources in the application's resource script file. The resource editors are included in the Microsoft Windows Software Development Kit (SDK). They are:

- SDKPaint (**SDKPAINT**), which creates icons, cursors, and bitmaps
- The Dialog Editor (**DIALOG**), which creates dialog-box descriptions
- The Font Editor (**FONTEDIT**), which creates font files

Because these editors are Windows applications, you run them within the Windows environment. For more information on the Windows resource editors, see *Tools*.

1.5.4 The Resource Compiler

Most Windows applications use a variety of resources, such as icons, cursors, menus, and dialog boxes. You define these resources in a file called a "resource script file," which always has the filename extension .RC. After creating the resource script (.RC) file, you use the Resource Compiler (**RC**) to compile the .RC file and add the compiled resources to the application's executable file. When the application runs, it can load and use the resources from the executable file.

The following is an example of a resource script file that defines two resources, a cursor and an icon:

```
Bullseye CURSOR BULLSEYE.CUR
Generic ICON GENERIC.ICO
```

The first statement defines a cursor resource by naming it (Bullseye), declaring its type (CURSOR), and specifing the file that contains the actual cursor image (BULLSEYE.CUR). The second statement does the same for an icon resource.

To compile a resource script file and add the compiled resources to an executable file, use the **RC** command. The following example shows a typical **RC** command:

```
RC GENERIC.RC
```

For a description of how to use the Resource Compiler, see *Tools*. For a description of the resource statements that make up a resource script file, see the *Reference, Volume 2*.

1.5.5 Debugging and Optimization Tools

The SDK includes several tools you can use to debug your Windows application and to optimize its peformance:

- CodeView for Windows (**CVW**) lets you debug Windows applications while running with Windows in standard mode or 386 enhanced mode. **CVW** lets you set breakpoints, view source-level code, and display symbolic information while debugging Windows applications.
- The Symbolic Debugger (**SYMDEB**) is a debugging tool you can use to debug Windows applications while running in real mode.
- The Spy (**SPY**) message watcher is a Windows application that lets you monitor the messages that Windows sends to an application. This can be particularly useful when debugging.

- Profiler (**PROFILER**) lets you find out the relative times it takes your application's code segments to execute; this lets you fine-tune your application's performance.
- The Swap (**SWAP**) swapping analyzer lets you analyze and fine-tune your application's memory-swapping behavior.
- Heap Walker (**HEAPWALK**) is a Windows application that lets you examine the contents of the local or global memory heap.

For more information about these tools, see *Tools*.

1.5.6 The Program Maintainer

The **MAKE** program is a program maintainer that updates programs by keeping track of the dates of its source files. **MAKE** is included with Microsoft C version 5.1. (**NMAKE** is a similar program that comes with version 6.0 of Microsoft C.) Both programs work equally well with Windows; the one you use will depend on the version of Microsoft C you have.

Although **MAKE** and **NMAKE** come with Microsoft C, not with the SDK, they are especially important for Windows applications because of the number of files required to create a Windows application. These program maintainers use a text file, called a "make file," that contains a list of the commands and files needed to build a Windows application. The commands compile and link the various files. The program maintainer executes the commands only if the files named in those commands have changed. This saves time if, for instance, you have made only a minor change to a single file.

Make files for **MAKE** and **NMAKE** are almost identical; the only difference is that **NMAKE** requires an additional line at the beginning.

The following example shows the content of a typical make file for a Windows application:

```
# The following line allows NMAKE to use this file as well
all: generic.exe

# Update the resources if necessary

GENERIC.RES: GENERIC.RC GENERIC.H
    RC -R GENERIC.RC

# Update the object file if necessary

GENERIC.OBJ: GENERIC.C GENERIC.H
    CL -AS -c -DLINT_ARGS -Gsw -Oat -W2 -Zped GENERIC.C
```

```
# Update the executable file if necessary; if so, add the resources
to it.

GENERIC.EXE: GENERIC.OBJ GENERIC.DEF
    LINK /NOD GENERIC, , , SLIBCEW LIBW, GENERIC.DEF
    MAPSYM GENERIC
    RC GENERIC.RES

# If the .RES file is new and the .EXE file is not,
# compile only the resources. Note that the .RC file can
# be updated without having to either recompile or
# relink the file.

GENERIC.EXE: GENERIC.RES
    RC GENERIC.RES
```

Typically, make files have the same name as the applications they build, although any name is allowed. The following example runs **MAKE** using the commands in the file GENERIC:

```
MAKE GENERIC
```

For more information about the **MAKE** program, see the documentation provided with the Microsoft C Optimizing Compiler.

1.6 Tips for Writing Windows Applications

There are some programming practices that work well for standard C or assembly-language applications, but will not work in the Windows environment. Chapter 14, "C and Assembly Language," provides detailed information on using those programming languages to write Windows applications.

In general, when writing Windows applications, remember the following rules:

- Do not take exclusive control of the CPU—it is a shared resource. Although Windows is a multitasking system, it is non-preemptive. This means it cannot take control back from an application until the application releases it. A cooperative application carefully manages access to the CPU and gives other applications ample opportunity to execute.
- Do not attempt to directly access memory or hardware devices such as the keyboard, mouse, timer, display, and serial and parallel ports. Windows requires absolute control of these resources to ensure equal, uninterrupted access for all applications that are running.

- Within your application, all functions that Windows can call must be defined with the **PASCAL** key word; this ensures that the function accesses arguments correctly. Functions that Windows can call are the WinMain function, callback functions, and window functions.

- Every application must have a WinMain function. This function is the entry point, or starting point, for the application. It contains statements and Windows function calls that create windows and read and dispatch input intended for the application. The function definition has the following form:

  ```
  int PASCAL WinMain(hInst,hPrevInst,lpCmdLine,nCmdShow)
  HANDLE hInst;
  HANDLE hPrevInst;
  LPSTR lpCmdLine;
  int nCmdShow;
  {
           .
           .
           .
  }
  ```

  The WinMain function must be declared with the **PASCAL** key word. Although Windows calls the function directly, WinMain must not be defined with the **FAR** key word, since it is called from linked-in start-up code.

- When using Windows functions, be sure to check the return values. It's not a good idea to ignore these return values, since unusual conditions sometimes occur when a function fails.

- Do not use C run-time console input and output functions, such as **getchar**, **putchar**, **scanf**, and **printf**.

- Do not use C run-time file input and output functions to access serial and parallel ports. Instead, use the communications functions, which are described in detail in the *Reference, Volume 1*.

- You can use the C run-time file input and output functions to access disk files. In particular, use the Windows **OpenFile** function and the low-level, C run-time input and output functions. Although you can use the C run-time stream input and output functions, you do not get the advantages that **OpenFile** provides.

- You can use the C run-time memory-management functions **malloc**, **calloc**, **realloc**, and **free**, but be aware that Windows translates these functions to its own local-heap functions, **LocalAlloc**, **LocalReAlloc**, and **LocalFree**. Since local-heap functions don't always operate exactly like C run-time memory-management functions, you may get unexpected results.

1.7 Summary

This chapter provided an overview of the Windows environment, and compared Windows applications with standard C applications. For additional information about Windows programming concepts, see the following:

Topic	Reference
The message loop	*Guide to Programming*: Chapter 2, "A Generic Windows Application"
A simple Windows application	*Guide to Programming*: Chapter 2, "A Generic Windows Application"
Menus	*Guide to Programming*: Chapter 7, "Menus"
Dialog boxes	*Guide to Programming*: Chapter 9, "Dialog Boxes"
Using C run-time routines and assembly language in Windows applications	*Guide to Programming*: Chapter 14, "C and Assembly Language"
Windows functions and messages	*Reference, Volume 1*
Software development tools	*Tools*

Chapter 2 A Generic Windows Application

This chapter explains how to create a simple Microsoft Windows application called Generic, which demonstrates the principles explained in Chapter 1, "An Overview of the Windows Environment."

This chapter covers the following topics:

- The essential parts of a Windows application
- Initializing a Windows application
- Writing the message loop
- Terminating an application
- The basic steps needed to build a Windows application

The Generic application will be used as basic code for all sample applications in Part 2 of this guide. (The source files for Generic and the other sample applications are included on the SDK Sample Source Code disk.)

2.1 The Generic Application

Generic is a standard Windows application; that is, it meets the recommendations for user-interface style given in the *System Application Architecture, Common User Access: Advanced Interface Design Guide*. Generic has a main window, a border, an application menu, and maximize and minimize boxes, but no other features. The application menu includes a Help menu with an About command, which, when chosen by the user, displays an About dialog box describing Generic. The completed Generic, with an About dialog box, looks like Figure 2.1 when displayed:

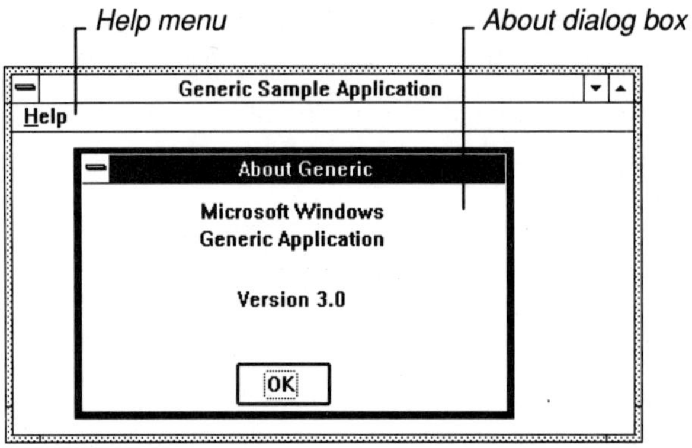

Figure 2.1 Generic: A Template for Writing Windows Applications

Generic is important not for what it can do, but for what it provides: a template for writing Windows applications. Building it helps you understand how Windows applications are put together and how they work.

2.2 A Windows Application

A Windows application is any application that is specifically written to run with Windows and that uses the Windows application program interface (API) to carry out its tasks. A Windows application has the following basic components:

- A main function named WinMain
- A window function

The WinMain function is the entry point for the application and is similar to the main function used in the standard C environment. It is always named WinMain.

A window function is something new. It is a "callback function" — a function within your application that Windows calls. Your application never calls its window functions directly. Instead, it waits for Windows to call the window function with requests to carry out specific tasks or to return information.

2.3 The WinMain Function

Much like the main function in standard C programs, the WinMain function is the entry point for a Windows application. Every Windows application must have a WinMain function; no Windows application can run without it. In most Windows applications, the WinMain function does the following:

- Calls initialization functions that register window classes, create windows, and perform any other necessary initializations
- Enters a message loop to process messages from the application queue
- Terminates the application when the message loop retrieves a WM_QUIT message

The WinMain function has the following form:

```
int PASCAL WinMain(hInstance, hPrevInstance, lpCmdLine, nCmdShow)
HANDLE hInstance;              /* current instance               */
HANDLE hPrevInstance;          /* previous instance              */
LPSTR lpCmdLine;               /* command line                   */
int nCmdShow;                  /* whether to show window or icon */
{

}
```

The WinMain function requires the **PASCAL** calling convention.

When the user starts an application, Windows passes the following four parameters to the application's WinMain function:

Parameter	Value Windows Passes to Application
hInstance	The instance handle of the application.
hPrevInstance	The handle of another instance of the application, if one is running. If no other instances of this application are running, Windows sets this parameter to NULL.
lpCmdLine	A long pointer to a null-terminated command line.
nCmdShow	An integer value that specifies whether to display the application's window as a window or as an icon. The application passes this value to the **ShowWindow** function when calling that function to display the application's main window.

For more information on handles, see Section 2.3.2, "Handles." For more information on the *lpCmdLine* parameter, see Section 2.3.11, "The Application Command-Line Parameter."

2.3.1 Data Types and Structures in Windows

The WinMain function uses several special data types to define its parameters. For example, it uses the **HANDLE** data type to define the *hInstance* and *hPrevInstance* parameters, and the **LPSTR** data type to define the *lpCmdLine* parameter. In general, Windows uses many more data types than you would find in a typical C program. Although the Windows data types are often equivalent to familiar C data types, they are intended to be more descriptive and should help you better understand the purpose of a given variable or parameter in an application.

The Windows data types are defined in the WINDOWS.H include file. The Windows include file is an ordinary C-language source file that contains definitions for all the Windows special constants, variables, data structures, and functions. To use these definitions, you must include the WINDOWS.H file in each source file. Place the following line at the beginning of your source file:

```
#include "WINDOWS.H" /* Required for all Windows applications */
```

The following is a list of some of the more common Windows data types:

Type	Meaning
WORD	Specifies a 16-bit, unsigned integer.
LONG	Specifies a 32-bit, signed integer.
HANDLE	Identifies a 16-bit, unsigned integer to be used as a handle.
HWND	Identifies a 16-bit, unsigned integer to be used as a handle to a window.
LPSTR	Specifies a 32-bit pointer to a **CHAR** type.
FARPROC	Specifies a 32-bit pointer to a function.

The following is a list of some commonly used structures:

Structure	Description
MSG	Defines the fields of an input message.
WNDCLASS	Defines a window class.
PAINTSTRUCT	Defines a paint structure used to draw within a window.
RECT	Defines a rectangle.

See the *Reference, Volume 2*, for a complete listing and description of Windows data types and structures.

2.3.2 Handles

The WinMain function has two parameters, *hPrevInstance* and *hInstance*, that are called "handles." A handle is a unique integer that Windows uses to identify an object created or used by an application. Windows uses a wide variety of handles, identifying objects such as application instances, windows, menus, controls, allocated memory, output devices, files, GDI pens and brushes, to name a few.

Most handles are index values for internal tables. Windows uses handle indexes to access the information stored in the table. Typically, your application has access only to the handle, and not to the data. When you need to examine or change the data, you supply the handle and Windows does the rest. This is one way that Windows protects data in its multitasking environment.

2.3.3 Instances

Not only can you run more than one application at a time in Windows, you can also run more than one copy, or "instance" of the same application at a time. To distinguish one instance from another, Windows supplies a unique "instance handle" each time it calls the WinMain function to start the application. An instance is a separately executing copy of an application, and an instance handle is an integer that uniquely identifies an instance.

In some multitasking systems, if you run multiple instances of the same application, the system loads a fresh copy of the application's code and data into memory and executes it. In Windows, when you start a new instance of the application, only the data for the application is loaded. Windows uses the same code for all instances of the application. This saves as much space as possible for other applications and for data. However, this method requires that the code segments of your application remain unchanged for the duration of the application. This means that you must not store data in a code segment or change the code while the program is running.

For most Windows applications, the first instance has a special role. Many of the resources an application creates, such as window classes, are generally available to all applications. Consequently, only the first instance of an application creates these resources. All subsequent instances may use the resources without creating them. To let you determine which is the first instance, Windows sets the *hPrevInstance* parameter of WinMain to NULL if there are no previous instances. The following example shows how to check that previous instance does not exist:

```
int PASCAL WinMain(hInstance, hPrevInstance, lpCmdLine, nCmdShow)
HANDLE hInstance;                /* current instance*/
HANDLE hPrevInstance;            /* previous instance*/
LPSTR lpCmdLine;                 /* command line */
int nCmdShow;                    /* whether to show window or icon */
{
    if (!hPrevInstance)
      .
      .
      .
}
```

To keep the user from starting more than one instance of your application, check the *hPrevInstance* parameter when the application starts; return to Windows immediately if the parameter is not NULL. The following example shows how to do this:

```
if (hPrevInstance)
    return (NULL);
```

2.3.4 Registering the Window Class

Before you can create any window, you must have a "window class." A window class is a template that defines the attributes of a window, such as the shape of the window's cursor and the name of the window's menu. The window class also specifies the window function that processes messages for all windows in the class. Although Windows provides some predefined window classes, most applications define their own window classes in order to control every aspect of the way their windows operate.

You must register a window class before you can create a window that belongs to that class. You register a window class by filling a **WNDCLASS** structure with information about the class, and passing it as a parameter to the **RegisterClass** function.

Filling the WNDCLASS Structure

The **WNDCLASS** provides information to Windows about the name, attributes, resources, and window function for a window class. The **WNDCLASS** data structure contains the following fields:

Field	Description
lpszClassName	Points to the name of the window class. A window class name must be unique; that is, different applications must use different class names.
hInstance	Specifies the application instance that is registering the class.
lpfnWndProc	Points to the window function used to carry out work on the window.
style	Specifies the class styles, such as automatic redrawing of the window when moved or sized.
hbrBackground	Specifies the brush used to paint the window background.
hCursor	Specifies the cursor used in the window.
hIcon	Specifies the icon used to represent a minimized window.
lpszMenuName	Points to the resource name of a menu.

Field	Description
cbClsExtra	Specifies the number of extra bytes to allocate for this class structure.
clWndExtra	Specifies the number of extra bytes to allocate for all the window structures created with this class.

See the *Reference, Volume 2*, for more information about these fields.

Some fields, such as **lpszClassName**, **hInstance**, and **lpfnWndProc**, must be assigned values. Other fields can be set to NULL. When these fields are set to NULL, Windows uses a default attribute for windows created using the class. The following example shows how to fill a window structure:

```
BOOL InitApplication(hInstance)
HANDLE hInstance;        /* current instance          */
{
  ❶ WNDCLASS  wc;

    /* Fill in window class structure with parameters that describe the       */
    /* main window. */

  ❷ wc.style = NULL;                     /* Class style(s).                  */
  ❸ wc.lpfnWndProc = MainWndProc;        /* Function to retrieve messages for */
                                         /* windows of this class. */

  ❹ wc.cbClsExtra = 0;                   /* No per-class extra data. */
    wc.cbWndExtra = 0;                   /* No per-window extra data. */

  ❺ wc.hInstance = hInstance;            /* Application that owns the class. */
  ❻ wc.hIcon = LoadIcon(NULL, IDI_APPLICATION);
  ❼ wc.hCursor = LoadCursor(NULL, IDC_ARROW);
  ❽ wc.hbrBackground = GetStockObject(WHITE_BRUSH);
  ❾ wc.lpszMenuName =  "GenericMenu";    /* Name of menu in .RC file. */
  ❿ wc.lpszClassName = "GenericWClass"; /* Name used with CreateWindow. */

    /* Register the window class and return success/failure code. */

    return (RegisterClass(&wc));

}
```

In this example of a window class structure:

❶ The example first declares that this is a **WNDCLASS** structure named “wc”.

❷ The **style** field is set to NULL.

❸ The **lpfnWndProc** field contains a pointer to the window function named MainWndProc. This means that the application’s MainWndProc function will then receive any messages that Windows sends to that window, and will be the function that carries out tasks for that window.

To assign the address of the MainWndProc function to the **lpfnWndProc** field, you must declare the function somewhere before the assignment statement. Windows applications should use function prototypes for function declaration in order to take advantage of the C Compiler's automatic type-checking and casting. The following is the correct prototype for a window function with the name MainWndProc:

```
long FAR PASCAL MainWndProc (HWND, unsigned, WORD, LONG);
```

Note that the MainWndProc function must be exported in the module-definition file.

❹ The **cbClsExtra** and **cbWndExtra** fields are set to zero, so there is no additional storage space associated with either the window class or each individual window. (You can set these fields to allocate additional storage space which you can then use to store information on a per-window basis. See Chapter 16, "More Memory Management," for information on using this extra space.)

❺ The **hInstance** field is set to hInstance, the instance handle that Windows passed to the WinMain function when the application was started.

❻ The **hIcon** field receives a handle to a built-in icon. The **LoadIcon** function can return a handle to either a built-in or an application-defined icon. In this case, the NULL and IDI_APPLICATION arguments specify the built-in application icon. (Most applications use their own icons instead of the built-in application icon. Chapter 5, "Icons," explains how to create and use your own icons.)

❼ The **hCursor** field receives a handle to the standard arrow-shaped cursor (pointer). The **LoadCursor** function can return a handle to either a built-in or an application-defined cursor. In this case, the NULL and IDC_ARROW arguments specify the built-in arrow cursor. (Some applications use their own cursors instead of built-in cursors. Chapter 6, "The Cursor, the Mouse, and the Keyboard," explains how to create and use your own cursors.)

❽ The **hbrBackground** field determines the color of the brush that Windows will use to paint the window's background. In this case, the application uses the **GetStockObject** function to get the handle of the standard white background brush.

❾ The **lpszMenuName** field specifies the name of the menu for this window class, "GenericMenu." This menu will then appear for all windows in this class. If the window class has no menu, this field is set to NULL.

❿ The **lpszClassName** field specifies "GenericWClass" as the class name for this window class.

Registering the Window Class

After you assign values to the **WNDCLASS** structure fields, you register the class by using the **RegisterClass** function. If registration is successful, the function returns TRUE; otherwise, it returns FALSE. Make sure you check the return value because you cannot create your windows without first registering the window class.

Although the **RegisterClass** function requires a 32-bit pointer to a **WNDCLASS** structure, in the previous example, the address operator (&) generates only a 16-bit address. This is an example of an implicit cast carried out by the C Compiler. The Windows include file contains prototypes for all Windows functions. These prototypes specify the correct types for each function parameter, and the compiler casts to these types automatically.

2.3.5 Creating a Window

You can create a window by using the **CreateWindow** function. This function tells Windows to create a window that has the specified style and belongs to the specified class. **CreateWindow** takes several parameters:

- The name of the window class
- The window title
- The window's style
- The window position
- The parent window handle
- The menu handle
- The instance handle
- Thirty-two bits of additional data

The following example creates a window belonging to the "GenericWClass" window class:

```
/* Create a main window for this application instance. */

    hWnd = CreateWindow(
     ❶ "GenericWClass",               /* See RegisterClass() call. */
     ❷ "Generic Sample Application",/* Text for window title bar. */
     ❸ WS_OVERLAPPEDWINDOW,           /* Window style. */
     ❹ CW_USEDEFAULT,                 /* Default horizontal position. */
     CW_USEDEFAULT,                    /* Default vertical position. */
     CW_USEDEFAULT,                    /* Default width. */
     CW_USEDEFAULT,                    /* Default height. */
     ❺ NULL,                          /* Overlapped windows have no parent. */
     ❻ NULL,                          /* Use the window class menu. */
     ❼ hInstance,                     /* This instance owns this window. */
     ❽ NULL                           /* Pointer not needed. */
    );
```

This example creates an overlapped window that has the style WS_OVERLAPPEDWINDOW and that belongs to the window class created by the code in the preceding example. In this example:

❶ The first parameter of the **CreateWindow** function specifies the name of the window class Windows should use when creating the window. In this example, the window class name is "GenericWClass."

❷ The second parameter of **CreateWindow** specifies the window caption as "Generic Sample Application".

❸ The WS_OVERLAPPEDWINDOW style specifies that the window is a normal "overlapped" window.

❹ The next four **CreateWindow** parameters specify the position and dimensions of the window. Since the CW_USEDEFAULT value is specified for the position, width, and height parameters, Windows will place the window at a default position and give it a default width and height. The default position and dimensions depend on the system and on how many other applications have been started. (Note that Windows does not display the window until you call the **ShowWindow** function.)

❺ When you create a window, you can specify its parent (used with controls and child windows). Because an overlapped window does not have a parent, this parameter is set to NULL.

❻ If you specify a menu when you create a window, the menu overrides the class menu (if any) for the window. Because this window will use the class menu, this parameter is set to NULL.

❼ You must specify the instance of the application that is creating the window. Windows uses this instance to make sure that the window function supporting the window uses the data for this instance.

❽ The last parameter is for additional data to be used by the window function when the window is created. This window takes no additional data, so the parameter is set to NULL.

When **CreateWindow** successfully creates the window, it returns a handle to the new window. You can use the handle to carry out tasks on the window, such as showing it or updating its client area.

If **CreateWindow** cannot create the window, it returns NULL. Whenever you create a window, you should check for a NULL handle and respond appropriately. For example, in the WinMain function, if you cannot create your application's main window, you should terminate the application; that is, return control to Windows.

2.3.6 Showing and Updating a Window

Although **CreateWindow** creates a window, it does not automatically display the window. Instead, it is up to you to display the window by using the **ShowWindow** function and to update the window's client area by using the **UpdateWindow** function.

The **ShowWindow** function tells Windows to display the new window. For the application's main window, WinMain should call **ShowWindow** soon after creating the window, and should pass the *nCmdShow* parameter to it. The *nCmdShow* parameter tells the application whether to display the window as an open window or as an icon. After calling **ShowWindow**, WinMain should call the **UpdateWindow** function. The following example illustrates how to show and update a window:

```
ShowWindow(hWnd, nCmdShow);  /* Shows the window      */
UpdateWindow(hWnd);          /* Sends WM_PAINT message*/
```

NOTE Normally, the *nCmdShow* parameter of the **ShowWindow** function can be set to any of the constants beginning with "SW_" that are defined in WINDOWS.H. The one exception is when the application calls **ShowWindow** to display its main window; then, it uses the *nCmdShow* parameter from the WinMain function. (See the *Reference, Volume 1*, for a complete list of these constants.)

2.3.7 Creating the Message Loop

Once you have created and displayed a window, the WinMain function can begin its primary duty: to read messages from the application queue and dispatch them to the appropriate window. WinMain does this by using a message loop. A "message loop" is a program loop, typically created by using a **while** statement, in which WinMain retrieves messages and dispatches them.

Windows does not send input directly to an application. Instead, it places all mouse and keyboard input into an application queue (along with messages posted by Windows and other applications). The application must read the application queue, retrieve the messages, and dispatch them so that the appropriate window function can process them.

The simplest possible message loop consists of the **GetMessage** and **DispatchMessage** functions. This loop has the following form:

```
MSG msg;
     .
     .
     .

while (GetMessage(&msg, NULL, NULL, NULL)) {
    DispatchMessage(&msg);
}
```

In this example, the **GetMessage** function retrieves a message from the application queue and copies it into the message structure named "msg". The NULL arguments indicate that all messages should be processed. The **DispatchMessage** function directs Windows to send each message to the appropriate window function. Every message an application receives, except the WM_QUIT message, belongs to one of the windows created by the application. Since an application must not call a window function directly, it instead uses the **DispatchMessage** function to pass each message to the appropriate function.

Depending on what your application does, you may need a more complicated message loop. In particular, to process character input from the keyboard, you must translate each message you receive by using the **TranslateMessage** function. Your message loop should then look like this:

```
while (GetMessage(&msg, NULL, NULL, NULL)) {
    TranslateMessage(&msg);
    DispatchMessage(&msg);
}
```

The **TranslateMessage** function looks for matching WM_KEYDOWN and WM_KEYUP messages and generates a corresponding WM_CHAR message for the window that contains the ANSI character code for the given key.

A message loop may also contain functions to process menu accelerators and key strokes within dialog boxes. Again, this depends on what your application actually does.

Windows places input messages in an application queue when the user moves the cursor in the window, presses or releases a mouse button when the cursor is in the window, or presses or releases a keyboard key when the window has the input focus. The window manager first collects all keyboard and mouse input in a system queue, then copies the corresponding messages to the appropriate application queue.

The message loop continues until **GetMessage** returns NULL, which it does only if it retrieves the WM_QUIT message. This message is a signal to terminate the application, and is usually posted (placed in the application queue) by the window function of the application's main window.

2.3.8 Yielding Control

Windows is a non-preemptive multitasking system. This means that Windows cannot take control from an application. The application must yield control before Windows can reassign control to another application.

To make sure that all applications have equal access to the CPU, the **Get-Message** function automatically yields control when there are no messages in an application queue. This means that if there is no work for the application to do, Windows can give control to another application. Since all applications have a message loop, this implicit yielding of control guarantees sharing of control.

In general, you should rely on the **GetMessage** function to yield for your application. Although a function (**Yield**) is available that explicitly yields control, you should avoid using it. Since there might be times when your application must keep control for a long time, such as when writing a large buffer to a disk file, you should try to minimize the work and provide a visual clue to the user that a lengthy operation is underway.

2.3.9 Terminating an Application

Your application terminates when the WinMain function returns control to Windows. You can return control at any time before starting the message loop. Typically, an application checks each step leading up to the message loop to make sure each window class is registered and each window is created. If there is an error, the application can display a message before terminating.

Once the WinMain function enters the message loop, however, the only way to terminate the loop is to post a WM_QUIT message in the application queue by using the **PostQuitMessage** function. When the **GetMessage** function retrieves a WM_QUIT message, it returns NULL, which terminates the message loop. Typically, the window function for the application's main window posts a WM_QUIT message when the main window is being destroyed (that is, when the window function has received a WM_DESTROY message).

Although WinMain specifies a data type for its return value, Windows does not currently use the return value. While you are debugging an application, however, a return value can be helpful. In general, you might use the same return-code conventions that standard C programs use: zero for successful execution, nonzero for error. The **PostQuitMessage** function lets the window function specify the return value. This value is then copied to the *wParam* parameter of the WM_QUIT message. To return this value after terminating the message loop, use the following statement:

```
return (msg.wParam);    /* Returns the value from PostQuitMessage */
```

Although standard C programs typically clean up and free resources just prior to termination, Windows applications should clean up as each window is destroyed. If you do not clean up as each window is destroyed, you lose some data. For example, when Windows itself terminates, it destroys each window, but does not return control to the application's message loop. This means that the loop never retrieves the WM_QUIT message and the statements after the loop are not executed. (Windows does send each application a message before terminating, so an application does have an opportunity to carry out tasks before terminating. See Chapter 10, "File Input and Output," for an illustration of the WM_QUERYENDSESSION message.)

2.3.10 Initialization Functions

Most applications use two locally defined initialization functions:

- The main initialization function carries out work that only needs to be done once for all instances of the application (for example, registering window classes).
- The instance initialization function performs tasks that must be done for every instance of the application.

Using initialization functions helps to keep the WinMain function simple and readable; it also organizes initialization tasks so that they can be placed in a separate code segment and discarded after use. The Generic application does not discard its initialization functions. (In Chapter 15, "Memory Management," you will encounter a sample application, Memory, that does discard its initialization functions.)

The Generic application's main initialization function looks like the following:

```
BOOL InitApplication(hInstance)
HANDLE hInstance;                            /* current instance     */
{
    WNDCLASS  wc;

    /* Fill in window class structure with parameters that describe the       */
    /* main window. */

    wc.style = NULL;                    /* Class style(s). */
    wc.lpfnWndProc = MainWndProc;       /* Function to retrieve messages for  */
                                        /* windows of this class. */

    wc.cbClsExtra = 0;                  /* No per-class extra data. */
    wc.cbWndExtra = 0;                  /* No per-window extra data. */

    wc.hInstance = hInstance;           /* Application that owns the class. */
    wc.hIcon = LoadIcon(NULL, IDI_APPLICATION);
```

```
    wc.hCursor = LoadCursor(NULL, IDC_ARROW);
    wc.hbrBackground = GetStockObject(WHITE_BRUSH);
    wc.lpszMenuName =  "GenericMenu";   /* Name of menu resource in .RC file. */
    wc.lpszClassName = "GenericWClass"; /* Name used in call to CreateWindow. */

    /* Register the window class and return success/failure code. */

    return (RegisterClass(&wc));

}
```

Generic's instance initialization function looks like the following:

```
BOOL InitInstance(hInstance, nCmdShow)
    HANDLE          hInstance;          /* Current instance identifier. */
    int             nCmdShow;           /* Param for first ShowWindow() call. */
{
    HWND            hWnd;               /* Main window handle. */

    /* Save the instance handle in static variable, which will be used in  */
    /* many subsequence calls from this application to Windows. */

    hInst = hInstance;

    /* Create a main window for this application instance. */

    hWnd = CreateWindow(
        "GenericWClass",                /* See RegisterClass() call. */
        "Generic Sample Application",   /* Text for window title bar. */
        WS_OVERLAPPEDWINDOW,            /* Window style. */
        CW_USEDEFAULT,                  /* Default horizontal position. */
        CW_USEDEFAULT,                  /* Default vertical position. */
        CW_USEDEFAULT,                  /* Default width. */
        CW_USEDEFAULT,                  /* Default height. */
        NULL,                           /* Overlapped windows have no parent. */
        NULL,                           /* Use the window class menu. */
        hInstance,                      /* This instance owns this window. */
        NULL                            /* Pointer not needed. */
    );

    /* If window could not be created, return "failure" */

    if (!hWnd)
        return (FALSE);

    /* Make the window visible; update its client area; and return "success" */

    ShowWindow(hWnd, nCmdShow);  /* Show the window                        */
    UpdateWindow(hWnd);          /* Sends WM_PAINT message                 */
    return (TRUE);
```

2.3.11 The Application Command-Line Parameter

You can examine the command line that starts your application by using the *lpCmdLine* parameter. The *lpCmdLine* parameter points to the start of a character array that contains the command exactly as it was typed by the user. To extract filenames or options from the command line, you need to parse the command line into individual values. Alternatively, you can use the **__argc** and **__argv** variables. For more information, see Chapter 14, "C and Assembly Language."

2.4 The Window Function

Every window must have a window function. The window function responds to input and window-management messages received from Windows. The window function can be a short function, processing only a message or two, or it can be complex, processing many types of messages for a variety of application windows.

A window function has the following form:

```
long FAR PASCAL MainWndProc(hWnd, message, wParam, lParam)
HWND hWnd;                  /* window handle           */
unsigned message;           /* type of message         */
WORD wParam;                /* additional information     */
LONG lParam;                /* additional information     */
{
          .
          .
          .
    switch (message) {
          .
          .
          .
        default:   /* Passes it on if unprocessed     */
            return (DefWindowProc(hWnd, message,
                                  wParam, lParam));
    }
    return (NULL);
}
```

The window function uses the **PASCAL** calling convention. Since Windows calls this function directly and always uses this convention, **PASCAL** is required. The window function also uses the **FAR** key word in its definition, since Windows uses a 32-bit address whenever it calls a function. Also, you must name the window function in an **EXPORTS** statement in the application's module-definition file. See Section 2.6, "Creating a Module-Definition File," for more information on module-definition files.

The window function receives messages from Windows. These may be input messages that have been dispatched by the WinMain function or window-management messages that come directly from Windows. The window function must examine each message; it then either carries out some specific action based on the message, or passes the message back to Windows for default processing through the **DefWindowProc** function.

The *message* parameter defines the message type. You use this parameter in a **switch** statement to direct processing to the correct case. The *lParam* and *wParam* parameters contain additional information about the message. The window function typically uses these parameters to carry out the requested action. If a window function doesn't process a message, it must pass it to the **DefWindowProc** function. Passing the message to **DefWindowProc** ensures that any special actions that affect the window, the application, or Windows itself can be carried out.

Most window functions process the WM_DESTROY message. Windows sends this message to the window function immediately after destroying the window. The message gives the window function the opportunity to finish its processing and, if it is the window function for the application's main window, to post a WM_QUIT message in the application queue. The following example shows how the main window function should process this message:

```
case WM_DESTROY:
    PostQuitMessage(0);
    break;
```

The **PostQuitMessage** function places a WM_QUIT message in the application's queue. When the **GetMessage** function retrieves this message, it will terminate the message loop and the application.

A window function receives messages from two sources. Input messages come from the message loop and window-management messages come from Windows. Input messages correspond to mouse input, keyboard input, and sometimes timer input. Typical input messages are WM_KEYDOWN, WM_KEYUP, WM_MOUSEMOVE, and WM_TIMER, all of which correspond directly to hardware input.

Windows sends window-management messages directly to a window function without going through the application queue or message loop. These window messages are typically requests for the window function to carry out some action, such as painting its client area or supplying information about the window. The messages may also inform the window function of changes that Windows has made to the window. Some typical window-management messages are WM_CREATE, WM_DESTROY, and WM_PAINT.

The window function should return a long value. The actual value to be returned depends on the message received. The *Reference, Volume 1,* describes the return values when they are significant (for most messages, the return value is arbitrary). If the window function doesn't process a message, it should return the **DefWindowProc** function's return value.

2.5 Creating an About Dialog Box

The *System Application Architecture, Common User Access: Advanced Interface Design Guide* recommends that you include an About dialog box with every application. A "dialog box" is a temporary window that displays information or prompts the user for input. The About dialog box displays such information as the application's name and copyright information. The user tells the application to display the About dialog box by choosing the About command from a menu. (See the *System Application Architecture, Common User Access: Advanced Interface Design Guide* for more information about design conventions for the About dialog box.)

You create and display a dialog box by using the **DialogBox** function. This function takes a dialog-box template, a procedure-instance address, and a handle to a parent window, and creates a dialog box through which you can display output and prompt the user for input.

To display and use an About dialog box, follow these steps:

1. Create a dialog-box template and add it to your resource script file.
2. Add a dialog function to your C-language source file.
3. Export the dialog function in your module-definition file.
4. Add a menu to your application's resource script file.
5. Process the WM_COMMAND message in your application code.

Once you have completed these steps, the user can display the dialog box by choosing the About command from your application's menu. The following sections explain these steps in more detail.

2.5.1 Creating a Dialog-Box Template

A dialog-box template is a textual description of the dialog style, contents, shape, and size. You can create a template by hand or by using the Windows version 3.0 Dialog Editor. In this example, the template is created by hand. *Tools* explains how to use the Dialog Editor to create a dialog box.

You create a dialog-box template by creating a resource script file. A resource script file contains definitions of resources to be used by the application, such as icons, cursors, and dialog-box templates. To create an About dialog-box template, you use a **DIALOG** statement and fill it with control statements, as shown in the following example:

```
❶ AboutBox DIALOG 22, 17, 144, 75
❷ STYLE DS_MODALFRAME | WS_CAPTION | WS_SYSMENU
CAPTION "About Generic"
```

```
❸ BEGIN
❹  CTEXT "Microsoft Windows"        -1, Ø,  5, 144,  8
    CTEXT "Generic Application"   -1, Ø, 14, 144,  8
    CTEXT "Version 3.Ø"           -1, Ø, 34, 144,  8
❺  DEFPUSHBUTTON "OK"              IDOK, 53, 59, 32, 14, WS_GROUP
END
```

In this example:

❶ The **DIALOG** statement starts the dialog-box template. The name, AboutBox, identifies the template when the **DialogBox** function is used to create the dialog box. The box's upper-left corner is placed at the point (22,17) in the parent window's client area. The box is 144 units wide by 75 units high. The horizontal units are ¼ of the dialog base width unit; the vertical units are ⅛ of the dialog base height unit. The current dialog base units are computed from the height and width of the current system font. The **GetDialogBaseUnits** function returns the dialog base units in pixels.

❷ The **STYLE** statement defines the dialog-box style. This particular style is a window with a framed border, a caption bar, and a system menu, which is the typical style used for modal dialog boxes.

❸ The **BEGIN** and **END** statements mark the beginning and end of the control definitions. The dialog box contains text and a default push button. The push button lets the user send input to the dialog function to terminate the dialog box.

The statements, strings, and integers contained between the **BEGIN** and **END** statements describe the contents of the dialog box. (Because you would normally create such a description using the Dialog Editor, this guide does not describe the numbers and statements that make up the description. See *Tools* for a complete description of how to use the Dialog Editor.)

❹ **CTEXT** creates a rectangle with the quoted text centered in a rectangle. This statement appears several times for the various texts that appear in the dialog box.

❺ **DEFPUSHBUTTON** creates a push button that allows the user to give a default response; in this case, to choose the "OK" button, causing the dialog box to disappear.

The DS_MODALFRAME, WS_CAPTION, WM_SYSMENU, IDOK, and WS_GROUP constants used in the dialog-box template are defined in the Windows include file. You should include this file in the resource script file by using the **#include** directive at the beginning of the script file.

The statements in this file were created with a text editor, and were based on a dialog box used in another application. You can create many such resources by copying them from other applications and modifying them using a text editor. You can also create new dialog boxes by using the Dialog Editor. (The files created by the Dialog Editor contain statements that are somewhat different from the statements shown here, and such files usually are edited only by using the Dialog Editor. For more information about using the Dialog Editor to create dialog boxes, see *Tools*.)

2.5.2 Creating an Include File

It is often useful to create an include file in which to define constants and function prototypes for your application. Most applications consist of at least two source files that share common constants: the C-language source file and the resource script file. Since the Resource Compiler (**RC**) carries out the same preprocessing as the C Compiler, it is useful and convenient to place constant definitions in a single include file and then include that file in both the C-language source file and the resource script file.

For example, for the Generic application, you can place the function prototypes for the WinMain, MainWndProc, About, InitApplication, and InitInstance functions, and the definition of the menu ID for the About command, in the GENERIC.H include file. The file should look like this:

```
#define IDM_ABOUT 100

int PASCAL                    WinMain (HANDLE, HANDLE, LPSTR, int);
BOOL                          InitApplication (HANDLE);
BOOL                          InitInstance (HANDLE, int);
long FAR PASCAL               MainWndProc (HWND, unsigned, WORD,
LONG);
BOOL FAR PASCAL               About (HWND, unsigned, WORD, LONG);
```

Since GENERIC.H refers to Windows data types, you must include it after WINDOWS.H, which defines those data types. That is, the beginning of your source files should look like this:

```
#include "WINDOWS.H"      /* required for all Windows applications */
#include "GENERIC.H"      /* specific to this program              */
```

2.5.3 Creating a Dialog Function

A "dialog box" is a special kind of window whose window procedure is built into Windows. For every dialog box an application has, the application must have a dialog function. Windows' built-in window procedure calls a dialog function to handle input messages that can be interpreted only by the application.

The function that processes input for Generic's About dialog box is called About. This function, like other dialog functions, uses the same parameters as a window function, but processes only messages that are not handled by Windows' default processing. (The dialog function returns TRUE if it processes a message, and FALSE if it does not.) The dialog function, like the window function, uses the **PASCAL** calling convention and the **FAR** key word in its definition. You must name the dialog function in an **EXPORTS** statement in the application's module-definition file. As with a window function, you must not call a dialog function directly from your application.

Unlike a window function, a dialog function usually processes only user-input messages, such as WM_COMMAND, and must not send unprocessed messages to the **DefWindowProc** function. Generic's dialog function, About, looks like this:

```
BOOL FAR PASCAL About(hDlg, message, wParam, lParam)
HWND hDlg;                        /* window handle of the dialog box */
unsigned message;                 /* type of message                 */
WORD wParam;                      /* message-specific information    */
LONG lParam;
{
   switch (message) {
        case WM_INITDIALOG:        /* message: initialize dialog box  */
            return (TRUE);

        case WM_COMMAND:                      /* message: received a command */
                    if (wParam == IDOK||      /* "OK" box selected?          */
                    wParam == IDCANCEL) {     /* System menu close command?  */
                EndDialog(hDlg, TRUE);        /* Exits the dialog box        */
                return (TRUE);
        }
            break;
    }
    return (FALSE);                /* Didn't process a message       */
}
```

The About dialog function processes two messages: WM_INITDIALOG and WM_COMMAND. Windows sends the WM_INITDIALOG message to a dialog function to let the function prepare before displaying the dialog box. In this case, WM_INITDIALOG returns TRUE so that the "focus" will be passed to the first control in the dialog box that has the WS_TABSTOP bit set (this control will be the default push button). If WM_INITDIALOG had returned FALSE, then Windows will not set the focus to any control.

In contrast to WM_INITDIALOG messages, WM_COMMAND messages are a result of user input. About responds to input to the OK button or the system-menu Close command by calling the **EndDialog** function, which directs Windows to remove the dialog box and continue execution of the application. The **EndDialog** function is used to terminate dialog boxes.

2.5.4 Defining a Menu with an About Command

Now that you have an About dialog box, you need some way to let the user tell your application when to display the dialog box. In most applications, the About command would appear as the last command on the application's Help menu. If the application does not have a Help menu, then it usually appears in the first menu, most often the File menu. In Generic, About is the only command, so it appears as the only item on the Help menu.

The most common way to create a menu is to define it in the resource script file. Put the following statements in GENERIC.RC:

```
GenericMenu MENU
BEGIN
    POPUP        "&Help"
    BEGIN
        MENUITEM "About Generic...", IDM_ABOUT
    END
END
```

These statements create a menu named "GenericMenu" with a single command on it, "Help." The command displays a pop-up menu with the single menu item "About Generic...".

Notice the ampersand (&) in the "&Help" string. This character immediately precedes the command mnemonic. A mnemonic is a unique letter or digit with which the user can access a menu or command. It is part of Windows' direct-access method. If a user presses the key for the mnemonic, together with the ALT key, Windows selects the menu or chooses the command. In the case of "&Help", Windows removes the ampersand and places an underscore under the letter "H" when displaying the menu.

The user will see the About command when he or she displays the Help menu. If the user chooses the About command, Windows sends the window function a WM_COMMAND message containing the About command's menu ID; in this case, IDM_ABOUT.

2.5.5 Processing the WM_COMMAND Message

Now that you've added a command to Generic's menu, you need to be able to respond when the user selects the command. To do this, you need to process the WM_COMMAND message. Windows sends this message to the window function when the user chooses a command from the window's menu. Windows passes the menu ID identifying the command in the *wParam* parameter, so you can check to see which command was chosen. (In this case, you can use **if** and **else** statements to direct the flow of control depending on the value of the *wParam* parameter. As your application's message-processing becomes more complex, you may want to use a **switch** statement instead.) You want to display the dialog box if the parameter is equal to IDM_ABOUT, the About command's menu ID. For any other value, you must pass the message on to the **DefWindowProc** function. If you do not, you effectively disable all other commands on the menu.

The WM_COMMAND case should look like this:

```
FARPROC lpProcAbout;
    .
    .
    .
case WM_COMMAND:    /* message: command from a menu      */
  if (wParam == IDM_ABOUT) {
    ❶ lpProcAbout = MakeProcInstance(About, hInst);

    ❷ DialogBox(hInst,  /* current instance               */
        "AboutBox",     /* resource to use                */
        hWnd,           /* parent handle                  */
        lpProcAbout);   /* About() inst. address          */
        ❸ FreeProcInstance(lpProcAbout);
        break;
    }
  else                  /* Let Windows process it         */
    return (DefWindowProc(hWnd, message, wParam, lParam));
```

❶ Before displaying the dialog box, you need the procedure-instance address of the dialog function. You create the procedure-instance address by using the **MakeProcInstance** function. This function binds the data segment of the current application instance to a function pointer. This guarantees that when Windows calls the dialog function, the dialog function will use the data in the current instance and not some other instance of the application.

MakeProcInstance returns the address of the procedure instance. This value should be assigned to a pointer variable that has the **FARPROC** type.

❷ The **DialogBox** function creates and displays the dialog box. It requires the current application's instance handle and the name of the dialog-box template. It uses this information to load the dialog-box template from the executable file. **DialogBox** also requires the handle of the parent window (the window to which the dialog box belongs) and the procedure-instance address of the dialog function.

DialogBox does not return control until the user has closed the dialog box. Typically, the dialog box contains at least a push-button control to permit the user to close the box.

❸ When the **DialogBox** function returns, the procedure-instance address of the dialog function is no longer needed, so the **FreeProcInstance** function frees the address. This invalidates the content of the pointer variable, making it an error to attempt to use the value again.

2.6 Creating a Module-Definition File

Every Windows application needs a module-definition file. This file defines the name, segments, memory requirements, and exported functions of the application. For a simple application, like Generic, you need at least the **NAME**, **STACKSIZE**, **HEAPSIZE**, **EXETYPE**, and **EXPORTS** statements. However, most applications include a complete definition of the module, as shown in the following example:

```
;module-definition file for Generic — used by LINK.EXE

❶ NAME     Generic        ; application's module name

❷ DESCRIPTION 'Sample Microsoft Windows Application'

❸ EXETYPE WINDOWS                 ; Required for all Windows applications

❹ STUB     'WINSTUB.EXE           ; Generates error message if applicatior
                                  ; is run without Windows

❺ CODE     MOVEABLE DISCARDABLE   ; code can be moved in memory and
                                  ; discarded/reloaded

;DATA must be MULTIPLE if program can be invoked more than once

❻ DATA     MOVEABLE MULTIPLE

❼ HEAPSIZE  1024
❽ STACKSIZE 5120  ; recommended minimum for Windows applications

; All functions that will be called by any Windows routine
; MUST be exported.

❾ EXPORTS
    MainWndProc    @1  ; name of window-processing function
    AboutDlgProc   @2  ; name of About processing function
```

The semicolon is the delimiter for comments in the module-definition file.

In this example:

❶ The **NAME** statement defines the name of the application. This name (in the example, Generic) is used by Windows to identify the application. The **NAME** statement is required.

❷ The **DESCRIPTION** statement is an optional statement that places the message "Sample Microsoft Windows Application" in the application's executable file. This statement is typically used to add version control or copyright information to the file.

❸ The **EXETYPE** statement marks the executable file as either a Windows or an OS/2 executable file. Windows application must contain the statement **EXETYPE WINDOWS**, since, by default, the linker creates executable files for the MS OS/2 environment.

❹ The **STUB** statement specifies another optional file that defines the executable stub to be placed at the beginning of the file. When a user tries to run the application without Windows, the stub is executed instead. Most Windows applications use the WINSTUB.EXE executable file supplied with the SDK. WINSTUB displays a warning message and terminates the application if the user attempts to run the application without Windows. You can also supply your own executable stub.

❺ The **CODE** statement defines the memory attributes of the application's code segment. The code segment contains the executable code that is generated when the GENERIC.C file is compiled. Generic is a small-model application with only one code segment, which is defined as **MOVEABLE DISCARDABLE**. If the application is not running and Windows needs additional space in memory, Windows can move the code segment to make room for other segments and, if necessary, discard it. A discarded code segment is automatically reloaded on demand by the Windows operating system.

❻ The **DATA** statement defines the memory requirements of the application's data segment. The data segment contains storage space for all the static variables declared in the GENERIC.C file. It also contains space for the program stack and local heap. The data segment, like the code segment, is **MOVEABLE**. The **MULTIPLE** key word directs Windows to create a new data segment for the application each time the user starts a new instance of the application. Although all instances share the same code segment, each has its own data segment. An application must have the **MULTIPLE** key word if the user can run more than one copy of it at a time.

❼ The **HEAPSIZE** statement defines the size, in bytes, of the application's local heap. Generic uses its heap to allocate the temporary structure used to register the window class, so it specifies 1024 bytes of storage. Applications that use the local heap frequently should specify larger amounts of memory.

❽ The **STACKSIZE** statement defines the size, in bytes, of the application's stack. The stack is used for temporary storage of function arguments. Any application, like Generic, that calls its own local function must have a stack. Generic specifies 5120 bytes of stack storage, the recommended minimum for a Windows application.

❾ The **EXPORTS** statement defines the names and ordinal values of the functions to be exported by the application. Generic exports its window function, MainWndProc, which has ordinal value 1 (this is an identifier; it could be any integer, but usually such values are assigned sequentially as the exports are listed). You must export all functions that Windows will call (except the WinMain function). These functions are referred to as "callback" functions. Callback functions include the following:

- All window functions
- All dialog functions
- Special callback functions, such as enumeration functions, that certain Windows API functions require
- Any other function that will be called from outside your application

For more information on callback functions, see Chapter 14, "C and Assembly Language."

For more information on module-definition statements, see the *Reference, Volume 2*.

2.7 Putting Generic Together

At this point you are ready to put the sample application, Generic, together. (You can find copies of the Generic source files on the SDK Sample Source Code disk.)

To create the Generic application, you need to do the following:

1. Create the C-language source (.C) file.
2. Create the header (.H) file.
3. Create the resource script (.RC) file.
4. Create the module-definition (.DEF) file.
5. Create the make file.
6. Run the **MAKE** utility on the file to compile and link the application.

The following sections describe each step.

NOTE Rather than typing the code presented in the following sections, you might find it more convenient to simply examine and compile the sample source files provided with the SDK.

2.7.1 Create the C-Language Source File

The C-language source file contains the WinMain function, the MainWndProc window function, the About dialog function, and the InitApplication and Init-Instance initialization functions. Name the file GENERIC.C.

The contents of the file GENERIC.C look like this:

```
/****************************************************************************
   PROGRAM: GENERIC.C

   PURPOSE: Generic template for Windows applications

   FUNCTIONS:

        WinMain() - calls initialization function, processes message loop
        InitApplication() - initializes window data and registers window
        InitInstance() - saves instance handle and creates main window
        MainWndProc() - processes messages
        About() - processes messages for "About" dialog box

   COMMENTS:

        Windows can have several copies of your application running
        at the same time. The variable hInst keeps track of which
        instance this application is so that processing will be to
        the correct window.

****************************************************************************/
#include "windows.h"                /* required for all Windows applications */
#include "generic.h"                /* specific to this program    */

HANDLE hInst;                       /* current instance     */

/****************************************************************************
    FUNCTION: WinMain(HANDLE, HANDLE, LPSTR, int)

    PURPOSE: calls initialization function, processes message loop

    COMMENTS:

        Windows recognizes this function by name as the initial entry point
        for the program. This function calls the application initialization
        routine, if no other instance of the program is running, and always
        calls the instance initialization routine. It then executes a message
        retrieval and dispatch loop that is the top-level control structure
        for the remainder of execution. The loop is terminated when a WM_QUIT
        message is received, at which time this function exits the application
        instance by returning the value passed by PostQuitMessage().

        If this function must abort before entering the message loop, it
        returns the conventional value NULL.

****************************************************************************/
int PASCAL WinMain(hInstance, hPrevInstance, lpCmdLine, nCmdShow)
HANDLE hInstance;                         /* current instance     */
HANDLE hPrevInstance;                     /* previous instance    */
LPSTR lpCmdLine;                          /* command line     */
int nCmdShow;                             /* show-window type (open/icon) */
```

```
{
    MSG msg;                                  /* message         */

    if (!hPrevInstance)                       /* Other instances of app running? */
        if (!InitApplication(hInstance))      /* Initialize shared things */
            return (FALSE);                   /* Exits if unable to initialize    */

    /* Perform initializations that apply to a specific instance */

    if (!InitInstance(hInstance, nCmdShow))
        return (FALSE);

    /* Acquire and dispatch messages until a WM_QUIT message is received. */

    while (GetMessage(&msg,          /* message structure     */
            NULL,                    /* handle of window receiving the message */
            NULL,                    /* lowest message to examine     */
            NULL))                   /* highest message to examine     */
        {
        TranslateMessage(&msg);      /* Translates virtual key codes    */
        DispatchMessage(&msg);       /* Dispatches message to window    */
    }
    return (msg.wParam);    /* Returns the value from PostQuitMessage */
}

/****************************************************************************
    FUNCTION: InitApplication(HANDLE)

    PURPOSE: Initializes window data and registers window class

    COMMENTS:

        This function is called at initialization time only if no other
        instances of the application are running. This function performs
        initialization tasks that can be done once for any number of running
        instances.

        In this case, we initialize a window class by filling out a data
        structure of type WNDCLASS and calling the Windows RegisterClass()
        function. Since all instances of this application use the same window
        class, we only need to do this when the first instance is initialized.


****************************************************************************/
BOOL InitApplication(hInstance)
HANDLE hInstance;                              /* current instance     */
{
    WNDCLASS  wc;

    /* Fill in window class structure with parameters that describe the      */
    /* main window. */
```

```
    wc.style = NULL;                    /* Class style(s). */
    wc.lpfnWndProc = MainWndProc;       /* Function to retrieve messages for */
                                        /* windows of this class. */
    wc.cbClsExtra = 0;                  /* No per-class extra data. */
    wc.cbWndExtra = 0;                  /* No per-window extra data. */
    wc.hInstance = hInstance;           /* Application that owns the class.  */
    wc.hIcon = LoadIcon(NULL, IDI_APPLICATION);
    wc.hCursor = LoadCursor(NULL, IDC_ARROW);
    wc.hbrBackground = GetStockObject(WHITE_BRUSH);
    wc.lpszMenuName =  "GenericMenu";  /* Name of menu resource in .RC file. */
    wc.lpszClassName = "GenericWClass";/* Name used in call to CreateWindow. */

    /* Register the window class and return success/failure code. */

    return (RegisterClass(&wc));

}

/****************************************************************************
    FUNCTION:  InitInstance(HANDLE, int)

    PURPOSE:  Saves instance handle and creates main window

    COMMENTS:

        This function is called at initialization time for every instance of
        this application. This function performs initialization tasks that
        cannot be shared by multiple instances.

        In this case, we save the instance handle in a static variable and
        create and display the main program window.

****************************************************************************/
BOOL InitInstance(hInstance, nCmdShow)
    HANDLE          hInstance;          /* Current instance identifier. */
    int             nCmdShow;           /* Param for first ShowWindow() call. */
{
    HWND            hWnd;               /* Main window handle. */

    /* Save the instance handle in static variable, which will be used in */
    /* many subsequence calls from this application to Windows. */

    hInst = hInstance;

    /* Create a main window for this application instance. */

    hWnd = CreateWindow(
        "GenericWClass",                /* See RegisterClass() call. */
        "Generic Sample Application",   /* Text for window title bar. */
        WS_OVERLAPPEDWINDOW,            /* Window style. */
        CW_USEDEFAULT,                  /* Default horizontal position. */
        CW_USEDEFAULT,                  /* Default vertical position. */
        CW_USEDEFAULT,                  /* Default width. */
```

```
        CW_USEDEFAULT,                  /* Default height. */
        NULL,                           /* Overlapped windows have no parent. */
        NULL,                           /* Use the window class menu. */
        hInstance,                      /* This instance owns this window. */
        NULL                            /* Pointer not needed. */
    );

    /* If window could not be created, return "failure" */

    if (!hWnd)
        return (FALSE);

    /* Make the window visible; update its client area; and return "success" */

    ShowWindow(hWnd, nCmdShow);  /* Show the window                        */
    UpdateWindow(hWnd);          /* Sends WM_PAINT message                 */
    return (TRUE);               /* Returns the value from PostQuitMessage */

}

/****************************************************************************
    FUNCTION: MainWndProc(HWND, unsigned, WORD, LONG)

    PURPOSE:  Processes messages

    MESSAGES:

        WM_COMMAND    - application menu (About dialog box)
        WM_DESTROY    - destroy window

    COMMENTS:

        To process the IDM_ABOUT message, call MakeProcInstance to get the
        current instance address of the About function. Then call DialogBox,
        which will create the box according to the information in your
        generic.rc file and turn control over to the About function. When
        it returns, free the instance address.

****************************************************************************/
long FAR PASCAL MainWndProc(hWnd, message, wParam, lParam)
HWND hWnd;                                /* window handle     */
unsigned message;                         /* type of message     */
WORD wParam;                              /* additional information     */
LONG lParam;                              /* additional information     */
{
    FARPROC lpProcAbout;          /* pointer to the "About" function */
```

```
    switch (message) {
      case WM_COMMAND:      /* message: command from application menu */
        if (wParam == IDM_ABOUT) {
                lpProcAbout = MakeProcInstance(About, hInst);

                DialogBox(hInst,                     /* current instance     */
                    "AboutBox",                      /* resource to use     */
                    hWnd,                            /* parent handle     */
                    lpProcAbout);                    /* About() instance address */

                FreeProcInstance(lpProcAbout);
                break;
            }
            else                          /* Lets Windows process it     */
                return (DefWindowProc(hWnd, message, wParam, lParam));

           case WM_DESTROY:                 /* message: window being destroyed */
            PostQuitMessage(0);
            break;

           default:                         /* Passes it on if unproccessed    */
            return (DefWindowProc(hWnd, message, wParam, lParam));
    }
    return (NULL);
}

/****************************************************************************
    FUNCTION: About(HWND, unsigned, WORD, LONG)

    PURPOSE:  Processes messages for "About" dialog box

    MESSAGES:

        WM_INITDIALOG - initialize dialog box
        WM_COMMAND    - Input received

    COMMENTS:

        No initialization is needed for this particular dialog box, but TRUE
        must be returned to Windows.

        Wait for user to click on "OK" button, then close the dialog box.

****************************************************************************/
BOOL FAR PASCAL About(hDlg, message, wParam, lParam)
HWND hDlg;                                /* window handle of the dialog box */
unsigned message;                         /* type of message                 */
WORD wParam;                              /* message-specific information    */
LONG lParam;
```

```
{
    switch (message) {
      case WM_INITDIALOG:                   /* message: initialize dialog box */
        return (TRUE);

      case WM_COMMAND:                      /* message: received a command */
        if (wParam == IDOK ||               /* "OK" box selected?          */
            wParam == IDCANCEL) {           /* System menu close command?  */
        EndDialog(hDlg, TRUE);              /* Exits the dialog box        */
        return (TRUE);
        }
              break;
    }
    return (FALSE);                         /* Didn't process a message    */
}
```

2.7.2 Create the Header File

The header file contains definitions and declarations required by the C-language source file which are incorporated into the source code by an **#include** directive. Name the file GENERIC.H and make sure it looks like this:

```
#define IDM_ABOUT 100

int PASCAL                  WinMain (HANDLE, HANDLE, LPSTR, int);
BOOL                        InitApplication (HANDLE);
BOOL                        InitInstance (HANDLE, int);
long FAR PASCAL             MainWndProc (HWND, unsigned, WORD, LONG);
BOOL FAR PASCAL             About (HWND, unsigned, WORD, LONG);
```

2.7.3 Create the Resource Script File

The resource script file must contain the Help menu and the dialog-box template for the About dialog box. Name the file GENERIC.RC and make sure it looks like this:

```
#include "windows.h"
#include "generic.h"

GenericMenu MENU
BEGIN
    POPUP        "&Help"
    BEGIN
        MENUITEM "About Generic...", IDM_ABOUT
    END
END
```

```
AboutBox DIALOG 22, 17, 144, 75
STYLE DS_MODALFRAME | WS_CAPTION | WS_SYSMENU
CAPTION "About Generic"
BEGIN
    CTEXT "Microsoft Windows"       -1,   0,   5,  144,  8
    CTEXT "Generic Application"     -1,   0,  14,  144,  8
    CTEXT "Version 3.0"             -1,   0,  34,  144,  8
    DEFPUSHBUTTON "OK"         IDOK, 53, 59, 32, 14, WS_GROUP
END
```

2.7.4 Create the Module-Definition File

The module-definition file must contain the module definitions for Generic. Name the file GENERIC.DEF and make sure it looks like this:

```
;module-definition file for Generic — used by LINK.EXE

NAME    Generic         ; application's module name

DESCRIPTION 'Sample Microsoft Windows Application'

EXETYPE WINDOWS         ; Required for all Windows applications

STUB    'WINSTUB.EXE'   ; Generates error message if application
                        ; is run without Windows

CODE    MOVEABLE DISCARDABLE; code can be moved in memory and discarded/reloaded

;DATA must be MULTIPLE if program can be invoked more than once

DATA    MOVEABLE MULTIPLE

HEAPSIZE  1024
STACKSIZE 5120  ; recommended minimum for Windows applications

; All functions that will be called by any Windows routine
; MUST be exported.

EXPORTS
    MainWndProc    @1  ; name of window-processing function
    AboutDlgProc   @2  ; name of About processing function
```

2.7.5 Create a Make File

Once you have the source files, you can create Generic's make file, then compile and link the application by using the **MAKE** program. To compile and link Generic, the make file must follow these steps:

- Use the C Compiler (**CL**) to compile the GENERIC.C file.
- Use the linker (**LINK**) to link the GENERIC.OBJ object file with the Windows library and the module-definition file, GENERIC.DEF.
- Use the Resource Compiler (**RC**) to create a binary resource file and add it to the executable file of the Windows application.

The following will properly compile and link the files created for Generic:

```
# Standard Windows make file. The utility MAKE.EXE compares the
# creation date of the file to the left of the colon with the file(s)
# to the right of the colon. If the file(s) on the right are newer
# then the file on the left, MAKE will execute all of the command lines
# following this line that are indented by at least one tab or space.
# Any valid MS-DOS command line may be used.

# Update the resource if necessary

❶ generic.res: generic.rc generic.h
    rc -r generic.rc

# Update the object file if necessary

❷ generic.obj: generic.c generic.h
    cl -c -Gsw -Oas -Zpe generic.c

# Update the executable file if necessary, and if so, add the resource back in.

❸ generic.exe: generic.obj generic.def
    link /NOD generic, , , slibcew libw, generic.def
    rc generic.res

# If the .res file is new and the .exe file is not, update the resource.
# Note that the .rc file can be updated without having to either
# compile or link the file.

❹ generic.exe: generic.res
    rc generic.res
```

❶ The first two lines direct **MAKE** to create a compiled resource file, GENERIC.RES, if the resource script file, GENERIC.RC, or the new include file, GENERIC.H, has been updated. The **–r** option of the **RC** command creates a compiled resource file without attempting to add it to an executable file, since this must be done as the last step in the process.

❷ The next two lines direct **MAKE** to create the GENERIC.OBJ file if GENERIC.C or GENERIC.H has a more recent access date than the current GENERIC.OBJ file. The **cl** command takes several command-line options that prepare the application for execution under Windows. The minimum required options are **–c**, **–Gw**, and **–Zp**. In this case, the C Compiler assumes that Generic is a small-model application. Generic and all other applications in this guide are small-model applications.

❸ The **MAKE** program then creates the GENERIC.EXE file if the GENERIC.OBJ or GENERIC.DEF file has a more recent access date than the current GENERIC.EXE file. Small Windows applications, like Generic, must be linked with the Windows SLIBW.LIB library and the Windows version of the C run-time library, SLIBCEW.LIB. The object file, GENERIC.OBJ, and the module-definition file, GENERIC.DEF, are used as arguments in the **LINK** command line.

❹ The last **RC** command automatically appends the compiled resources in the file GENERIC.RES to the executable file, GENERIC.EXE.

2.7.6 Run the MAKE Program

Once you have created the make file, you can compile and link your application by running the **MAKE** utility. The following example runs **MAKE** using the commands in the file GENERIC:

```
MAKE GENERIC
```

2.8 Using Generic as a Template

Generic provides essentials that make it an appropriate starting point for your applications. It conforms to the standards given in the *System Application Architecture, Common User Access: Advanced Interface Design Guide* for appearance and cooperation with other applications. It contains all the files an application can have: .DEF, .H, .RC, .C, and a make file. The About dialog box, an application standard, is included, as is the About Generic... command on the Help menu.

You can use Generic as a template to build your own applications. To do this, copy and rename the sources of an existing application, such as Generic, then change relevant function names, and insert new code. All sample applications in this guide have been created by copying and renaming Generic's source files, then modifying some of the function and resource names to make them unique to each new application.

The following procedure explains how to use Generic as a template and adapt its source files to your application:

1. Choose your application's filename.
2. Copy the following Generic source files, renaming them to match your application's filename: GENERIC.C, GENERIC.H, GENERIC.DEF, GENERIC.RC, and GENERIC.

3. Use a text editor to change each occurrence of "Generic" in your application's C-language source file to your application's name. This includes changing the following:
   - The class name: GenericWClass
   - The class menu: GenericMenu
   - The window title: Generic Sample Application
   - The include filename: GENERIC.H
4. Use a text editor to change each occurrence of "Generic" in your application's module-definition file to your application's name. This includes changing the following:
   - The application name: Generic
5. Use a text editor to change each occurrence of "Generic" in your application's resource script file to your application's name. This includes changing the following:
   - The include filename: GENERIC.H
   - The application title: Generic Application
   - The menu name: GenericMenu
6. Use a text editor to change each occurrence of "Generic" in your application's make file to your application's name. This includes changing the following:
   - The C-language source filename: GENERIC.C
   - The object filename: GENERIC.OBJ
   - The executable filename: GENERIC.EXE
   - The module-definition filename: GENERIC.DEF

As you add new resources and include files to your applications, be sure to use your application's filename to ensure that these names are unique.

2.9 Summary

This chapter described the required elements of a Windows application, and explained how to build Generic, a simple application that contains those elements. You can use Generic as a template on which to build your own Windows applications.

A Windows application must contain a WinMain function and a window function. The WinMain function performs initializations, processes messages, and terminates the application. The window function responds to input and window-management messages that it receives from Windows.

For more information on topics related to simple Windows applications, see the following:

Topic	Reference
The Windows programming model	*Guide to Programming*: Chapter 1, "An Overview of the Windows Environment"
The message loop	*Guide to Programming*: Chapter 2, "A Generic Windows Application"
Menus	*Guide to Programming*: Chapter 7, "Menus"
Dialog boxes	*Guide to Programming*: Chapter 9, "Dialog Boxes"
Using C run-time routines and assembly language in Windows applications	*Guide to Programming*: Chapter 14, "C and Assembly Language"
Windows functions and messages	*Reference, Volume 1*
The WM_COMMAND message	*Reference, Volume 1*: Chapter 6, "Messages Directory"
Data types and structures	*Reference, Volume 2*: Chapter 7, "Data Types and Structures"
Software development tools	*Tools*

Part 2 Programming Windows Applications

Like most applications, Windows applications receive input from the user and send output to the screen and printer. Unlike standard applications, however, Windows applications must cooperate within a multitasking, graphics-based environment. For this reason, they cannot read directly from the keyboard or write directly to output devices. Instead, they must allow Windows to mediate between the application and shared system resources. The apparent penalty this imposes upon an application is offset by the built-in support Windows provides an application for advanced user-interface and system-interface features.

For example, a user typically provides input to a Windows application by choosing commands from menus, and by entering and selecting information in dialog boxes. In the Windows environment, you do not have to implement the details of how these menus and dialog boxes are displayed and respond to the user's input. Instead, you simply provide a high-level description of their contents and specify the messages that your application will receive when the user interacts with the item. Windows provides the low-level tasks of displaying the menus and dialog boxes and of tracking the user's interaction with them.

Part 1 provided an overview of the Windows environment and the basic structure of a Windows application, and introduced some typical application features, such as windows, menus and dialog boxes.

Part 2 explains each of the major aspects of a Windows application in more detail. In the chapters that follow, you'll learn how to create and work with windows, icons, cursors, menus, dialog boxes, and other features that make a Windows application distinctive and easy to use.

Each chapter in Part 2 covers a particular topic in Windows programming, and provides a sample application that illustrates the concepts in that chapter.

CHAPTERS

Chapter 3 Output to a Window

In Microsoft Windows, all output to a window is performed by the graphics device interface (GDI).

This chapter covers the following topics:

- How the painting and drawing process works in the Windows environment
- The purpose of the display context and the WM_PAINT message
- Using GDI functions to draw within the client area of a window
- Drawing lines and figures, writing text, and creating pens and brushes

This chapter also explains how to build a sample application, Output, that illustrates some of these concepts.

3.1 The Display Context

A display context defines the output device and the current drawing tools, colors, and other drawing information used by GDI to generate output. All GDI output functions require a display-context handle. No output can be performed without one.

To draw within a window, you need the handle to the window. You can then use the window handle to get a handle to the display context of the window's client area.

The method you use to retrieve the handle to the display context depends on where you plan to perform the output operations. Although you can draw and write anywhere within an application, including within the WinMain function, most applications do so only in the window function. The most common time to draw and write is in response to a WM_PAINT message. Windows sends this message to a window function when changes to the window may have altered the content of the client area. Since only the application knows what is in the client area, Windows sends the message to the window function so that this function can restore the client area.

For the WM_PAINT message, you typically use the **BeginPaint** function. If you plan to draw within the client area at any time other than in response to a

WM_PAINT message, you must use the **GetDC** function to retrieve the handle to the display context.

Whenever you retrieve a display context for a window, that context is only on temporary loan from Windows to your application. A display context is a shared resource; as long as one application has it, no other application can retrieve it. Therefore, you must release the display context as soon as possible after using it to draw within the window. If you retrieve a display context by using the **GetDC** function, you must use the **ReleaseDC** function to release it. Similarly, for **BeginPaint**, you use the **EndPaint** function.

3.1.1 Using the GetDC Function

You typically use the **GetDC** function to provide instant feedback to some action by the user, such as drawing a line as the user moves the cursor (pointer) through the window. The function returns a display-context handle that you can use in any GDI output function.

The following example shows how to use the **GetDC** function to retrieve a display-context handle and write the string "Hello Windows!" in the client area:

```
hDC = GetDC(hWnd);
TextOut(hDC, 10,10, "Hello Windows!", 14);
ReleaseDC(hWnd, hDC);
```

In this example, the **GetDC** function returns the display context for the window identified by the *hWnd* parameter, and the **TextOut** function writes the string at the point (10,10) in the window's client area. The **ReleaseDC** function releases the display context.

Anything you draw in the client area will be erased the next time the window function receives a WM_PAINT message that affects that part of the client area. The reason is that Windows sends a WM_ERASEBKGND message to the window function while processing the WM_PAINT message. If you pass WM_ERASEBKGND on to the **DefWindowProc** function, **DefWindowProc** fills the affected area by using the class background brush, erasing any output you may have previously drawn there.

3.1.2 The WM_PAINT Message

Windows posts a WM_PAINT message when the user has changed the window. For example, Windows posts a WM_PAINT message when the user closes a window that covers part of another window. Since a window shares the screen with other windows, anything the user does in one window can have an impact on the content and appearance of another window. However, you can do nothing about the change until your application receives the WM_PAINT message.

Windows posts a WM_PAINT message by making it the last message in the application queue. This means any input is processed before the WM_PAINT message. In fact, the **GetMessage** function also retrieves any input generated after the WM_PAINT message is posted. That is, **GetMessage** retrieves the WM_PAINT message from the queue only when there are no other messages. The reason for this is to let the application carry out any operations that might affect the appearance of the window. In general, output operations should be carried out as infrequently as possible to avoid flicker and other distracting effects. Windows helps ensure this by holding the WM_PAINT message until it is the last message.

The following example shows how to process a WM_PAINT message:

```
PAINTSTRUCT ps;
    .
    .
    .
case WM_PAINT:
    hDC = BeginPaint(hWnd, &ps);
    /* Output operations */
    EndPaint(hWnd, &ps);
    break;
```

The **BeginPaint** and **EndPaint** functions are required. **BeginPaint** fills the **PAINTSTRUCT** structure, ps, with information about the paint request, such as the part of the client area that needs redrawing, and returns a handle to the display context. You can use the handle in any GDI output functions. The **EndPaint** function ends the paint request and releases the display context.

You must not use the **GetDC** and **ReleaseDC** functions in place of the **BeginPaint** and **EndPaint** functions. **BeginPaint** and **EndPaint** carry out special tasks, such as validating the client area and sending the WM_ERASEBKGND message, that ensure that the paint request is processed properly. If you use **GetDC** instead of **BeginPaint**, the painting request will never be satisfied and your window function will continue to receive the same paint request.

3.1.3 Invalidating the Client Area

Windows is not the only source of WM_PAINT messages. You can also generate WM_PAINT messages for your windows by using the **InvalidateRect** or **InvalidateRgn** functions. These functions mark all or part of a client area as invalid (in need of redrawing). For example, the following function invalidates the entire client area:

```
InvalidateRect(hWnd, NULL, TRUE);
```

This example invalidates the entire client area for the window identified by the *hWnd* parameter. The NULL argument, used in place of a rectangle structure, specifies the entire client area. The TRUE argument causes the background to be erased.

When the client area is marked as invalid, Windows posts a WM_PAINT message. If other parts of the client area are marked as invalid, Windows does not post another WM_PAINT message. Instead, it adds the invalidated areas to the previous area, so that all areas are processed by the same WM_PAINT message.

If you change your mind about redrawing the client area, you can validate parts of it by using the **ValidateRect** and **ValidateRgn** functions. These functions remove any previous invalidation and will remove the WM_PAINT message if no other invalidated area remains.

If you do not want to wait for the WM_PAINT message to be retrieved from the application queue, you can force an immediate WM_PAINT message by using the **UpdateWindow** function. If there is any invalid part of the client area, **UpdateWindow** pulls the WM_PAINT message for the given window from the queue and sends it directly to the window function.

3.1.4 Display Contexts and Device Contexts

A display context is actually a type of "device context" that has been especially prepared for output to the client area of a window. A device context defines the device, drawing tools, and drawing information for a complete device, such as a display or printer; a display context defines these things only for a window's client area. To prepare a display context, Windows adjusts the device origin so that it aligns with the upper-left corner of the client area instead of with the upper-left corner of the display. It also sets a clipping rectangle so that output to a display context is "clipped" to the client area. This means any output that would otherwise appear outside the client area is not sent to the display.

3.1.5 The Coordinate System

The default coordinate system for a display context is very simple. The upper-left corner of the client area is the origin, or point (0,0). Each pixel to the right represents one unit along the positive *x*-axis. Each pixel down represents one unit along the positive *y*-axis.

You can modify this coordinate system by changing the mapping mode and display origins. The mapping mode defines the coordinate-system units. The default mode is MM_TEXT, or one pixel per unit. You can also specify mapping modes that use inches or millimeters as units. The **SetMapMode** function changes the mapping mode for a device. The origin of the coordinate system can be moved to any point by calling the **SetViewportOrg** function.

For simplicity, the examples in this chapter and throughout this guide use the default coordinate system.

3.2 Creating, Selecting, and Deleting Drawing Tools

GDI lets you use a variety of drawing tools to draw within a window. It provides pens to draw lines, brushes to fill interiors, and fonts to write text. To create these tools, use functions such as **CreatePen** and **CreateSolidBrush**. Then select them into the display context by using the **SelectObject** function. When you are done using a drawing tool, you can delete it by using the **DeleteObject** function.

Use the **CreatePen** function to create a pen for drawing lines and borders. The function returns a handle to a pen that has the specified style, width, and color. (Be sure to check the return value of **CreatePen** to ensure that it is a valid handle.)

The following example creates a dashed, black pen, one pixel wide:

```
HPEN hDashPen;
     .
     .
     .

hDashPen = CreatePen(PS_DASH, 1, RGB(0, 0, 0));
if (hDashPen)      /* make sure handle is valid  */
     .
     .
     .
```

The **RGB** utility creates a 32-bit value representing a red, green, and blue color value. The three arguments specify the intensity of the colors red, green, and blue, respectively. In this example, all colors have zero intensity, so the specified color is black.

You can create solid brushes for drawing and filling by using the **Create-SolidBrush** function. This function returns a handle to a brush that contains the specified solid color. (Be sure to check the return value of **CreateSolidBrush** to ensure that it is a valid handle.)

The following example shows how to create a red brush:

```
HBRUSH hRedBrush
     .
     .
     .

hRedBrush = CreateSolidBrush(RGB(255, 0, 0));
if (hRedBrush)    /* make sure handle is valid */
     .
     .
     .
```

Once you have created a drawing tool, you can select it into a display context by using the **SelectObject** function. The following example selects the red brush for drawing:

```
HBRUSH hOldBrush;
      .
      .
      .
hOldBrush = SelectObject(hDC, hRedBrush);
```

In this example, **SelectObject** returns a handle to the previous brush. In general, you should save the handle of the previous drawing tool so that you can restore it later.

You do not have to create or select a drawing tool before using a display context. Windows provides default drawing tools with each display context; for example, a black pen, a white brush, and the system font.

You can delete drawing objects you no longer need by using the **DeleteObject** function. The following example deletes the brush identified by the handle hRedBrush:

```
DeleteObject(hRedBrush);
```

You must not delete a selected drawing tool. You should use the **SelectObject** function to restore a previous drawing tool and remove the tool to be deleted from the selection, as shown in the following example:

```
SelectObject(hDC, hOldBrush);
DeleteObject(hRedBrush);
```

Although you can create and select fonts for writing text, working with fonts is a fairly involved process and is not described in this chapter. For a full discussion of how to create and select fonts, see Chapter 18, "Fonts."

3.3 Drawing and Writing

GDI provides a wide variety of output operations, from drawing lines to writing text. Specifically, you can use the **LineTo**, **Rectangle**, **Ellipse**, **Arc**, **Pie**, **TextOut**, and **DrawText** functions to draw lines, rectangles, circles, arcs, pie wedges, and text, respectively. All these functions use the selected pen and brush to draw borders and fill interiors, and the selected font to write text.

You can draw lines by using the **LineTo** function. You usually combine the **MoveTo** and **LineTo** functions to draw lines. The following example draws a line from the point (10,90) to the point (360,90):

```
MoveTo(hDC, 10, 90);
LineTo(hDC, 360, 90);
```

You can draw a rectangle by using the **Rectangle** function. This function uses the selected pen to draw the border, and the selected brush to fill the interior. The following example draws a rectangle that has its upper-left and lower-right corners at the points (10,30) and (60,80), respectively:

```
Rectangle (hDC, 10, 30, 60, 80);
```

You can draw an ellipse or circle by using the **Ellipse** function. The function uses the selected pen to draw the border, and the selected brush to fill the interior. The following example draws an ellipse that is bounded by the rectangle specified by the points (160,30) and (210,80):

```
Ellipse (hDC, 160, 30, 210, 80);
```

You can draw arcs by using the **Arc** function. You draw an arc by defining a bounding rectangle for the circle containing the arc, then specifying on which points the arc starts and ends. The following example draws an arc within the rectangle defined by the points (10,90) and (360,120); it draws the arc from the point (10,90) to the point (360,90):

```
Arc(hDC, 10, 90, 360, 120, 10, 90, 360, 90);
```

You can draw a pie wedge by using the **Pie** function. A pie wedge consists of an arc and two radii extending from the focus of the arc to its endpoints. The **Pie** function uses the selected pen to draw the border, and the selected brush to fill the interior. The following example draws a pie wedge that is bounded by the rectangle specified by the points (310,30) and (360,80) and that starts and ends at the points (360,30) and (360,80), respectively:

```
Pie (hDC, 310, 30, 360, 80, 360, 30, 360, 80);
```

You can display text by using the **TextOut** function. The function displays a string starting at the specified point. The following example displays the string "A Sample String" at the point (1,1):

```
TextOut(hDC, 1, 1, "A Sample String", 15);
```

You can also use the **DrawText** function to display text. This function is similar to **TextOut**, except that it lets you write text on multiple lines. The following example displays the string "This long string illustrates the DrawText function" on multiple lines in the specified rectangle:

```
RECT rcTextBox;
LPSTR lpText = "This long string illustrates the DrawText function";
    .
    .
    .

SetRect(&rcTextBox, 1, 10, 160, 40);
DrawText(hDC, lpText, strlen(lpText), &rcTextBox, DT_LEFT);
```

This example displays the string pointed to by the lpText variable as one or more left-aligned lines in the rectangle specified by the points (1,10) and (160,40).

Although you can also create and display bitmaps in a window, the process is not described in this chapter. For details, see Chapter 11, "Bitmaps."

3.4 A Sample Application: Output

The sample application Output illustrates how to use the WM_PAINT message to draw within the client area, as well as how to create and use drawing tools. The Output application is a simple extension of the Generic application described in the previous chapter. To create the Output application, copy and rename the source files of the Generic application, then make the following modifications:

1. Add new variables.
2. Modify the WM_CREATE case.
3. Add a WM_PAINT case.
4. Modify the WM_DESTROY case.
5. Compile and link the application.

You can find the source files for Output on the SDK Sample Source Code disk.

This sample assumes that you have a color display. If you do not, GDI will simulate some of the color output by "dithering." Dithering is a method of simulating a color by creating a unique pattern with two or more available colors. On a color monitor that cannot display orange, for example, Windows simulates orange by using a pattern of red and yellow pixels. On a monochrome monitor, Windows represents colors with black, white, and shades of gray, instead of colors.

NOTE Rather than typing the code presented in the following sections, you might find it more convenient to simply examine and compile the sample source files provided with the SDK.

3.4.1 Add New Variables

You need several new global variables for this sample application. Add the following variables at the beginning of your C-language source file:

```
HPEN hDashPen;              /* "--" pen handle     */
HPEN hDotPen;               /* "..." pen handle    */
HBRUSH hOldBrush;           /* old brush handle    */
HBRUSH hRedBrush;           /* red brush handle    */
```

```
HBRUSH hGreenBrush;          /* green brush handle */
HBRUSH hBlueBrush;           /* blue brush handle  */
```

You also need new local variables in the window function. Declare the following at the beginning of the MainWndProc function:

```
HDC hDC;               /* display-context variable  */
PAINTSTRUCT ps;        /* paint structure           */
RECT rcTextBox;        /* rectangle around the text */
HPEN hOldPen;          /* old pen handle            */
```

3.4.2 Add the WM_CREATE Case

You must create the drawing tools to be used in Output's client area before any drawing is carried out. Since you need to create these tools only once, a convenient place to do so is in the WM_CREATE message. Add the following statements to the MainWndProc function:

```
case WM_CREATE:

    /* Create the brush objects */

    hRedBrush =   CreateSolidBrush(RGB(255,   0,   0));
    hGreenBrush = CreateSolidBrush(RGB(  0, 255,   0));
    hBlueBrush =  CreateSolidBrush(RGB(  0,   0, 255));

    /* Create the "--" pen */

    hDashPen = CreatePen(PS_DASH,             /* style */
        1,                                    /* width */
        RGB(0, 0, 0));                        /* color */

    /* Create the "..." pen */

    hDotPen = CreatePen(PS_DOT,               /* style */
        1,                                    /* width */
        RGB(0, 0, 0));                        /* color */
    break;
```

The **CreateSolidBrush** functions create the solid brushes to be used to fill the rectangle, the ellipse, and the circle that Output draws on the screen in response to the WM_PAINT message. The **CreatePen** functions create the dotted and dashed lines used to draw borders.

3.4.3 Add the WM_PAINT Case

The WM_PAINT message informs your application when it should redraw all or part of its client area. To handle this message, add to the window function the following **case** statement:

```
case WM_PAINT:
    {
        TEXTMETRIC textmetric;
        int nDrawX;
        int nDrawY;
        char szText[300];

        /* Set up a display context to begin painting */

        hDC = BeginPaint (hWnd, &ps);

        /* Get the size characteristics of the current font. */
        /* This information will be used for determining the  */
        /* vertical spacing of text on the screen. */

        GetTextMetrics (hDC, &textmetric);

        /* Initialize drawing position to 1/4 inch from the top */
        /* and from the left of the top, left corner of the     */
        /* client area of the main window. */

        nDrawX = GetDeviceCaps (hDC, LOGPIXELSX) / 4;   /* 1/4 inch */
        nDrawY = GetDeviceCaps (hDC, LOGPIXELSY) / 4;   /* 1/4 inch */

        /* Send characters to the screen. After displaying each  */
        /* line of text, advance the vertical position for the    */
        /* next line of text. The pixel distance between the top  */
        /* of each line of text is equal to the standard height of */
        /* the font characters (tmHeight), plus the standard      */
        /* amount of spacing (tmExternalLeading) between adjacent */
        /* lines. */

        strcpy (szText, "These characters are being painted using ");
        TextOut (hDC, nDrawX, nDrawY, szText, strlen (szText));
        nDrawY += textmetric.tmExternalLeading + textmetric.tmHeight;

        strcpy (szText, "the TextOut() function, which is fast and ");
        TextOut (hDC, nDrawX, nDrawY, szText, strlen (szText));
        nDrawY += textmetric.tmExternalLeading + textmetric.tmHeight;

        strcpy (szText, "allows programmer control of placement and ");
        TextOut (hDC, nDrawX, nDrawY, szText, strlen (szText));
        nDrawY += textmetric.tmExternalLeading + textmetric.tmHeight;

        strcpy (szText, "formatting details. However, TextOut() ");
        TextOut (hDC, nDrawX, nDrawY, szText, strlen (szText));
        nDrawY += textmetric.tmExternalLeading + textmetric.tmHeight;

        strcpy (szText, "does not provide any automatic formatting.");
        TextOut (hDC, nDrawX, nDrawY, szText, strlen (szText));
        nDrawY += textmetric.tmExternalLeading + textmetric.tmHeight;
```

```
/* Put text in a 5-inch by 1-inch rectangle and display it. */
/* First define the size of the rectangle around the text  */

nDrawY += GetDeviceCaps (hDC, LOGPIXELSY) / 4;  /* 1/4 inch */
SetRect (
      &rcTextBox
    , nDrawX
    , nDrawY
    , nDrawX + (5 * GetDeviceCaps (hDC, LOGPIXELSX)) /* 5" */
    , nDrawY + (1 * GetDeviceCaps (hDC, LOGPIXELSY)) /* 1" */
);

/* Draw the text within the bounds of the above rectangle */

strcpy (szText, "This text is being displayed with a single "
            "call to DrawText(). DrawText() isn't as fast "
            "as TextOut(), and it is somewhat more "
            "constrained, but it provides numerous optional "
            "formatting features, such as the centering and "
            "line breaking used in this example.");
DrawText (
      hDC
    , szText
    , strlen (szText)
    , &rcTextBox
    , DT_CENTER | DT_EXTERNALLEADING | DT_NOCLIP
                                    | DT_NOPREFIX | DT_WORDBREAK
);

/*  Paint the next object immediately below the bottom of  */
/*  the above rectangle in which the text was drawn. */

nDrawY = rcTextBox.bottom;

/* The (x,y) pixel coordinates of the objects about to be  */
/* drawn are below, and to the right of, the current       */
/* coordinate (nDrawX,nDrawY). */

/* Draw a red rectangle.. */

hOldBrush = SelectObject(hDC, hRedBrush);
Rectangle (
      hDC
    , nDrawX
    , nDrawY
    , nDrawX + 50
    , nDrawY + 30
);
```

```
/* Draw a green ellipse */

SelectObject(hDC, hGreenBrush);
Ellipse (
      hDC
    , nDrawX + 150
    , nDrawY
    , nDrawX + 150 + 50
    , nDrawY + 30
);

/* Draw a blue pie shape */

SelectObject(hDC, hBlueBrush);
Pie (
      hDC
    , nDrawX + 300
    , nDrawY
    , nDrawX + 300 + 50
    , nDrawY + 50
    , nDrawX + 300 + 50
    , nDrawY
    , nDrawX + 300 + 50
    , nDrawY + 50
);

nDrawY += 50;

/* Restore the old brush */

SelectObject(hDC, hOldBrush);

/* Select a "--" pen, save the old value */

nDrawY += GetDeviceCaps (hDC, LOGPIXELSY) / 4;  /* 1/4 inch */
hOldPen = SelectObject(hDC, hDashPen);

/* Move to a specified point */

MoveTo(hDC, nDrawX, nDrawY);

/* Draw a line */

LineTo(hDC, nDrawX + 350, nDrawY);

/* Select a "..." pen */

SelectObject(hDC, hDotPen);
```

```
    /* Draw an arc connecting the line */

    Arc (
          hDC
        , nDrawX
        , nDrawY - 20
        , nDrawX + 350
        , nDrawY + 20
        , nDrawX
        , nDrawY
        , nDrawX + 350
        , nDrawY
    );

    /* Restore the old pen */

    SelectObject(hDC, hOldPen);

    /* Tell Windows you are done painting */

    EndPaint (hWnd,  &ps);
}
break;
```

NOTE "Hard-coding" strings using functions such as **strcpy** can make it difficult to translate your application into other languages. If you plan to distribute your application in more than one language, you should use string tables instead. See the *Reference, Volume 2*, for more information about string tables.

3.4.4 Modify the WM_DESTROY Case

Before terminating the Output application, you should delete the drawing tools created for Output's window; this frees the memory that each drawing tool uses. To do this, use the **DeleteObject** function to delete the various pens and brushes in the WM_DESTROY case. Modify the WM_DESTROY case so that it looks like this:

```
case WM_DESTROY:

    DeleteObject(hRedBrush);
    DeleteObject(hGreenBrush);
    DeleteObject(hBlueBrush);
    DeleteObject(hDashPen);
    DeleteObject(hDotPen);
    PostQuitMessage(0);
    break;
```

You must include one **DeleteObject** function call for each object to be deleted.

3.4.5 Compile and Link

No changes are required to the make file to recompile and link the Output application. After compiling and linking Output, start Windows and the application. The application should look like Figure 3.1:

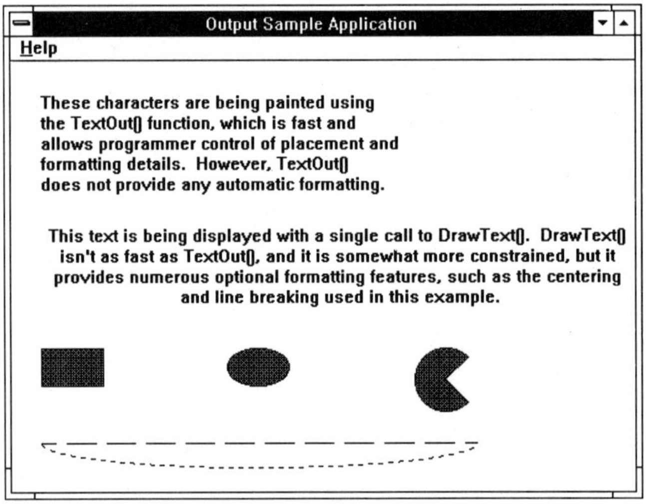

Figure 3.1 The Output Application's Window

You can use the WM_PAINT case of this application to experiment with a variety of GDI functions. For information about other GDI output functions, see the *Reference, Volume 1*.

3.5 Summary

This chapter described how the graphics device interface (GDI) portion of Windows handles output to a window. GDI uses a "display context" to generate output. A display context is a data structure, maintained by GDI, that contains information about the display device you are using.

GDI lets you use a variety of drawing tools and output operations to draw within a window.

For more information on topics related to output, see the following:

Topic	Reference
Working with bitmaps	*Guide to Programming*: Chapter 11, "Bitmaps"
	Tools: Chapter 4, "Designing Images: SDKPaint"
Working with fonts	*Guide to Programming*: Chapter 18, "Fonts"
	Tools: Chapter 6, "Designing Fonts: The Font Editor"
Window functions and class and private display contexts	*Reference, Volume 1*: Chapter 1, "Window Manager Interface Functions"
Painting functions	*Reference, Volume 1*: Chapter 2, "Graphics Device Interface Functions," and Chapter 4, "Functions Directory"
WM_PAINT, WM_CREATE, and WM_DESTROY messages	*Reference, Volume 1*: Chapter 6, "Messages Directory"
Data types and structures	*Reference, Volume 2*: Chapter 7, "Data Types and Structures"

Chapter 4 Keyboard and Mouse Input

Most applications require input from the user. Typically, input from the user comes via the keyboard or the mouse. In Microsoft Windows, applications receive keyboard and mouse input in the form of input messages.

This chapter covers the following topics:

- The input messages that Windows sends your application
- Responding to Windows input messages

This chapter also explains how to build a sample application, Input, that responds to various types of input messages.

4.1 Windows Input Messages

Whenever the user presses a key, moves the mouse, or clicks a mouse button, Windows responds by sending input messages to the appropriate application. Windows also sends input messages in response to timer input.

Windows provides several types of input messages:

Message	Description
Keyboard	User input through the keyboard.
Character	Keyboard input translated into character codes.
Mouse	User input through the mouse.
Timer	Input from the system timer.
Scroll-bar	User input through a window's scroll bars and the mouse.
Menu	User input through a window's menus and the mouse.

The keyboard, mouse, and timer input messages correspond directly to hardware input. Windows passes these messages to your application through the application queue.

The character, menu, and scroll-bar messages are created in response to mouse and keyboard actions in the nonclient area of a window, or are the result of translated keyboard messages. Normally, Windows sends these messages directly to the appropriate window function.

4.1.1 Message Formats

Input messages come in two formats, depending on how your application receives them:

- Messages that Windows places in the application queue take the form of a **MSG** structure.

  The **MSG** structure contains fields that identify and contain information about the message. Your application's message loop retrieves this structure from the application queue and dispatches it to the appropriate window function.

- Messages that Windows sends directly to a window function take the form of four arguments. The arguments correspond to the window function's *hWnd*, *message*, *wParam*, and *lParam* parameters.

The only difference between these two message forms is that the **MSG** structure contains two additional pieces of information: the current location of the cursor (pointer) and the current system time. Windows does not pass this information to the window function.

4.1.2 Keyboard Input

Much of an application's user input comes from the keyboard. Windows sends keyboard input to an application when the user presses or releases a key. Windows generates keyboard messages in response to the following keyboard events:

Message	Event
WM_KEYDOWN	User presses a key.
WM_KEYUP	User releases a key.
WM_SYSKEYDOWN	User presses a system key.
WM_SYSKEYUP	User releases a system key.

The *wParam* parameter of a keyboard message specifies the "virtual-key code" of the key the user pressed. A virtual-key code is a device-independent value for a specific keyboard key. Windows uses virtual-key codes so that it can provide consistent keyboard input no matter what computer your application is running on.

The *lParam* parameter contains the keyboard's actual scan code for the key, as well as additional information about the keyboard, such as the state of the SHIFT key and whether the current key was previously up or down.

Windows generates system-key messages, WM_SYSKEYUP and WM_SYSKEYDOWN. These are special keys, such as the ALT and F10 keys, that belong to the Windows user interface and cannot be used by an application in any other way.

An application receives keyboard messages only when it has the "input focus." Your application receives the input focus when it is the active application; that is, when the user has selected your application's window. You can also use the **SetFocus** function to explicitly set the input focus for a given window, and the **GetFocus** function to determine which window has the focus.

4.1.3 Character Input

Applications that read character input from the keyboard need to use the **TranslateMessage** function in their message loops. **TranslateMessage** translates a keyboard-input message into a corresponding ANSI-character message, WM_CHAR or WM_SYSCHAR. These messages contain the ANSI character codes for the given key in the *wParam* parameter. The *lParam* parameter is identical to *lParam* in the keyboard-input message.

4.1.4 Mouse Input

User input can also come from the mouse. Windows sends mouse messages to the application when the user moves the cursor into and through a window or presses or releases a mouse button while the cursor is in the window. Windows generates mouse messages in response to the following events:

Message	Event
WM_MOUSEMOVE	User moves the cursor into or through the window.
WM_LBUTTONDOWN	User presses the left button.
WM_LBUTTONUP	User releases the left button.
WM_LBUTTONDBLCLK	User presses, releases, and presses again the left button within the system's defined double-click time.
WM_MBUTTONDOWN	User presses the middle button.
WM_MBUTTONUP	User releases the middle button.

Message	Event
WM_MBUTTONDBLCLK	User presses, releases, and presses again the middle button within the system's defined double-click time.
WM_RBUTTONDOWN	User presses the right button.
WM_RBUTTONUP	User releases the right button.
WM_RBUTTONDBLCLK	User presses, releases, and presses again the right button within the system's defined double-click time.

The *wParam* parameter of each button includes a bitmask specifying the current state of the keyboard and mouse buttons, such as whether the mouse buttons, SHIFT key, and CONTROL key are down. The *lParam* parameter contains the the *x*- and *y*-coordinates of the cursor.

Windows sends mouse messages to a window only if the cursor is in the window or if you have captured mouse input by using the **SetCapture** function. The **SetCapture** function directs Windows to send all mouse input, regardless of where the cursor is, to the specified window. Applications typically use this function to take control of the mouse when carrying out some critical operation with the mouse, such as selecting something in the client area. Capturing the mouse prevents other applications from taking control of the mouse before the operation is completed.

Since the mouse is a shared resource, it is important to release the captured mouse as soon as you have finished the operation. You release the mouse by using the **ReleaseCapture** function. Use the **GetCapture** function to determine which window, if any, has the captured mouse.

Windows sends double-click messages to a window function only if the corresponding window class has the CS_DBLCLKS style. You must set this style while registering the window class. A double-click message is always the third message in a four-message series. The first two messages are the first button press and release. The second button press is replaced with the double-click message. The last message is the second release. Remember that a double-click message occurs only if the first and second press occur within the system's defined double-click time. You can retrieve the current double-click time by using the **GetDoubleClickTime** function. You can set it by using the **SetDoubleClickTime** function, but be aware that this sets the double-click time for all applications, not just your own.

4.1.5 Timer Input

Windows sends timer input to your application when the specified interval elapses for a particular timer. To receive timer input, you must set a timer by using the **SetTimer** function.

You can receive timer input in two ways:

- Windows can place a WM_TIMER message in your application's queue.
- Windows can call a callback function defined in your application. You specify the callback function when you call the **SetTimer** function.

The following example shows how to set timer input for a five-second interval:

```
idTimer = SetTimer (hWnd, 1, 5000, (FARPROC) NULL);
```

This example sets a timer interval of 5000 milliseconds. This means that the timer will generate input every five seconds. The second argument is any non-zero value that your application uses to identify the particular timer. The last argument specifies the callback function that will receive timer input. Setting this argument to NULL tells Windows to provide timer input as a WM_TIMER message. Because there is no callback function specified for timer input, Windows sends the timer input through the application queue.

The **SetTimer** function returns a "timer ID"—an integer that identifies the timer. You can use this timer ID to turn the timer off by using it in the **KillTimer** function.

4.1.6 Scroll-Bar Input

Windows sends a scroll-bar input message, either WM_HSCROLL or WM_VSCROLL, to a window function when the user clicks with the cursor in a scroll bar. Applications use the scroll-bar messages to direct scrolling within the window. Applications that display text or other data that does not all fit in the client area usually provide some form of scrolling. Scroll bars are an easy way to let the user direct scrolling actions.

To get scroll-bar input, add scroll bars to the window. You can do this by specifying the WS_HSCROLL and WS_VSCROLL styles when you create the window. These direct the **CreateWindow** function to create horizontal and vertical scroll bars for the window. The following example creates scroll bars for the given window:

```
hWnd = CreateWindow("InputWCLass",  /* window class      */
    "Input Sample Application",     /* window name       */
    WS_OVERLAPPEDWINDOW | WS_HSCROLL | WS_VSCROLL,
    CW_USEDEFAULT,                  /* x position        */
    CW_USEDEFAULT,                  /* y position        */
    CW_USEDEFAULT,                  /* width             */
    CW_USEDEFAULT,                  /* height            */
    NULL,                           /* parent handle     */
    NULL,                           /* menu or child ID */
    hInstance,                      /* instance          */
    NULL);                          /* additional info  */
```

Windows displays the scroll bars when it displays the window. It automatically maintains the scroll bars and sends scroll-bar messages to the window function when the user moves the thumb of the scroll bar.

When Windows sends a scroll-bar message, it sets the *wParam* parameter of the message to indicate the type of scrolling request made. For example, if the user clicks the Up arrow of a vertical scroll bar, Windows sets the *wParam* parameter to the value SB_LINEUP. Depending on the event, Windows sets the *wParam* parameter to one of the following values:

Value	Event
SB_LINEUP	User clicks the Up or Left arrow.
SB_LINEDOWN	User clicks the Down or Right arrow.
SB_PAGEUP	User clicks between the scroll box and the Up or Left arrow.
SB_PAGEDOWN	User clicks between the scroll box and the Down or Right arrow.
SB_THUMBPOSITION	User releases the mouse button when the cursor is in the scroll box, typically after dragging the box.
SB_THUMBTRACK	User drags the scroll box with the mouse.

4.1.7 Menu Input

Whenever the user chooses a command from a menu, Windows sends a menu-input message to the window function for that window.

There are two types of menu-input messages:

- WM_SYSCOMMAND, which indicates that the user has selected a command from the System menu.
- WM_COMMAND, which indicates that the user has selected a command from the application's menu.

Since menu input is often the primary source of input for an application, its processing can be complex. See Chapter 7, "Menus," for more information on menus and menu input.

4.2 A Sample Application: Input

This sample application, Input, illustrates how to process input messages from the keyboard, mouse, timer, and scroll bars. The Input application displays the current or most recent state of each of these input mechanisms. To create the

Input application, copy and rename the source files of the Generic application, then make the following modifications:

1. Add new variables.
2. Set the window-class style.
3. Modify the **CreateWindow** function.
4. Set the text rectangles.
5. Add the WM_CREATE case.
6. Modify the WM_DESTROY case.
7. Add the WM_KEYUP and WM_KEYDOWN cases.
8. Add the WM_CHAR case.
9. Add the WM_MOUSEMOVE case.
10. Add the WM_LBUTTONUP and WM_RBUTTONUP cases.
11. Add the WM_LBUTTONDBLCLK case.
12. Add the WM_TIMER case.
13. Add the WM_HSCROLL and WM_VSCROLL cases.
14. Add the WM_PAINT case.
15. Compile and link the Input application.

Although Windows does not require a pointing device, this sample assumes that you have a mouse or other pointing device. If you do not have a mouse, the application will not receive mouse-input messages.

NOTE Rather than typing the code presented in the following sections, you might find it more convenient to simply examine and compile the sample source files provided in the SDK.

4.2.1 How the Input Application Displays Output

The Input application responds to input messages by displaying text that indicates the type of input message. It uses some simple functions to format and display the output.

To create a formatted string, use **wsprintf**, the Windows version of the C run-time function **sprintf**. The Windows **wsprintf** function copies a formatted string to a buffer; you can then pass the buffer address as an argument to the **TextOut** function. In small-model applications, such as the sample applications described in this guide, be careful when using the **wsprintf** function; the buffer you specify must be defined within the application's data segment or stack. The following example shows how to create a formatted string:

```
char MouseText[48];
     .
     .
     .

wsprintf(MouseText, "WM_MOUSEMOVE: %x, %d, %d", wParam,
    LOWORD(lParam), HIWORD(lParam));
```

This example copies the formatted string to the MouseText array. The array is declared a local variable so that it can be passed to the **wsprintf** function.

4.2.2 Add New Variables

You need several new global variables. Declare the following variables at the beginning of the C-language source file:

```
char MouseText[48];      /* mouse state          */
char ButtonText[48];     /* mouse-button state   */
char KeyboardText[48];   /* keyboard state       */
char CharacterText[48];  /* latest character     */
char ScrollText[48];     /* scroll status        */
char TimerText[48];      /* timer state          */
RECT rectMouse;
RECT rectButton;
RECT rectKeyboard;
RECT rectCharacter;
RECT rectScroll;
RECT rectTimer;
int idTimer;             /* timer ID             */
int nTimerCount = 0;     /* current timer count */
```

The character arrays hold strings that describe the current state of the keyboard, mouse, and timer. The rectangles keep track of where the strings appear on the screen; they facilitate the invalidation technique explained in Section 4.2.15, "Add the WM_PAINT Case."

You also need some local variables for the window function. Declare the following variables at the beginning of the MainWndProc window function:

```
HDC hDC;                /* display-context variable     */
PAINTSTRUCT ps;         /* paint structure              */
char HorzOrVertText[12];
char ScrollTypeText[20];
RECT rect;
```

Add the following variables to the InitInstance function:

```
HDC           hdc;
TEXTMETRIC    textmetric;
RECT          rect;
int           nLineHeight;
```

4.2.3 Set the Window-Class Style

Set the window-class style to CS_DBLCLKS to enable double-click processing. In the initialization function, find this statement:

```
wc.style = NULL;
```

Change it to the following:

```
wc.style = CS_DBLCLKS;
```

This enables double-click processing for windows that belong to this class.

4.2.4 Modify the CreateWindow Function

Modify the call to the **CreateWindow** function in order to create a window that has vertical and horizontal scroll bars. Change the **CreateWindow** function call in the WinMain function so that it looks like this:

```
hWnd = CreateWindow("InputWClass",
    "Input Sample Window",
    WS_OVERLAPPEDWINDOW | WS_HSCROLL | WS_VSCROLL,
    CW_USEDEFAULT,
    CW_USEDEFAULT,
    CW_USEDEFAULT,
    CW_USEDEFAULT,
    NULL,
    NULL,
    hInstance,
    NULL);
```

4.2.5 Set the Text Rectangles

Add the following statements to the InitInstance function to establish the client-area rectangles in which different messages are displayed:

```
hDC = GetDC(hWnd);
GetTextMetrics(hDC, &textmetric);
ReleaseDC(hWnd, hDC);
nLineHeight = textmetric.tmExternalLeading + textmetric.tmHeight;
```

```
rect.left   = GetDeviceCaps(hDC, LOGPIXELSX) / 4;  /* 1/4 inch */
rect.right  = GetDeviceCaps(hDC, HORZRES);
rect.top    = GetDeviceCaps(hDC, LOGPIXELSY) / 4;  /* 1/4 inch */
rect.bottom = rect.top + nLineHeight;
rectMouse   = rect;

rect.top += nLineHeight;
rect.bottom += nLineHeight;
rectButton = rect;

rect.top += nLineHeight;
rect.bottom += nLineHeight;
rectKeyboard = rect;

rect.top += nLineHeight;
rect.bottom += nLineHeight;
rectCharacter = rect;

rect.top += nLineHeight;
rect.bottom += nLineHeight;
rectScroll = rect;

rect.top += nLineHeight;
rect.bottom += nLineHeight;
rectTimer = rect;
```

4.2.6 Add the WM_CREATE Case

Set a timer by using the **SetTimer** function. You can do this in the WM_CREATE case. Add the following statements:

```
case WM_CREATE:
    /* Set the timer for five-second intervals */
    idTimer =  SetTimer(hWnd, NULL, 5000, (FARPROC) NULL);
    break;
```

4.2.7 Modify the WM_DESTROY Case

You also need to stop the timer before terminating the application. You can do this in the WM_DESTROY case. Add the following statement:

```
KillTimer(hWnd, idTimer);
```

4.2.8 Add the WM_KEYUP and WM_KEYDOWN Cases

Add the WM_KEYUP and WM_KEYDOWN cases to process key presses. Add the following statements to the window function:

```
case WM_KEYDOWN:
    wsprintf(KeyboardText, "WM_KEYDOWN: %x, %x, %x",
        wParam, LOWORD(lParam), HIWORD(lParam));
    InvalidateRect(hWnd, &rectKeyboard, TRUE);
    break;

case WM_KEYUP:
    wsprintf(KeyboardText, "WM_KEYUP: %x, %x, %x",
        wParam, LOWORD(lParam), HIWORD(lParam));
    InvalidateRect(hWnd, &rectKeyboard, TRUE);
    break;
```

4.2.9 Add the WM_CHAR Case

Add a WM_CHAR case to process ANSI-character input. Add the following statements to the window function:

```
case WM_CHAR:
    wsprintf(CharacterText, "WM_CHAR: %c, %x, %x",
        wParam, LOWORD(lParam), HIWORD(lParam));
    InvalidateRect(hWnd, &rectCharacter, TRUE);
    break;
```

4.2.10 Add the WM_MOUSEMOVE Case

Add a WM_MOUSEMOVE case to process mouse-motion messages. Add the following statements to the window function:

```
case WM_MOUSEMOVE:
    wsprintf(MouseText, "WM_MOUSEMOVE: %x, %d, %d",
        wParam, LOWORD(lParam), HIWORD(lParam));
    InvalidateRect(hWnd, &rectMouse, TRUE);
    break;
```

4.2.11 Add the WM_LBUTTONUP and WM_LBUTTONDOWN Cases

Add the WM_LBUTTONUP and WM_LBUTTONDOWN cases to process mouse-button input messages. Add the following statements to the window function:

```
case WM_LBUTTONDOWN:
    wsprintf(ButtonText, "WM_LBUTTONDOWN: %x, %d, %d",
        wParam, LOWORD(lParam), HIWORD(lParam));
    InvalidateRect(hWnd, &rectButton, TRUE);
    break;
```

```
case WM_LBUTTONUP:
    wsprintf(ButtonText, "WM_LBUTTONUP: %x, %d, %d",
        wParam, LOWORD(lParam), HIWORD(lParam));
    InvalidateRect(hWnd, &rectButton, TRUE);
    break;
```

4.2.12 Add the WM_LBUTTONDBLCLK Case

Add a WM_LBUTTONDBLCLK case to process mouse-button input messages. Add the following statements to the window function:

```
case WM_LBUTTONDBLCLK:
    wsprintf(ButtonText, "WM_LBUTTONDBLCLK: %x, %d, %d",
        wParam, LOWORD(lParam), HIWORD(lParam));
    InvalidateRect(hWnd, &rectButton, TRUE);
    break;
```

4.2.13 Add the WM_TIMER Case

Add a WM_TIMER case to process timer messages. Add the following statements to the window function:

```
case WM_TIMER:
    wsprintf(TimerText, "WM_TIMER: %d seconds",
        nTimerCount += 5);
    InvalidateRect(hWnd, &rectTimer, TRUE);
    break;
```

4.2.14 Add the WM_HSCROLL and WM_VSCROLL Cases

Add the WM_HSCROLL and WM_VSCROLL cases to process scroll-bar messages. Add the following statements to the window function:

```
case WM_HSCROLL:
case WM_VSCROLL:
    strcpy(HorzOrVertText,
        (message == WM_HSCROLL) ? "WM_HSCROLL" : "WM_VSCROLL");
    strcpy(ScrollTypeText,
        (wParam == SB_LINEUP) ? "SB_LINEUP" :
        (wParam == SB_LINEDOWN) ? "SB_LINEDOWN" :
        (wParam == SB_PAGEUP) ? "SB_PAGEUP" :
        (wParam == SB_PAGEDOWN) ? "SB_PAGEDOWN" :
        (wParam == SB_THUMBPOSITION) ? "SB_THUMBPOSITION" :
        (wParam == SB_THUMBTRACK) ? "SB_THUMBTRACK" :
        (wParam == SB_ENDSCROLL) ? "SB_ENDSCROLL" : "unknown");
```

```
        wsprintf(ScrollText, "%s: %s, %x, %x",
            (LPSTR)HorzOrVertText,
            (LPSTR)ScrollTypeText,
            LOWORD(lParam),
            HIWORD(lParam));
        InvalidateRect(hWnd, &rectScroll, TRUE);
        break;
```

4.2.15 Add the WM_PAINT Case

You need to display the current state of the mouse, keyboard, and timer. The most convenient way to do this is to use the WM_PAINT message to display the states. Your application only repaints the parts of its client area that need repainting.

Add the following statements to the window function:

```
case WM_PAINT:
    hDC = BeginPaint (hWnd, &ps);

    if (IntersectRect(&rect, &rectMouse, &ps.rcPaint))
        TextOut(hDC, rectMouse.left, rectMouse.top,
                MouseText, strlen(MouseText));
    if (IntersectRect(&rect, &rectButton, &ps.rcPaint))
        TextOut(hDC, rectButton.left, rectButton.top,
                ButtonText, strlen(ButtonText));
    if (IntersectRect(&rect, &rectKeyboard, &ps.rcPaint))
        TextOut(hDC, rectKeyboard.left, rectKeyboard.top,
                KeyboardText, strlen(KeyboardText));
    if (IntersectRect(&rect, &rectCharacter, &ps.rcPaint))
        TextOut(hDC, rectCharacter.left, rectCharacter.top,
                CharacterText, strlen(CharacterText));
    if (IntersectRect(&rect, &rectTimer, &ps.rcPaint))
        TextOut(hDC, rectTimer.left, rectTimer.top,
                TimerText, strlen(TimerText));
    if (IntersectRect(&rect, &rectScroll, &ps.rcPaint))
        TextOut(hDC, rectScroll.left, rectScroll.top,
                ScrollText, strlen(ScrollText));

    EndPaint(hWnd, &ps);
    break;
```

4.2.16 Compile and Link

You can compile and link the Input application without changing the make file. Once the application is compiled, start Windows and then the Input application. To test the application, press keys on the keyboard, click the mouse button, move the mouse, and use the scroll bars. The application should look like Figure 4.1:

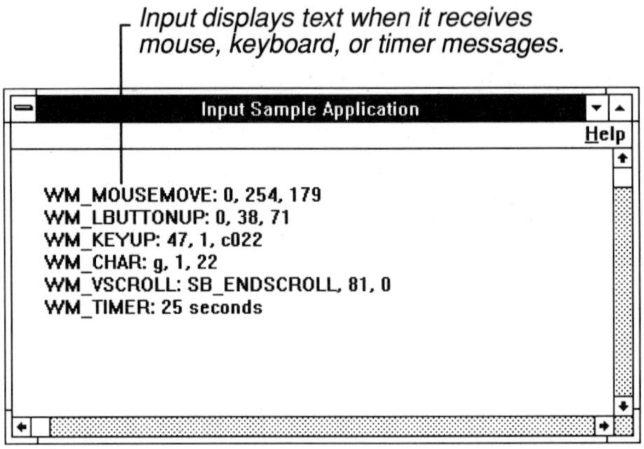

Figure 4.1 The Input Application's Window

4.3 Summary

This chapter explained how a Windows application receives input from the user. All user input goes first to Windows, which then translates the input to an input message and forwards it to the appropriate application. The application can recieve input messages either directly, through a window function's four arguments, or indirectly, via the application queue.

This chapter also described the different types of input messages and explained how to respond to each type.

For more information on topics related to input, see the following:

Topic	Reference
The Windows message-based programming model	*Guide to Programming*: Chapter 1, "An Overview of the Windows Environment"
Using the cursor for mouse and keyboard input	*Guide to Programming*: Chapter 6, "The Cursor, the Mouse, and the Keyboard"
Menus and menu input	*Guide to Programming*: Chapter 7, "Menus"
Scroll-bar controls	*Guide to Programming*: Chapter 8, "Controls"

Topic	Reference
Input functions	*Reference, Volume 1*: Chapter 1, "Window Manager Interface Functions," and Chapter 4, "Functions Directory"
Input messages	*Reference, Volume 1*: Chapter 5, "Messages Overview" and Chapter 6, "Messages Directory"

Chapter 5 Icons

A typical Windows application uses an icon to represent itself when its main window is minimized.

This chapter covers the following topics:

- What an icon is
- Creating and using your own predefined icons
- Specifying an icon for your application's window class
- Changing your application's icon "on the fly"
- Displaying an icon in a dialog box

This chapter also explains how to create a sample application, Icon, that illustrates many of these concepts.

5.1 What is an Icon?

To the user, an icon is a small graphic image that represents an application when that application's main window is minimized. For example, Microsoft Paintbrush uses an icon that looks like a painter's palette to represent its minimized window. Icons are also used in message and dialog boxes.

To the application, an icon is a type of resource. Before resource compilation, each icon is a separate file that contains a set of bitmap images. The images may be similar in appearance, but each is targeted for a different display device. When the application wants to use an icon, it simply requests the icon resource by name. Windows then decides which of that icon's images is most appropriate for the current display. Because Windows handles this decision, the application doesn't need to check the display type or determine which icon image is best suited for the current display. Figure 5.1 illustrates what happens when an application requests an icon resource.

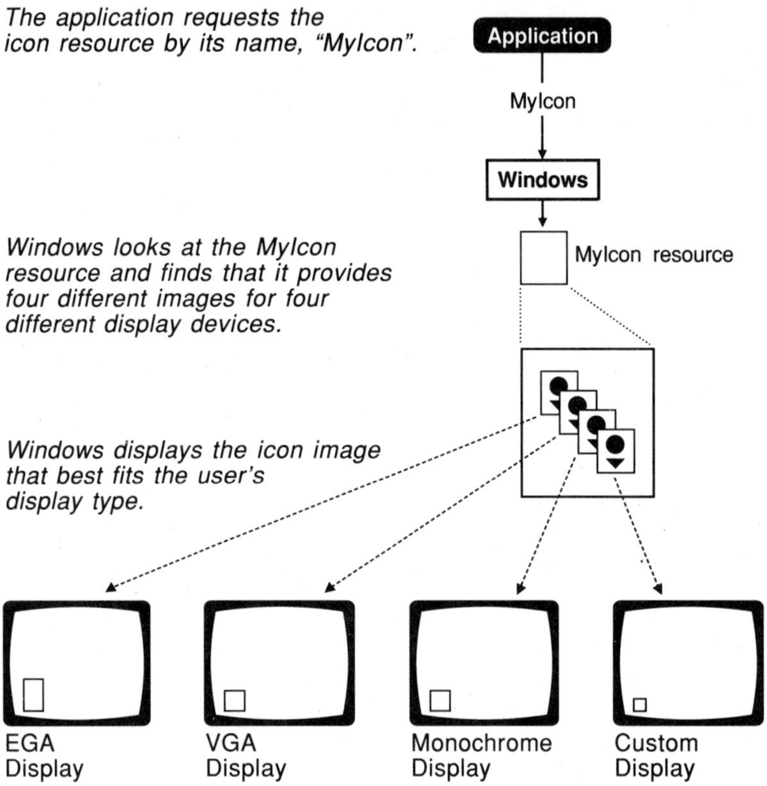

Figure 5.1 Using an Icon

5.1.1 Using Built-In Icons

Windows provides several built-in icons. You can use any of these icons in your applications. Windows uses several built-in icons in message boxes to indicate notes, cautions, warnings, and errors.

To use a built-in icon, you must first load it. To do this, you retrieve a handle to it by using the **LoadIcon** function. The first argument to the function must be NULL, indicating that you are requesting a built-in icon. The second argument identifies the icon you want. For example, the following statement loads the built-in "exclamation" icon:

```
hHandIcon = LoadIcon(NULL, IDI_EXCLAMATION);
```

After loading a built-in icon, your application can use it. For example, the application could specify the icon as the class icon for a particular window class. Or, you could include the icon in a message box. For more information, see Section 5.3, "Specifying a Class Icon," and Section 5.4, "Displaying Your Own Icons."

5.2 Using Your Own Icons

Using an icon requires three steps:

1. Create the icon file with the SDKPaint tool.
2. Define the icon resource by using an **ICON** statement in your application's resource script file.
3. Load the icon resource, when needed, by using the **LoadIcon** function in your application code.

After loading an icon, you can use it; for example, you can then specify it as the class icon.

The following sections explain each step in detail.

5.2.1 Creating an Icon File

An icon file contains one or more icon images. You use the SDKPaint tool to paint the images and save them in an icon file.

Follow the directions given in *Tools* for creating and saving an icon. The recommended file extension for an icon file is .ICO.

5.2.2 Defining the Icon Resource

Once you have an icon file, you must define that icon in your application's resource script (.RC) file.

To define an icon resource, add an **ICON** statement to your resource script file. The **ICON** statement defines a name for the icon, and specifies the icon file that contains the icon. For example, the following resource statement adds the icon named "MyIcon" to your application's resources:

```
MyIcon ICON MYICON.ICO
```

The filename MYICON.ICO specifies the file that contains the images for the icon named "MyIcon." When the resource script file is compiled, the icon images will be copied from the file MYICON.ICO into your application's resources.

5.2.3 Loading the Icon Resource

Once you have created an icon file and defined the icon resource in the .RC file, your application can load the icon from its resources.

To load the icon from your resources, you use the **LoadIcon** function. The **LoadIcon** function takes the application's instance handle and the icon's name, and returns a handle to the icon. The following example loads "MyIcon" and stores its handle in the variable hMyIcon.

```
hMyIcon = LoadIcon (hInstance, "MyIcon");
```

After loading it, the application can display the icon.

5.3 Specifying a Class Icon

A "class icon" is an icon that represents a particular window class whenever a window in that class is minimized. You specify a class icon by supplying an icon handle in the **hIcon** field of the window-class structure before registering the class. Once the class icon is set, Windows automatically displays that icon when any window you create using that window class is minimized.

The following example shows a definition of the window class "wc" before registering the class. In this definition, the field **hIcon** is set to the handle returned by **LoadIcon**.

```
wc.style = NULL;
wc.lpfnWndProc = MainWndProc;
wc.cbClsExtra = 0;
wc.cbWndExtra = 0;
wc.hInstance = hInstance;
❶ wc.hIcon = LoadIcon (NULL, IDI_APPLICATION);
wc.hCursor = LoadCursor (NULL, IDC_ARROW);
wc.hbrBackground = COLOR_WINDOW + 1;
wc.lpszMenuName =  NULL;
wc.lpszClassName = "Generic";
```

❶ The **LoadIcon** function returns a handle to the built-in application icon identified by IDI_APPLICATION. If you minimize a window that has this class, you will see a white rectangle with a black border. This is the built-in application icon.

5.4 Displaying Your Own Icons

Windows displays a class icon when the application is minimized, and removes it when the application is maximized. All the application does is specify it as the class icon. This meets the needs of most applications, since most applications do not need to display additional information to the user when the application is minimized.

However, sometimes your application may need to display its icon itself, instead of letting Windows display a prespecified class icon. This is particularly useful when you want your application's icon to be dynamic, like the icon in the Clock application. (The Clock application continues to show the time even when it has been minimized.) Windows lets applications paint within the client area of an iconic window, so that they can paint their own icons.

If you want your application to display its own icon:

1. In the window class structure, set the class icon to NULL before registering the window class. Use the following statement:

   ```
   wc.hIcon = NULL;
   ```

   This step is required because it signals Windows to continue sending WM_PAINT messages, as necessary, to the window function even though the window has been minimized.

2. Add a WM_PAINT case to your window function that draws within the icon's client area if the window receives a WM_PAINT message when the window is iconic (minimized). Use the following statements:

   ```
   PAINTSTRUCT ps;
   HDC hDC;
       .
       .
       .
   case WM_PAINT:
       hDC = BeginPaint(hWnd, &ps);
       if (IsIconic(hWnd))
           {
           /* Output functions for iconic state */
           }
       else
           {
           /* Output functions for non-iconic state */
           }
       EndPaint(hWnd, &ps);
       break;
   ```

Applications need to determine whether the window is iconic, since what they paint in the icon may be different from what they paint in the open window. The **IsIconic** function returns TRUE if the window is iconic.

The **BeginPaint** function returns a handle to the display context of the icon's client area. **BeginPaint** takes the window handle, hWnd, and a long pointer to the paint structure, ps. **BeginPaint** fills the paint structure with information about the area to be painted. As with any painting operation, after each call to **Begin-Paint**, the **EndPaint** function is required. **EndPaint** releases any resources that **BeginPaint** retrieved and signals the end of the application's repainting of the client area.

You can retrieve the size of the icon's client area by using the **rcPaint** field of the paint structure. For example, to draw an ellipse that fills the icon, you can use the following statement:

```
Ellipse(hDC, ps.rcPaint.left, ps.rcPaint.top,
        ps.rcPaint.right, ps.rcPaint.bottom);
```

You can use any GDI output functions to draw the icon, including the **TextOut** function. The only limitation is the size of the icon, which varies from display to display, so make sure that your painting does not depend on a specific icon size.

5.5 Displaying an Icon in a Dialog Box

You can place icons in dialog boxes by using the **ICON** control statement in the **DIALOG** statement. You have already seen an example of a **DIALOG** statement in the About dialog box described with the Generic application. The **DIALOG** statement for that box looks like this:

```
AboutBox DIALOG 22, 17, 144, 75
STYLE DS_MODALFRAME | WS_CAPTION | WS_SYSMENU
CAPTION "About Icon"
BEGIN
    CTEXT "Microsoft Windows"                    -1, 37,  5,  68, 8
    CTEXT "Generic Application"                  -1,  0, 14, 144, 8
    CTEXT "Version 3.0"                          -1, 38, 34,  64, 8
    DEFPUSHBUTTON "OK"              IDOK, 53, 59, 32, 14, WS_GROUP
END
```

You can add an icon to the dialog box by inserting the following **ICON** statement immediately after the **DEFPUSHBUTTON** statement:

```
ICON "MyIcon", -1, 25, 14, 16, 21
```

When an icon is added to a dialog box, it is treated like any other control. It must have a control ID, a position for its upper-left corner, a width, and a height. In this example, –1 is the control ID, 25 and 14 specify the location of the icon in the dialog box, and 16 and 21 specify the height and width of the icon, respectively. However, Windows ignores the height and width, sizing the icon automatically.

The name "MyIcon" identifies the icon you want to use. The icon must be defined in an **ICON** statement elsewhere within the resource script file. For example, the following statement defines the icon "MyIcon."

```
MyIcon ICON MYICON.ICO
```

5.6 A Sample Application: Icon

This sample application shows how to incorporate icons in your applications, in particular, how to do the following:

- Use a custom icon as the class icon.
- Use an icon in the About dialog box.

To create the Icon application, copy and rename the source files of the Generic application, then do the following:

1. Add an **ICON** statement to the resource script file.
2. Add an **ICON** control statement to the **DIALOG** statement in the resource script file.
3. Load the custom icon and use it to set the class icon in the initialization function.
4. Modify the make file to cause the Resource Compiler to add the icon to the application's executable file.
5. Compile and link the application.

This sample assumes that you have created an icon using SDKPaint, and have saved the icon in a file named MYICON.ICO.

NOTE Rather than typing the code provided in the following sections, you might find it more convenient to simply examine and compile the sample source files provided with the SDK.

5.6.1 Add an ICON Statement

Add an **ICON** statement to your resource script file. Insert the following line at the beginning of the resource script file, immediately after the **#include** directives:

```
MyIcon ICON MYICON.ICO
```

5.6.2 Add an ICON Control Statement

Add an **ICON** control statement to the **DIALOG** statement. Insert the following line immediately after the **DEFPUSHBUTTON** statement:

```
ICON "MyIcon", -1, 25, 14, 16, 21
```

5.6.3 Set the Class Icon

Set the class icon by adding the following statement to the initialization function in the C-language source file:

```
wc.hIcon = LoadIcon (hInstance, "MyIcon");
```

5.6.4 Add MYICON.ICO to the Make File

In the make file, add the file MYICON.ICO to the list of files on which ICON.RES is dependent. The relevant lines in the make file should look like the following:

```
ICON.RES: ICON.RC ICON.H MYICON.ICO
     RC -r ICON.RC
```

This ensures that, if the file MYICON.ICO changes, ICON.RC will be recompiled to form a new ICON.RES file.

No other changes are required.

5.6.5 Compile and Link

Recompile and link the Icon application. When the application is recompiled, start Windows and the Icon application. Now, if you choose the About command, Icon displays the About dialog box, which now contains an icon.

5.7 Summary

This chapter explained how to create and use icons in your application. An icon is a small graphic image that can represent an application when that application is minimized. You can use one of Windows' built-in icons, or you can use the SDKPaint tool to create your own icons. You can specify an icon when you register a window class; then, Windows will automatically display that icon whenever a window in that class is minimized. Your application can also display icons itself, using the **BeginPaint** and **EndPaint** functions.

For more information on topics related to icons, see the following:

Topic	Reference
LoadIcon, **IsIconic, BeginPaint, EndPaint**, and **TextOut** functions	*Reference, Volume 1*: Chapter 4, "Functions Directory"
Resource script statements	*Reference, Volume 2*: Chapter 8, "Resource Script Statements"

Topic	Reference
Using SDKPaint	*Tools*: Chapter 4, "Designing Images: SDKPaint"
Using the Dialog Editor to add an icon to a dialog box	Tools: Chapter 5, "Designing Dialog Boxes: The Dialog Editor"

Chapter 6

The Cursor, the Mouse, and the Keyboard

The cursor is a special bitmap that shows the user where actions initiated by the mouse will take place. In most Windows applications, the user makes selections, chooses commands, and directs other actions by using either the mouse or the keyboard.

This chapter covers the following topics:

- Controlling the shape of the cursor
- Displaying the cursor
- Letting the user select information using the mouse
- Letting the user move the cursor using the keyboard

This chapter also explains how to create a sample application, Cursor, that illustrates some of these concepts.

6.1 Controlling the Shape of the Cursor

Since no one cursor shape can satisfy the needs of all applications, Windows lets your application change the shape of the cursor to suit its own needs.

In order to use a particular cursor shape, you must first retrieve a handle to it using the **LoadCursor** function. Once your application has loaded a cursor, it can use that cursor shape whenever it needs to.

Your application can control the shape of the cursor using either of two methods:

- It can take advantage of the built-in cursor shapes that Windows provides.
- It can use its own customized cursor shapes.

The following sections explain each method.

6.1.1 Using Built-In Cursor Shapes

Windows provides several built-in cursor shapes. These include the arrow, hourglass, I-beam, and cross-hair cursors. Most of the built-in cursor shapes have specialized uses. For example, the I-beam cursor is normally used when the user is editing text; the hourglass cursor is used to indicate that a lengthy operation is in progress, such as reading a disk file.

To use a built-in cursor, use the **LoadCursor** function to retrieve a handle to the built-in cursor. The first argument to **LoadCursor** must be NULL (indicating that a built-in cursor is requested); the second argument must specify the cursor to load. The following example loads the I-beam cursor, IDC_IBEAM, and assigns the resulting cursor handle to the variable hCursor.

```
hCursor = LoadCursor(NULL, IDC_IBEAM);
```

Once you have loaded a cursor, you can use it. For example, you could display the I-beam cursor to indicate that the user is currently editing text. Section 6.2, "Displaying the Cursor," explains methods for displaying the cursor.

6.1.2 Using Your Own Cursor Shapes

To create and use your own cursor shapes, follow these steps:

1. Create the cursor shape itself by using the SDKPaint tool.
2. Define the cursor in your resource script file by using the **CURSOR** statement.
3. Load the cursor by using the **LoadCursor** function.
4. Display the cursor using one of the techniques described in Section 6.2, "Displaying the Cursor."

The following sections explain each step.

Creating a Cursor Shape

The first step is to create the cursor shape itself. You do this by using SDKPaint, which lets you see an actual-size version of the cursor shape while you're editing it.

When you have created the cursor, save it in a cursor file. The recommended extension for cursor files is .CUR.

For information about using SDKPaint, see *Tools*.

Adding the Cursor to Your Application Resources

Next, add a **CURSOR** statement to your resource script file. The **CURSOR** statement specifies the file that contains the cursor, and defines a name for the cursor. The application will use this cursor name when loading the cursor. The following is an example of a **CURSOR** statement:

```
bullseye CURSOR BULLSEYE.CUR
```

In this example, the name of the cursor is "bullseye", and the cursor is in the file BULLSEYE.CUR.

Loading the Cursor Resource

In your application code, retrieve a handle to the cursor using the **LoadCursor** function. For example, the following code loads the cursor resource named "bullseye" and assigns its handle to the variable hCursor:

```
hCursor = LoadCursor(hInstance,(LPSTR) "bullseye");
```

In this example, the **LoadCursor** function loads the cursor from the application's resources. The instance handle, hInstance, identifies the application's resources and is required. The name "bullseye" identifies the cursor. It is the same name given in the resource script file.

6.2 Displaying the Cursor

Once you have loaded a cursor shape, you can display it using one of two methods:

- Specifying it as the "class cursor" for all windows in a window class
- Explicitly setting the cursor shape when the cursor moves within the client area of a particular window

The following sections explain each method.

6.2.1 Specifying a Class Cursor

The "class cursor" defines the shape the cursor will take when it enters the client area of a window that belongs to that window class. To specify a class cursor, load the cursor you want, and assign its handle to the **hCursor** field of the window-class structure before registering the class. For example, to use the built-in arrow cursor (IDC_ARROW) in your window, add the following statement to your initialization function:

```
wc.hCursor = LoadCursor(NULL, IDC_ARROW);
```

For each window created using this class, the built-in arrow cursor will appear automatically when the user moves the cursor into the window.

6.2.2 Explicitly Setting the Cursor Shape

Your application does not have to specify a class cursor. Instead, you can set the **hCursor** field to NULL to indicate that the window class has no class cursor. If a window has no class cursor, Windows will not automatically change the shape of the cursor when it moves into the client area of the window. This means that your application will need to display the cursor itself.

To use any cursor, whether built-in or custom, you must load it first. For example, to load the custom cursor "MyCursor" (defined in your application's resource script file) add the following statements to your initialization function:

```
static HCURSOR hMyCursor; /* static variable */
hMyCursor = LoadCursor (hInstance, (LPSTR) "MyCursor");
```

Then, to change the cursor shape, use the **SetCursor** function to set the shape each time the cursor moves in the client area. Since Windows sends a WM_MOUSEMOVE message to the window on each cursor movement, you can manage the cursor by adding the following statements to the window function:

```
case WM_MOUSEMOVE:
    SetCursor(hMyCursor);
    break;
```

NOTE If your application needs to display the cursor itself, you must set the class-cursor field to NULL. Otherwise, Windows will attempt to set the cursor shape on each WM_MOUSEMOVE message, even though your application is also setting the cursor shape. This will result in a noticeable flicker as you move the cursor through the window.

6.2.3 Example: Displaying the Hourglass on a Lengthy Operation

Whenever your application begins a lengthy operation, such as reading or writing a large block of data to a disk file, you should change the shape of the cursor to the hourglass. This lets users know that a lengthy operation is in progress and that they should wait before attempting to continue their work. Once the operation is complete, your application should restore the cursor to its previous shape.

To change the cursor to an hourglass, use the following statements:

```
❶ HCURSOR hSaveCursor;
HCURSOR hHourGlass;
    .
    .
    .
hHourGlass = LoadCursor(NULL, IDC_WAIT);
```

```
      .
      .
      .
❷ SetCapture(hWnd);
❸ hSaveCursor = SetCursor(hHourGlass);

/* Lengthy operation */

❹ SetCursor(hSaveCursor);
❺ ReleaseCapture();
      .
      .
      .
```

In this example:

❶ The application defines the variables that will be used to store the cursor handles. Both variables are type **HCURSOR**.

❷ The application first captures the mouse input, using the **SetCapture** function. This keeps the user from attempting to use the mouse to carry out work in another application while the lengthy operation is in progress. When the mouse input is captured, Windows directs all mouse input messages to the specified window, regardless of whether the mouse is in that window. The application can then process the messages as appropriate.

❸ The application then changes the cursor shape using the **SetCursor** function. **SetCursor** returns a handle to the previous cursor shape, so that the shape can be restored later. The application saves this handle in the variable hSave-Cursor.

❹ After the lengthy operation is complete, the application restores the previous cursor shape.

❺ The **ReleaseCapture** function releases the mouse input.

6.3 Letting the User Select Information with the Mouse

The mouse is a hardware device that lets the user move the cursor and enter simple input by pressing a button. In a typical Windows application, the user performs many types of tasks with the mouse; for example, choosing commands from a menu, selecting text or graphics, or directing scrolling operations. For most of these tasks, Windows automatically handles the mouse input; for example, when the user chooses a menu command, Windows automatically sends the application a message that contains the command ID.

However, one common task, selection of information within the client area, must be handled by the application itself. In order to let the user select such information using the mouse, the application must perform the following tasks:

- Start processing the selection.

  When the user presses the mouse button to start selecting information, the application must note the location of the cursor and temporarily capture all mouse input to ensure that other applications do not interfere with the selection process.

- Provide visual feedback during the selection.

  While the user drags the mouse across the screen, the application should show the user what information is currently being selected. For example, some applications highlight selected information; others draw a dotted rectangle around it.

- Complete the selection.

  When the user releases the mouse button, the application must note the final location of the cursor and signal the end of the selection process.

When the selection process is complete, the user can then choose an action to perform on the selected information. For example, in a word processor, the user might select several words, then choose a command that changes the selected text to a different font. The following sections discuss each step in more detail, and explain how to let the user select graphics in a window's client area.

NOTE The mouse is just one of many possible system pointing devices. Other pointing devices such as graphics tablets, joysticks, and light pens may operate differently but still provide input identical to that of a mouse. The following examples can be used with these devices as well. Remember that when a pointing device is present, Windows automatically controls the position and shape of the cursor as the user moves the pointing device.

6.3.1 Starting a Graphics Selection

Because graphics can be virtually any shape, they are potentially more difficult to select than simple text. The simplest approach to selecting graphics is to let the user "stretch" a selection rectangle so that it encloses the desired information.

This section explains how to use the "rubber rectangle" method of selecting graphics. You can use the messages WM_LBUTTONDOWN, WM_LBUTTONUP, and WM_MOUSEMOVE to create the rectangle. This lets the user create the selection by choosing a point, pressing the left button, and dragging to another point before releasing. While the user drags the mouse, the application can provide instant feedback by inverting the border of the rectangle described by the starting and current points.

For this method, you start the selection when you receive the message WM_LBUTTONDOWN. You need to do three things: capture the mouse input, save the starting (original) point, and save the current point, as follows:

```
BOOL bTrack = FALSE;    /* these are global variables */
int OrgX = 0, OrgY = 0;
int PrevX = 0, PrevY = 0;
int X = 0, Y = 0;
      .
      .
      .
❶ case WM_LBUTTONDOWN:
    bTrack = TRUE;
    PrevX = LOWORD(lParam);
    PrevY = HIWORD(lParam);
    OrgX = LOWORD(lParam);
    OrgY = HIWORD(lParam);
    ❷ InvalidateRect (hWnd, NULL, TRUE);
    UpdateWindow (hWnd);

    /* Capture all input even if the mouse goes outside of window */

    ❸ SetCapture(hWnd);
    break;
```

❶ When the application receives the WM_LBUTTONDOWN message, the bTrack variable is set to TRUE to indicate that a selection is in progress. As with any mouse message, the *lParam* parameter contains the current *x*- and *y*-coordinates of the mouse in the low- and high-order words, respectively. These are saved as the origin *x* and *y* values, OrgX and OrgY, as well as the previous values, PrevX and PrevY. The PrevX and PrevY variables will be updated immediately on the next WM_MOUSEMOVE message. The OrgX and OrgY variables remain unchanged and will be used to determine a corner of the bitmap to be copied. (The variables bTrack, OrgX, OrgY, PrevX, and PrevY must be global variables.)

❷ To provide immediate visual feedback in response to the WM_LBUTTON-DOWN message, the application invalidates the screen and notifies the window function that it needs to repaint the screen. It does this by calling **InvalidateRect** and **UpdateWindow**.

❸ The **SetCapture** function directs all subsequent mouse input to the window even if the cursor moves outside of the window. This ensures that the selection process will continue uninterrupted.

Respond to the WM_PAINT message by redrawing the invalidated portions of the screen:

```
case WM_PAINT:
    {
        PAINTSTRUCT     ps;
        HDC             hDC;

        hDC = BeginPaint (hWnd, &ps);
        if (OrgX != PrevX || OrgY != PrevY) {
            MoveTo(hDC, OrgX, OrgY);
            LineTo(hDC, OrgX, PrevY);
            LineTo(hDC, PrevX, PrevY);
            LineTo(hDC, PrevX, OrgY);
            LineTo(hDC, OrgX, OrgY);
        }
        EndPaint (hWnd, &ps);
    }
    break;
```

In some applications, you might want to be able to extend an existing selection. One way to do this is to have the user hold the SHIFT key when making a selection. Since the *wParam* parameter contains a flag that specifies whether the SHIFT key is being pressed, it is easy to check for this, and to extend the selection as necessary. In this case, extending a selection means preserving its previous OrgX and OrgY values when you start it. To do this, change the WM_LBUTTONDOWN case so it looks like this:

```
case WM_LBUTTONDOWN:
    bTrack = TRUE;
    PrevX = LOWORD(lParam);
    PrevY = HIWORD(lParam);
    if (!(wParam & MK_SHIFT)) {          /* If shift key is
                                            not pressed */
        OrgX = LOWORD(lParam);
        OrgY = HIWORD(lParam);
    }
    InvalidateRect (hWnd, NULL, TRUE);
    UpdateWindow (hWnd);

    /* Capture all input even if the mouse goes
       outside the window */

    SetCapture(hWnd);
    break;
```

6.3.2 Showing the Selection

As the user makes the selection, you need to provide feedback about his or her progress. You can do this by drawing a border around the rectangle by using the **LineTo** function on each new WM_MOUSEMOVE message. To prevent losing information already on the display, you need to draw a line that inverts the screen rather than drawing over it. You can do this by using the **SetROP2** function to set the binary raster mode to R2_NOT. The following statements perform this function:

```
case WM_MOUSEMOVE:
    {
        RECT        rectClient;
        int         NextX;
        int         NextY;

        if (bTrack) {
            NextX = LOWORD(lParam);
            NextY = HIWORD(lParam);

            /* Do not draw outside the window's client area */

            GetClientRect (hWnd, &rectClient);
            if (NextX < rectClient.left) {
                NextX = rectClient.left;
            } else if (NextX >= rectClient.right) {
                NextX = rectClient.right - 1;
            }
            if (NextY < rectClient.top) {
                NextY = rectClient.top;
            } else if (NextY >= rectClient.bottom) {
                NextY = rectClient.bottom - 1;
            }

            /* If the mouse position has changed, then clear the */
            /* previous rectangle and draw the new one. */

            if ((NextX != PrevX) || (NextY != PrevY)) {
                hDC = GetDC(hWnd);
                SetROP2(hDC, R2_NOT);           /* Erases the previous box */
                MoveTo(hDC, OrgX, OrgY);
                LineTo(hDC, OrgX, PrevY);
                LineTo(hDC, PrevX, PrevY);
                LineTo(hDC, PrevX, OrgY);
                LineTo(hDC, OrgX, OrgY);
```

```
                /* Get the current mouse position */

                PrevX = NextX;
                PrevY = NextY;
                MoveTo(hDC, OrgX, OrgY);        /* Draws the new box */
                LineTo(hDC, OrgX, PrevY);
                LineTo(hDC, PrevX, PrevY);
                LineTo(hDC, PrevX, OrgY);
                LineTo(hDC, OrgX, OrgY);
                ReleaseDC(hWnd, hDC);
            }
        }
    }
    break;
```

The application processes the WM_MOUSEMOVE message only if bTrack is TRUE (that is, if a selection is in progress). The purpose of the WM_MOUSE-MOVE processing is to remove the border around the previous rectangle and draw a new border around the rectangle described by the current and original positions. Since the border is actually the inverse of what was originally on the display, inverting again restores it completely. The first four **LineTo** functions remove the previous border. The next four draw a new border. Before drawing the new border, the PrevX and PrevY values are updated by assigning them the current values contained in the *lParam* parameter.

6.3.3 Ending the Selection

Finally, when the user releases the left button, save the final point and signal the end of the selection process. The following statements complete the selection:

```
case WM_LBUTTONUP:
     bTrack = FALSE;          /* No longer carrying out a selection */
     ReleaseCapture();        /* Release hold on mouse input */

     X = LOWORD(lParam);      /* Save the current value     */
     Y = HIWORD(lParam);
     break;
```

When the application receives a WM_LBUTTONUP message, it immediately sets bTrack to FALSE to indicate that selection processing has been completed. It also releases the mouse capture by using the **ReleaseCapture** function. It then saves the current mouse position in the variables, X and Y. This, together with the selection-origin information saved on WM_LBUTTONDOWN, records the selection the user has made. The application can now operate on the selection, and can redraw the selection rectangle when necessary.

For some applications, you might want to check the final cursor position to make sure it represents a point to the lower right of the original point. This is the way most rectangles are described—by their upper-left and lower-right corners.

The **ReleaseCapture** function is required since a corresponding **SetCapture** function was called. In general, you should release the mouse immediately after the mouse capture is no longer needed.

6.4 Using the Cursor with the Keyboard

Because Windows does not require a pointing device, applications should provide the user with a way to duplicate mouse actions with the keyboard. To allow the user to move the cursor using the keyboard, use the **SetCursorPos**, **SetCursor**, **GetCursorPos**, **ClipCursor**, and **ShowCursor** functions to display and move the cursor.

6.4.1 Using the Keyboard to Move the Cursor

You can use the **SetCursorPos** function to move the cursor directly from your application. This function is typically used to let the user move the cursor by using the keyboard.

To move the cursor, use the WM_KEYDOWN message and filter for the virtual-key values of the direction keys: VK_LEFT, VK_RIGHT, VK_UP, and VK_DOWN. On each key stroke, the application should update the position of the cursor. The following example shows how to retrieve the cursor position and convert the coordinates to client coordinates:

```
POINT ptCursor;      /* these are global variables */
int repeat = 1;
RECT Rect;
    .
    .
    .
case WM_KEYDOWN:
    ❶ if (wParam != VK_LEFT && wParam != VK_RIGHT
             && wParam != VK_UP && wParam != VK_DOWN)
        break;

    ❷ GetCursorPos(&ptCursor);

    /* Convert screen coordinates to client coordinates */

    ❸ ScreenToClient(hWnd, &ptCursor);
    ❹ repeat++;                       /* Increases the repeat rate  */
```

```
    switch (wParam) {

    /* Adjust cursor position according to which key was pressed. */
    /* Accelerate by adding the repeat variable to the cursor
       position. */

        case VK_LEFT:
            ptCursor.x -= repeat;
            break;

        case VK_RIGHT:
            ptCursor.x += repeat;
            break;

        case VK_UP:
            ptCursor.y -= repeat;
            break;

        case VK_DOWN:
            ptCursor.y += repeat;
            break;

        default:
            return (NULL);

    }

    /* ensure that cursor doesn't go outside client area */
    ❺ GetClientRect(hWnd, &Rect);

    ❻ if (ptCursor.x >= Rect.right)
       ptCursor.x = Rect.right - 1;
    else if (ptCursor.x < Rect.left)
       ptCursor.x = Rect.left;
    if (ptCursor.y >= Rect.bottom)
       ptCursor.y = Rect.bottom - 1;
    else if (ptCursor.y < Rect.top)
       ptCursor.y = Rect.top;

    ❼ ClientToScreen(hWnd, &ptCursor);
    ❽ SetCursorPos(ptCursor.x, ptCursor.y);
    break;

case WM_KEYUP:
    ❾ repeat = 1;                 /* Clears the repeat rate  */
    break;
```

In this example:

❶ The first **if** statement filters for the virtual-key values of the direction keys VK_LEFT, VK_RIGHT, VK_UP, and VK_DOWN.

❷ The **GetCursorPos** function retrieves the current cursor position. If the mouse is available, the user could potentially move the cursor with the mouse at any time; therefore, there is no guarantee that the position values you saved on the last key stroke are correct.

❸ The **ScreenToClient** function converts the cursor position to client coordinates. The application does this for two reasons: mouse messages give the mouse position in client coordinates, and client coordinates do not need to be updated if the window moves. In other words, it is convenient to use client coordinates because the system uses them and because it usually means less work for the application.

❹ The repeat variable provides accelerated cursor motion. Advancing the cursor one unit for each key stroke can be frustrating for users if they need to move to the other side of the screen. You can accelerate the cursor motion by increasing the number of units the cursor advances when the user holds down a key. When the user holds down a key, Windows sends multiple WM_KEYDOWN messages without matching WM_KEYUP messages. To accelerate the cursor, you simply increase the number of units to advance on each WM_KEYDOWN message.

❺ The **GetClientRect** function retrieves the current size of the client area and stores it in the Rect structure. You then use that information to ensure that the cursor motion remains within the client area.

❻ These **if** statements check the current cursor position to ensure that it is within the client area. If necessary, the application then adjusts the cursor position.

❼ In preparation for the **SetCursorPos** function, the **ClientToScreen** function converts the values in the ptCursor structure from client coordinates to screen coordinates. Because **SetCursorPos** requires screen coordinates rather than client coordinates, you must convert the coordinates before calling **SetCursorPos**.

❽ The **SetCursorPos** function moves the cursor to the desired location.

❾ Within the WM_KEYUP case, the application restores the initial value of the repeat variable when the user releases the key.

6.4.2 Using the Cursor when No Mouse Is Available

When no mouse is available, the application must display and move the cursor in response to keyboard actions. To determine whether a mouse is present, you can use the **GetSystemMetrics** function and specify the SM_MOUSEPRESENT option:

```
GetSystemMetrics(SM_MOUSEPRESENT);
```

This function returns TRUE if the mouse is present.

You will need to display the cursor and update the cursor position when the application is activated, and hide the cursor when the application is deactivated. The following statements carry out both activation functions:

```
case WM_ACTIVATE:
    if (!GetSystemMetrics(SM_MOUSEPRESENT)) {
        if (!HIWORD(lParam)) {
            if (wParam) {
                SetCursor(hMyCursor);
                ClientToScreen(hWnd, &ptCursor);
                SetCursorPos(ptCursor.x, ptCursor.y);
            }
            ShowCursor(wParam);
        }
    }
    break;
```

The cursor functions are called only if the system has no mouse; that is, if the **GetSystemMetrics** function returns FALSE. Since Windows positions and updates the cursor automatically if a mouse is present, the cursor functions, if carried out, would disrupt this processing.

The next step is to determine whether the window is iconic. The cursor must not be displayed or updated if the window is an icon. In a WM_ACTIVATE message, the high-order word is nonzero if the window is iconic, so the cursor functions are called only if this value is zero.

The final step is to check the *wParam* parameter to determine whether the window is being activated or deactivated. This parameter is nonzero if the window is being activated. When a window is activated, the **SetCursor** function sets the shape and the **SetCursorPos** function positions it. The **ClientToScreen** function converts the cursor position to screen coordinates as required by the **SetCursorPos** function. Finally, the **ShowCursor** function shows or hides the cursor depending on the value of *wParam.*

When the system has no mouse installed, applications must be careful when using the cursor. In general, applications must hide the cursor when the window is closed, destroyed, or relinquishes control. If an application fails to hide the cursor, it prevents subsequent windows from using the cursor. For example, if an application sets the cursor to the hourglass, displays the cursor, then relinquishes control to a dialog box, the cursor remains on the screen (possibly in a new shape), but cannot be used by the dialog box.

6.5 A Sample Application: Cursor

This sample application, Cursor, illustrates how to incorporate cursors and how to use the mouse and keyboard in your applications. It illustrates the following:

- Using a custom cursor as the class cursor
- Showing the hourglass cursor during a lengthy operation
- Using the mouse to select a portion of the client area
- Using the keyboard to move the cursor

To create the Cursor application, copy and rename the source files of the Generic application, then make the following modifications:

1. Add a **CURSOR** statement to your resource script file.
2. Add new variables.
3. Load the custom cursor and use it to set the class cursor in the initialization function.
4. Prepare the hourglass cursor.
5. Add a lengthy operation to the window function (for simplicity, use the ENTER key to trigger the operation).
6. Add the WM_LBUTTONDOWN, WM_MOUSEMOVE, and WM_LBUTTONUP cases to the window function to support selection.
7. Add the WM_KEYDOWN case to the window function to support keyboard-controlled cursor movement.
8. Add the WM_PAINT case to the window function to redraw the client area after it has been invalidated.
9. Add BULLSEYE.CUR to the make file.
10. Compile and link the application.

This sample assumes that your system has a mouse; if your system does not, the application might not operate as described. However, it is a fairly straightforward task to adjust the sample to work with both the mouse and the keyboard or with only the keyboard.

NOTE Rather than typing the code provided in the following sections, you might find it more convenient to simply compile and execute the sample source files provided with the SDK.

6.5.1 Add the CURSOR Statement

To use a custom cursor, you need to create a cursor file using SDKPaint, and give the name of the file in a **CURSOR** statement in the resource script file. Add the following statement to your resource script file:

```
bullseye CURSOR BULLSEYE.CUR
```

Make sure that the cursor file, BULLSEYE.CUR, contains a cursor.

6.5.2 Add New Variables

You will need several new variables for this sample application. Place the following statements at the beginning of your C-language source file:

```
char str[255];                  /* general-purpose string buffer */

HCURSOR hSaveCursor;            /* handle to current cursor      */
HCURSOR hHourGlass;             /* handle to hourglass cursor    */

BOOL bTrack = FALSE;            /* TRUE if left button clicked   */
int OrgX = 0, OrgY = 0;         /* original cursor position      */
int PrevX = 0, PrevY = 0;       /* current cursor position       */
int X = 0, Y = 0;               /* last cursor position          */
RECT Rect;                      /* selection rectangle           */

POINT ptCursor;                 /* x and y coordinates of cursor */
int repeat = 1;                 /* repeat count of key stroke    */
```

The hSaveCursor and hHourGlass variables hold the cursor handles to be used for the lengthy operation. The bTrack variable holds a Boolean flag indicating whether a selection is in progress. The variables OrgX, OrgY, PrevX, and PrevY hold the original and current cursor positions as a selection is being made. OrgX and OrgY, along with the variables X and Y, hold the original and final coordinates of the selection when the selection process is complete. The ptCursor structure holds the current position of the cursor in the client area. This is updated when the user presses a DIRECTION key. The Rect structure holds the current dimensions of the client area and is used to make sure the cursor stays within the client area. The repeat variable holds the current repeat count for each keyboard motion.

6.5.3 Set the Class Cursor

To set the class cursor, you need to modify a statement in the initialization function. Specifically, you need to assign the cursor handle to the **hCursor** field of the window-class structure. Make the following change in the C-language source file. Find this line:

```
wc.hCursor = LoadCursor(NULL, IDC_ARROW);
```

Change it to the following:

```
wc.hCursor = LoadCursor(hInstance, "bullseye");
```

6.5.4 Prepare the Hourglass Cursor

Since you will be using the hourglass cursor during a lengthy operation, you need to load it. The most convenient place to load it is during the initialization tasks handled by the InitInstance function. Add the following statement to InitInstance:

```
hHourGlass = LoadCursor(NULL, IDC_WAIT);
```

This makes the hourglass cursor available whenever it is needed.

6.5.5 Add a Lengthy Operation

A lengthy operation can take many forms. This sample is a function named "sieve" that computes several hundred prime numbers. The operation begins when the user presses ENTER. Add the following statements to the window function:

```
case WM_CHAR:
    if (wParam == '\r') {
    SetCapture(hWnd);

    /* Set the cursor to an hourglass */

    hSaveCursor = SetCursor(hHourGlass);

    strcpy (str, "Calculating prime numbers...");
    InvalidateRect (hWnd, NULL, TRUE);
    UpdateWindow (hWnd);
    sprintf(str, "Calculated %d primes. ", sieve());
    InvalidateRect (hWnd, NULL, TRUE);
    UpdateWindow (hWnd);

    SetCursor(hSaveCursor); /* Restores previous cursor */
    ReleaseCapture();
}
break;
```

When the user presses ENTER, Windows generates a WM_CHAR message whose *wParam* parameter contains an ANSI value representing the carriage return. When the window function receives a WM_CHAR message, it checks for this value and carries out the sample lengthy operation, sieve. This function, called Eratosthenes Sieve Prime-Number Program, is from *Byte*, January 1983. It is defined as follows:

```
#define NITER 20
#define SIZE 8190
```

```
char flags[SIZE+1] = { 0};

sieve() {
    int i,k;
    int iter, count;

    for (iter = 1; iter <= NITER; iter++) {
        count = 0;
        for (i = 0; i <= SIZE; i++)
            flags[i] = TRUE;

        for (i = 2; i <= SIZE; i++) {
            if (flags[i] ) {
                for (k = i + i; k <= SIZE; k += i)
                    flags[k] = FALSE;
                count++;
            }
        }
    }
    return (count);
}
```

6.5.6 Add the WM_LBUTTONDOWN, WM_MOUSEMOVE, and WM_LBUTTONUP Cases

To carry out a selection, you can use the statements described in Section 6.3, "Letting the User Select Information with the Mouse." Add the following statements to your window function:

```
case WM_LBUTTONDOWN:
    bTrack = TRUE;
    strcpy (str, "");
    PrevX = LOWORD(lParam);
    PrevY = HIWORD(lParam);
    if (!(wParam & MK_SHIFT)) {        /* If shift key is not pressed */
        OrgX = LOWORD(lParam);
        OrgY = HIWORD(lParam);
    }
    InvalidateRect (hWnd, NULL, TRUE);
    UpdateWindow (hWnd);

    /* Capture all input even if the mouse goes outside of window */

    SetCapture(hWnd);
    break;
```

```
case WM_MOUSEMOVE:
    {
        RECT          rectClient;
        int           NextX;
        int           NextY;

        if (bTrack) {
            NextX = LOWORD(lParam);
            NextY = HIWORD(lParam);

            /* Do not draw outside the window's client area */

            GetClientRect (hWnd, &rectClient);
            if (NextX < rectClient.left) {
                NextX = rectClient.left;
            } else if (NextX >= rectClient.right) {
                NextX = rectClient.right - 1;
            }
            if (NextY < rectClient.top) {
                NextY = rectClient.top;
            } else if (NextY >= rectClient.bottom) {
                NextY = rectClient.bottom - 1;
            }

            /* If the mouse position has changed, then clear the */
            /* previous rectangle and draw the new one. */

            if ((NextX != PrevX) || (NextY != PrevY)) {
                hDC = GetDC(hWnd);
                SetROP2(hDC, R2_NOT);           /* Erases the previous box */
                MoveTo(hDC, OrgX, OrgY);
                LineTo(hDC, OrgX, PrevY);
                LineTo(hDC, PrevX, PrevY);
                LineTo(hDC, PrevX, OrgY);
                LincTo(hDC, OrgX, OrgY);

                /* Get the current mouse position */

                PrevX = NextX;
                PrevY = NextY;
                MoveTo(hDC, OrgX, OrgY);         /* Draws the new box */
                LineTo(hDC, OrgX, PrevY);
                LineTo(hDC, PrevX, PrevY);
                LineTo(hDC, PrevX, OrgY);
                LineTo(hDC, OrgX, OrgY);
                ReleaseDC(hWnd, hDC);
            }
        }
    }
    break;
```

```
case WM_LBUTTONUP:
    bTrack = FALSE;                    /* Ignores mouse input         */
    ReleaseCapture();                  /* Releases hold on mouse input */

    X = LOWORD(lParam);                /* Saves the current value     */
    Y = HIWORD(lParam);
    break;
```

6.5.7 Add the WM_KEYDOWN and WM_KEYUP Cases

In order to use the keyboard to control the cursor, you need to add WM_KEYDOWN and WM_KEYUP cases to the window function.

The statements in the WM_KEYDOWN case retrieve the current position of the cursor and update the position when a DIRECTION key is pressed. Add the following statements to the window function:

```
case WM_KEYDOWN:
    GetCursorPos(&ptCursor);
    if (wParam != VK_LEFT || wParam != VK_RIGHT ||
        wParam != VK_UP || wParam != VK_DOWN )
        break;

    ScreenToClient(hWnd, &ptCursor);
    repeat++;                   /* Increases the repeat rate */

    switch (wParam) {

        case VK_LEFT:
            ptCursor.x -= repeat;
            break;

        case VK_RIGHT:
            ptCursor.x += repeat;
            break;

        case VK_UP:
            ptCursor.y -= repeat;
            break;

        case VK_DOWN:
            ptCursor.y += repeat;
            break;

        default:
            return (NULL);
    }

    GetClientRect(hWnd, &Rect); /* Gets the client boundaries */
```

```
        if (ptCursor.x >= Rect.right)
            ptCursor.x = Rect.right - 1;
        else if (ptCursor.x < Rect.left)
            ptCursor.x = Rect.left;
        if (ptCursor.y >= Rect.bottom)
            ptCursor.y = Rect.bottom - 1;
        else if (ptCursor.y < Rect.top)
            ptCursor.y = Rect.top;

    ClientToScreen(hWnd, &ptCursor);
    SetCursorPos(ptCursor.x, ptCursor.y);
    break;
```

The **GetCursorPos** function retrieves the cursor position in screen coordinates. To check the position of the cursor within the client area, the coordinates are converted to client coordinates by using the **ScreenToClient** function. The **switch** statement checks for the DIRECTION keys; each time it encounters a DIRECTION key, the statement adds the current contents of the repeat variable to the appropriate coordinate of the cursor location.

The new position is checked to make sure it is still in the client area, using the **GetClientRect** function to retrieve the dimensions of the client area. The position is adjusted, if necessary. Finally, the **ClientToScreen** function converts the position back to screen coordinates and the **SetCursorPos** function sets the new position.

The WM_KEYUP case restores the initial value of the repeat variable when the user releases the key, as shown in the following example:

```
case WM_KEYUP:
    repeat = 1;                       /* Clears the repeat count  */
    break;
```

6.5.8 Add the WM_PAINT Case

To be sure that the text string and selection rectangle are redrawn when necessary (for example, when another window has temporarily covered the client area), add the following case to the window function:

```
case WM_PAINT:
            {
                PAINTSTRUCT     ps;

                hDC = BeginPaint (hWnd, &ps);
                if (OrgX != PrevX || OrgY != PrevY) {
                    MoveTo(hDC, OrgX, OrgY);
                    LineTo(hDC, OrgX, PrevY);
                    LineTo(hDC, PrevX, PrevY);
                    LineTo(hDC, PrevX, OrgY);
                    LineTo(hDC, OrgX, OrgY);
                }
```

```
        TextOut (hDC, 1, 1, str, strlen (str));
        EndPaint (hWnd, &ps);
    }
    break;
```

6.5.9 Add BULLSEYE.CUR to the Make File

In the make file, add the file BULLSEYE.CUR to the list of files on which CURSOR.RES is dependent. The relevant lines in the make file should look like the following:

```
CURSOR.RES: CURSOR.RC CURSOR.H BULLSEYE.CUR
     RC -r CURSOR.RC
```

This ensures that, if the file BULLSEYE.CUR changes, CURSOR.RC will be re-compiled to form a new CURSOR.RES file.

6.5.10 Compile and Link

Recompile and link the Cursor application. When the application is recompiled, start Windows and the Cursor application. When you move the cursor into the client area, it changes to the bull's-eye shape.

Press and hold down the left mouse button, then drag the mouse to a new position and release the mouse button. You should see a selection that looks like Figure 6.1:

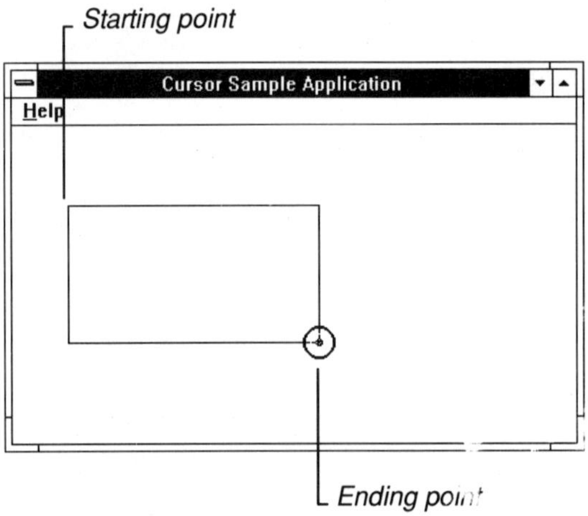

Figure 6.1 A Selection in the Cursor Application

Now press the DIRECTION keys to move the cursor. Then press ENTER to see the application display the hourglass cursor to indicate that the lengthy operation is in progress.

6.6 Summary

This chapter explained how to use the cursor in a Windows application. A cursor is a special bitmap that allows the user to track actions initiated via the mouse. Windows lets you change the shape of the cursor to suit your application's needs. You can use one of Windows' built-in cursor shapes, or create your own cursors using SDKPaint.

Windows automatically carries out most mouse actions; however, one action, selection, must be carried out by the application.

Because Windows does not require a mouse or other pointing device, you will probably want to include functions that allow the user to move the cursor using the keyboard.

For more information on topics related to cursors, see the following:

Topic	Reference
Mouse and keyboard input	*Guide to Programming*: Chapter 4, "Keyboard and Mouse Input"
Cursor functions	*Reference, Volume 1*: Chapter 1, "Window Manager Interface Functions" and Chapter 4, "Functions Directory"
Window-management messages and input messages	*Reference, Volume 1*: Chapter 5, "Messages Overview" and Chapter 6, "Messages Directory"
Resource script statements	*Reference, Volume 2*: Chapter 8, "Resource Script Statements"
Using SDKPaint	*Tools*: Chapter 4, "Designing Images: SDKPaint"

Chapter 7 Menus

Most Windows applications use menus to let the user select commands or actions.

This chapter covers the following topics:

- What a menu is
- Defining a menu
- Including a menu in your application
- Processing input from a menu
- Modifying an existing menu
- Working with special menu features

This chapter also explains how to create a sample application, EditMenu, that uses and processes input from menus.

7.1 What is a Menu?

A menu is a list of items which, to the user, are the application's commands. A menu item can be displayed using text or a bitmap. The user tells the application to perform a command by selecting a menu item using the mouse or the keyboard. When a user chooses a menu item, Windows sends the application a message that indicates which item the user selected.

To use a menu in your application, follow these general steps:

1. Define the menu in your resource script file.
2. Specify the menu in your application code. There are two common ways to do this:
   - When registering the window class, specify a menu for that entire window class (the "class menu").
   - When creating a window, specify a menu for that window.
3. Initialize the menu, if necessary.

Once the menu exists and has been initialized, the following can take place:

- The user can select commands from the menu.

  When the user selects a command (menu item), Windows sends your application an input message that includes the identifier for that menu item.

- Your application can add, change or replace menu items, or even the entire menu, as necessary.

7.2 Defining a Menu

The first step in using a menu is to define it in your application's resource script (.RC) file using a **MENU** statement. The **MENU** statement specifies:

- The name of the menu
- Items on the menu
- The menu ID of each item
- The text or bitmap that appears for each item
- Special attributes of each item

A **MENU** statement consists of the menu name, the **MENU** key word, and a pair of **BEGIN** and **END** key words that enclose one or more of the following menu-definition statements:

- The **MENUITEM** statement defines a menu item, its appearance, and its identifier.

  When the user chooses a menu item, Windows notifies the application of the user's selection.

- The **POPUP** statement defines a pop-up menu, which contains a list of menu items.

  When the user selects a pop-up menu, Windows displays the list of items. The user can then select an item from the pop-up menu; Windows then notifies the application of the user's selection.

For example, the following **MENU** statement defines a menu named SampleMenu:

```
❶ SampleMenu MENU
   BEGIN
       ❷ MENUITEM "Exit!", IDM_EXIT
       MENUITEM "Recalculate!", IDM_RECALC
       ❸ POPUP "Options"
```

```
        BEGIN
            ❹ MENUITEM "Scylla", IDM_SCYLLA
            MENUITEM "Charybdis", IDM_CHARYBDIS
        END
    END
```

In this example:

❶ This line tells the Resource Compiler that this is the beginning of a menu definition, and names the menu SampleMenu. A **MENU** statement consists of the menu name, the **MENU** key word, and a pair of **BEGIN** and **END** key words which enclose the item-definition statements for that menu.

❷ This **MENUITEM** statement defines the first item on the menu. The text "Exit!" will appear as the leftmost command on the menu bar. When the user selects the Exit! command, Windows sends the application a WM_COMMAND message that specifies the menu ID "IDM_EXIT" in the message's *wParam* parameter. The next **MENUITEM** statement defines the Recalculate! command in the same way.

❸ The **POPUP** statement defines a pop-up menu. The text "Options" appears on the menu bar. When the user selects the Options command, a menu appears that lets the user choose between the Scylla and Charybdis commands.

❹ Within the **POPUP** statement are the definitions for the items on that pop-up menu. For the Options pop-up menu, there are two menu items, each with its own text and menu ID.

When the user selects the Exit!, Recalculate!, Scylla or Charybdis command, Windows notifies the application of the user's selection by passing it that item's menu ID. Note that Windows does not notify the application when the user selects the Options command; instead, Windows simply displays the Options pop-up mcnu.

For more information about the **MENU**, **POPUP** and **MENUITEM** resource statements, see the *Reference*, *Volume 2*.

7.2.1 Menu IDs

Each menu item has a unique identifier, usually called a "menu ID." When the user chooses a command, Windows passes the command's menu ID to the application. Menu IDs must be unique constants. You can define each menu ID as a constant by using the **#define** directive in the resource script file or the include file. For example:

```
#define IDM_EXIT        111
#define IDM_RECALC      112
#define IDM_SCYLLA      113
#define IDM_CHARYBDIS   114
```

You use a menu ID to direct the flow of control depending on which menu item the user selects. For more information on handling menu input, see Section 7.4, "Processing Input from a Menu."

7.3 Including a Menu in Your Application

Once you have defined a menu in the resource script file, you can include it in your application code. You specify a menu by associating it with a window. Any overlapped or pop-up window can have a menu; a child window cannot (although child windows can have system menus).

There are two common ways to specify a menu in your application:

- Specify the menu as the class menu when registering a window class. All windows of that class will then include that menu.
- Specify the menu when creating a window. That window will then include that menu.

The following sections explain these two methods.

7.3.1 Specifying the Menu for a Window Class

When you register a window class, you are setting the default attributes for windows in that class. You can specify a menu as the default menu for a window class; this default menu is known as the class menu. You specify the class menu when you register the window class. To do so, you assign the name of the menu, as given in the resource file, to the **lpszMenuName** field of the window-class structure. For example:

```
wc.lpszMenuName = "SampleMenu";
```

In this example, the **lpszMenuName** field is part of a **WNDCLASS** data structure named **wc**. The menu name "SampleMenu" is the name given to the menu in the application's resource script file.

Once a window class has been registered, each window of that class will have the specified class menu. You can override this default menu by explicitly supplying a menu handle when you create a window of that class.

7.3.2 Specifying a Menu for a Specific Window

A window need not use the class menu; the class menu is simply a default, not a requirement. To use a menu other than the class menu, specify the menu you want when you create the window.

To specify a menu when creating a window:

1. Load the menu from your application resources using the **LoadMenu** function. This function returns a menu handle.

2. When you call **CreateWindow** to create the window, pass the menu handle as the function's *hMenu* parameter.

The following example shows how to load and specify a menu by using **CreateWindow**:

```
HWND hWnd;          /* Initialize a variable to hold the
                       handle to the current window*/

HMENU hSampleMenu;/* Initialize a variable to hold the
                       handle to the menu */
   .
   .
   .

❶ hSampleMenu = LoadMenu (hInstance, "SampleMenu");
❷ hWnd = CreateWindow ("SampleWindow",
              "SampleWindow",
              WS_OVERLAPPEDWINDOW,
              CW_USEDEFAULT,
              CW_USEDEFAULT,
              CW_USEDEFAULT,
              CW_USEDEFAULT,
              (HWND) NULL,
          ❸  hSampleMenu,
              hInstance,
              (LPSTR) NULL );
```

In this example:

❶ The **LoadMenu** function loads the menu named SampleMenu. The hInstance variable specifies that the resource is to be loaded from the application's resources. **LoadMenu** returns a menu handle, which is stored in the hSampleMenu variable.

❷ The application then calls **CreateWindow** to create a new window named SampleWindow.

❸ The application passes hSampleMenu, the menu handle that **LoadMenu** returned, to the **CreateWindow** function. This tells Windows to use SampleMenu for this window, instead of the class menu (if any).

7.4 Processing Input from a Menu

When a user chooses a command in a menu, Windows sends a WM_COMMAND message to the corresponding window function. The message contains the menu ID of the command in its *wParam* parameter.

The window function is responsible for carrying out any tasks associated with the selected command. For example, if the user chooses the Open command, the window function prompts for the filename, opens the file, and displays the file in the window's client area.

The most common way to process menu input is with a **switch** statement in the window function. Usually, the **switch** statement directs processing according to the value of the *wParam* parameter of the WM_COMMAND message. Each case processes a different menu ID.

For example:

```
case WM_COMMAND:
❶ switch (wParam)
  {
      ❷ case IDM_NEW:
    /* perform operations for creating a new file */
      break;
    case IDM_OPEN:
      /* perform operations for opening a file */
      break;
    case IDM_SAVE:
      /* perform operations for saving this file */
      break;
    case IDM_SAVEAS:
      /* perform operations for saving this file */
      break;
    case IDM_EXIT:
      /* perform operations for exiting the application */
      break;
  }
  break;
```

In this example:

❶ The *wParam* parameter contains the menu ID of the item the user just selected.

❷ For each menu ID (menu item), the application performs the appropriate operations.

7.5 Working with Menus from Your Application

Windows provides functions you can use to change existing menus and create new menus, while your application runs. This section explains:

- How to enable and disable menu items
- How to check and uncheck menu items
- How to add, change, and delete menu items
- How to use bitmaps as menu items
- How to replace a menu
- How to create and initialize a menu from your application

When a window is created, it receives a private copy of the class menu. The application can alter that window's copy of the menu without affecting other windows' menus.

NOTE Whenever you make changes to items on the menu bar, you need to call the **DrawMenuBar** function to display the changes.

7.5.1 Enabling and Disabling Menu Items

Normally, a menu item is enabled; its text appears normal, and the user can select it. A disabled menu item appears normal, but does not respond to mouse clicks or keyboard selection. A "grayed" item has dimmed text, and does not respond to mouse clicks or keyboard selection. Typically, you disable or gray a menu item when the action it represents is not appropriate. For example, you might gray the Print command in the File menu when the system does not have a printer installed.

Setting the Initial State of a Menu Item

In the resource script file, you can specify whether a menu item is initially disabled or grayed. To do so, use the **INACTIVE** or **GRAYED** options with the **MENUITEM** statement. For example, the following statement specifies that the Print command is initially grayed:

```
MENUITEM "Print", IDM_PRINT, GRAYED
```

The information in the resource script file applies only to the initial state of the menu. You can change the menu item's state later, using the **EnableMenuItem** function in your C-language source file. **EnableMenuItem** enables, disables, or grays a menu item.

Disabling a Menu Item

A "disabled" menu item appears normal, but does not respond to mouse clicks or selection by the keyboard. A disabled menu item is commonly used as a title for related menu options. The following statement disables a menu item:

```
EnableMenuItem (hMenu, IDM_SAVE, MF_DISABLED);
```

This example disables a command on the menu represented by the menu handle hMenu. The menu ID of the command is IDM_SAVE. By specifying the value MF_DISABLED, you tell Windows to disable the specified menu item.

Disabling and Graying a Menu Item

So that the user can tell that a menu item is not currently available, it's a good idea to disable a menu item by "graying" it rather than simply disabling it. Graying a menu item disables the item and redisplays the item text in dimmed letters.

To disable and gray a menu item, specify the value MF_GRAYED when you call **EnableMenuItem**. For example:

```
EnableMenuItem (hMenu, IDM_PRINT, MF_GRAYED);
```

This example disables a command on the menu represented by the menu handle hMenu. The menu ID of the command is IDM_PRINT. By specifying the value MF_GRAYED, you tell Windows to disable the specified menu item, and redisplay the item text in gray letters.

Enabling a Menu Item

You can enable a disabled menu item by calling **EnableMenuItem** and specifying the MF_ENABLED value.

The following example enables the command identified by ID_EXIT:

```
EnableMenuItem (hMenu, ID_EXIT, MF_ENABLED);
```

7.5.2 Checking and Unchecking Menu Items

You can display a checkmark next to an item to indicate that the user has selected it. Typically, you check a menu item when it is part of a group of items that are mutually exclusive. The checkmark indicates the user's latest choice. For example, if a group consists of the items Left, Right, and Center, you might check the Left item to indicate that the user chose that item most recently.

Setting an Initial Checkmark

In the resource script file, you can specify whether a menu item is initially checked. To do so, use the **CHECKED** option in the **MENUITEM** statement. For example, the following **MENUITEM** statement specifies that the Left command is initially checked:

```
MENUITEM "Left", IDM_LEFT, CHECKED
```

Checking a Menu Item

The information in the resource script file applies only to the initial state of the menu. You can check or remove a checkmark from a menu item later, using the **CheckMenuItem** function in your C-language source file. **CheckMenuItem** checks or removes a checkmark from a specified menu item.

The following example places a checkmark next to the item whose menu ID is IDM_LEFT:

```
CheckMenuItem (hMenu, IDM_LEFT, MF_CHECKED);
```

Removing a Menu-Item Checkmark

To remove a checkmark from a menu item, you call the **CheckMenuItem** function and specify the value MF_UNCHECKED. The following example removes the check (if any) from the item whose menu ID is IDM_RIGHT:

```
CheckMenuItem (hMenu, IDM_RIGHT, MF_UNCHECKED);
```

If you change menu items in the menu bar, you need to call the **DrawMenuBar** function to display the changes.

7.5.3 Adding Menu Items

You can add a new menu item to the end of an existing menu, or insert one after a particular menu item.

Appending a Menu Item

To append an item to the end of an existing menu, you use the **AppendMenu** function. This function adds a new item to the end of the specified menu, and lets you specify whether the new item is checked, enabled, grayed, and so on.

The following example appends the item "Raspberries" to the end of the Fruit menu. The example disables and grays the new item if raspberries are not currently in season.

```
if (!RasberriesInSeason)
   AppendMenu (hFruitMenu,
               MF_GRAYED,
               IDM_RASPBERRIES,
               "Raspberries");
 else
   AppendMenu (hFruitMenu,
               MF_ENABLED,
               IDM_RASPBERRIES,
               "Raspberries");
```

Inserting a Menu Item

To insert an item in an existing menu, you use the **InsertMenu** function. This function inserts the specified item at the specified position, and moves subsequent items down to accommodate the new item. Like **AppendMenu**, **InsertMenu** lets you specify the state of the new item when you insert it.

The following example inserts the item "Kumquats" before the existing item "Melons." The example disables and grays the new item.

```
InsertMenu (hFruitMenu,
                 IDM_MELONS,
                 MF_BYCOMMAND | MF_GRAYED,
                 IDM_KUMQUATS,
                 "Kumquats");
```

You can also insert items by numerical position rather than before a specific item. The following example inserts the item "Bananas" so that it becomes the third item in the Fruit menu. (The first item has position 0, the second item 1, and so on.)

```
InsertMenu (hFruitMenu,
                 2,
                 MF_BYPOSITION | MF_GRAYED,
                 IDM_BANANAS,
                 "Bananas");
```

7.5.4 Changing Existing Menus

You can change existing menus and menu items by using the **ModifyMenu** function. For example, you might need to change the text of a menu item. **ModifyMenu** lets you enable, disable, gray, check or uncheck the item.

In the following example, the **ModifyMenu** function changes the text of the Water command to "Wine". The example also changes the item's menu ID.

```
ModifyMenu (hMenu,
            IDM_WATER,
            MF_BYCOMMAND,
            IDM_WINE,
            "Wine");
```

When you use **ModifyMenu**, you are essentially telling Windows to replace a specific menu item with a new item. The third, fourth and fifth **ModifyMenu** parameters specify the attributes of the new item.

For example, the following statement changes the item text from "Wine" to "Cabernet". Although only the menu item's text is changing, the statement nonetheless respecifies all the attributes of the item (in this case, just the menu ID).

```
ModifyMenu (hMenu,
            IDM_WINE,
            MF_BYCOMMAND,
            IDM_WINE,
            "Cabernet");
```

Performing Several Changes at Once

When you use **ModifyMenu** to change a menu item, you can also check or uncheck the item, and can enable, disable, or gray it as well.

The following example not only changes the Water command to "Wine"; it enables the command (if not already enabled), checks it, and changes its menu ID.

```
ModifyMenu (hMenu,
            IDM_WATER,
            MF_BYCOMMAND | MF_ENABLED | MF_CHECKED,
            IDM_WINE,
            "Wine");
```

7.5.5 Deleting a Menu Item

You can remove a menu item, and any pop-up menus associated with that item, by using the **DeleteMenu** function. **DeleteMenu** permanently removes the specified menu item from the specified menu, and moves subsequent items up to fill the gap.

```
DeleteMenu (hFruitMenu,         /* handle to menu */
            1,                  /* delete the second item */
            MF_BYPOSITION);     /* we are specifying the
                                   item by its position
                                   on the menu */
```

This example deletes the Fruit menu's second item. Windows moves any subsequent items up to fill the gap.

The following example deletes the same item, but specifies it by its menu ID rather than by its position on the menu:

```
DeleteMenu (hFruitMenu,         /* handle to menu */
            IDM_ORANGES,        /* delete "Oranges" item */
            MF_BYCOMMAND);      /* we are specifying the
                                   item by its menu ID */
```

7.5.6 Using a Bitmap as a Menu Item

Windows lets you use bitmaps as menu items. There are two ways to do this:

- When you insert or append a new menu item, specify that you want to use a bitmap instead of text for that item.
- Use the **ModifyMenu** function to change an existing item so that it appears as a bitmap instead of text.

You cannot specify a bitmap as a menu item in the .RC file.

The following example loads a bitmap named "Apples", then uses the **Modify-Menu** function to replace the text of the Apples command with a bitmap image of an apple.

```
  HMENU hMenu;
  HBITMAP hBitmap;
     .
     .
     .
❶ hBitmap = LoadBitmap (hInstance, "Apples");

❷ hMenu = GetMenu(hWnd);
  ModifyMenu (hMenu,
❸             IDM_APPLES,       /* item to replace */
❹             MF_BYCOMMAND | MF_BITMAP,
❺             IDM_APPLES,      /* Menu ID of new item */
❻             (LPSTR) MAKELONG (hBitmap, 0))
```

In this example:

❶ The **LoadBitmap** function loads the bitmap from the file and returns a handle to the bitmap, saved in the hBitmap variable.

❷ The **GetMenu** function retrieves the handle of the current window's menu, and places it in the variable hMenu. This variable is then passed as the first parameter of the **ModifyMenu** function, which specifies which menu to change.

❸ The second parameter of the **ModifyMenu** function, in this case set to IDM_APPLES, specifies the menu item to modify.

❹ The third parameter specifies how to make the changes. MF_BYCOMMAND tells Windows that we are specifying the item to change by its menu ID rather than by its position. MF_BITMAP indicates that the new item will be a bitmap rather than text.

❺ The fourth parameter of the **ModifyMenu** function, set to IDM_APPLES, specifies the new menu ID for the item we are modifying. In this example, the menu ID does not change.

❻ The new bitmap handle must be passed as the low-order word of the fifth parameter of **ModifyMenu**. The **MAKELONG** utility combines the 16-bit handle with a 16-bit constant to make the 32-bit argument. Casting the parameter to an **LPSTR** prevents the compiler from issuing a warning, since the compiler expects this parameter to be a string.

7.5.7 Replacing a Menu

You can replace a window's menu by using the **SetMenu** function. Typically, you replace a menu when the application changes modes and needs a completely new set of commands. For example, an application might replace a spreadsheet menu with a charting menu when the user changes from a spreadsheet to a charting mode.

In the following example, the **GetMenu** function retrieves the menu handle of the spreadsheet menu and saves it for restoring the menu later. The **SetMenu** function replaces the spreadsheet menu with a charting menu loaded from the application's resources.

```
HMENU hMenu;
HMENU hSpreadsheetMenu;
    .
    .
    .
hOldMenu = GetMenu(hWnd);
hMenu = LoadMenu(hInstance, "ChartMenu");
SetMenu(hWnd, hMenu);
    .
    .
    .
```

You can also load menus from resources other than those belonging to the application (by using the module handle of a library).

7.5.8 Creating a New Menu

You can create new menus while your application runs, using the **CreateMenu** function. **CreateMenu** creates a new, empty menu; you can then add items to it using **AppendMenu** or **InsertMenu**.

The following example creates an empty pop-up menu and appends it to the window's menu. It then appends three items to the new pop-up menu.

```
HMENU hWinMenu;
HMENU hVeggieMenu;
           .
           .
           .
hVeggieMenu = CreateMenu ();

AppendMenu (hWinMenu,
            MF_POPUP | MF_ENABLED,
            hVeggieMenu,
            "Veggies");

AppendMenu (hVeggieMenu,
            MF_ENABLED,
            IDM_CELERY,
            "Celery");

AppendMenu (hVeggieMenu,
            MF_ENABLED,
            IDM_LETTUCE,
            "Lettuce");

AppendMenu (hVeggieMenu,
            MF_ENABLED,
            IDM_PEAS,
            "Peas");
```

7.5.9 Initializing a Menu

If necessary, your application can initialize a menu before Windows displays that menu. Although you can specify a menu item's initial state (disabled, grayed, or checked) in the resource script file, this method doesn't work if the initialization differs from time to time. For example, to disable the Print menu item only if the user's system has no printer installed, you could disable the Print item when you initialize that menu. (Disabling "Print" in the .RC file wouldn't work, since you won't know whether or not there's a printer available until the application is running.)

Just before Windows displays a menu, it sends a WM_INITMENU message to the window function for the window that owns that menu. This lets the window function check the state of the menu items and, if necessary, modify them, before

Windows displays the menu. In the following example, the window function processes the WM_INITMENU message, and sets the state of a command based on the value of the wChecked variable:

```
WORD wChecked = IDM_LEFT;
      .
      .
      .
❶ case WM_INITMENU:
❷   if (GetMenu(hWnd)!= wParam)
        break;
    CheckMenuItem(wParam, IDM_LEFT,
        IDM_LEFT == wChecked ? MF_CHECKED : MF_UNCHECKED);
    CheckMenuItem(wParam, IDM_CENTER,
        IDM_CENTER == wChecked ? MF_CHECKED : MF_UNCHECKED);
    CheckMenuItem(wParam, IDM_RIGHT,
        IDM_RIGHT == wChecked ? MF_CHECKED : MF_UNCHECKED);
    break;
```

In this example:

❶ The WM_INITMENU message passes the given menu handle in the *wParam* message parameter.

❷ To make sure that Windows is about to display the correct menu, the **Get-Menu** function retrieves a handle to the current window's menu and compares that handle with the value of *wParam*. If these are not equal, the window's menu should not be initialized. Otherwise, the menu is correct, and you can use the **CheckMenuItem** function to initialize the commands in the menu.

7.6 Special Menu Features

So far, this chapter has discussed "standard" menus, which drop down from a menu bar, and which contain items the user selects using the mouse, the DIRECTION keys, or command mnemonics. In addition to these menu features, Windows provides the following special features:

- Accelerator keys, which provide a keyboard shortcut for selecting menu items
- Cascading menus, which let you have several levels of pop-up menus
- Floating pop-up menus, which are normal pop-up menus except that they can appear anywhere on the screen (usually at the current mouse position)
- Customized checkmarks, which let you use your own bitmaps for checkmarks instead of the standard Windows checkmark

The rest of this section explains how to use these features.

7.6.1 Providing Menu-Accelerator Keys

Accelerator keys are shortcut keys that let the user choose a command from a menu using a single key stroke. For example, an application could let the user select the Delete command simply by pressing the DELETE key. Accelerator keys are part of the resource script file, and are tied into the application through the C-language source code.

To provide menu-accelerator keys in your application:

1. In the resource script file, mark the accelerator key for each menu item in the **MENUITEM** statements.
2. In the resource script file, create an accelerator table. An accelerator table lists the accelerator keys and corresponding menu IDs. You create it using the **ACCELERATORS** resource statement.
3. In the C-language source file, load the accelerator table by using the **LoadAccelerators** function.
4. Change the message loop so that it processes accelerator-key messages.

The remainder of this section describes each step in more detail.

Adding Accelerator Text to a Menu Item

The menu text should indicate each item's accelerator key so that the user can tell which key to use. Add the key designations to the **MENUITEM** definitions in the .RC file.

For example, suppose your application has the following pop-up menu defined in its resource script file:

```
GroceryMenu MENU
    POPUP       "&Meats"
    BEGIN
        MENUITEM    "&Beef\tF9",             IDM_BEEF
        MENUITEM    "&Chicken\tShift+F9",    IDM_CHICKEN
        MENUITEM    "&Lamb\tCtrl+F9",        IDM_LAMB
        MENUITEM    "&Pork\tAlt+F9",         IDM_PORK
    END
END
```

The pop-up menu "Meats" has the four menu items Beef, Chicken, Lamb, and Pork. Each menu item has a mnemonic, indicated by the ampersand (&), and an accelerator key separated from the name with a tab (\t). Whenever a command has a corresponding accelerator, it should be displayed in this way. The accelerator keys in this sample are F9, SHIFT+F9, CONTROL+F9, and ALT+F9.

Creating an Accelerator Table

To use accelerator keys, add an accelerator table to the resource script file using the **ACCELERATORS** statement. The statement lists the accelerator keys and the corresponding menu IDs of the associated commands. In the **ACCELERATORS** statement, as with other resource statements, **BEGIN** starts the entry and **END** marks its end. For example:

```
GroceryMenu ACCELERATORS
BEGIN
    VK_F9,   IDM_BEEF,      VIRTKEY
    VK_F9,   IDM_CHICKEN,   VIRTKEY, SHIFT
    VK_F9,   IDM_LAMB,      VIRTKEY, CONTROL
    VK_F9,   IDM_PORK,      VIRTKEY, ALT
END
```

This example defines four accelerator keys, one for each command. The first accelerator key is simply the F9 key; the other three accelerators are key-stroke combinations using the ALT, SHIFT, or CONTROL key in combination with the F9 key.

The accelerator keys are defined using the Windows virtual-key code, as indicated by the **VIRTKEY** option. Virtual keys are device-independent key values that Windows translates for each computer. They are a way to guarantee that the same key is used on all computers without knowing what the actual value of the key is on any computer. You may also use ASCII key codes for accelerators, in which case, you would use the ASCII option.

The **ACCELERATORS** statement associates each accelerator with a menu ID. In the preceding example, the IDM_BEEF, IDM_CHICKEN, IDM_LAMB, and IDM_PORK constants are the menu IDs of the commands on the Grocery menu. When the user presses an accelerator key, these are the values that are passed to the window function.

Loading the Accelerator Table

The accelerator table, like any other resource, needs to be loaded before your application can use it. To load the accelerator table, use the **LoadAccelerators** function. This function takes a handle to the current instance of the application and the name of the accelerator table (as defined in the .RC file); it returns a handle to the accelerator table for the associated menu. Typically, you load a menu's accelerator table when that menu's window has just been created—that is, within the WM_CREATE case of the window function. For example:

```
HANDLE hInst;          /* handle to current instance */
HANDLE hAccTable;      /* handle to accelerator table */
    .
    .
    .
case WM_CREATE:

➊ hAccTable = LoadAccelerators (hInst, "GroceryMenu");
   break;
```

In this example:

➊ This statement loads the accelerator table for GroceryMenu into memory; it assigns the handle identifying the table to the hAccTable variable. The hInst variable identifies the application's resource file; "GroceryMenu" is the name of the accelerator table.

Once the table is loaded, the application can use the **TranslateAccelerator** function to translate accelerators for that menu.

Changing the Message Loop to Process Accelerators

To use the accelerator table, you must add the **TranslateAccelerator** function to the message loop. When the message loop receives a keyboard-input message containing an accelerator key, **TranslateAccelerator** converts the message to a WM_COMMAND message containing the appropriate menu ID for that accelerator, and sends the resulting WM_COMMAND message to the window function.

The message loop should test each message to see if it is an accelerator-key message. If it is, the loop should translate and dispatch the message using **TranslateAccelerator**. If the message is not an accelerator-key message, the loop should process it normally.

NOTE **TranslateAccelerator** also translates accelerators for commands chosen from the system menu. In such cases, it translates the message into a WM_SYSCOMMAND message.

After you add the **TranslateAccelerator** function, the message loop should look like this:

```
while (GetMessage(&msg, NULL, NULL, NULL)) {

❶       if (!TranslateAccelerator(hWnd, hAccTable, &msg))
        {
❷         TranslateMessage(&msg);
          DispatchMessage(&msg);
        }
}
```

In this example:

❶ This statement checks each message to see whether it is an accelerator-key message. The window handle, hWnd, identifies the window whose messages are to be translated. The window handle must identify the window that contains the menu with the accelerators. The accelerator handle, hAccTable, specifies the accelerator table to use when translating the accelerators.

If the message was generated via an accelerator key, the **TranslateAccelerator** function converts the keystroke to a WM_COMMAND message containing the appropriate menu ID, and sends that WM_COMMAND message to the window function.

❷ If the message is not an accelerator-key message, the application processes it as usual, by using the **TranslateMessage** and **DispatchMessage** functions.

7.6.2 Using Cascading Menus

Windows lets you provide more than one level of pop-up menus. Such multilevel pop-up menus are called cascading menus. Such a menu structure can help minimize the number of commands on a single pop-up menu, without requiring a dialog box to let the user refine his or her choice.

Figure 7.1 shows an example of cascading menus.

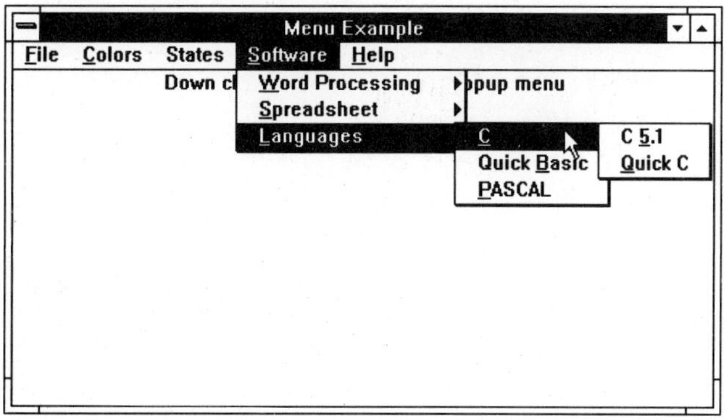

Figure 7.1 Cascading Menus

In this example, the user chose the Software menu, then chose the Languages command from the Software menu. At this point, the Languages pop-up menu appeared to the right of the cursor. The user then moved the cursor over the Languages pop-up menu and chose "C." The C pop-up menu then appeared, and let the user choose either C version 5.1 or QuickC.

Cascading menus are simply nested pop-up menus. The menu definition for the example in Figure 7.1 looks like this:

```
MenuMenu MENU
BEGIN
  .
  .
  .
  POPUP "&Software"
     BEGIN

     POPUP "&Word Processing"
          BEGIN
          MENUITEM  "&Word 5.0", IDM_WORD
          MENUITEM  "W&rite", IDM_WRITE
          END

     POPUP "&Spreadsheet"
          BEGIN
          MENUITEM "&Microsoft Excel", IDM_EXCEL
          MENUITEM "&1+2=4", IDM_124
          END

     POPUP "&Languages"
          BEGIN
          POPUP "&C"
               BEGIN
               MENUITEM "C &5.1", IDM_C51
               MENUITEM "&Quick C", IDM_QUICKC
               END
          MENUITEM  "Quick &Basic", IDM_QUICKBASIC
          MENUITEM  "&PASCAL", IDM_PASCAL
          END
     END
  .
  .
  .
END
```

NOTE A cascading pop-up menu has its own menu handle. To manipulate items on a cascading pop-up menu, you must first get its menu handle by calling the **GetSubMenu** function.

7.6.3 Using Floating Pop-up Menus

Usually, pop-up menus are "attached" to another menu; they appear when the user selects a command on that menu. However, Windows also lets you provide "floating" pop-up menus, which appear at the current cursor position when the user presses a certain key or clicks a mouse button.

To provide a floating pop-up menu, you use the **CreatePopupMenu** and **Track-PopupMenu** functions. If you want the floating pop-up menu to appear when the user presses a certain key or mouse button, create the floating pop-up menu within the **case** statement that handles the input message from that key or button.

The following example displays a floating pop-up menu when the user depresses the right mouse button:

```
POINT currentpoint;
        .
        .
        .
case WM_RBUTTONDOWN:
   {
      HWND hWnd;                /* handle to current window */
      HMENU hFloatingPopup;     /* handle for floating pop-up */
   ❶  currentpoint = MAKEPOINT (lParam);
                                /* point at which the user
                                   pressed the button */
        .
        .
        .
   ❷  hFloatingPopup = CreatePopupMenu();

   ❸  AppendMenu (hFloatingPopup,
                  MF_ENABLED,
                  IDM_CALC,
                  "Calculator");

      AppendMenu (hFloatingPopup,
                  MF_ENABLED,
                  IDM_CARDFILE,
                  "Cardfile");

      AppendMenu (hFloatingPopup,
                  MF_ENABLED,
                  IDM_NOTEPAD,
                  "Notepad");

   ❹  ClientToScreen (hWnd, (LPPOINT)&currentpoint);
```

```
❺ TrackPopupMenu (hFloatingPopup,
                  NULL,
                  ❻ currentpoint.x,
                  currentpoint.y,
                  NULL,
                  hWnd,
                  NULL);

❼ DestroyMenu (hFloatingPopup);

break;
}
```

In this example:

❶ The *lParam* parameter of the WM_RBUTTONDOWN message contains the current position of the mouse. The **MAKEPOINT** function converts this long value to a point, which is then stored in the **currentpoint** data structure.

❷ The **CreatePopupMenu** function creates an empty pop-up menu, and returns a handle to that menu. The new menu's handle is placed in the variable hFloatingPopup.

❸ After creating the empty pop-up menu, the application appends three items to it: Calculator, Cardfile, and Notepad.

❹ The **ClientToScreen** function converts the coordinates of the current cursor position so that they describe the position relative to the entire screen's upper-left corner. (Initially, the coordinates describe the cursor position relative to the client window instead).

❺ Once the menu is complete, the application displays it at the current cursor position by calling **TrackPopupMenu**.

❻ The **x** and **y** fields of the **currentpoint** data structure contain the current screen coordinates of the cursor.

❼ After the user has made a selection from the menu, the application destroys the menu, thereby freeing up the memory the menu used. The application re-creates the menu each time the user depresses the right mouse button.

7.6.4 Designing Your Own Checkmarks

Normally, when you check a menu item, Windows displays the standard Windows checkmark next to the item text. A menu item that is not checked has no special mark next to it at all.

However, you can specify a bitmap, instead of the standard Windows checkmark, to display when an item is checked. You can also specify a bitmap to display when a menu item is not checked.

Custom checkmarks can be particularly useful for helping the user distinguish between menu commands that perform an action and commands that can be checked but are not currently checked. Some Windows applications use the following conventions:

Type of Menu Item	Convention
Menu items that perform an action (for example, display another menu or a dialog box)	Do not display a checkmark for such an item.
Menu items that are currently checked	Display either a normal Windows checkmark or a custom checkmark. When the user chooses a checked item again, remove the checkmark.
Menu items that can be checked but are not currently checked	Display a custom checkmark. When the user chooses an unchecked item, display either a standard Windows checkmark or a different custom checkmark.

To provide your own checkmark bitmaps:

1. Use SDKPaint to create the bitmaps you want to use as checkmarks.

   Windows requires that your checkmark bitmaps be the same size as the standard checkmarks. Although you can, during run time, stretch or shrink your checkmark bitmaps to the right size, it's a good idea to start with a bitmap that's close to the right size. (The size of the standard checkmarks depends on the current display device. To find out the current size of the standard checkmarks, use the **GetMenuCheckMarkDimensions** function.)

   You can also create a bitmap "by hand" — by coding the individual bits. Chapter 11, "Bitmaps," explains how to do this.

2. In your application's resource script file, define each bitmap's name and source file using the **BITMAP** statement. For example:

   ```
   BitmapChecked BITMAP CHECK.BMP
   BitmapNotChecked BITMAP NOCHECK.BMP
   ```

3. In your application source code, use the **LoadBitmap** function to load each bitmap from your application resources.

4. Use the **GetMenuCheckMarkDimensions** function to find out the size of the standard checkmarks on the current display device.

5. If necessary, use the **StretchBlt** function to stretch or shrink each bitmap to the right size.

6. Use the **SetMenuItemBitmaps** function to specify the checkmark bitmaps for each menu item.

7. Before your application terminates, it should destroy the bitmaps to free memory.

The following example shows how to specify checkmark bitmaps for a menu item:

```
SetMenuItemBitmaps (hMenu,        /* handle to menu */
                    0,            /* position of menu item */
                    MF_BYPOSITION,
                    hbmCheckOff,  /* bitmap for unchecked item */
                    hbmCheckOn);  /* bitmap for checked item */
```

7.6.5 Using Owner-Draw Menus

Your application can take complete control over the appearance of menu items by using owner-draw menu items. An owner-draw menu item is a menu for which the application has total responsibility for drawing the item in its normal, selected (highlighted), checked, and unchecked states.

For example, suppose your application provides a menu that allows the user to select a font. Your application could draw each menu item using the font that the menu item represents: the item for roman would be drawn with a roman font, the item for italic would be drawn in italic, and so on.

You cannot define an owner-draw menu item in your application's resource-script (.RC) file. Instead, you must create a new menu item or modify an existing menu item with the MF_OWNERDRAW menu flag. You can use any of the following functions to specify an owner-draw menu item:

- **AppendMenu**
- **InsertMenu**
- **ModifyMenu**

When you call any of these functions, you can pass a 32-bit value as the *lpNewItem* parameter. This 32-bit value can represent any information that is meaningful to your application, and will be available to your application when the menu item is to be displayed. For example, the 32-bit value could contain a pointer to a data structure; the data structure, in turn, might contain a string and the handle of a logical font that your application will use to draw the string.

Before Windows displays an owner-draw menu item for the first time, it sends the WM_MEASUREITEM message to the window that owns the menu. This message's *lParam* parameter points to a **MEASUREITEMSTRUCT** data structure that identifies the menu item and contains the optional 32-bit value for the item. When your application receives the WM_MEASUREITEM message, it must fill in the **itemWidth** and **itemHeight** fields of the data structure before returning from processing the message. Windows uses the information in these fields when creating the bounding rectangle in which your application draws the menu item; it also uses the information to detect the user's interaction with the item.

When the item needs to be drawn (for example, when it is first displayed, or when the user chooses it), Windows sends the WM_DRAWITEM message to the window that owns the menu. The *lParam* parameter of the WM_DRAWITEM message points to a **DRAWITEMSTRUCT** data structure. Like **MEASURE-ITEMSTRUCT**, the **DRAWITEMSTRUCT** data structure contains identifying information about the menu item and its optional 32-bit data. In addition, **DRAWITEMSTRUCT** contains flags that indicate the state of the item (such as grayed or checked) as well as a bounding rectangle and device context with which your application will draw the item.

In response to the WM_DRAWITEM message, your application must perform the following actions before returning from processing the message:

1. Determine the type of drawing that is needed. To do so, check the **item-Action** field of the **DRAWITEMSTRUCT** data structure.
2. Draw the menu item appropriately, using the rectangle and device context obtained from the **DRAWITEMSTRUCT** data structure. Your application must draw only within the bounding rectangle. For performance reasons, Windows does not clip portions of the image that are drawn outside the rectangle.
3. Restore all GDI objects selected for the menu item's device context.

For example, if the menu item is selected, Windows sets the **itemAction** field of the **DRAWITEMSTRUCT** data structure to ODA_SELECT, and sets the ODS_SELECTED bit in the **itemState** field. This is your application's cue to redraw the menu item so that the item indiates that it has been selected.

7.7 A Sample Application: EditMenu

The EditMenu sample application illustrates the following:

- The two most common menus, the Edit menu and the File menu
- How to use accelerator keys in an application

NOTE The accelerator keys shown in this sample are specifically reserved, and should be used only as accelerator keys for the Edit menu. See the *System Application Architecture, Common User Access: Advanced Interface Design Guide* for more information about standard accelerator-key assignments.

To create the EditMenu application, copy and rename the Generic source files. Then do the following:

1. Add the Edit and File menus to the resource script file.
2. Add definitions to the include file.
3. Add an accelerator table to the resource file.
4. Add a new variable.
5. Load the accelerator table.
6. Modify the message loop in WinMain.
7. Modify the WM_COMMAND case.
8. Compile and link the application.

EditMenu does not show how to use the clipboard. This task is described in Chapter 13, "The Clipboard."

NOTE Rather than typing the code provided in the following sections, you might find it more convenient to simply examine and compile the sample source files provided in the SDK.

7.7.1 Add New Menus to the Resource File

You need to add an Edit and a File menu to the **MENU** statement in the resource file. The **MENU** statement should now look like this:

```
EditMenuMenu MENU
BEGIN
    POPUP        "&File"
    BEGIN
        MENUITEM    "&New",              IDM_NEW
        MENUITEM    "&Open...",          IDM_OPEN
        MENUITEM    "&Save",             IDM_SAVE
        MENUITEM    "Save &As...",       IDM_SAVEAS
        MENUITEM    "&Print",            IDM_PRINT
        MENUITEM    SEPARATOR
        MENUITEM    "E&xit",             IDM_EXIT
        MENUITEM    SEPARATOR
        MENUITEM    "&About EditMenu...",        IDM_ABOUT
    END
```

```
    POPUP        "&Edit"
    BEGIN
        MENUITEM    "&Undo\tAlt+BkSp",     IDM_UNDO   ,GRAYED
        MENUITEM    SEPARATOR
        MENUITEM    "Cu&t\tShift+Del",     IDM_CUT
        MENUITEM    "&Copy\tCtrl+Ins",     IDM_COPY
        MENUITEM    "&Paste\tShift+Ins",   IDM_PASTE  ,GRAYED
        MENUITEM    "C&lear\tDel",         IDM_CLEAR  ,GRAYED
    END

END
```

The File menu has seven commands and two separators; each command has a mnemonic, indicated by the ampersand (&).

The Edit menu has five commands and a separator. Each command has both a mnemonic and an accelerator key, separated from the name with a tab (\t). Whenever a command has a corresponding accelerator, it should be displayed in this way. In the Edit menu, the five accelerator keys are ALT+BACKSPACE, DELETE, CONTROL+INSERT, SHIFT+INSERT, and SHIFT+DELETE. The separator between the Undo and Cut commands places a horizontal bar between these commands in the menu. A separator is recommended between menu commands that otherwise have nothing in common. For example, Undo affects only the application, whereas the remaining commands affect the clipboard.

NOTE The purpose and content of the File and Edit menus are described in the *System Application Architecture, Common User Access: Advanced Interface Design Guide.*

7.7.2 Add Definitions to the Include File

You must declare each menu ID in your application's include file. These constants are used both in the C-language source file and in the resource script file.

A menu ID can have any integer value. The only restriction is that menu IDs must be unique within a menu; no two commands in a menu can have the same menu ID.

Add the following to the include file:

```
 #define IDM_ABOUT 100

/* file menu items */

#define     IDM_NEW       101
#define     IDM_OPEN      102
#define     IDM_SAVE      103
#define     IDM_SAVEAS    104
#define     IDM_PRINT     105
#define     IDM_EXIT      106
```

```
/* edit menu items */

#define     IDM_UNDO     200
#define     IDM_CUT      201
#define     IDM_COPY     202
#define     IDM_PASTE    203
#define     IDM_CLEAR    204
```

7.7.3 Add an Accelerator Table to the Resource Script File

Add the following **ACCELERATORS** statement to the resource script file:

```
EditMenu ACCELERATORS
BEGIN
    VK_BACK,   IDM_UNDO,  VIRTKEY, ALT
    VK_DELETE, IDM_CUT,   VIRTKEY, SHIFT
    VK_INSERT, IDM_COPY,  VIRTKEY, CONTROL
    VK_INSERT, IDM_PASTE, VIRTKEY, SHIFT
    VK_DELETE, IDM_CLEAR, VIRTKEY
END
```

This statement defines five accelerator keys, one for each command. Four accelerators are key-stroke combinations using the ALT, SHIFT, or CONTROL key.

The **ACCELERATORS** statement associates each accelerator with a menu ID. The IDM_UNDO, IDM_CUT, IDM_COPY, IDM_PASTE, and IDM_CLEAR constants are the menu IDs of the Edit-menu commands. When the user presses an accelerator key, these are the values that are passed to the window function.

7.7.4 Add a New Variable

Add the following statement to the beginning of the source file:

```
HANDLE hAccTable;       /* handle to accelerator table */
```

The hAccTable variable is a handle to the accelerator table. It receives the return value of the **LoadAccelerators** function and is used in the **Translate-Accelerator** function to identify the accelerator table.

7.7.5 Load the Accelerator Table

Before using the accelerator table, you must load it from the application's resources. Add the following statements to the application's InitInstance function:

```
hAccTable = LoadAccelerators(hInst, "EditMenu");
```

This statement loads the accelerator table into memory and assigns the handle identifying the table to the hAccTable variable. The hInstance variable identifies the application's resource file, and EditMenu is the name of the accelerator table. Once the table is loaded, it can be used in the **TranslateAccelerator** function.

7.7.6 Modify the Message Loop

To use the accelerator table, you must add the **TranslateAccelerator** function to the message loop. After you add the function, the message loop should look like this:

```
while (GetMessage(&msg, NULL, NULL, NULL)) {

    if (!TranslateAccelerator(hWnd, hAccTable, &msg)) {
        TranslateMessage(&msg);
        DispatchMessage(&msg);
```

7.7.7 Modify the WM_COMMAND Case

You need to process menu commands. In this application, instead of performing tasks, all menu commands activate a "Command not implemented" message box. Replace the WM_COMMAND case with the following statements:

```
case WM_COMMAND:
     switch (wParam) {
         case IDM_ABOUT:
             lpProcAbout = MakeProcInstance(About, hInst);
             DialogBox(hInst, "AboutBox", hWnd, lpProcAbout);
             FreeProcInstance(lpProcAbout);
             break;

         /* file menu commands */

         case IDM_NEW:
         case IDM_OPEN:
         case IDM_SAVE:
         case IDM_SAVEAS:
         case IDM_PRINT:
             MessageBox (
                   GetFocus(),
                   "Command not implemented",
                   "EditMenu Sample Application",
                   MB_ICONASTERISK | MB_OK);
             break;

         case IDM_EXIT:
             DestroyWindow(hWnd);
             break;
```

```
        /* edit menu commands */

        case IDM_UNDO:
        case IDM_CUT:
        case IDM_COPY:
        case IDM_PASTE:
        case IDM_CLEAR:
            MessageBox (
                  GetFocus(),
                  "Command not implemented",
                  "EditMenu Sample Application",
                  MB_ICONASTERISK | MB_OK);
            break;
    }
    break;
```

7.7.8 Compile and Link

No changes are required to the make file to compile and link the EditMenu application. Start Windows, then the EditMenu application, and, without opening the pop-up menus, press any of the five accelerator keys. You will notice that the "Command not implemented" message appears when a command is chosen.

7.8 Summary

This chapter explained how to use menus in your application. A menu provides and organizes a list of commands the user can choose. Windows handles most menu features automatically; for example, when the user chooses a command on the menu bar, Windows automatically displays the menu associated with that command. When the user chooses a command from a menu, Windows sends the application a WM_COMMAND message that contains the command ID. The application can then carry out the action appropriate to that command.

Windows also provides advanced menu features such as cascading menus, custom checkmarks, and owner-draw menus.

For more information on topics related to menus, see the following:

Topic	Reference
Processing input messages	*Guide to Programming*: Chapter 4, "Keyboard and Mouse Input"
Bitmaps	*Guide to Programming*: Chapter 11, "Bitmaps"
	Tools: Chapter 4, "Designing Images: SDKPaint"

Topic	Reference
Menu functions	*Reference, Volume 1*: Chapter 1, "Window Manager Interface Functions," and Chapter 4, "Functions Directory"
Resource script statements	*Reference, Volume 2*: Chapter 8, "Resource Script Statements"
The sample application MENU.EXE, which illustrates the use of cascading menus, custom checkmarks, and owner-draw menus	SDK Sample Source Code disk

Chapter 8 Controls

Controls are special windows that provide easy methods for interaction with the user.

This chapter covers the following topics:

- What is a control?
- Creating a control
- Using controls in application windows

This chapter also explains how to create a sample application, EditCntl, that illustrates those concepts.

8.1 What is a Control?

A "control" is a predefined child window that carries out a specific kind of input or output. For example, to get a filename from the user, you can create and display an edit control to let the user type the name. An "edit control" is a predefined child window that receives and displays keyboard input.

A control, like any other window, belongs to a window class. The window class defines the control's window function and the default attributes of the control. The window function is important because it determines what the control will look like and how it will respond to user input. Control window functions are predefined in Windows, so no extra coding is required in your application when you use a control.

8.2 Creating a Control

Windows provides two ways to create a control:

- Within a dialog box
- Within the client area of any other type of window

This chapter discusses using controls in a standard window. Chapter 9, "Dialog Boxes," explains how to create controls within a dialog box.

To create a control in a window other than a dialog box, use the **CreateWindow** function, just as you would to create any window. When creating a control, specify the following information:

- The control's window class
- The control style
- The control's parent window
- The control ID

The **CreateWindow** function returns a handle to the control that you can use in subsequent functions to move, size, paint, or destroy a window, or to direct a window to carry out tasks.

The following example shows how to create a push-button control:

```
hButtonWnd = CreateWindow(
    "Button",                              /* window control class */
    "OK",                                  /* button label         */
    BS_PUSHBUTTON | WS_CHILD | WS_VISIBLE, /* control styles       */
    20,                                    /* x-coordinate         */
    40,                                    /* y-coordinate         */
    30,                                    /* width in pixels      */
    12,                                    /* height in pixels     */
    hWnd,                                  /* parent window        */
    IDOK,                                  /* control ID           */
    hInstance,                             /* instance handle      */
    NULL);
```

This example creates a push-button control that belongs to the "Button" window class and has the BS_PUSHBUTTON style. The control is a child window and will be visible when first created. The WS_CHILD style is required, but you do not need to specify the WS_VISIBLE style if you plan to use the **ShowWindow** function to show the control. **CreateWindow** places the control at the point (20,40) in the parent window's client area. The width and height are 30 and 12 pixels, respectively. The parent window is identified by the hWnd handle. The constant IDOK is the control identifier.

The rest of this section explains how to specify the control's window class, control style, parent window, and control ID.

8.2.1 Specifying a Control Class

The control's window class, or "control class," defines the control window function and the default attributes of the control. You specify a control class when you create the control. To do so, include the class name (for example, BUTTON) as the *lpClassName* parameter for the **CreateWindow** function.

Windows provides the following built-in control classes:

Class	Description
BUTTON	Produces small, labeled windows that the user can choose to generate yes/no, on/off type of input.
EDIT	Produces windows in which the user can enter and edit text.
LISTBOX	Produces windows that contain lists of names from which the user can select one or more names.
COMBOBOX	Produces combination controls consisting of an edit or static control linked with a list box. The user can select items from the list box and/or enter text in the edit box.
SCROLLBAR	Produces windows that look and function like scroll bars in a window.
STATIC	Produces small windows containing text or simple graphics. These are often used to label other controls or to separate a group of controls.

8.2.2 Choosing a Control Style

The control styles, which depend on the control class, determine the control's appearance and function. You specify a control style when you create the control. To do so, include the control style (for example, BS_PUSHBUTTON) as the *dwStyle* parameter for the **CreateWindow** function.

Windows provides many predefined control styles. The following styles are some of the most commonly used:

Style	Description
BS_PUSHBUTTON	Specifies a push-button control. This is a small window containing a label that the user can choose in order to notify the parent window.
BS_DEFPUSHBUTTON	Specifies a default push-button control. A default push-button control is identical to a push-button control except that it has a special border.
BS_CHECKBOX	Specifies a check-box control. The user can select the box to turn the control on and off. When the control is on, the box contains an "X".

Style	Description
BS_RADIOBUTTON	Specifies a radio-button control. The user can select a circle to turn the control on and off. When the control is on, the circle contains a solid bullet.
ES_LEFT	Specifies a single-line, left-adjusted edit control.
ES_MULTILINE	Specifies a multiple-line edit control.
SS_LEFT	Specifies a left-adjusted, static text control.
SS_RIGHT	Specifies a right-adjusted, static text control.
LBS_STANDARD	Specifies a standard list box. A standard list box includes a scroll bar and notifies its parent window when the user makes a selection.
CBS_DROPDOWN	Specifies a combo box consisting of an edit control and a list box that is displayed when the user selects a box next to the selection field. If an item in the list box is selected, the edit control displays the selected item.

For a complete list of control styles, see the *Reference*, *Volume 2*.

8.2.3 Setting the Parent Window

Because every control is a child window, it requires a parent window. You specify the parent window when you create the control. To do so, include the handle of the parent window as the *hWndParent* parameter for the **CreateWindow** function.

As with any child window, a control is affected by changes to its parent window. For example, if Windows disables the parent window, it disables the control as well. If Windows paints, moves, or destroys the parent window, it also paints, moves, or destroys the control.

Although a control can be any size, and can be moved to any position, it is restricted to the client area of the parent window. Windows clips the control if you move it outside the parent window's client area or make it bigger than the client area.

8.2.4 Choosing a Control ID

When you create a control, you give it a unique identifier, or control ID. You specify the control ID when you create the control. To do so, include the control ID as the *hMenu* parameter for the **CreateWindow** function. The control supplies the control ID in any notification message it sends to the window function of the parent window. The control ID is especially useful if you have several controls in a window. It is the quickest, easiest way to distinguish one control from another.

8.3 Using a Control

Once you have created a control, you can:

- Receive user input through the control.
- Tell the control to perform specialized tasks, such as returning a string of text.
- Enable or disable input to the control.
- Move or size the control.
- Destroy the control.

This section explains how to perform these tasks.

8.3.1 Receiving User Input

As the user interacts with the control, the control sends information about that interaction, in the form of a notification message, to the parent window. A notification message is a WM_COMMAND message in which:

- The *wParam* parameter contains the control ID.
- The *lParam* parameter contains the notification code and the control handle.

For example, when the user clicks a button control, that control sends a WM_COMMAND message to the window function of the parent window. The WM_COMMAND message's *wParam* parameter contains the button control's ID; the high-order word of *lParam* parameter contains the notification code BN_CLICKED, which indicates that the user has clicked that control.

Since a notification message has the same basic form as menu input, you process notification messages much as you would menu input. If you have carefully selected control IDs so that they do not conflict with menu IDs, you can process notification messages in the same **switch** statement you use to process menu input.

8.3.2 Sending Control Messages

Most controls accept and process a variety of control messages—special messages that tell the control to carry out some task that is unique to the control. For example, the WM_GETTEXTLENGTH message tells an edit control to return the length of a selected line of text.

To send a control message to a control, use the **SendMessage** function. Supply the message number and any required *wParam* and *lParam* parameter values. For example, the following statement sends the WM_GETTEXTLENGTH message to the edit control identified by the handle hEditWnd; it then returns the length of the selected line in the edit control:

```
nLength = SendMessage(hEditWnd, WM_GETTEXTLENGTH, 0, 0L);
```

Many controls also process standard window messages, such as WM_HSCROLL and WM_VSCROLL. To send such messages to controls, use the same method you use to send control messages.

8.3.3 Disabling and Enabling Input to a Control

To disable or enable input to a control, use the **EnableWindow** function.

When you disable a control, it does not respond to user input. Windows "grays" the control (displays it dimly) so that the user can tell that the control is disabled. To disable a control, use **EnableWindow**; specify the value FALSE, as follows:

```
EnableWindow(hButton, FALSE);
```

To restore input to the disabled control, enable it using the **EnableWindow** function with the value TRUE, as follows:

```
EnableWindow(hButton, TRUE);
```

8.3.4 Moving and Sizing a Control

To move or size a control, use the **MoveWindow** function. This function moves the control to the specified point in the parent window's client area and sets the control to the given width and height. The following example shows how to move and size a control:

```
MoveWindow(hButtonWnd, 10,10, 30,12, TRUE);
```

This example moves a control to the point (10,10) in the client area and sets the width and height to 30 and 12 pixels, respectively. The value TRUE specifies that the control should be repainted after moving.

Windows automatically moves a control when it moves the parent window. A control's position is always relative to the upper-left corner of the parent's client area, so when the parent moves, the control remains fixed in the client area but moves relative to the display. Although Windows does not size a control when it sizes the parent window, it sends a WM_SIZE message to the parent to indicate the new size of the parent window. You can use this message to give the control a new size.

8.3.5 Destroying a Control

To destroy a control, use the **DestroyWindow** function. This function deletes any internal record of the control and removes the control from the parent window's client area. The following example shows how to destroy a control:

```
DestroyWindow(hEditWnd);
```

Windows automatically destroys a control when it destroys the parent window. In general, you will need to destroy a control only if you no longer need it in the parent window.

8.4 Creating and Using Some Common Controls

The rest of this chapter explains more about the following common controls:

- Button controls
- Static controls
- List-box controls
- Combo-box controls
- Edit controls
- Scroll-bar controls

8.4.1 Button Controls

A button control is a small window used for simple yes/no, on/off type of input. The following are some of the most commonly used types of button controls:

- Push button
- Default push button
- Check box
- Radio button
- Owner-draw button
- Group box

Push Buttons

A push button is a button that the user can select to carry out a specific action. The button contains text that indicates what that button does. When the user clicks a push button, the application normally carries out the associated action immediately. For example, if the user clicks the Cancel button in a dialog box, the application immediately removes the dialog box and cancels the user's changes to the dialog (if any).

To create a button control, specify "Button" as the control's window class, and specify the button style(s) in the *dwStyle* parameter. For example, the following call to the **CreateWindow** function creates a push-button control with the label "Cancel":

```
HWND hCancelButton;
    .
    .
    .
hCancelButton = CreateWindow(
    "Button", "Cancel",
    BS_PUSHBUTTON | WS_CHILD | WS_VISIBLE,
    20,40, 80,20, hWnd, IDCANCEL, hInstance, NULL);
```

Because this example specifies the WS_VISIBLE style, Windows displays the control after creating it. The control ID is IDCANCEL. This constant is defined in the WINDOWS.H file and is intended to be used with Cancel push buttons.

Default Push Buttons

A default push button typically lets the user signal the completion of some activity, such as filling in an edit control with a filename. A default push-button control, as with other button controls, responds to both mouse and keyboard input. If the user moves the cursor into the control and clicks it, the button sends a BN_CLICKED notification message to the parent window. The button does not have to have the input focus in order to respond to mouse input. It does, however, require the focus in order to respond to keyboard input. To let the user use the keyboard, use the **SetFocus** function to give the input focus to the button. The user can then press the SPACEBAR to direct the button to send a BN_CLICKED notification message to the parent window.

Creating a default push-button control is similar to creating a push-button control. Specify "Button" as the control's window class, and specify the button style(s) in the *dwStyle* parameter. For example, the following call to the **CreateWindow** function creates a default push-button control with the label "OK":

```
HWND hDefButton;
    .
    .
    .
hDefButton = CreateWindow(
    "Button", "OK",
    BS_DEFPUSHBUTTON | WS_CHILD | WS_VISIBLE,
    20,40, 80,20, hWnd, IDOK, hInstance, NULL);
```

This example specifies the WS_VISIBLE style, so Windows displays the control after creating it. The control ID is IDOK. This constant is defined in the WINDOWS.H file and is intended to be used with default push buttons, such as this OK button.

Check Boxes

A check box typically lets the user select an option to use in the current task. By convention, within a group of check boxes, the user can select more than one option. (To present options that are mutually exclusive, use radio buttons instead of check boxes.)

For example, you might present a group of check boxes that lets the user select font properties for the next output operation. The user could choose both bold and italic by checking both the “Bold” and the “Italic” check boxes.

To create a check-box control, use the BS_CHECKBOX style, as in the following example:

```
#define IDC_ITALIC    201
HWND hCheckBox;
     .
     .
     .

hCheckBox = CreateWindow("Button", "Italic",
    BS_CHECKBOX | WS_CHILD | WS_VISIBLE,
    20,40, 80,20, hWnd, IDC_ITALIC, hInstance, NULL);
```

In this example, the check-box label is “Italic” and the control ID is IDC_ITALIC.

A check box responds to mouse and keyboard input much as a push-button control would. That is, it sends a notification message to the parent window when the user clicks the control or presses the SPACEBAR. However, a check box can display a check (an “X”) in its box to show that it is currently on (it has been selected).

To tell a control to display a check, send the control the BM_SETCHECK message. You can also test to see if the check box has a check by sending the control the BM_GETCHECK message. For example, to place a check in the check box, use the following function:

```
SendMessage(hCheckBox, BM_SETCHECK, 1, 0L);
```

This means you can place or remove a check in the check box whenever you want; for example, when the parent window function receives a BN_CLICKED notification message. Windows also provides a BS_AUTOCHECKBOX style that automatically toggles its state (places or removes a check) each time the user clicks it.

Radio Buttons

Radio-button controls work in much the same way as check boxes. However, radio buttons are usually used in groups and represent mutually exclusive options. For example, you might use a group of radio buttons to let the user specify text justification (right-justified, left-justified, or centered). The radio buttons would let the user select only one type of justification at a time.

Create a radio-button control as you would any button control. Specify "Button" as the control's window class, and specify the button style(s) in the *dwStyle* parameter. For example, the following call to the **CreateWindow** function creates a radio-button control with the label "Right":

```
HWND HRightJustifyButton
#define IDC_RIGHTJUST
    .
    .
    .
hRightJustifyButton = CreateWindow("Button", "Right",
    BS_RADIOBUTTON | WS_CHILD | WS_VISIBLE,
    20,40, 80,20, hWnd, IDC_RIGHTJUST, hInstance, NULL);
```

As with a check box, you must send a BM_SETCHECK message to the radio button to display a "check" (actually, a solid circle) in the button when the user selects that button. Also, since radio buttons represent mutually exclusive choices, you should also send the BM_SETCHECK message to the previously checked radio button (if any) to clear its check. You can determine which radio button in a group is checked by sending the BM_GETCHECK message to each button.

In a dialog box, you can create radio buttons with the BS_AUTORADIOBUTTON style. When all the radio buttons in a group box have the BS_AUTORADIOBUTTON style, Windows automatically removes the check from the previously checked button when the user selects a different radio button.

You can also use the **CheckRadioButton** function to check a radio button and remove the check from other buttons in a dialog box. When you call **CheckRadioButton**, you specify the IDs of the first and last buttons in a range of buttons and the ID of the radio button (within that range) that is to be checked. Windows removes the check from all the buttons in the specified range and then checks the appropriate radio button. For example, in a group of buttons representing types of text justification, you would call **CheckRadioButton** to check the "Right" button, as in the following example:

```
CheckRadioButton(hDlg, ID_RIGHTLEFTJUST, ID_LEFTJUST,
                 ID_RIGHTJUST)
```

In this example, **CheckRadioButton** would check the radio button identified by ID_RIGHTJUST and remove the check from all the other buttons whose IDs fall within the range specified by ID_RIGHTLEFTJUST and ID_LEFTJUST.

Owner-Draw Buttons

An owner-draw button is similar to other button styles, except that the application is responsible for maintaining the button's appearance, including whether the button has focus, is disabled, or is selected. Windows simply notifies your application when the button has been clicked.

To create an owner-draw button, use the BS_OWNERDRAW style, as shown in the following example:

```
hMyOwnButton = CreateWindow("Button", NULL,
                    BS_OWNERDRAW | WS_CHILD | WS_VISIBLE,
                    20, 40, 30, 12, hWnd, ID_MYBUTTON,
                    hInstance, NULL);
```

Whenever the button needs to be drawn, Windows sends the WM_DRAWITEM message to the window that owns the button. The *lParam* parameter of the WM_DRAWITEM message contains a pointer to a **DRAWITEMSTRUCT** data structure. This structure contains, among other information, the control ID, a value specifying the type of drawing action required, a value indicating the state of the button, a bounding rectangle for the button, and a handle to the device context of the button.

In response to the WM_DRAWITEM message, your application must perform the following actions before returning from processing the message:

1. Determine the type of drawing that is needed. To do so, examine the **itemAction** field of the **DRAWITEMSTRUCT** data structure.
2. Draw the button appropriately, using the rectangle and device context obtained from the **DRAWITEMSTRUCT** data structure.
3. Restore all GDI objects selected for the button's device context.

For example, if the button has lost input focus, Windows sets the **itemAction** field of the **DRAWITEMSTRUCT** data structure to ODA_FOCUS, but not the ODS_FOCUS bit in the **itemState** field. This is your application's cue to redraw the button so that it no longer appears to have focus.

Group Boxes

Group boxes are rectangles that enclose two or more related buttons or other controls. You can send the WM_SETTEXT message to the group box to place a caption in the upper-left corner of the box. Group boxes do not respond to user input; that is, they do not generate notification messages.

8.4.2 Static Controls

A static control is a small window that contains text or graphics. You typically use a static control to label some other control or to create boxes and lines that separate one group of controls from another.

The most commonly used static control is the SS_LEFT style—a left-adjusted line of text. That is, the control writes the line's text starting at the left end of the control, displaying as much of the label as will fit in the control and clipping the rest. The control uses the system font for the text, so you can compute an appropriate size for the control by retrieving the font metrics for this font (see Chapter 18, "Fonts," for details).

Like group boxes, static controls do not respond to user input; that is, they do not generate notification messages when chosen. However, you can change the appearance and location of a static control at any time. For example, you can change the text associated with a static control by using the **SetWindowText** function or the WM_SETTEXT message.

8.4.3 List Boxes

A list box is a box that contains a list of selectable items, such as filenames. You typically use a list box to display a list of items from which the user can select one or more. There are several styles associated with a list box. The following are the most commonly used styles:

List-Box Style	Description
LBS_BORDER	The list box has a surrounding border.
LBS_NOTIFY	The list box sends notification messages to the parent window when the user selects an item.
LBS_SORT	The list box alphabetically sorts its items.
WS_VSCROLL	The list box has a vertical scroll bar.

These four styles are included in the LBS_STANDARD style. The following example creates a standard list box:

```
HWND hListBox
#define IDC_LISTBOX 203
    .
    .
    .
hListBox = CreateWindow("Listbox", NULL,
                    LBS_STANDARD | WS_CHILD | WS_VISIBLE,
                    20, 40, 120, 56, hWnd, IDC_LISTBOX,
                    hInstance, NULL);
```

Adding a String to a List Box

Use the LB_ADDSTRING message to add a string to a list box. This message copies the given string to the list box, which displays it in the list. If the list box has the LBS_SORT style, the string is sorted alphabetically. Otherwise, Windows simply places the string at the end of the list. The following example shows how to add a string:

```
int nIndex;
    .
    .
    .
nIndex = SendMessage(hListBox,
                    LB_ADDSTRING,NULL,
                    (LONG)(LPSTR) "Horseradish");
```

The LB_ADDSTRING message returns an integer that represents the index of the string in the list. You can use this index in subsequent list-box messages to identify the string, but only as long as you do not add, delete, or insert any other string. Doing so may change the string's index.

Deleting a String from a List Box

You can delete a string from the list box by supplying the index of the string with the LB_DELETESTRING message, as in the following example:

```
SendMessage(hListBox, LB_DELETESTRING, nIndex, (LPSTR) NULL);
```

You can also add a string to a list box is by sending the LB_INSERTSTRING message to the list box. Unlike LB_ADDSTRING, LB_INSERTSTRING lets you specify where Windows should place the new string in the list box. When it receives the LB_INSERTSTRING message, the list box does not sort the list, even if the list box was created with the LBS_SORT style.

Adding Filenames to a List Box

As noted earlier, a common use for a list box is to display a list of filenames, directories, and/or disk drives. The LB_DIR message instructs the list box to fill itself with such a list. The message's *wParam* parameter contains a value specifying the DOS attributes of the files, and the *lParam* parameter points to a string containing a file specification.

For example, to fill a list box with the names of all files in the current directory that have the .TXT extension, plus a list of subdirectories and disk drives, you would send the LB_DIR message as shown in the following example:

```
#define FILE_LIST 4010;
    .
    .
    .
int nFiles;
```

```
    .
    .
    .

nFiles = SendMessage(hListBox, LB_DIR, FILE_LIST,
                     (LPSTR) "*.TXT");
```

The return value of the LB_DIR message indicates how many items the list box contains.

NOTE If the list box is in a dialog box, you can call the **DlgDirList** function to perform the same task.

A list box responds to both mouse and keyboard input. If the user clicks a string or presses the SPACEBAR in the list box, the list box selects the string and indicates the selection by inverting the string text and removing the selection from the last item that was selected, if any. The user can also press a character key to select an item in the list box; the next item in the list box that begins with the character is selected. If the list box has the LBS_NOTIFY style, the list box also sends an LBN_SELCHANGE notification message to the parent window. If the user double-clicks a string and LBS_NOTIFY is specified, the list box sends the LBN_SELCHANGE and LBN_DBLCLK messages to the parent window.

You can always retrieve the index of the selected string by using the LB_GETCURSEL and LB_GETTEXT messages. The LB_GETCURSEL message retrieves the selection's index in the list box, and the LB_GETTEXT message retrieves the selection from the list box, copying it to a buffer that you supply.

Table 8.1 summarizes the mouse and keyboard interface for a standard list box.

Table 8.1 User Interface for Standard List Box

Action	Result
Mouse Interface	
Single click	Selects the item and removes the selection from the previously selected item (if any).
Double click	Is the same as a single click.
Keyboard Interface	
SPACEBAR	Selects the item.
RIGHT ARROW, DOWN ARROW	Selects the next item in the list and removes the selection from the previously selected item (if any).
LEFT ARROW, UP ARROW	Selects the preceding item in the list and removes the selection from the previously selected item (if any).

Table 8.1 User Interface for Standard List Box *(continued)*

Action	Result
PAGE UP	Scrolls the currently selected item to the bottom of the list box, selects the first visible item in the list box, and removes the selection from the previously selected item (if any).
PAGE DOWN	Scrolls the currently selected item to the top of the list box, selects the last visible item in the list box, and removes the selection from the previously selected item (if any).
HOME	Scrolls the first item in the list box to the top of the list box, selects the first item, and removes the selection from the previously selected item (if any).
END	Scrolls the last item in the list box to the bottom of the list box, selects the last item, and removes the selection from the previously selected item (if any).

Using Multiple-Selection List Boxes

By default, a list box lets the user select only one item at a time. To allow the user to select more than one item from a list box, create the list box with either of the following styles:

Style	Description
LBS_MULTIPLESEL	A list box created with the LBS_MULTIPLESEL style is essentially the same as a standard list box, except that the user can select more than one item in the list box.
LBS_EXTENDEDSEL	A list box created with the LBS_EXTENDEDSEL style provides an easy method for selecting several contiguous items in the list box, as well as for selecting separate items.

The rest of this section describes each style of multiple-selection list box.

List Boxes with the LBS_MULTIPLESEL Style

A list box created with the LBS_MULTIPLESEL style is essentially the same as a standard list box, except that the user can select more than one item in the list box. Clicking or pressing the SPACEBAR on an item in the list box toggles the selection state of the item. If the user presses a character key while the list box has focus, the list-box cursor moves to the next item in the list that begins with that character; the item is not actually selected unless the user presses the SPACEBAR. Table 8.2 describes the mouse and keyboard interface for a list box with the LBS_MULTIPLESEL style.

Table 8.2 User Interface for LBS_MULTIPLESEL List Box

Action	Result
Mouse Interface	
Single click	Toggles the selection status of the item, but does not remove the selection from other selected items (if any).
Double click	Is the same as a single click.
Keyboard Interface	
SPACEBAR	Toggles the selection status of item, but does not remove the selection from other selected items (if any).
RIGHT ARROW, DOWN ARROW	Moves the list-box cursor to next item in the list.
LEFT ARROW, UP ARROW	Moves the list-box cursor to the preceding item in the list.
PAGE UP	Scrolls the currently selected item to the bottom of the list box and moves the list-box cursor to the first visible item in the list box.
PAGE DOWN	Scrolls the currently selected item to the top of the list box and moves the list-box cursor to the last visible item in the list box.
HOME	Scrolls the first item in the list box to the top of the list box and moves the list-box cursor to the first item.
END	Scrolls the last item in the list box to the bottom of the list box and moves the list-box cursor to the last item.

List Boxes with the LBS_EXTENDEDSEL Style

A list box created with the LBS_EXTENDEDSEL style provides an easy method for selecting several contiguous items in the list box, as well as for selecting separate items. Table 8.3 describes the mouse and keyboard interface for a list box with the LBS_EXTENDEDSEL style.

Table 8.3 User Interface for LBS_EXTENDEDSEL List Box

Action	Result (Add mode disabled)	Result (Add mode enabled)
Mouse Interface		
Single click	Selects the item, removes the selection from other items, and drops the selection anchor on the selected item.	Same as if add mode is disabled; in addition, disables add mode.
SHIFT+single click	Selects all items between the selection anchor and the selected item, and removes the selection from items not in that range.	Same as if add mode is disabled, plus disables add mode.
Double click, SHIFT+double click	Same as single click and SHIFT+single click.	Same as if add mode is disabled, plus disables add mode.
CONTROL+single click	Drops the selection anchor and toggles the selection state of the selected item, but does not remove the selection from other items.	Same as if add mode is disabled, plus disables add mode.
CONTROL+SHIFT+single click	Does not remove the selection from other items (except for those that are part of the selection range established by the most recent selection anchor) and toggles all items (to the same selection state as the item at the anchor point) from the anchor point to the selected item. Does not move the selection anchor.	Same as if add mode is disabled, plus disables add mode.
Drag	Drops the selection anchor where the user pressed the mouse button, selects items from the selection anchor to the item where the the user released the button, and removes the selection from all other items.	Same as if add mode is disabled, plus disables add mode.

Table 8.3 User Interface for LBS_EXTENDEDSEL List Box *(continued)*

Action	Result (Add mode disabled)	Result (Add mode enabled)
SHIFT+drag	Selects items from the selection anchor to the item where the user released the button and removes the selection from all other items. Does not move the selection anchor.	Same as if add mode is disabled, plus disables add mode.
CONTROL+drag	Drops the selection anchor on the item where the user pressed the mouse button. Does not remove the selection from other items, but toggles all items (to the same selection state as the item at the anchor point) from the anchor point to the item where the user released the mouse button.	Same as if add mode is disabled, plus disables add mode.
CONTROL+SHIFT+drag	Does not remove the selection from other items (except for those that are part of the selection range established by the most recent selection anchor), but toggles all items (to the same selection state as the item at the anchor point) from the anchor point to the item where the user released the mouse button. Does not move the selection anchor.	Same as if add mode is disabled, plus disables add mode.
Keyboard Interface[a]		
SHIFT+F8	Enables add mode. Add mode is indicated by a flashing list-box cursor.	Disables add mode.
SPACEBAR	Selects the item, removes the selection from previously selected items, and drops the selection anchor.	Toggles the selection status of the item and drops the selection anchor, but does not remove the selection from other items.

Table 8.3 User Interface for LBS_EXTENDEDSEL List Box *(continued)*

Action	Result (Add mode disabled)	Result (Add mode enabled)
SHIFT+SPACEBAR	Removes the selection from previously selected items and toggles all items (to the same selection state as the item at the selection anchor) from the anchor point to the current position. Does not move the selection anchor.	Does not remove the selection from other items (except for those that are part of the selection established by the most recent anchor point) and toggles all items (to the same selection state as the item at the selection anchor) from the selection anchor to the current position. Does not move the selection anchor.
Navigation key[b]	Moves the list-box cursor as defined by the key and selects the item at the cursor, drops the selection anchor at selected item, and removes the selection from all previously selected items.	Moves the list-box cursor as defined by the key, but does not select the item, remove the selection from other items, or move the selection anchor.
SHIFT+Navigation key	Removes the selection from all other items, moves the list-box cursor as defined by the key, toggles all items (to the same selection state as the item at the selection anchor) from the selection anchor to the item at the cursor. Does not move the selection anchor.	Does not remove the selection from other items (except for those that are part of the selection range established by the most recent selection anchor), moves the list-box cursor as defined by the key, and toggles all items (to the same selection state as the item at the anchor point) from the anchor point to the item at the list-box cursor. Does not move the selection anchor.

[a] Except for the SHIFT+F8, all keys and key combinations can be combined with CONTROL. For example, CONTROL+SHIFT+SPACEBAR has the same effect as SHIFT+SPACEBAR.

[b] Navigation keys include the DIRECTION (arrow) keys and the HOME, END, PAGE UP, and PAGE DOWN keys. See Table 8.2, "User Interface for LBS_MULTIPLESEL List Box," for a description of how each key moves the list-box cursor.

Using Multicolumn List Boxes

Normally, a list box displays its items in a single column. If you anticipate that a list box will contain a large number of items, you may want to create the list box with the LBS_MULTICOLUMN style. This style specifies a list box that can display its items in several columns. A multicolumn list box "snakes" its items from the bottom of one column to the next. Because of this, the list box never needs to be scrolled vertically. However, if the list box may contain more items than it can display at one time, you should create it with the WM_HSCROLL style to allow the user to scroll the list box horizontally. The following example shows how to create a multicolumn list box that occupies the entire client area of the parent window:

```
#define IDC_MULTILISTBOX
RECT Rect;
HWND hMultiListBox
     .
     .
     .
GetClientRect(hWnd, (LPRECT) &Rect);

hMultiListBox = CreateWindow("Listbox",
     NULL,
     WS_CHILD | WS_VISIBLE | LBS_SORT |
     LBS_MULTICOLUMN | WS_HSCROLL | LBS_NOTIFY,
     Rect.left,
     Rect.top,
     Rect.right,
     Rect.bottom,
     hWnd,
     IDC_MULTILISTBOX,
     hInst,
     NULL);
```

In this example, the **GetClientRect** function retrieves the coordinates of the client area of the parent window, which are then passed to **CreateWindow** to set the location and size of the list box.

The directory window displayed by the Windows File Manager is an example of a window that contains a multicolumn list box.

To set the width of the columns in a multicolumn list box, send the LB_SETCOLUMNWIDTH message to the list box.

Using Owner-Draw List Boxes

Like a button, a list box can be created as an owner-draw control. In the case of list boxes, however, your application is responsible for drawing only the items in the list box.

To create an owner-draw list box, use either the LBS_OWNERDRAWFIXED or LBS_OWNERDRAWVARIABLE style. LBS_OWNERDRAWFIXED designates an owner-draw list box in which all the items are the same height; LBS_OWNERDRAWVARIABLE specifies a list box whose items can vary in height.

To add an item to the list box, send the LB_ADDSTRING or LB_INSERT-STRING message to the list box. The *lParam* parameter can contain any 32-bit value that you want to associate with the item. If *lParam* contains a pointer to a string, the LBS_HASSTRINGS list-box style lets the list box maintain the memory and pointers for the string. This allows the application to use the LB_GETTEXT message to retrieve the text for the particular item. Also, if you created the list box with the LBS_SORT and LBS_HASSTRINGS style, Windows automatically sorts the items in the list box.

If you create the list box with the LBS_SORT style but without LBS_HAS-STRINGS, Windows has no way to determine the order of the items within the list box. In this case, when you add an item to the list box (using the LB_ADD-STRING message), Windows will send one or more WM_COMPAREITEM messages to the owner of the list box. This message's *lParam* parameter points to a **COMPAREITEMSTRUCT** data structure containing identifying information for two items in the list box. When your application returns from processing the message, the return value specifies which, if any, of two items should appear above the other. Windows sends this message repeatedly until it has sorted all the items in the list box.

When you add or insert an item in a list box, Windows determines the size of the item by sending the WM_MEASUREITEM message to the owner of the list box. Windows needs this information so it can detect the user's interaction with items in the list box. If you created the list box with the LBS_OWNERDRAWFIXED style, Windows sends the message only once, since all the items in the list box will be the same size. For a list box that was created with the LBS_OWNER-DRAWVARIABLE style, Windows sends a WM_MEASUREITEM message for each item when that item is added to the list box.

The *lParam* parameter of WM_MEASUREITEM contains a pointer to a **MEASUREITEMSTRUCT** data structure. In addition to the control type and ID, this data structure also contains the list-box item number of the item to be measured (if the list box is the LBS_OWNERDRAWVARIABLE style) and optional 32-bit data associated with the item. Each time the owner window receives the WM_MEASUREITEM message, it must fill in the **itemHeight** field of the **MEASUREITEMSTRUCT** structure with the height of the item before returning from processing the message. The height is measured in vertical dialog units. A vertical dialog unit is ⅛ of the current vertical dialog base unit, which is computed from the height of the system font. To determine the size in pixels of the dialog base units, call the **GetDialogBaseUnits** function.

When Windows displays the list box, or whenever the appearance of an item in the list box should change, Windows sends the WM_DRAWITEM message to the window that owns the list box. The *lParam* parameter of the WM_DRAW-ITEM message contains a pointer to a **DRAWITEMSTRUCT** data structure. This structure contains information identifying the list box item and the type of drawing required. As with an owner-draw button, your application uses this information to determine how to draw the item.

To delete an item from an owner-draw list box, send the LB_DELETESTRING message to the list box. When this happens, Windows in turn sends the WM_DELETEITEM message to the owner window. (Windows also sends this message for each item when the list box is destroyed.) The *lParam* parameter of this message points to a **DELETEITEMSTRUCT** data structure; this structure identifies the list box and list-box item that is being deleted and the 32-bit optional data associated with the item. Your application should use this information to clean up any memory which was used for the item.

8.4.4 Combo Boxes

A combo box is a single control that consists of a list box combined with a static or edit control. Depending on the style you use to create the list box, the list box can be displayed at all times, or the list box can be hidden until the user displays it. Except where noted, the mouse and keyboard interface for the edit field and list box of a combo box is identical to that of a standard edit control or list box.

The CBS_SIMPLE style creates a combo box with an edit field and a list box that is always displayed below the edit field. When the combo box has focus, the user can type in the edit field. If an item in the list box matches what the user has typed, the matching item moves to the top of the list box. The user can also select items from the list box by using the DOWN ARROW and UP ARROW keys or the mouse.

The CBS_DROPDOWN style is similar to CBS_SIMPLE except that the list box is displayed only if the user selects the icon next to the edit field or presses ALT+DOWN ARROW or ALT+UP ARROW. Even when the list box is hidden, the user can select items from the list box by using UP ARROW and DOWN ARROW.

A combo box created with the CBS_DROPDOWNLIST appears identical to a CBS_DROPDOWN combo box, except that the edit field is replaced with a static text field. Instead of typing in the edit field, the user can select items from the list box by typing the first letter of the item. Of course, the user can also use the UP ARROW and DOWN ARROW keys or the mouse to select items in the combo box.

You add and delete items to the list-box portion of a combo box in much the same way as a plain list box, but using the CB_ADDSTRING, CB_INSERTSTRING, CB_DIR, and CB_DELETESTRING messages. Windows also provides additional combo-box messages for retrieving the contents of the edit field, matching text with a list-box item, and dealing with the contents of the edit field.

In many respects, a combo box is quite similar to a list box in the way it reports the user's interaction with the control. All of the list-box notification codes have parallel combo-box notification codes. In addition to these, Windows sends notification codes to indicate the following:

- The list box of the combo box is being dropped down (CBN_DROPDOWN).
- The user has changed the text in the edit field, and Windows has updated the display (CBN_EDITCHANGE).
- The user has changed the text in the edit field, but Windows has not yet updated the display (CBN_EDITUPDATE).
- The combo box has lost input focus (CBN_KILLFOCUS). In the case of CBS_DROPDOWN and CBS_DROPDOWNLIST combo boxes, this causes Windows to remove the list box from the display.
- The combo box has gained focus (CBN_SETFOCUS).

Like a list box, a combo box can be created with a fixed- or variable-height owner-draw style. In the case of combo boxes, however, the owner is responsible for drawing items in the list box and in the selection (edit or static) field. For example, if the user selects an item in the list box, the owner of the combo box receives a WM_DRAWITEM message for the list-box item (to draw it as selected) and another WM_DRAWITEM message for the selection field.

You can also designate the CBS_SORT style for a combo box; Windows sorts owner-draw combo boxes in the same manner as owner-draw list boxes.

There is no multicolumn style for combo boxes.

8.4.5 Edit Controls

An edit control is a rectangular child window in which the user can enter and edit text. Edit controls have a variety of features, such as multiple-line editing and scrolling. You specify the features you want by specifying a control style.

Edit control styles define how the edit control will appear and operate. For example, the ES_MULTILINE style creates an edit control in which you can enter more than one line of text. The ES_AUTOHSCROLL and ES_AUTOVSCROLL styles direct the edit control to scroll horizontally or vertically if the user enters more text than can fit in the control's client area. If these styles are not specified and the user enters more text than can fit on one line, the text wraps to the next line if it is a multiline edit control. You can also use the WS_HSCROLL and (for a multiline edit control) WS_VSCROLL styles to an edit control to allow the user to scroll the text in the control.

Your application can use an edit control to let a user enter a password or other private text without displaying the password. The ES_PASSWORD style creates an edit control that does not display text as the user types it; instead, the edit control displays an arbitrary character for each character that the user types. By default, this character is an asterisk (*). To change the character displayed by the edit control, send the EM_SETPASSWORDCHAR message to the control.

You can set tab stops in a multiline edit control by sending the EM_SETTAB-STOPS message to the control. This message specifies the number of tab stops the edit control should contain and the distances between the tab stops.

An edit control sends notification messages to its parent window. For example, an edit control sends an EN_CHANGE message when the user makes a change to the text. An edit control can also receive messages, such as EM_GETLINE and EM_LINELENGTH. An edit control carries out the specified action when it receives a message.

A particularly powerful feature of edit controls allows you to "undo" a change to the contents of the edit control. To determine whether an edit control can undo an action, send the EM_CANUNDO message to the control; the control will return a nonzero value if it can undo the last change. If it can, your application can send the EM_UNDO message to the control to reverse the last change made to the edit control.

Table 8.4 describes the mouse and keyboard interface for edit controls.

Table 8.4 User Interface for Edit Control

Action	Result
Mouse Interface	
Single click	Positions the insertion point and drops the selection anchor.
Double click	Selects a word.
SHIFT+Single click	Positions the insertion point and extends the selection from the selection anchor to the insertion point.
Drag	Drops the selection anchor, moves the insertion point, and extends the selection from the selection anchor to the insertion point.
Keyboard Interface	
DIRECTION	Removes the selection from any text and moves the insertion point in the indicated direction.
SHIFT+DIRECTION	Drops the selection anchor (if it is not already dropped), moves the insertion point, and selects all text between the selection anchor and the insertion point.
CONTROL+LEFT ARROW, CONTROL+RIGHT ARROW	Moves the insertion point to the beginning of the word in the indicated direction.
SHIFT+CONTROL+LEFT ARROW, SHIFT+CONTROL+RIGHT ARROW	Drops the selection anchor (if it is not already dropped), moves the insertion point to the beginning of the word in the indicated direction, and selects all text between the selection anchor and the insertion point.

Table 8.4 User Interface for Edit Control *(continued)*

Action	Result
HOME	Removes the selection from any text and moves the insertion point to the beginning of the line.
SHIFT+HOME	Drops the selection anchor (if it is not already dropped), moves the insertion point to the beginning of the line, and selects all text between the selection anchor and the insertion point.
CONTROL+HOME	Places the insertion point before the first character in the edit control.
SHIFT+CONTROL+HOME	Drops the selection anchor (if it is not already dropped), places the insertion point before the first character in the edit control, and selects all text between the selection anchor and the insertion point.
END	Removes the selection from any text and moves the insertion point to the end of the line.
SHIFT+END	Drops the selection anchor (if it is not already dropped), moves the insertion point to the end of the line, and selects all text between the selection anchor and the insertion point.
CONTROL+END	Places the insertion point after the last character in the edit control.
SHIFT+CONTROL+END	Drops the selection anchor (if it is not already dropped), places the insertion point after the last character in the edit control, and selects all text between the selection anchor and the insertion point.
DELETE	If text is selected, deletes (clears) the text. Otherwise, deletes the character following the insertion point.
SHIFT+DELETE	If text is selected, cuts the text to the clipboard. Otherwise, deletes the character before the insertion point.
SHIFT+INSERT	Pastes (inserts) the contents of the clipboard at the insertion point.
CONTROL+INSERT	Copies selected text to the clipboard, but does not delete it.
PAGE UP	In a multiline edit control, scrolls text up one line less than the height of the edit control.
CONTROL+PAGE UP	In a multiline edit control, scrolls text left one character less than the width of the edit control.
PAGE DOWN	In a multiline edit control, scrolls text down one line less than the height of the edit control.
CONTROL+PAGE DOWN	In a multiline edit control, scrolls text right one character less than the width of the edit control.

Table 8.4 User Interface for Edit Control *(continued)*

Action	Result
CONTROL+ENTER	In a multiline edit control in a dialog box, ends the line and moves the cursor to the next line.
CONTROL+TAB	In a multiline edit control in a dialog box, inserts a tab character.

The EditCntl sample application described at the end of this chapter illustrates how to use a multiline edit control to provide basic text entry and editing.

8.4.6 Scroll Bars

Scroll bars are predefined controls that can be positioned anywhere in a window. They allow a user to select a value from a continuous range of values. The scroll bar sends a notification message to its parent window whenever the user clicks the control with the mouse or moves the scroll-bar thumb using the keyboard; this allows the parent window to process the messages so that it can determine the value selected by the user and position the thumb appropriately.

To create a child-window scroll bar, use the SBS_HORZ or SBS_VERT style. You can create a scroll bar with any desired size. If you want the width (of a vertical scroll bar) or height (of a horizontal scroll bar) to match the size of a window scroll bar, you can use the appropriate system metrics, as shown in the following example:

```
hScrollBar = CreateWindow("Scrollbar", NULL,
                   WS_CHILD | WS_VISIBLE | SBS_VERT,
                   20, 20,
                   GetSystemMetrics (SM_CXVSCROLL), 50,
                   hWnd, IDSCROLLBAR, hInst, NULL);
```

The **GetSystemMetrics** function returns the current value for SM_CXVSCROLL, which is the width of a standard window scroll bar.

Scroll-bar controls do not have a special set of notification messages. Instead, they send the same messages (WM_HSCROLL and WM_VSCROLL) sent by window scroll bars. The *wParam* parameter of these messages contains a value that indicates what kind of scrolling is being performed. Your application uses this information to determine how to position the scroll-bar thumb and what that position means to your application. Table 8.5 lists these *wParam* values and describes the user action which generates them.

Table 8.5 User Interface for Scroll Bar

Message *wParam* Value	Mouse	Keyboard
SB_LINEUP	User clicked the Up or Left arrow of the scroll bar.	User pressed LEFT ARROW or UP ARROW.
SB_LINEDOWN	User clicked the Down or Right arrow of the scroll bar.	User pressed RIGHT ARROW or DOWN ARROW.
SB_PAGEUP	User clicked above or to the left of the scroll-bar thumb.	User pressed PAGE UP.
SB_PAGEDOWN	User clicked below or to the right of the scroll-bar thumb.	User pressed PAGE DOWN.
SB_ENDSCROLL	User clicked anywhere on the scroll bar except the thumb.	None.
SB_THUMBTRACK	User is dragging the thumb.	None.
SB_THUMBPOSITION	User stopped dragging the thumb.	None.
SB_TOP	None.	User pressed HOME.
SB_BOTTOM	None.	User pressed END.

Windows is capable of properly positioning the thumb of a scroll bar associated with a list box or an edit control based on the contents of the control. However, a scroll bar that is a child-window control represents a range of values known only to your application. As a result, it is the responsibility of your application to set the scrolling range for the scroll bar and to position the thumb each time the user moves it.

The **SetScrollRange** function establishes the range of values that the scroll bar represents. For example, if your application has a scroll bar with which the user can select a day in a given month, you would call **SetScrollRange** to set the scroll range to the number of days in a particular month. The following shows how your application could set the range from the month of January:

```
SetScrollRange(hScrollBar, SB_CTL, 1, 31, 1)
```

In this example, SB_CTL informs Windows that the scroll bar is a separate scroll-bar control, not a scroll bar associated with a window. The third and fourth parameters specify the scroll-bar range, and the fourth parameter is set to 1 to direct windows to redraw the scroll bar to reflect the new range.

Even though you have established the range of values that the scroll bar represents, Windows still cannot properly position the thumb of the scroll bar when the user moves it; that remains the responsibility of your application. Each time your application receives a WM_HSCROLL or WM_VSCROLL message for the scroll bar, you must check the *wParam* parameter of the message to determine how far the user moved the thumb. You then call the **SetScrollPos** function to position the thumb. Also, if your application allows the user to change the value represented by the thumb position without using the scroll bar (such as by typing in an edit control), your application must reposition the thumb based on the new value.

8.5 A Sample Application: EditCntl

This sample application illustrates how you can use an edit control in an application's main window to provide multiple-line text entry and editing. The EditCntl application fills the client area of its main window with a multiple-line edit control and monitors the size of the client area to ensure that the edit control always just fits. When completed, the EditCntl application appears as shown in Figure 8.1:

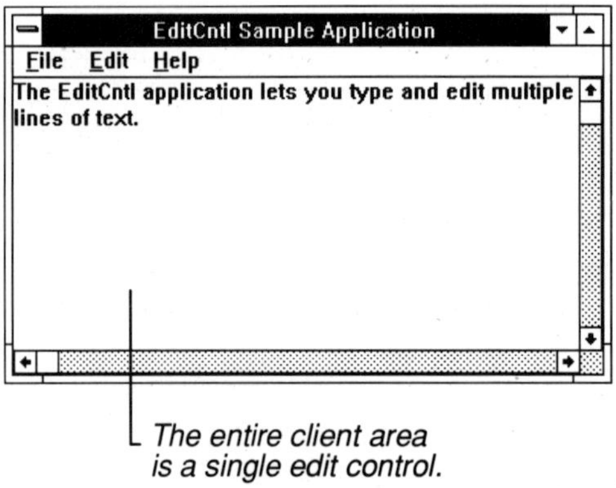

Figure 8.1 The EditCntl Application's Window

To create the application, copy and rename the source files of the EditMenu application, then make the following modifications:

1. Add a new constant to the include file.
2. Add new variables.
3. Add a **CreateWindow** function.
4. Modify the WM_COMMAND case.
5. Add a WM_SETFOCUS case.
6. Add a WM_SIZE case.
7. Compile and link the application.

NOTE Rather than typing the code presented in the following sections, you might find it more convenient to simply examine and compile the sample source files provided with the SDK.

8.5.1 Add a Constant to the Include File

You need to add a constant to the include file to serve as the control ID for the edit control. Add the following statement:

```
#define IDC_EDIT 300
```

8.5.2 Add New Variables

You need a global variable to hold the window handle of the edit control. Add the following statement to the beginning of the C-language source file:

```
HWND hEditWnd /* handle to edit window */
```

You also need a local variable in the WinMain function to hold the coordinates of the client-area rectangle. These coordinates are used to determine the size of the control. Add the following statement to the beginning of the WinMain function:

```
RECT Rect;
```

8.5.3 Add a CreateWindow Function

First, you need to retrieve the dimensions of the client area so that you can set the size of the control. Once you have the dimensions of the client area, use the **CreateWindow** function to create the edit control.

Add the following statements to the WinMain function immediately after creating the main window:

```
GetClientRect(hWnd, (LPRECT) &Rect);

hEditWnd = CreateWindow("Edit",
    NULL,
    WS_CHILD | WS_VISIBLE |
    ES_MULTILINE |
    WS_VSCROLL | WS_HSCROLL |
    ES_AUTOHSCROLL | ES_AUTOVSCROLL,
    0,
    0,
    (Rect.right-Rect.left),
    (Rect.bottom-Rect.top),
    hWnd,
    IDC_EDIT,
    hInst,
    NULL);

if (!hEditWnd) {
   DestroyWindow(hWnd);
   return (NULL);
}
```

The **GetClientRect** function retrieves the dimensions of the the main window's client area and places that information in the Rect structure. The **CreateWindow** function creates the edit control, using the width and height computed by the Rect structure.

The **CreateWindow** function creates the edit window. To create an edit control, you need to use the predefined "Edit" control class and you need to specify the WS_CHILD window style. The predefined controls may be used as child windows only. They cannot be used as main or pop-up windows. Since a child window requires a parent window, the handle of the main window, hWnd, is specified in the function call.

For this edit control, a number of edit-control styles are also specified. Edit-control styles, like window styles, define how the control will look and operate. This edit control is a multiple-line control, meaning the user will be able to enter more than one line of text in the control window. Also, the control will automatically scroll horizontally or vertically if the user types more text than can fit in the window.

The upper-left corner of the edit control is placed at the upper-left corner of the parent window's client area. A child window's coordinates are always relative to the parent window's client area. The next two arguments, Rect.right–Rect.left and Rect.bottom–Rect.top, define the height and width of the edit control, ensuring that the edit control fills the client area when the window is first displayed.

Since an edit control sends notification messages to its parent window, the control must be given a control ID. Child windows cannot have menus, so the menu argument in the **CreateWindow** function is used to specify the control ID instead. For this edit control, the ID is set to IDC_EDIT. Any notification messages sent to the parent window by the edit control will contain this ID.

If the edit control cannot be created, the **CreateWindow** function returns NULL. In this case, the application cannot continue, so the **DestroyWindow** function is used to destroy the main window before terminating the application.

8.5.4 Modify the WM_COMMAND Case

Child-window controls notify the parent window of events by using a WM_COMMAND message. The *wParam* parameter of the WM_COMMAND message identifies the control that generated the message.

To recognize an out-of-memory notification from the edit control, add the following code to the WM_COMMAND case:

```
case IDC_EDIT:
    if (HIWORD (lParam) == EN_ERRSPACE) {
        MessageBox (
            GetFocus (),
            "Out of memory.",
            "EditCntl Sample Application",
            MB_ICONHAND | MB_OK
        );
    }
    break;
```

8.5.5 Add a WM_SETFOCUS Case

To set the input focus to the edit control whenever the parent window is activated, add the following statements to the window procedure:

```
case WM_SETFOCUS:
      SetFocus (hEditWnd);
      break;
```

8.5.6 Add a WM_SIZE Case

You need to add a WM_SIZE case to the window function. Windows sends a WM_SIZE message to the window function whenever the width or height of a window changes. Since changing the main window size does not automatically change the size of the edit control, the WM_SIZE case is needed to change the size of the control.

Add the following statements to the window function:

```
case WM_SIZE:
    MoveWindow(hEditWnd, 0, 0, LOWORD(lParam),
        HIWORD(lParam), TRUE);
    break;
```

8.5.7 Compile and Link

No changes are required to the make file. Compile and link the EditCntl application, then start Windows and run the application. Now, you can insert text, backspace to delete text, and you can use the mouse instead of the keyboard to select text. And since you specified ES_MULTILINE, ES_AUTOVSCROLL, and ES_AUTOHSCROLL when creating the control, the control can edit a full screen of text, then scroll and edit more.

The EditCntl application illustrates the first step required to make a simple text editor. To make a complete editor, you can add a File menu to the main window to open and save text files and to copy or retrieve text from the edit control, and add an Edit menu to the main window to copy, cut, and paste text through the clipboard. Later chapters illustrate some simple ways to incorporate these features into your application.

8.6 Summary

This chapter explained how to provide controls in your application. A control is a special type of child window that you can add to your application's windows to facilitate user input. Windows provides automatic support for most types of controls. For example, Windows can automatically draw a control in the location you specify; when the user selects a control, Windows sends your application a message containing the control ID.

This chapter also explained how to use each of the most common types of controls.

For more information on topics related to controls, see the following:

Topic	Reference
Processing input messages	*Guide to Programming*: Chapter 4, "Keyboard and Mouse Input"
Using controls in dialog boxes	*Guide to Programming*: Chapter 9, "Dialog Boxes"
Control functions	*Reference, Volume 1*: Chapter 1, "Window Manager Interface Functions"

Topic	Reference
Resource script statements	*Reference, Volume 2*: Chapter 8, "Resource Script Statements"
The sample application OWN-COMBO.EXE, which illustrates the use of combo boxes and owner-draw controls	SDK Sample Source Code disk

Chapter 9 Dialog Boxes

Dialog boxes are pop-up windows that applications use to interact with the user. Typically, dialog boxes contain one or more controls.

This chapter covers the following topics:

- What is a dialog box?
- Creating and using both modal and modeless dialog boxes
- Creating a dialog function
- Using controls in dialog boxes

This chapter also explains how to create a sample application, FileOpen, which shows how to build and use a modal dialog box that contains controls.

9.1 What Is a Dialog Box?

A dialog box is a pop-up window that an application uses to display or prompt for information. Dialog boxes are typically used to prompt the user for the information needed to complete a command. A dialog box contains one or more controls with which the user can enter text, choose options, and direct the action of a particular command.

You have already seen a dialog box in the Generic application: the About dialog box. This dialog box contains static text controls that provide information about the application, and a push-button control that the user can use to close the dialog box and return to the main window. To process a dialog box, you need to supply a dialog-box template, a dialog function, and some means to call up the dialog box.

A dialog-box template is text that describes the dialog box and the controls it contains. You can use either a text editor or the Windows 3.0 Dialog Editor to create the template. Once you have created the template, add it to your resource script file.

A dialog function is a callback function; Windows calls the dialog function and passes it messages for the dialog box. Although a dialog function is similar to a window function, Windows carries out special processing for dialog boxes.

Therefore, the dialog function does not have the same responsibilities as a window function.

The most common way to display a dialog box is in response to menu input. For example, the Open and Save As commands in the File menu both require additional information to complete their tasks; both display dialog boxes to prompt for the additional information.

There are two types of dialog boxes: modal and modeless.

9.1.1 Modal Dialog Boxes

You have already seen a modal dialog box (About) in the Generic application. A modal dialog box temporarily disables the parent window and forces the user to complete the requested action before returning control to the parent window. Modal dialog boxes are particularly useful for gathering information your application requires in order to proceed. For example, Windows Notepad displays a modal dialog box when the user chooses the Open command from the File menu. Notepad cannot proceed with the Open command until the user specifies a file.

Although you can give a modal dialog box almost any window style, the recommended styles are DS_MODALFRAME, WS_CAPTION, and WS_SYSMENU. The DS_MODALFRAME style gives the dialog box its characteristic thick border.

A modal dialog box starts its own message loop to process messages from the application queue without returning to the WinMain function. To keep input from going to the parent window, the dialog box disables the parent window before processing input. For this reason, a modal dialog box must never be created using the WS_CHILD style, since disabling the parent window also disables all child windows belonging to the parent.

To display a modal dialog box, use the **DialogBox** function. To terminate a modal dialog box, use the **EndDialog** function.

9.1.2 Modeless Dialog Boxes

A modeless dialog box, unlike a modal dialog box, does not disable the parent window. This means that the user can continue to work in the parent window while the modeless dialog box is displayed. For example, Windows Write uses a modeless dialog box for its Find command. This allows the user to continue editing the document without having to close the Find dialog box.

Most modeless dialog boxes have the WS_POPUP, WS_CAPTION, WS_BORDER, and WS_SYSTEMMENU styles. The typical modeless dialog box has a system menu, a title bar, and a thin black border.

Although Windows automatically disables some of the system-menu commands for the dialog box, the menu still contains a Close command. The user can use this command instead of a push button to terminate the dialog box. You can also include controls in the dialog box, such as edit controls and check boxes.

A modeless dialog box receives its input through the message loop in the WinMain function. If the dialog box has controls, and you want to let the user move to and select those controls using the keyboard, call the **IsDialogMessage** function in the main message loop. This function determines whether a keyboard input message is for the dialog box and, if necessary, processes it. The WinMain message loop for an application that has a modeless dialog box will look like this:

```
while (GetMessage(&msg, NULL, NULL, NULL) {
    if (hDlg == NULL || !IsDialogMessage(hDlg, &msg)) {
        TranslateMessage(&msg);
        DispatchMessage(&msg);
    }
}
```

Since a modeless dialog box may not be present at all times, you need to check the hDlg variable that holds the handle in order to see if it is valid. If it is valid, **IsDialogMessage** determines whether the message is for the dialog box. If so, the message is processed and must not be further processed by the **TranslateMessage** and **DispatchMessage** functions.

To terminate a modeless dialog box, use the **DestroyWindow** function.

9.2 Using a Dialog Box

To create and use a dialog box, follow these steps:

1. Create a dialog-box template and add it to the resource script file.
2. Create a dialog function to support the box.
3. Export the dialog function.
4. Display the dialog box by calling either the **DialogBox** function (for a modal dialog box) or the **CreateDialog** function (for a modeless dialog box).
5. Close the dialog box by calling either the **EndDialog** function (for modal dialog boxes) or the **DestroyWindow** function (for modeless dialog boxes).

The following sections explain each step.

9.2.1 Creating a Dialog Function

A dialog function has the following form:

```
BOOL FAR PASCAL DlgFunc(hDlg, message, wParam, lParam)
HWND hDlg;
unsigned message;
WORD wParam;
DWORD lParam;
{
    switch (message) {

        /* Place message cases here */

        default:
             return FALSE;
    }
}
```

This is basically a window function, except that the **DefWindowProc** function is not called. Default processing of dialog-box messages is handled internally, so the dialog function must not call the **DefWindowProc** function.

The dialog function must be defined as a **FAR PASCAL** procedure, and must have the parameters given here. **BOOL** is the required return type.

Just as it does with window functions, Windows sends messages to a dialog function when it has information to give the function or wants the function to carry out some action. Unlike a window function, a dialog function responds to a message by returning a Boolean value. If the function processes the message, it returns TRUE. Otherwise, it returns FALSE.

In this function, the hDlg variable receives the handle of the dialog box. The other parameters serve the same purpose as in a window function. The **switch** statement is used as a filter for different messages. Most dialog functions process the WM_INITDIALOG and WM_COMMAND messages, but very little else.

The WM_INITDIALOG message, sent to the dialog box just before it is displayed, gives the dialog function the opportunity to give the input focus to any control in the dialog box. If the function returns TRUE, Windows will set the input focus to the control of its choosing.

The WM_COMMAND message is sent to the dialog function by the controls in the dialog box. If there are controls in the dialog box, they send notification messages when the user carries out some action within them. For example, a dialog function with a push button can check WM_COMMAND messages for the control ID of the push button. The control ID is in the message's *wParam* parameter. When it finds the ID, the dialog function can carry out the corresponding task.

If you create the dialog box with the WS_SYSMENU style, you should include a WM_COMMAND **switch** statement for the IDCANCEL control ID which is sent when the user chooses the close option in the dialog-box system menu. The statement should include a call to the **EndDialog** function.

9.2.2 Using Controls in Dialog Boxes

You use controls in dialog boxes much as you use them in regular windows. When a control is in a dialog box, however, you can use several special functions to access the control and send messages to it. For example, the **SendDlgItem-Message** function sends a message to a control in the dialog box, and the **Set-DlgItemText** function sets the text of a control. You do not need to supply the control handle in these functions. Instead, you supply the dialog handle and the control ID. If you want the control handle, you can use the **GetDlgItem** function.

9.3 A Sample Application: FileOpen

This sample application shows how to build and use a modal dialog box to support the Open command in the File menu. The purpose and operation of the dialog box is fully described in the *System Application Architecture, Common User Access: Advanced Interface Design Guide*. Figure 9.1 shows the dialog box that the FileOpen application displays when the user chooses the Open command:

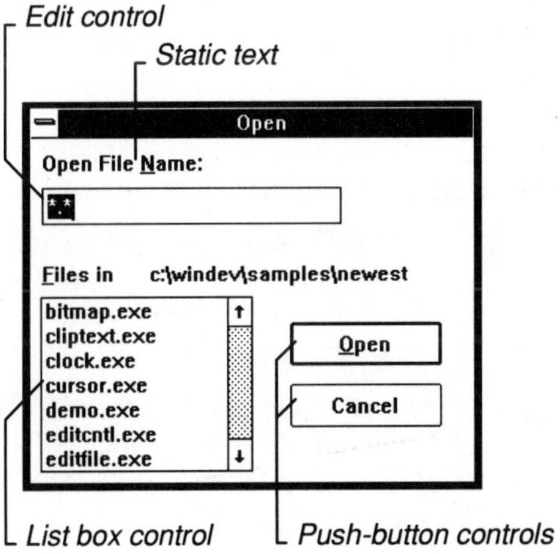

Figure 9.1 The FileOpen Application's Dialog Box

The dialog box contains the following controls:

- A default push-button control labeled "Open" that lets the user tell the application to open the selected file.
- A button control labeled "Cancel" that lets the user cancel the Open command.

- A single-line edit control in which the user can enter the name of the file to open.
- A list box containing the names of files in the current directory from which the user can select the file to be opened.

  The list box also contains directory and drive names that the user can select to change the current directory or drive.
- Several static text controls that label the list box and edit control, and display the current directory name.

To create the FileOpen application, copy and rename the source files for the EditCntl application, then make the following modifications:

1. Add new constants to the include file.
2. Create the Open dialog-box template and add it to the resource script file.
3. Add new variables.
4. Add an IDM_OPEN case to the WM_COMMAND case.
5. Create the OpenDlg dialog function.
6. Add helper functions to support the OpenDlg dialog function.
7. Export the OpenDlg dialog function.
8. Compile and link the application.

NOTE Rather than typing the code provided in the following sections, you might find it more convenient to simply examine and compile the sample source files provided with the SDK.

9.3.1 Add Constants to the Include File

You need several new constants in the include file to identify the controls of the FileOpen dialog box. Add the following statements:

```
#define     IDC_FILENAME  400
#define     IDC_EDIT      401
#define     IDC_FILES     402
#define     IDC_PATH      403
#define     IDC_LISTBOX   404
```

Although you may choose any integer for a control ID, the ID for each control in a given dialog box must be unique. By convention, a predefined ID, such as IDOK or IDCANCEL, is less than 100, so any number greater than 100 can be used for other controls.

9.3.2 Create the Open Dialog-Box Template

You need a dialog-box template in your resource script file to define the size and appearance of the Open dialog box. The **DIALOG** statement specifies the name and dimensions of a dialog box, as well as the controls the dialog box contains. Add the following statements:

```
❶ Open DIALOG 10, 10, 148, 112
STYLE DS_MODALFRAME | WS_CAPTION | WS_SYSMENU
CAPTION "About FileOpen"
❷ BEGIN
    ❸ LTEXT "Open File &Name:", IDC_FILENAME, 4, 4, 60, 10
    ❹ EDITTEXT IDC_EDIT, 4, 16, 100, 12, ES_AUTOHSCROLL
    LTEXT "&Files in", IDC_FILES, 4, 40, 32, 10
    ❺ LISTBOX, IDC_LISTBOX, 4, 52, 70, 56, WS_TABSTOP
    ❻ LTEXT "", IDC_PATH, 40, 40, 100, 10
    ❼ DEFPUSHBUTTON "&Open", IDOK, 87, 60, 50, 14
    ❽ PUSHBUTTON "Cancel", IDCANCEL, 87, 80, 50, 14
END
```

In this **DIALOG** statement:

❶ The dialog box has a width and height (in dialog units) of 148 and 112, respectively. Dialog units are fractions of the default system-font character size and are used with dialog boxes to ensure that a dialog box has the same relative size, no matter which computer it is displayed on.

❷ The **BEGIN** and **END** statements are required.

❸ The first **LTEXT** statement creates a left-adjusted static control that contains the string, "Open File &Name:". This string serves as the label to the list box. In some dialog boxes, all static controls have this same ID. Although the general rule is to have a unique ID for each control in a dialog box, it is acceptable to use –1 for static controls, as long as the dialog function does not need to distinguish between them (for example, as long as the dialog function does not attempt to change the static-control text or position).

❹ The **EDITTEXT** statement adds an edit control to the dialog box and identifies it with IDC_EDIT. The ES_AUTOHSCROLL style is given so that the user can enter filenames that are longer than the control is wide.

❺ The **LISTBOX** statement creates a list box. The ID of the list box is IDC_LISTBOX. The width and height (in dialog units) of the list box are 70 and 56, respectively. The WS_TABSTOP style is given so that the user can move the focus to the list box using the keyboard. Without this style, the user can get to the list box only by clicking it with the mouse.

❻ The last **LTEXT** statement creates a left-adjusted static control used to display the current directory and drive. The control is initially empty; the pathname is added later. This control also has a unique control ID, IDC_PATH, to distinguish it from other static controls. This is important since you will use the **DlgDirList** function to fill the control.

❼ The **DEFPUSHBUTTON** statement creates a default push button that is labeled “Open” and has the control ID IDOK, a predefined ID found in the WINDOWS.H file. In modal dialog boxes, pressing ENTER generates a notification message that uses the same ID, so you can permit the user to click the button or press ENTER to open the selected file.

❽ The **PUSHBUTTON** statement creates the “Cancel” push button. Its ID is IDCANCEL, a predefined ID found in the WINDOWS.H file. In modal dialog boxes, pressing ESCAPE generates a notification message by using the same ID, so you can permit the user to click the button or press ESCAPE to cancel the Open command.

9.3.3 Add New Variables

You need to declare several new global and local variables in order to hold the filename and the various pieces used to build the filename. Add the following statements at the beginning of your source file:

```
char FileName[128];              /* current filename          */
char PathName[128];              /* current pathname          */
char OpenName[128];              /* filename to open          */
char DefPath[128];               /* default path for list box */
char DefSpec[13] = "*.*";        /* default search spec       */
char DefExt[] = ".txt";          /* default extension         */
char str[255];                   /* string for sprintf() calls */
```

You need a new local variable to hold the procedure-instance address of the FileOpen dialog box. Add the following statement at the beginning of the window function:

```
FARPROC lpOpenDlg;
```

9.3.4 Add the IDM_OPEN Case

You need to fill in the IDM_OPEN case for the WM_COMMAND message. When the user chooses the command, the application should display the Open dialog box. Add the following statements to the window function:

```
case IDM_OPEN:
    lpOpenDlg = MakeProcInstance((FARPROC) OpenDlg, hInst));
    DialogBox(hInst, "Open", hWnd, lpOpenDlg);
    FreeProcInstance(lpOpenDlg);
    break;
```

The **MakeProcInstance** function creates a procedure-instance address for the OpenDlg function. The function ensures that the data segment for the current instance is used when the dialog function is called. Functions, such as OpenDlg, that are exported by an application may be called only through a procedure-instance address and must not be called directly.

The **FreeProcInstance** function is used to free a procedure-instance address when it is no longer needed. After the **DialogBox** function returns, the procedure-instance address, lpOpenDlg, is not needed and can be freed. It will be re-created the next time the dialog box is invoked.

The **DialogBox** function returns control to WinMain only after the dialog function has terminated the dialog box. This means the dialog box will complete any actions the user requests, before the application can continue execution. Such a dialog box is called a modal dialog box, since while it remains on the screen, the application is in a new mode of operation. This means the user can respond only to the dialog box. It also means that commands that apply to the application are not available while the dialog box is present.

9.3.5 Create the OpenDlg Function

You need to create a dialog-box function to process the controls in the Open dialog box. When the dialog box is first displayed, the dialog function needs to fill the list box and the edit control, then give the input focus to the edit control and select the entire specification. If the user selects a filename in the list box, the dialog function should copy the name to the edit control. If the user clicks the Open button, the dialog function should retrieve the filename from the edit control and prepare to open the file. If the user double-clicks a filename in the list box, the dialog function should retrieve the filename, copy it to the edit control, and prepare to open the file.

Add the following function to your source file:

```
HANDLE FAR PASCAL OpenDlg(hDlg, message, wParam, lParam)
HWND hDlg;
unsigned message;
WORD wParam;
LONG lParam;
{
    WORD index;          /* index to the filenames in the list box */
    PSTR pTptr;          /* temporary pointer                      */
    HANDLE hFile;        /* handle to the opened file              */

    switch (message) {
        case WM_COMMAND:
            switch (wParam) {
                case IDC_LISTBOX:
                    switch (HIWORD(lParam)) {
                        case LBN_SELCHANGE:
                            if (!DlgDirSelect(hDlg, str, IDC_LISTBOX)) {
                                SetDlgItemText(hDlg, IDC_EDIT, str);
                                SendDlgItemMessage(hDlg, IDC_EDIT,
```

```
                                  EM_SETSEL,
                                  NULL,
                                  MAKELONG(Ø, Øx7fff));
                          }
                          else {
                              strcat(str, DefSpec);
                              DlgDirList(hDlg, str, IDC_LISTBOX,
                                  IDC_PATH, Øx4Ø1Ø);
                          }
                          break;
                      case LBN_DBLCLK:
                          goto openfile;
                  }                       /* Ends IDC_LISTBOX case */
                  return (TRUE);

              case IDOK:
openfile:
                  GetDlgItemText(hDlg, IDC_EDIT, OpenName, 128);
                  if (strchr(OpenName, '*') ||
                      strchr(OpenName, '?')) {
                      SeparateFile(hDlg, (LPSTR) str, (LPSTR) DefSpec,
                          (LPSTR) OpenName);
                      if (str[Ø])
                          strcpy(DefPath, str);
                      ChangeDefExt(DefExt, DefSpec);
                      UpdateListBox(hDlg);
                      return (TRUE);
                  }
                  if (!OpenName[Ø]) {
                      MessageBox(hDlg, "No filename specified.",
                          NULL, MB_OK | MB_ICONQUESTION);
                      return (TRUE);
                  }
                  AddExt(OpenName, DefExt);
                  EndDialog(hDlg, NULL);
                  return(TRUE);

              case IDCANCEL:
                  EndDialog(hDlg, NULL);
                  return(TRUE);
          }
          break;

      case WM_INITDIALOG:                /* Request to initalize   */
          UpdateListBox(hDlg);
          SetDlgItemText(hDlg, IDC_EDIT, DefSpec);
          SendDlgItemMessage(hDlg,       /* dialog handle          */
              IDC_EDIT,                  /* where to send message  */
              EM_SETSEL,                 /* select characters      */
              NULL,                      /* additional information */
              MAKELONG(Ø, Øx7fff));      /* Accept entire contents */
          SetFocus(GetDlgItem(hDlg, IDC_EDIT));
          return (FALSE); /* Indicates focus is set to a control */
```

```
    }
    return (FALSE);
}
```

When the dialog function receives the WM_INITDIALOG message, the **SetDlgItemText** function copies the initial filename to the edit control, and the **SendDlgItemMessage** function sends the EM_SETSEL message to the control in order to select the entire contents of the edit control for editing. The **SetFocus** function gives the input focus to the edit control. (The **GetDlgItem** function retrieves the window handle of the edit control.) The UpdateListBox function, given at the beginning of the WM_INITDIALOG case, is a locally defined function that fills the list box with a list of files in the current directory.

When the dialog function receives the WM_COMMAND message, it looks for three different values: IDC_LISTBOX, IDOK, and IDCANCEL.

For IDC_LISTBOX, the dialog function checks the notification-message type. If it is LBN_SELCHANGE, the dialog function retrieves the new selection using the **DlgDirSelect** function. It then copies the new filename to the edit control using the **SetDlgItemText** function and selects it for editing by sending a EM_SETSEL message. If the current selection is not a filename, the dialog function uses **DlgDirList** to copy the default specification to the list box. This fills the list box with all files in the current directory.

If the IDC_LISTBOX notification type is LBN_DBLCLK, the dialog function carries out the same action as for the IDOK case. A list box sends an LBN_DBLCLK message only after sending an LBN_SELCHANGE message. This means you do not have to retrieve the new filename when you receive a double-click notification.

For IDOK, the dialog function retrieves the contents of the edit control and checks the filename to see if it is valid. The **strchr** function searches for wildcard characters in the name. If it finds a wildcard character, it divides the filename into separate path and filename parts using the locally defined SeparateFile function. The **strcpy** function updates the DefPath variable with a new default path, if any. The locally defined ChangeDefExt function updates the DefExt variable with a new default filename extension, if any. After the default path, filename, and filename extension are updated, the UpdateListBox function updates the contents of the list box, and the dialog function returns to let the user select a valid filename from the new list.

If a filename has no wildcard characters, the dialog function makes sure the file is not empty. If it is empty, the dialog function displays a warning message, but does not terminate the dialog box. This lets the user try again. If the filename has no wildcards and the file is not empty, and if the user has entered a filename that does not have an extension, the dialog function uses the locally defined AddExt function to append the default filename extension. The dialog function then calls the **EndDialog** function to terminate the modal dialog box and sets the dialog-box return value to NULL.

For IDCANCEL, the dialog function calls the **EndDialog** function to terminate the dialog box and cancel the command. The return value is set to NULL.

The dialog function can also check the existence and access mode of the given file before terminating the dialog box. The existence check, not given in this example, is entirely up to the application. Some simple ways of checking whether a file exists and is accessible are shown in Chapter 10, "File Input and Output."

9.3.6 Add Helper Functions

You need to add several functions to your C-language source file to support the OpenDlg dialog function. These functions are listed as follows:

Function	Description
UpdateListBox	Fills the list box in the Open dialog box with the specified files.
SeparateFile	Divides a pathname into separate path and filename parts.
ChangeDefExt	Copies the filename extension from a filename to a buffer, as long as the extension has no wildcard characters.
AddExt	Appends an extension to a filename if one does not already exist.

The UpdateListBox function builds a pathname by concatenating the default path and filename, then passes this pathname to the list box using the **DlgDirList** function. This function fills the list box with the names of the files and directories identified by the pathname. Add the following statements to the C-language source file:

```
void UpdateListBox(hDlg)
HWND hDlg;
{
    strcpy(str, DefPath);
    strcat(str, DefSpec);
    DlgDirList(hDlg, str, IDC_LISTBOX, IDC_PATH, 0x4010);
    SetDlgItemText(hDlg, IDC_EDIT, DefSpec);
}
```

The **SetDlgItemText** function copies the default filename to the dialog box's edit control.

The SeparateFile function divides a pathname into two parts and copies them to separate buffers. It first moves to the end of the pathname and uses the **AnsiPrev** function to back through it, looking for a drive or directory separator. Add the following statements to your C-language source file:

```
void SeparateFile(hDlg, lpDestPath, lpDestFileName, lpSrcFileName)
HWND hDlg;
LPSTR lpDestPath, lpDestFileName, lpSrcFileName;
{
    LPSTR lpTmp;
    CHAR  cTmp;

    lpTmp = lpSrcFileName + (long) lstrlen(lpSrcFileName);

    while (*lpTmp != ':' && *lpTmp != '\\' && lpTmp > lpSrcFileName)
        lpTmp = AnsiPrev(lpSrcFileName, lpTmp);

    if (*lpTmp != ':' && *lpTmp != '\\') {
        lstrcpy(lpDestFileName, lpSrcFileName);
        lpDestPath[0] = 0;
        return;
    }
    lstrcpy(lpDestFileName, lpTmp + 1);
    cTmp = *(lpTmp + 1);
    lstrcpy(lpDestPath, lpSrcFileName);
    *(lpTmp + 1) = cTmp;
    lpDestPath[(lpTmp - lpSrcFileName) + 1] = 0;
}
```

The ChangeDefExt and AddExt functions all use standard C-language statements to carry out their tasks. Add the following statements to the C-language source file:

```
void ChangeDefExt(Ext, Name)
PSTR Ext, Name;
{
    PSTR pTptr;

    pTptr = Name;
    while (*pTptr && *pTptr != '.')
        pTptr++;
    if (*pTptr)                    /* true if this is an extension */
        if (!strchr(pTptr, '*') && !strchr(pTptr, '?'))
            strcpy(Ext, pTptr);            /* Copies the extension */
}

void AddExt(Name, Ext)
PSTR Name, Ext;
{
    PSTR pTptr;

    pTptr = Name;
    while (*pTptr && *pTptr != '.')
        pTptr++;
    if (*pTptr != '.')            /* If no extension, add the default */
        strcat(Name, Ext);
}
```

9.3.7 Export the Dialog Function

You need to export the OpenDlg dialog function, since it is a callback function and will be called by Windows. Add the following line to the **EXPORTS** statement in your module-definition file:

```
OpenDlg @3
```

9.3.8 Compile and Link

No changes are required to the make file. Compile and link the application, start Windows, then run the FileOpen application. When you open the File menu and choose the Open command, the FileOpen application displays the Open dialog box, as shown in Figure 9.1 at the beginning of this section. You can select a file from the list box, or enter a filename in the edit control, then choose the Open button.

9.4 Summary

This chapter explained how to create and use dialog boxes in your application. A dialog box is a special type of window that overlaps your application's main window. There are two types of dialog boxes: modal and modeless. Modal dialog boxes require the user to complete them before returning to the main application window. Modeless dialog boxes do not require completion before the user can move to other application windows.

Windows provides a special set of functions for handling controls in dialog boxes.

You can use the Dialog Editor to design dialog boxes.

For more information on topics related to dialog boxes, see the following:

Topic	Reference
Processing input messages	*Guide to Programming*: Chapter 4, "Keyboard and Mouse Input"
Controls	*Guide to Programming*: Chapter 8, "Controls"
Control and dialog-box functions	*Reference, Volume 1*: Chapter 1, "Window Manager Interface Functions"
Resource script statements	*Reference, Volume 2*: Chapter 8, "Resource Script Statements"

Topic	Reference
Using the Dialog Editor	*Tools*: Chapter 5, "Designing Dialog Boxes: The Dialog Editor"
The sample application OWN-COMBO.EXE, which illustrates the use of combo boxes and owner-draw controls in dialog boxes	SDK Sample Source Code disk

Chapter 10 File Input and Output

File input and output in Microsoft Windows applications are similar to file input and output in standard C run-time programs. However, there are enough differences between the two environments to make a review of file input and output important. For example, although you can use C run-time, stream input and output (I/O) functions in Windows, it's preferable to use the low-level, C run-time input and output functions. Also, since Windows is a multitasking environment, you need to manage open files carefully.

In Windows, your application should use the **OpenFile** function to work with files. **OpenFile** opens and manages your files; it returns a file handle that you can use with the low-level, C run-time functions to read and write data.

This chapter covers the following topics:

- Handling files in the Windows environment
- Using the **OpenFile** function to create, open, close, reopen, prompt for, and check the status of disk files
- Using the low-level, C run-time input and output functions to read from and write to disk files

This chapter also explains how to create a sample application, EditFile, that illustrates some of these concepts.

10.1 Rules for Handling Files in the Windows Environment

In the Windows environment, multitasking imposes some special restrictions on file access that you do not encounter in the standard C environment. Since there may be several applications working with files at the same time, you need to follow some simple rules to avoid conflicts and potential overwriting of files.

The rest of this section lists and explains these rules.

Keep a file open only while you have execution control.

You should close the file before calling the **GetMessage** function, or any other function that may yield execution control. Closing the file prevents it from being affected by changes in the disk environment that may be caused by other applications. For example, suppose your application is writing to a floppy disk and affected by changes in the disk environment that may be caused by other applications. For example, suppose your application is writing to a floppy disk and temporarily relinquishes control to another application, and the other application tells the user to remove the floppy disk and replace it with another. When your application gets control back and tries to write to the disk as before, without having closed and reopened the file, it could destroy data on the new disk.

Another reason to keep files closed is the DOS open-file limit. DOS sets a limit on the number of open files that can exist at one time. If many applications attempt to open and use files, they can quickly exhaust the available files.

To prevent open-file problems, the **OpenFile** function provides an OF_REOPEN option that lets you easily close and reopen files. Whenever you open or create a file, **OpenFile** automatically copies the relevant facts about the file, including the full pathname and the current position of the file pointer, in an **OFSTRUCT** structure. This means you can close the file, then reopen it by supplying nothing more than the structure.

If the user changes disks while working in another application, when your application calls the **OpenFile** function, the function will fail to reopen your file. If your application specifies the OF_PROMPT option when reopening a file, **OpenFile** automatically displays a message box asking the user to insert the correct disk.

Follow DOS conventions when carrying out file operations.

Ultimately, Windows depends on the DOS file-handling functions to carry out all file input and output. This means that you must follow DOS conventions when carrying out file operations. For example, with DOS, a filename can have from one to eight characters and a filename extension can have from zero to three characters. The name must not contain spaces or special-purpose characters. Furthermore, filenames must be specified in the OEM character set, not the Windows default character set, ANSI.

It is up to you to make sure that your application uses filenames that are the appropriate length and contain the appropriate characters. However, if you use the **OpenFile** function, you do not have to worry about translating character sets; **OpenFile** automatically translates filenames from the ANSI character set to the OEM set. It does so using the **AnsiToOem** function.

NOTE All edit controls and list boxes use the ANSI character set by default, so if you plan to display DOS filenames or let users enter filenames, they may see unexpected characters wherever an OEM character is not identical to an ANSI character.

If your application processes international filenames, it must be prepared to handle filenames that do not contain conventional single-byte character values. For such filenames, use the **AnsiNext** and **AnsiPrev** functions to move forward and backward in a string. These functions correctly handle strings that contain characters that are not one byte in length, such as strings in machines that are using Japanese characters.

Use unique filenames for each instance of your application.

Since more than one instance of an application can run at a time, one instance can end up overwriting the temporary file of another instance. You can prevent this by using unique filenames for each instance of your application.

To create unique filenames, use the **GetTempFilename** function. This function creates a unique name by combining a unique integer with a prefix and filename extension that you supply. **GetTempFilename** creates names that follow the DOS filename requirements.

NOTE The **GetTempFileName** function uses the TEMP environment variable to create the full pathname of the temporary file. If the user has not set the variable, the temporary file will be placed in the root directory of the current drive. If the variable does not specify a valid directory, you will not be able to create the temporary file.

Close files before displaying a message box, or use system-modal error message boxes.

As mentioned earlier, your application should not relinquish control while it has open files on floppy disks. If your application uses a message box that's not system-modal, the user can move to another application while the message box is on display. If your application still has open files, switching applications like this can cause file I/O problems.

To avoid such problems, whenever your application displays an alert or error message by using the **MessageBox** function, it should do at least one of the following:

- Close any open files before displaying the message box.
- If closing files is not feasible, make the message box system-modal.

10.2 Creating Files

To create a new file, use the **OpenFile** function with the OF_CREATE option. When you call the **OpenFile** function, you specify:

- A null-terminated filename for the file you're creating
- A buffer with the type **OFSTRUCT**
- The OF_CREATE option

The following example creates the FILE.TXT file and returns a handle to the file. The application can then use this file handle with low-level, C run-time I/O functions:

```
int hFile;
OFSTRUCT OfStruct;
        .
        .
        .
hFile = OpenFile("FILE.TXT", &OfStruct, OF_CREATE);
```

The **OpenFile** function creates the file, if necessary, and opens it for writing. If the file already exists, the function truncates it to zero length and opens it for writing.

If you want to avoid overwriting an existing file, you can check whether the file exists, before creating a new file, by calling **OpenFile** as follows:

```
hFile = OpenFile("FILE.TXT", &OfStruct, OF_EXIST);
if (hFile >= 0) {
    wAction = MessageBox(hWnd,
        (LPSTR) "File exists. Overwrite?",
        (LPSTR) "File",
        MB_OKCANCEL);
    if (wAction == IDCANCEL)

/* End this processing */
    }
}

/* Open the file */
```

10.3 Opening Existing Files

You can open an existing file by using the OF_READ, OF_WRITE, or OF_READWRITE option. These options direct the **OpenFile** function to open existing files for reading, writing, or reading and writing. The following example opens the FILE.TXT file for reading:

```
hFile = OpenFile("FILE.TXT", &OfStruct, OF_READ);
```

If the file fails to open, you can display a dialog box to indicate that the file was not found. You can also use **OpenFile** to prompt for the file, as described in Section 10.6, "Prompting for Files."

10.4 Reading From and Writing To Files

Once you have opened a file, you can read from it or write to it using low-level, C run-time functions. The following example opens the FILE.TXT file for reading and then reads 512 bytes from it:

```
char buffer[512];
int count;
        .
        .
        .
hFile = OpenFile("FILE.TXT", &OfStruct, OF_READ);
if (hFile >= 0) {
    count = read(hFile, buffer, 512);
    close(hFile);
}
```

In this example, the file handle is checked before bytes are read from the file. **OpenFile** returns –1 if the file could not be found or opened. The **close** function closes the file immediately after reading.

The following example opens the FILE.TMP file for writing and then writes bytes from the character-array buffer:

```
hFile = OpenFile("FILE.TMP", &OfStruct, OF_WRITE);
if (hFile >= 0) {
    write(hFile, buffer, count);
    close(hFile);
}
```

You should always close floppy-disk files after reading or writing. This is to prevent problems if you remove the current disk while working with another application. You can always reopen a disk file by using the OF_REOPEN option.

10.5 Reopening Files

If you open a file on a floppy disk, you should close it before your application relinquishes control to another application. The most convenient time is immediately after reading or writing the file. The file can always be reopened using **OpenFile** with the OF_REOPEN option:

```
hFile = OpenFile((LPSTR) NULL, &OfStruct, OF_REOPEN | OF_READ);
```

In this example, **OpenFile** uses the filename in the OfStruct structure to open the file. When a file is reopened, the file pointer marking the current position in the file is moved to the same position it was in just before the file was closed.

10.6 Prompting for Files

You can automatically prompt the user to insert the correct disk before reopening a file by using the OF_PROMPT option. **OpenFile** uses the filename to create a prompt string. If you are reopening a file, you need to use the OF_REOPEN and OF_PROMPT options in addition to specifying how you want to open the file:

```
hFile = OpenFile((LPSTR)NULL, &OfStruct, OF_PROMPT | OF_REOPEN
    | OF_READ);
```

If you reopen a file as read only, Windows will check whether the date and time match the date and time of the file when it was first opened.

10.7 Checking File Status

You can retrieve the current status of an open file by using the low-level, C run-time function **fstat**. This function fills a structure with information about a file, such as its length in bytes (specified in the **size** field) and the date and time it was created. The following example fills the FileStatus structure with information about the FILE.TXT file:

```
stat FileStatus;
          .
          .
          .
fstat(hFile, FileStatus);
```

10.8 A Simple File Editor: EditFile

This example shows how to create a simple Windows application that uses the **OpenFile** and C run-time functions to open and save small text files. To create the EditFile sample application, copy and rename the FileOpen application sources, described in Chapter 9, "Dialog Boxes," and modify them as follows:

1. Add constants to the include file.
2. Create a SaveAs dialog-box template and add it to the resource script file.
3. Add new include statements to the C-language source file.
4. Add new variables.
5. Replace the WM_COMMAND case.
6. Add the WM_QUERYENDSESSION and WM_CLOSE cases.
7. Modify the OpenDlg dialog function.
8. Create a SaveAsDlg dialog function.

9. Create helper functions for the SaveAsDlg dialog function.
10. Export the SaveAsDlg dialog function.
11. Modify the application's **HEAPSIZE** statement.
12. Compile and link the application.

When this application is completed, you will be able to view text files in an edit control. The application's Open command in the File menu will let you specify the file to be opened. You will also be able to make changes to a file or enter new text, and save the text using the Save or Save As command in the dialog box.

NOTE Rather than typing the code provided in the following sections, you might find it more convenient to simply examine and compile the sample source files provided with the SDK.

10.8.1 Add a Constant to the Include File

You need to add a constant definition to the include file to support the SaveAs dialog box. Add the following statement to the include file:

```
#define MAXFILESIZE 0x7FFF
```

10.8.2 Add a SaveAs Dialog Box

You need a new dialog box to support the Save As command. The SaveAs dialog box prompts for a filename, and lets the user enter the name in an edit control. Add the following **DIALOG** statement to the resource file:

```
SaveAs DIALOG 10, 10, 180, 53
STYLE DS_MODALFRAME | WS_CAPTION | WS_SYSMENU
CAPTION "Save As"
BEGIN
    LTEXT "Save As File &Name:", IDC_FILENAME, 4,  4,  72, 10
    LTEXT "",                    IDC_PATH,    84,  4,  92, 10
    EDITTEXT                     IDC_EDIT,     4, 16, 100, 12
    DEFPUSHBUTTON  "Save",       IDOK,       120, 16,  50, 14
    PUSHBUTTON     "Cancel",     IDCANCEL,   120, 36,  50, 14
END
```

The constants, IDC_PATH, IDC_FILENAME, IDC_EDIT, IDCANCEL, and IDOK, are the same as those used in the Open dialog box. Since the Open and SaveAs dialog boxes will never be open at the same time, there is no need to worry about conflicting control IDs.

10.8.3 Add Include Statements

You need to include additional C run-time include files to support the file input and output operations. Add the following statements to the beginning of the C-language source file:

```
#include <sys\types.h>
#include <sys\stat.h>
```

10.8.4 Add New Variables

The following global variables should be declared at the beginning of the file:

```
HANDLE hEditBuffer;              /* handle to editing buffer       */
HANDLE hOldBuffer;               /* old buffer handle              */
HANDLE hHourGlass;               /* handle to hourglass cursor     */
HANDLE hSaveCursor;              /* current cursor handle          */
int hFile;                       /* file handle                    */
int count;                       /* number of chars read or written */
PSTR pBuffer;                    /* address of read/write buffer   */
OFSTRUCT OfStruct;               /* information from OpenFile()    */
struct stat FileStatus;          /* information from fstat()       */
BOOL bChanges = FALSE;           /* TRUE if the file is changed    */
BOOL bSaveEnabled = FALSE;       /* TRUE if text in the edit buffer */
PSTR pEditBuffer;                /* address of the edit buffer     */

char Untitled[] =                /* default window title           */
    "Edit File - (untitled)";
```

The hEditBuffer variable holds the handle of the current editing buffer. This buffer, located in the application's heap, contains the current file text. To load a file, you allocate the buffer, load the file, then pass the buffer handle to the edit control. The hOldBuffer variable is used to replace an old buffer with a new one. The hHourGlass and hSaveCursor handles hold cursor handles for lengthy operations.

The hFile variable holds the file handle returned by the **OpenFile** function. The count variable holds a count of the number of characters to be read or written. The pBuffer variable is a pointer, and holds the address of the character that contains the characters to be read or written. The OfStruct structure holds information about the file.

The FileStatus structure holds information about the file. The bChanges variable is TRUE if the user has changed the contents of the file. The bSaveEnabled variable is TRUE if the user has given a valid name for the file to be saved. The Untitled variable holds the main window's caption, which changes whenever a new file is loaded.

10.8.5 Replace the WM_COMMAND Case

Replace the WM_COMMAND case so that it processes all File-menu commands except Print. The New command should clear the current filename and empty the edit control if there is any text in it. The Open command should retrieve the selected filename, open the file, and fill the edit control. The Save command should write the contents of the edit control back to the current file. Finally, the Save As command should prompt the user for a filename and write the contents of the edit control.

If the user chooses the New command and there is text in the current file that has been modified, you should prompt the user with a message box to determine whether the changes should be saved. Add the following statements to the WM_COMMAND case:

```
case IDM_NEW:
    if (!QuerySaveFile(hWnd))
        return (NULL);
    bChanges = FALSE;
    FileName[0] = 0;
    SetNewBuffer(hWnd, NULL, Untitled);
    break;
```

The locally defined QuerySaveFile function checks the file for changes and prompts the user to save the changes. If the changes are saved, the filename is cleared and the editing buffer is emptied by using the locally-defined SetNew-Buffer function.

If the user chooses the Open command and there is text in the current file that has been modified, you should prompt the user to determine whether the changes should be saved before opening the new file. Add the following statements to the WM_COMMAND case:

```
case IDM_OPEN:
    if (!QuerySaveFile(hWnd))
        return (NULL);
    lpOpenDlg = MakeProcInstance((FARPROC) OpenDlg, hInst);
    hFile = DialogBox(hInst, "Open", hWnd, lpOpenDlg);
    FreeProcInstance(lpOpenDlg);
    if (!hFile)
        return (NULL);
    hEditBuffer =
        LocalAlloc(LMEM_MOVEABLE | LMEM_ZEROINIT,
            FileStatus.st_size+1);
    if (!hEditBuffer) {
        MessageBox(hWnd, "Not enough memory.",
            NULL, MB_OK | MB_ICONHAND);
        return (NULL);
    }
    hSaveCursor = SetCursor(hHourGlass);
    pEditBuffer = LocalLock(hEditBuffer);
```

```
IOStatus = read(hFile, pEditBuffer, FileStatus.st_size);
close(hFile);
if (IOStatus != FileStatus.st_size) {
    sprintf(str, "Error reading %s.", FileName);
    SetCursor(hSaveCursor);          /* Remove the hourglass */
    MessageBox(hWnd, str, NULL,
        MB_OK | MB_ICONEXCLAMATION);
}
LocalUnlock(hEditBuffer);
sprintf(str, "EditFile - %s", FileName);
SetNewBuffer(hWnd, hEditBuffer, str);
SetCursor(hSaveCursor);              /* Restore the cursor */
break;
```

When the IDM_OPEN case is processed, the QuerySaveFile function checks the existing file for changes before displaying the Open dialog box. The **DialogBox** function returns a file handle to the open file. This handle is created in the OpenDlg dialog function. If the file can't be opened, the function returns NULL and processing ends. Otherwise, the **LocalAlloc** function allocates the space needed to load the file into memory. The amount of space needed is determined by the FileStatus structure, which is filled with information about the open file by the OpenDlg dialog function. If there is no available memory, a message box is displayed and processing ends. Otherwise, the **SetCursor** function displays the hourglass, the **LocalLock** function locks the new buffer, and the C run-time **read** function copies the contents of the file into memory. If the file was not read completely, a message box is displayed. **SetCursor** restores the cursor before the **MessageBox** function is called. The **LocalUnlock** function unlocks the editing buffer, and after a new window caption is created, the locally defined SetNew-Buffer function changes the editing buffer and caption.

If the user chooses the Save command and there is no current filename, carry out the same action as the Save As command. Add the following statements to the WM_COMMAND case:

```
case IDM_SAVE:
    if (!FileName[0])
        goto saveas;
    if (bChanges)
        SaveFile(hWnd);
    break;
```

The IDM_SAVE case checks for a filename and, if none exists, skips to the IDM_SAVEAS case. If a filename does exist, the locally defined SaveFile function saves the file only if changes have been made to it.

The Save As command should always prompt for a filename. You should save the file only if the user gives a valid filename. Add the following statements to the WM_COMMAND case:

```
case IDM_SAVEAS:
saveas:
    lpSaveAsDlg = MakeProcInstance(SaveAsDlg, hInst);
    Success = DialogBox(hInst, "SaveAs", hWnd, lpSaveAsDlg);
    FreeProcInstance(lpSaveAsDlg);
    if (Success == IDOK) {
        sprintf(str, "EditFile - %s", FileName);
        SetWindowText(hWnd, str);
        SaveFile(hWnd);
    }
    break;                          /* User canceled */
```

The **DialogBox** function displays the SaveAs dialog box. The **MakeProc-Instance** and **FreeProcInstance** functions create and free the procedure-instance address for the SaveAsDlg dialog function. The **DialogBox** function returns IDOK from the SaveAsDlg dialog function if the user enters a valid filename. The **SetWindowText** function then changes the window caption, and the Save-File function saves the contents of the editing buffer to the file.

The Exit command should now prompt the user to determine whether the current file should be saved. Also, to keep track of the changes to the file, you should process notification messages from the edit-control window. Modify the IDM_EXIT case and add the IDC_EDIT case to the WM_COMMAND case, as follows:

```
case IDM_EXIT:
    QuerySaveFile(hWnd);
    DestroyWindow(hWnd);
    break;

case IDC_EDIT:
    if (HIWORD(lParam) == EN_CHANGE)
        bChanges = TRUE;
    return (NULL);
```

10.8.6 Add the WM_QUERYENDSESSION and WM_CLOSE Cases

You need to process the WM_QUERYENDSESSION and WM_CLOSE messages to prevent the contents of your files from being lost when the user closes a file or ends a session. Add the following statements to the window function:

```
case WM_QUERYENDSESSION:       /* message: to end the session? */
    return (QuerySaveFile(hWnd));

case WM_CLOSE:                 /* message: close the window   */
    if (QuerySaveFile(hWnd))
        DestroyWindow(hWnd);
    break;
```

Windows sends a WM_QUERYENDSESSION message to the window function when the user has chosen to exit Windows. The session ends only if TRUE is returned. The QuerySaveFile function checks for changes to the file, saves them if desired, and returns TRUE or FALSE depending on whether the user canceled or confirmed the operation.

Windows sends the WM_CLOSE message to the window function when the user has chosen the Close command in the main window's system menu. The QuerySaveFile function carries out the same task as in the WM_QUERYENDSESSION message, but in order to complete the WM_CLOSE case, you must also destroy the main window by using the **DestroyWindow** function.

10.8.7 Modify the OpenDlg Dialog Function

You need to modify the IDOK case in the OpenDlg function in order to open and check the size of the file that is selected by the user. Add the following statements immediately after the call to the AddExt function in the IDOK case of the OpenDlg function:

```
if ((hFile = OpenFile(OpenName, (LPOFSTRUCT) &OfStruct,
        OF_READ)) < 0) {
    sprintf(str, "Error %d opening %s.",
        OfStruct.nErrCode, OpenName);
    MessageBox(hDlg, str, NULL, MB_OK | MB_ICONHAND);
}
else {
    fstat(hFile, &FileStatus);
    if (FileStatus.st_size > MAXFILESIZE) {
        sprintf(str,
            "Not enough memory to load %s.\n%s exceeds %ld bytes.",
            OpenName, OpenName, MAXFILESIZE);
        MessageBox(hDlg, str, NULL,
            MB_OK | MB_ICONHAND);
        return (TRUE);
    }
    strcpy(FileName, OpenName);
    EndDialog(hDlg, hFile);
    return (TRUE);
    }
```

The **OpenFile** function opens the specified file for reading and, if successful, returns a file handle. If the file cannot be opened, the case displays a message box containing the error number generated by DOS. If the file is opened, the C run-time **fstat** function copies information about the file into the FileStatus structure. The file size is checked to make sure the file does not exceed the maximum size given by the MAXFILESIZE constant. The case displays an error message if the size is too big. Otherwise, the **strcpy** function copies the new name to the FileName variable and the **EndDialog** function terminates the dialog box and returns the file handle, hFile, to the **DialogBox** function.

10.8.8 Add the SaveAsDlg Dialog Function

You need to supply a dialog function for the SaveAs dialog box. The function will retrieve a filename from the edit control and copy the name to the global variable, FileName. The dialog function should look like this:

```
int FAR PASCAL SaveAsDlg(hDlg, message, wParam, lParam)
HWND hDlg;
unsigned message;
WORD wParam;
LONG lParam;
{
    char TempName[128];

    switch (message) {
        case WM_INITDIALOG:
            if (!FileName[0])
                bSaveEnabled = FALSE;
            else {
                bSaveEnabled = TRUE;
                DlgDirList(hDlg, DefPath, NULL, IDC_PATH, 0x4010);
                SetDlgItemText(hDlg, IDC_EDIT, FileName);
                SendDlgItemMessage(hDlg, IDC_EDIT, EM_SETSEL, 0,
                    MAKELONG(0, 0x7fff));
            }
            EnableWindow(GetDlgItem(hDlg, IDOK), bSaveEnabled);
            SetFocus(GetDlgItem(hDlg, IDC_EDIT));
            return (FALSE);         /* FALSE since Focus was changed */
        case WM_COMMAND:
            switch (wParam) {
                case IDC_EDIT:
                    if (HIWORD(lParam) == EN_CHANGE && !bSaveEnabled)
                        EnableWindow(GetDlgItem(hDlg, IDOK),
                        bSaveEnabled = TRUE);
                    return (TRUE);
                case IDOK:
                    GetDlgItemText(hDlg, IDC_EDIT, TempName, 128);
                    if (CheckFileName(hDlg, FileName, TempName)) {
                        SeparateFile(hDlg, (LPSTR) str, (LPSTR) DefSpec,
                            (LPSTR) FileName);
                        if (str[0]) strcpy(DefPath, str);
                        EndDialog(hDlg, IDOK);
                    }
                    return (TRUE);
                case IDCANCEL:
                    EndDialog(hDlg, IDCANCEL);
                    return (TRUE);
            }
            break;
    }
    return (FALSE);
}
```

The WM_INITDIALOG case enables or disables the Save button. The button should be disabled if there is no current filename. The **EnableWindow** function, along with the bSaveEnabled variable, enables or disables the button. If there is a current filename, it should be the proposed name. The **SetDlgItemText** function copies the filename to the edit control, and the **SendDlgItemMessage** function selects the entire name for editing. The **DlgDirList** function sets the IDC_PATH control to the current directory. Since there is no list box to fill, no list-box ID is given.

The WM_COMMAND case processes notification messages from the controls in the dialog box. When the function receives the EN_CHANGE notification from the edit control, IDC_EDIT, it uses the **EnableWindow** function to enable the Save button, if it is not already enabled.

When the function receives a notification from the Save button, it uses the **GetDlgItemText** function to retrieve the filename in the edit control, then checks the validity of the filename by using the locally defined CheckFileName function. This function checks the filename to make sure it contains no path separators or wildcard characters. It then checks to see if the file already exists; if it does, CheckFileName uses the **MessageBox** function to ask the user whether the file should be overwritten. Finally, the dialog function uses the SeparateFile function to copy the filename to the DefSpec and DefPath variables.

10.8.9 Add Helper Functions

You need to add several functions to your C-language source file to support the EditFile application. These functions are as follows:

Function	Description
CheckFileName	Checks a filename for wildcards, adds the default filename extension if one is needed, and checks for the existence of the file.
SaveFile	Saves the contents of the editing buffer in a file.
QuerySaveFile	Prompts the user to save changes if the file has changed without having been saved.
SetNewBuffer	Frees the existing editing buffer and replaces it with a new one.

The CheckFileName function verifies that a filename is not empty and that it contains no wildcards. It also checks to see whether the file already exists by using the **OpenFile** function and the OF_EXIST option. If the file exists, CheckFileName prompts the user to see whether the file should be overwritten. Add the following statements:

```
BOOL CheckFileName(hWnd, pDest, pSrc)
HWND hWnd;
PSTR pDest, pSrc;
{
    PSTR pTmp;

    if (!pSrc[0])
        return (FALSE);       /* Indicates no filename was specified */

    pTmp = pSrc;
    while (*pTmp) {            /* Searches the string for wildcards */
        switch (*pTmp++) {
            case '*':
            case '?':
                MessageBox(hWnd, "Wildcards not allowed.",
                    NULL, MB_OK | MB_ICONEXCLAMATION);
                return (FALSE);
        }
    }

    AddExt(pSrc, DefExt);  /* Adds the default extension if needed */

    if (OpenFile(pSrc, (LPOFSTRUCT) &OfStruct, OF_EXIST) >= 0) {
        sprintf(str, "Replace existing %s?", pSrc);
        if (MessageBox(hWnd, str, "EditFile",
            MB_OKCANCEL | MB_ICONHAND) == IDCANCEL);
            return (FALSE);
    }
    strcpy(pDest, pSrc);
    return (TRUE);
}
```

The SaveFile function uses the OF_CREATE option of the **OpenFile** function in order to open a file for writing. The OF_CREATE option directs **OpenFile** to delete the existing contents of the file. The SaveFile function then retrieves a file-buffer handle from the edit control, locks the buffer, and copies the contents to the file. Add the following statements:

```
BOOL SaveFile(hWnd)
HWND hWnd;
{
    BOOL bSuccess;
    int IOStatus;                        /* result of a file write */

    if ((hFile = OpenFile(FileName, &OfStruct,
        OF_PROMPT | OF_CANCEL | OF_CREATE)) < 0) {
        sprintf(str, "Cannot write to %s.", FileName);
        MessageBox(hWnd, str, NULL, MB_OK | MB_ICONEXCLAMATION);
        return (FALSE);
    }
    hEditBuffer = SendMessage(hEditWnd, EM_GETHANDLE, 0, 0L);
    pEditBuffer = LocalLock(hEditBuffer);
```

```
    hSaveCursor = SetCursor(hHourGlass);
    IOStatus = write(hFile, pEditBuffer, strlen(pEditBuffer));
    close(hFile);
    SetCursor(hSaveCursor);
    if (IOStatus != strlen(pEditBuffer)) {
        sprintf(str, "Error writing to %s.", FileName);
        MessageBox(hWnd, str, NULL, MB_OK | MB_ICONHAND);
        bSuccess = FALSE;
    }
    else {
        bSuccess = TRUE;       /* Indicates the file was saved      */
        bChanges = FALSE;      /* Indicates changes have been saved */
    }
    LocalUnlock(hEditBuffer);
    return (bSuccess);
}
```

The EM_GETHANDLE message, sent by using the **SendMessage** function, directs the edit control to return the handle of its editing buffer. This buffer is located in local memory, so it is locked by using the **LocalLock** function. Once locked, the contents are written to the file by using the C run-time **write** function. The **SetCursor** function displays the hourglass cursor to indicate a lengthy operation. If **write** fails to write all bytes, the SaveFile function displays a message box. The **LocalUnlock** function unlocks the editing buffer before the SaveFile function returns.

The QuerySaveFile function checks for changes to the file and prompts the user to save or delete the changes, or cancel the operation. If the user wants to save the changes, the function prompts the user for a filename by using the SaveAs dialog box. Add the following statements:

```
BOOL QuerySaveFile(hWnd)
HWND hWnd;
{
    int Response;
    FARPROC lpSaveAsDlg;

    if (bChanges) {
        sprintf(str, "Save current changes: %s", FileName);
        Response = MessageBox(hWnd, str,
            "EditFile",  MB_YESNOCANCEL | MB_ICONEXCLAMATION);
        if (Response == IDYES) {
check_name:
            if (!FileName[0]) {
                lpSaveAsDlg = MakeProcInstance(SaveAsDlg, hInst);
                Response = DialogBox(hInst, "SaveAs",
                    hWnd, lpSaveAsDlg);
                FreeProcInstance(lpSaveAsDlg);
                if (Response == IDOK)
                    goto check_name;
                else
                    return (FALSE);
```

```
            }
            SaveFile(hWnd);
        }
        else if (Response == IDCANCEL)
            return (FALSE);
    }
    else
        return (TRUE);
}
```

The SetNewBuffer function retrieves and frees the editing buffer before allocating and setting a new editing buffer. It then updates the edit control window. Add the following statements to the C-language source file:

```
void SetNewBuffer(hWnd, hNewBuffer, Title)
HWND hWnd;
HANDLE hNewBuffer;
PSTR Title;
{
    HANDLE hOldBuffer;

    hOldBuffer = SendMessage(hEditWnd, EM_GETHANDLE, 0, 0L);
    LocalFree(hOldBuffer);
    if (!hNewBuffer)          /* Allocates a buffer if none exists */
        hNewBuffer = LocalAlloc(LMEM_MOVEABLE | LMEM_ZEROINIT, 1);

    SendMessage(hEditWnd, EM_SETHANDLE, hNewBuffer, 0L);
    InvalidateRect(hEditWnd, NULL, TRUE);    /* Updates the buffer */
    UpdateWindow(hEditWnd);
    SetWindowText(hWnd, Title);
    SetFocus(hEditWnd);
    bChanges = FALSE;
}
```

The new text will not be displayed until the edit control repaints its client area. The **InvalidateRect** function invalidates part of the edit control's client area. The NULL argument means that the entire control needs repainting, and TRUE specifies that the background should be erased before repainting. All of this prepares the control for painting. The **UpdateWindow** function causes Windows to send the edit control a WM_PAINT message immediately.

10.8.10 Export the SaveAsDlg Dialog Function

You need to export the SaveAsDlg dialog function. Add the following line to the **EXPORTS** statement in your module-definition file:

```
SaveAsDlg @4
```

10.8.11 Add Space to the Heap

You need to add extra space to the local heap. This space is required to support the edit control, which uses memory from the local heap to store its current text. Make the following change to the module-definition file:

```
HEAPSIZE 0xAFFF
```

This statement limits the size of the edit-control buffer to slightly less than 32,767 (32K – 1) bytes. Files larger than this cannot be opened.

10.8.12 Compile and Link

No changes are required to the make file. Compile and link the application, then start Windows and the EditFile application. Choose the Open command, select a file, and EditFile will read and display the file. If the file is larger than can fit in the window, you can use the DIRECTION keys to scroll left and right or up and down.

10.9 Summary

This chapter explained how to work with files in the Windows environment, and provided a list of file-management guidelines.

Because Windows is a multitasking system, your application needs to manage files carefully to avoid conflicts with other applications. You use the Windows **OpenFile** function to create, open, close and otherwise work with disk files. When performing file input and output, use the low-level, C run-time input and output functions rather than the C run-time stream input and output functions.

For more information on topics related to files, see the following:

Topic	Reference
A comparison of the Windows environment to the standard C environment	Guide to Programming: Chapter 1, "An Overview of the Windows Environment"
Using C and assembly language in a Windows application	*Guide to Programming*: Chapter 14, "C and Assembly Language"
The **OpenFile** message	*Reference, Volume 1*: Chapter 3, "System Services Interface Functions" and Chapter 4, "Functions Directory"

Chapter 11 Bitmaps

Your application can use bitmaps to display images that are otherwise too cumbersome to draw using GDI output functions. This chapter shows how to create and display bitmaps for monochrome as well as color displays.

This chapter covers the following topics:

- What is a bitmap?
- Creating bitmaps
- Displaying bitmaps
- Adding color to monochrome bitmaps
- Deleting bitmaps

This chapter also explains how to create a sample application, Bitmap, which illustrates many of the concepts explained in this chapter.

11.1 What is a Bitmap?

In general, the term "bitmap" refers to an image formed by a pattern of bits, rather than by a pattern of lines. In Microsoft Windows, there are two kinds of bitmaps:

- A "device-dependent" bitmap is a pattern of bits in memory which can be displayed on an output device. Because there is a close correlation between the bits in memory and the pixels on the display device, a memory bitmap is said to be device dependent. For such bitmaps, the way the bits are arranged in memory depends on the intended output device.
- A "device-independent" bitmap (DIB) describes the actual appearance of an image, rather than the way that image is internally represented by a particular display device. Because this external definition can be applied to any display device, it is referred to as device independent.

11.2 Creating Bitmaps

You create a bitmap by supplying GDI with the dimensions and color format of the bitmap, and, optionally, the initial value of the bitmap bits. GDI then returns a handle to the bitmap. You can use this handle in subsequent GDI functions to select and display the bitmap.

You can create bitmaps in the following ways:

- You can use the Windows SDKPaint application to draw the bitmap image and save it in a file. You then add the bitmap file to your application's resources. Your application loads the bitmap using the **LoadBitmap** function.
- Your application can first create a blank bitmap and then use GDI output functions to draw the bitmap bits.
- To hard-code a bitmap, your application can create a blank bitmap and initialize its bits using an array of bits.
- Your application can create a bitmap and initialize its bits using the image in an existing DIB.

The following sections explain how to use each of these methods to create bitmaps.

11.2.1 Creating and Loading Bitmap Files

You can create bitmaps with SDKPaint. SDKPaint lets you specify the dimensions of a bitmap, then fill it in by "painting" in the blank area with such tools as a brush, spray can, and even text. Any of these tools can produce images using colors from a palette of up to 28 colors, which you can define.

To create and load a bitmap using this method, follow these steps:

1. Start SDKPaint and create the bitmap by following the directions given in *Tools*.
2. After creating the bitmap image, save it in a file that has the filename extension .BMP.
3. In your application's resource script (.RC) file, add a **BITMAP** statement that defines that bitmap as an application resource.

   For example, the following statement specifies that the bitmap resource named "dog" resides in the file DOG.BMP:

   ```
   dog BITMAP DOG.BMP
   ```

   The name "dog" identifies the bitmap; the filename DOG.BMP specifies the file that contains the bitmap.

4. In your application's source file, load the bitmap using the **LoadBitmap** function.

   The **LoadBitmap** function takes the bitmap's resource name, loads the bitmap into memory, and returns a handle to the bitmap. For example, the following statement loads the bitmap resource named "dog", and stores the resulting bitmap handle in the variable hDogBitmap:

   ```
   hDogBitmap = LoadBitmap (hInstance, "dog");
   ```

5. Select the bitmap into a device context using the **SelectObject** function.

   For example, the following statement loads the bitmap specified by hDogBitmap into the device context specified by hMemoryDC:

   ```
   SelectObject(hMemoryDC, hDogBitmap);
   ```

6. Display the bitmap using the **BitBlt** function.

   For example, the following statement displays a copy of the bitmap in the memory device context hMemoryDC on the device represented by hDC:

   ```
   BitBlt (hDC, 10, 10, 100, 150, hMemoryDC, 0, 0, SRCCOPY)
   ```

   This example displays the bitmap beginning at location (10, 10) of the destination device context. The bitmap is 100 units wide and 150 units high. The bitmap is taken from the memory device context beginning at location (0,0). The SRCCOPY value specifies that Windows should copy the source bitmap to the destination.

11.2.2 Creating and Filling a Blank Bitmap

You can create a bitmap "on the fly" by creating a blank bitmap and then filling it in using GDI output functions. With this method, your application is not limited to external bitmap files, preloaded bitmap resources, or bitmaps that are hard-coded in your application source code.

Follow these general steps:

1. Create a blank bitmap by using the **CreateBitmap** or **CreateCompatibleBitmap** functions.
2. Select the bitmap into a memory device context using the **SelectObject** function.
3. Draw in the bitmap image using GDI output functions.

The following example creates a "star" bitmap by first making a bitmap that is compatible with the display, and then filling the compatible bitmap using the **Polygon** function:

```
HDC hDC;
HDC hMemoryDC;
HBITMAP hBitmap;
HBITMAP hOldBitmap;
POINT Points[5] = { 32,0, 16,63, 63,16, 0,16, 48,63 };
      .
      .
      .
❶ hDC = GetDC(hWnd);
❷ hMemoryDC = CreateCompatibleDC(hDC);
❸ hBitmap = CreateCompatibleBitmap(hDC, 64, 64);
❹ hOldBitmap = SelectObject(hMemoryDC, hBitmap);
❺ PatBlt(hMemoryDC, 0, 0, 64, 64, WHITENESS);
❻ Polygon(hMemoryDC, Points, 5);
❼ BitBlt (hDC, 0, 0, 64, hMemoryDC, 0, 0, SRCCOPY);
❽ SelectObject(hMemoryDC, hOldBitmap);
DeleteDC(hMemoryDC);
❾ ReleaseDC(hWnd, hDC);
```

In this example:

❶ The **GetDC** function retrieves a handle to the device context. The bitmap will be compatible with the display. (If you want a bitmap that is compatible with some other device, you should use the **CreateDC** function to retrieve a handle to that device.)

❷ The **CreateCompatibleDC** function creates the memory device context in which the image of the bitmap will be drawn.

❸ The **CreateCompatibleBitmap** function creates the blank bitmap. The size of the bitmap is set to 64 by 64 pixels. The actual number of bits in the bitmap depends on the color format of the display. If the display is a color display, the bitmap will be a color bitmap and might have many bits for each pixel.

❹ The **SelectObject** function selects the bitmap into the memory device context and prepares it for drawing. The handle of the previously selected bitmap is saved in the variable hOldBitmap.

❺ The **PatBlt** function clears the bitmap and sets all pixels white. This, or a similar function, is required since, initially, the image in a blank bitmap is undefined. You cannot depend on having a clean bitmap in which to draw.

❻ The **Polygon** function draws the star by using the endpoints specified in the array of structures, Points.

❼ The **BitBlt** function copies the bitmap from the memory device context to the display.

❽ The **SelectObject** and **DeleteDC** functions restore the previous bitmap and delete the memory device context. Once the bitmap has been drawn, the memory device context is no longer needed. You cannot delete a device context when any bitmap other than the context's original bitmap is selected.

❾ Finally, the **ReleaseDC** function releases the device context. The bitmap handle, hBitmap, may now be used in subsequent GDI functions.

11.2.3 Creating a Bitmap with Hard-Coded Bits

You can create a bitmap and set its initial image to an array of bitmap bits by using the **CreateDIBitmap** function. This function creates a memory bitmap of a given size with a device-dependent color format; it initializes the bitmap image by translating a device-independent bitmap definition into the device-dependent format required by the display device and copying this device-dependent information to the memory bitmap. Typically, this method is used to create small bitmaps for use with pattern brushes, but it can also be used to create larger bitmaps.

NOTE Unless the bitmap is monochrome (that is, a bitmap having a single color plane and one bit per pixel), the memory bitmap created by **CreateBitmap** is device-specific, and therefore might not be suitable for display on some devices.

The following example creates a 64-by-32-pixel, monochrome bitmap; the example initializes the bitmap by using the bits in the array Square.

```
HBITMAP hBitmap;
HDC hDC;
BYTE Square[] = {
0x00,0x00,0x00,0x00,0x00,0x00,0x00,0x00,
0x00,0x00,0x00,0x00,0x00,0x00,0x00,0x00,
0x00,0x00,0x00,0x00,0x00,0x00,0x00,0x00,
0x00,0x00,0x00,0x00,0x00,0x00,0x00,0x00,
0x00,0x00,0x00,0x00,0x00,0x00,0x00,0x00,
0x00,0x00,0x00,0x00,0x00,0x00,0x00,0x00,
0x00,0x00,0x00,0x00,0x00,0x00,0x00,0x00,
0x00,0x00,0x00,0x00,0x00,0x00,0x00,0x00,
0x00,0x00,0x00,0x00,0x00,0x00,0x00,0x00,
0x00,0x00,0x00,0x00,0x00,0x00,0x00,0x00,
0x00,0x00,0x00,0x00,0x00,0x00,0x00,0x00,
0x00,0x00,0xff,0xff,0xff,0xff,0x00,0x00,
0x00,0x00,0xff,0xff,0xff,0xff,0x00,0x00,
0x00,0x00,0xff,0xff,0xff,0xff,0x00,0x00,
0x00,0x00,0xff,0xff,0xff,0xff,0x00,0x00,
0x00,0x00,0xff,0xff,0xff,0xff,0x00,0x00,
0x00,0x00,0xff,0xff,0xff,0xff,0x00,0x00,
0x00,0x00,0xff,0xff,0xff,0xff,0x00,0x00,
0x00,0x00,0xff,0xff,0xff,0xff,0x00,0x00,
0x00,0x00,0xff,0xff,0xff,0xff,0x00,0x00,
```

```
0x00,0x00,0xff,0xff,0xff,0xff,0x00,0x00,
0x00,0x00,0x00,0x00,0x00,0x00,0x00,0x00,
0x00,0x00,0x00,0x00,0x00,0x00,0x00,0x00,
0x00,0x00,0x00,0x00,0x00,0x00,0x00,0x00,
0x00,0x00,0x00,0x00,0x00,0x00,0x00,0x00,
0x00,0x00,0x00,0x00,0x00,0x00,0x00,0x00,
0x00,0x00,0x00,0x00,0x00,0x00,0x00,0x00,
0x00,0x00,0x00,0x00,0x00,0x00,0x00,0x00,
0x00,0x00,0x00,0x00,0x00,0x00,0x00,0x00,
0x00,0x00,0x00,0x00,0x00,0x00,0x00,0x00,
0x00,0x00,0x00,0x00,0x00,0x00,0x00,0x00,
0x00,0x00,0x00,0x00,0x00,0x00,0x00,0x00 };
    .
    .
    .
HANDLE          hDibInfo;
PBITMAPINFO     pDibInfo;

      if (pDibInfo = (PBITMAPINFO)LocalAlloc(LMEM_FIXED,
                     sizeof(BITMAPINFOHEADER)+2*sizeof(RGBQUAD)))
      {
         HBRUSH hOldBrush,hBrush;
         pDibInfo->bmiHeader.biSize =
                                 (long)sizeof(BITMAPINFOHEADER);
         pDibInfo->bmiHeader.biWidth = 64L;
         pDibInfo->bmiHeader.biHeight = 32;
         pDibInfo->bmiHeader.biPlanes = 1;
         pDibInfo->bmiHeader.biBitCount = 1;
         pDibInfo->bmiHeader.biCompression=0L;
         pDibInfo->bmiHeader.biSizeImage=0L;
         pDibInfo->bmiHeader.biXPelsPerMeter=0L;
         pDibInfo->bmiHeader.biYPelsPerMeter=0L;
         pDibInfo->bmiHeader.biClrUsed=0L;
         pDibInfo->bmiHeader.biClrImportant=0L;
         pDibInfo->bmiColors[0].rgbRed = 0;
         pDibInfo->bmiColors[0].rgbGreen = 0;
         pDibInfo->bmiColors[0].rgbBlue = 0;
         pDibInfo->bmiColors[1].rgbRed = 0xff;
         pDibInfo->bmiColors[1].rgbGreen = 0xff;
         pDibInfo->bmiColors[1].rgbBlue = 0xff;
         hDC = GetDC(hWnd);
         hBitmap = CreateDIBitmap (hDC,
                         (LPBITMAPINFOHEADER)&(pDibInfo->bmiHeader),
                         CBM_INIT,
               (LPSTR) Square,
                  (LPBITMAPINFO)pDibInfo, DIB_RGB_COLORS);
         ReleaseDC (hWnd, hDC);
         DeleteObject(hBitmap);
         LocalFree((HANDLE)pDibInfo);
      }
```

The **CreateDIBitmap** function creates and initializes the bitmap before returning the bitmap handle. The width and height of the bitmap are 64 and 32 pixels, respectively. The bitmap has one bit for each pixel, making it a monochrome bitmap.

The Square array contains the bits used to initialize the bitmap. The **BITMAP-INFO** data structure determines how the bits in the array are interpreted. It defines the width and height of the bitmap, how many bits (1, 4, 8 or 24) are used in the array to represent each pixel, and a table of colors for the pixels. Since the Square array defines a monochrome bitmap, the bit count per pixel is one and the color table contains only two entries, one for black and one for white. If a given bit in the array is zero, then GDI draws a black pixel for that bit; if it is one, then GDI draws a white pixel.

Since the Square array defines a monochrome bitmap, you could also call **CreateBitmap** to create the bitmap:

```
hBitmap = CreateBitmap (64, 32, 1, 1, (LPSTR) Square);
```

This is possible because all monochrome memory bitmaps are device independent. For color bitmaps, however, **CreateBitmap** cannot use the same bitmap-bit specification as can **CreateDIBitmap**.

Once you have created and initialized the bitmap, you can use its handle in subsequent GDI functions. If you want to change the bitmap, you can draw in it by selecting it into a memory device context as described in Section 11.2.2, "Creating and Filling a Blank Bitmap." If you want to replace the bitmap image with another or change a portion of it, you can use the **SetDIBits** function to copy another array of bits into the bitmap. For example, the following function call replaces the current bitmap image with the bits in the array Circle:

```
BYTE Circle[] = {
      .
      .
      .
};

SetDIBits(hDC, hBitmap, 0, 32, (LPSTR) Circle,
        (LPBITMAPINFO)&myDIBInfo, DIB_RGB_COLORS);
```

The **SetDIBits** function copies the bits in the Circle array into the bitmap specified by the hBitmap variable. The array contains 32 scan lines, representing the image of a 64-by-32-pixel monochrome bitmap. If you want to retrieve the current bits in a bitmap before replacing them, you can use the **GetDIBits** function. It copies a specified number of scan lines from the bitmap into a device-independent bitmap specification. You can also use **GetBitmapBits** to retrieve bits from a monochrome bitmap.

Again, since the Circle array defines a monochrome bitmap, you could call **SetBitmapBits** instead to change the bitmap:

```
SetBitmapBits (hBitmap, 256, (LPSTR) Circle);
```

The preceding examples show how to create and modify a small bitmap. Typically you will not want to hard-code larger bitmaps in your application source code. Instead, you can store a larger bitmap in a device-independent bitmap file created by SDKPaint or other tools. A device-independent bitmap file consists of a **BITMAPFILEHEADER** data structure followed by a **BITMAPINFO** structure and an array of bytes that together define the bitmap.

The sample application ShowDIB demonstrates how to display device-independent bitmaps with colors controlled by a color palette. ShowDIB is located on the Sample Source Code disk, supplied with the SDK. See Chapter 19, "Color Palettes," for more information on Windows color palettes.

11.2.4 Drawing a Color Bitmap

Since hard-coding a color bitmap may require considerable effort, it is usually simpler to create a compatible bitmap and draw in it. For example, to create a color bitmap that has a red, green, and blue plaid pattern, you simply create a blank bitmap and use the **PatBlt** function, with the red, green, and blue brushes, to draw the pattern. This method has the advantage of generating a reasonable bitmap even if the display does not support color. This is because GDI provides dithered brushes for monochrome displays when a color brush is requested. A dithered brush is a unique pattern of pixels that represents a color when that color is not available for the device.

The following statements create the color bitmap by drawing it:

```
# define PATORDEST      0x00FA0089L
HDC hDC;
HDC hMemoryDC;
HBITMAP hBitmap;
HBITMAP hOldBitmap;
HBRUSH hRedBrush;
HBRUSH hGreenBrush;
HBRUSH hBlueBrush;
HBRUSH hOldBrush;
    .
    .
    .
hDC = GetDC(hWnd);
hMemoryDC = CreateCompatibleDC(hDC);
hBitmap = CreateCompatibleBitmap(hDC, 64, 32);
hOldBitmap = SelectObject(hMemoryDC, hBitmap);

hRedBrush = CreateSolidBrush(RGB(255,0,0));
hGreenBrush = CreateSolidBrush(RGB(0,255,0));
hBlueBrush = CreateSolidBrush(RGB(0,0,255));

PatBlt(hMemoryDC, 0, 0, 64, 32, BLACKNESS);
hOldBrush = SelectObject(hMemoryDC, hRedBrush);
PatBlt(hMemoryDC, 0, 0, 24, 11, PATORDEST);
```

```
PatBlt(hMemoryDC, 40, 10, 24, 12, PATORDEST);
PatBlt(hMemoryDC, 24, 22, 24, 11, PATORDEST);
SelectObject(hMemoryDC, hGreenBrush);
PatBlt(hMemoryDC, 24, 0, 24, 11, PATORDEST);
PatBlt(hMemoryDC, 0, 10, 24, 12, PATORDEST);
PatBlt(hMemoryDC, 40, 22, 24, 11, PATORDEST);
SelectObject(hMemoryDC, hBlueBrush);
PatBlt(hMemoryDC, 40, 0, 24, 11, PATORDEST);
PatBlt(hMemoryDC, 24, 10, 24, 12, PATORDEST);
PatBlt(hMemoryDC, 0, 22, 24, 11, PATORDEST);

BitBlt(hDC, 0, 0, 64, 32, hMemoryDC, 0, 0, SRCCOPY)

SelectObject(hMemoryDC, hOldBrush);
DeleteObject(hRedBrush);
DeleteObject(hGreenBrush);
DeleteObject(hBlueBrush);

SelectObject(hMemoryDC, hOldBitmap);
DeleteDC(hMemoryDC);
ReleaseDC(hWnd, hDC);
```

In this example, the **CreateSolidBrush** function creates the red, green, and blue brushes needed to make the plaid pattern. The **SelectObject** function selects each brush into the memory device context as that brush is needed, and the **PatBlt** function paints the colors into the bitmap. Each color is painted three times, each time into a small rectangle. In this example, the application instructs **PatBlt** to overlap the different color rectangles a little. Since the PATORDEST raster-operation code is given, **PatBlt** combines the brush color with the color already in the bitmap by using a Boolean OR operator. The result is a different color border around each rectangle. After the bitmap is complete, **BitBlt** copies it from the memory device context to the screen.

11.3 Displaying Bitmaps

Windows provides several ways to display a bitmap:

- You can display a memory bitmap by using the **BitBlt** function to copy the bitmap from the memory device context to a device surface.
- You can use the **StretchBlt** function to copy a stretched or compressed bitmap from a memory device context to a device surface.
- You can use the **CreatePatternBrush** function to create a brush that incorporates the bitmap. Any subsequent GDI functions that use the brush, such as **PatBlt**, will display that bitmap.
- You can use the **SetDIBitsToDevice** function to display a device-independent bitmap directly on the output device.

- You can display the bitmap in a menu. In such a case, the bitmap is used as a menu item that the user can choose to carry out an action. For details, see Chapter 7, "Menus."

This section explains each method of displaying a bitmap.

11.3.1 Using the BitBlt Function to Display a Memory Bitmap

You can display any bitmap by using the **BitBlt** function. This function copies a bitmap from a source to a destination device context. To display a bitmap with **BitBlt**, you need to create a memory device context and select the bitmap into it first. The following example displays the bitmap by using **BitBlt**:

```
HDC hDC, hMemoryDC;
    .
    .
    .
hDC = GetDC(hWnd);
hMemoryDC = CreateCompatibleDC(hDC);

hOldBitmap = SelectObject(hMemoryDC, hBitmap);

if (hOldbitmap)
{
   BitBlt(hDC, 100, 30, 64, 32, hMemoryDC, 0, 0, SRCCOPY);

   SelectObject(hMemoryDC, hOldBitmap);
}
DeleteDC(hMemoryDC);
ReleaseDC(hWnd, hDC);
```

The **GetDC** function specifies the device context for the client area of the window identified by the hWnd variable. The **CreateCompatibleDC** function creates a memory device context that is compatible with the device context. The **SelectObject** function selects the bitmap, identified by the hBitmap variable, into the memory device context and returns the previously selected bitmap. If **Select-Object** cannot select the bitmap, it returns zero.

The **BitBlt** function copies the bitmap from the memory device context to the screen device context. The function places the upper-left corner of the bitmap at the point (100,30). The entire bitmap, 64 bits wide by 32 bits high, is copied. The hDC and hMemoryDC variables identify the destination and source context-s, respectively. The constant, SRCCOPY, is the raster-operation code. It directs **BitBlt** to copy the source bitmap without combining it with patterns or colors al-ready at the destination.

The **SelectObject**, **DeleteDC**, and **ReleaseDC** functions clean up after the bit-map has been displayed. In general, when you have finished using memory and device contexts, you should release them as soon as possible—especially device contexts, which are a limited resource. Windows maintains a cache of device contexts that all applications draw from. If an application does not release a device context after using it, other applications might not be able to retrieve a context when needed. If you get a device context by using **GetDC**, you must later release it using **ReleaseDC**; if you instead create the device context using **CreateCompatibleDC**, you must later delete it using **DeleteDC**. Before deleting a device context, you must call **SelectObject**, since you must not delete a device context while any bitmap other than the context's original bitmap is selected.

In the previous example, the width and height of the bitmap were assumed to be 64 and 32 pixels, respectively. Another way to specify the width and height of the bitmap to be displayed is to retrieve them from the bitmap itself. You can do this by using the **GetObject** function, which fills a specified structure with the dimensions of the given object. For example, to retrieve the width and height of a bitmap, you would use the following statements:

```
BITMAP Bitmap;
     .
     .
     .
GetObject(hBitmap, sizeof(BITMAP), (LPSTR) &Bitmap);
```

The next example copies the width and height of the bitmap to the **bmWidth** and **bmHeight** fields of the structure, Bitmap. You can use these values in **BitBlt** as follows:

```
BitBlt(hDC, 100, 30, Bitmap.bmWidth, Bitmap.bmHeight,
    hMemoryDC, 0, 0, SRCCOPY);
```

The **BitBlt** function can display both monochrome and color bitmaps. No special steps are required to display bitmaps of different formats. However, you should be aware that **BitBlt** may convert the bitmap if its color format is not the same as that of the destination device. For example, when displaying a color bitmap on a monochrome display, **BitBlt** converts the pixels having the current background color to white and all other pixels to black.

11.3.2 Stretching a Bitmap

Your bitmaps are not limited to their original size. You can stretch or compress them by using the **StretchBlt** function in place of **BitBlt**. For example, you can double the size of a 64-by-32-pixel bitmap by using the following statement:

```
StretchBlt(hDC, 100, 30, 128, 64, hMemoryDC,
        0, 0, 64, 32, SRCCOPY);
```

The **StretchBlt** function has two additional parameters that **BitBlt** does not. In particular, **StretchBlt** specifies the width and height of the source bitmap. The first width and height, given as 128 and 64 pixels in the previous example, apply only to the final size of the bitmap on the destination device context.

To compress a bitmap, **StretchBlt** removes pixels from the copied bitmap. This means that some of the information in the bitmap is lost when it is displayed. To minimize the loss, you can set the current stretching mode to tell **StretchBlt** to combine some of the information with the pixels that will be displayed. The stretching mode can be one of the following:

Mode	Purpose
WHITEONBLACK	Preserves white pixels at the expense of black pixels; for example, a white outline on a black background.
BLACKONWHITE	Preserves black pixels at the expense of white pixels; for example, a black outline on a white background.
COLORONCOLOR	Displays color bitmaps. Attempting to combine colors in a bitmap can lead to undesirable effects.

The **SetStretchBltMode** function sets the stretching mode. In the following example, **SetStretchBltMode** sets the stretching mode to WHITEONBLACK:

```
SetStretchBltMode(hDC, WHITEONBLACK);
```

11.3.3 Using a Bitmap in a Pattern Brush

You can use bitmaps in a brush by creating a pattern brush. Once the pattern brush is created, you can select the brush into a device context and use the **PatBlt** function to copy it to the screen; or the **Rectangle**, **Ellipse**, and other drawing functions can use the brush to fill interiors. When Windows draws with a pattern brush, it fills the specified area by repeatedly copying the bitmap horizontally and vertically as necessary. It does not adjust the size of the bitmap to fit in the area as the **StretchBlt** function does.

If you use a bitmap in a pattern brush, the bitmap should be at least 8 pixels wide by 8 pixels high—the default pattern size used by most display drivers. (You can use large bitmaps, but only the upper-left, 8-by-8 corner will be used.) You may hard-code the bitmap, create and draw it, or load it as a resource. In any case, once you have the bitmap handle, you can create the pattern brush by using the **CreatePatternBrush** function. The following example loads a bitmap and uses it to create a pattern brush:

```
hBitmap = LoadBitmap(hInstance, "checks");
hBrush = CreatePatternBrush(hBitmap);
```

Once a pattern brush is created, you can select it into a device context by using the **SelectObject** function:

```
hOldBrush = SelectObject(hDC, hBrush);
```

Since the bitmap is part of the brush, this call to the **SelectObject** function does not affect the device context's selected bitmap.

After selecting the brush, you can use the **PatBlt** function to fill a specified area with the bitmap. For example, the following statement fills the upper-left corner of a window with the bitmap:

```
PatBlt(hDC, 0, 0, 100, 100, PATCOPY);
```

The PATCOPY raster operation directs **PatBlt** to completely replace the destination image with the pattern brush.

You can also use a pattern brush as a window's background brush. To do this, simply assign the brush handle to the **hbrBackground** field of the window-class structure as in the following example:

```
pWndClass->hbrBackground = CreatePatternBrush(hBitmap);
```

Thereafter, Windows uses the pattern brush when it erases the window's background. You can also change the current background brush for a window class by using the **SetClassWord** function. For example, if you want to use a new pattern brush after a window has been created, you can use the following statement:

```
SetClassWord(hWnd, GCW_HBRBACKGROUND, hBrush);
```

Be aware that this statement changes the background brush for all windows of this class. If you only want to change the background for one window, you need to explicitly process the WM_ERASEBKGND messages that the window receives. The following example shows how to process this message:

```
RECT Rect;
HBRUSH hOldBrush;
    .
    .
    .
case WM_ERASEBKGND:
    UnrealizeObject(hMyBkgndBrush);
    hOldBrush = SelectObject(wParam, hMyBkgndBrush);
    GetUpdateRect(wParam, (LPRECT)&Rect, FALSE);
    PatBlt(wParam, Rect.left, Rect.top,
        Rect.right - Rect.left, Rect.bottom - Rect.top,
        PATCOPY);
    SelectObject(wParam, hOldBrush);
    break;
```

The WM_ERASEBKGND message passes a handle to a device context in the *wParam* parameter. The **SelectObject** function selects the desired background brush into the device context. The **GetUpdateRect** function retrieves the area that needs to be erased (this is not always the entire client area). The **PatBlt** function copies the pattern, overwriting anything already in the update rectangle. The final **SelectObject** function restores the previous brush to the device context.

The **UnrealizeObject** function is used in the preceding example. Whenever your application or the user moves a window in which you have used or will use a pattern brush, you need to align your pattern brushes to the new position by using the **UnrealizeObject** function. This function resets a brush's drawing origin so that any patterns displayed after the move match the patterns displayed before the move.

You can use the **DeleteObject** function to delete a pattern brush when it is no longer needed. This function does not, however, delete the bitmap along with the brush. To delete the bitmap, you need to use **DeleteObject** again and specify the bitmap handle.

11.3.4 Displaying a Device-Independent Bitmap

One of the advantages of device-independent bitmaps is that you can display them directly without having to create an intermediate memory bitmap. The **SetDIBitsToDevice** function sets all or part of a device-independent bitmap directly to an output device, significantly reducing the memory required to display the bitmap. When you call **SetDIBitsToDevice** to display a bitmap, you supply it this information:

- The device context of the target output device
- The location in the device context where the bitmap will appear
- The size of the bitmap on the output device
- The number of scan lines in the source bitmap buffer from which you are copying the bitmap
- The location of the first pixel in the source bitmap to copy to the output device
- The device-independent bitmap information structure and a buffer containing the bitmap to be displayed
- Whether the color table of the DIB specification contains literal RGB color values or logical-palette indexes

NOTE The origin for device-independent bitmaps is the lower-left corner of the bitmap, not the upper-left corner as for other graphics operations.

The following is an example of how an application calls **SetDIBitsToDevice**:

```
SetDIBitsToDevice(hDC, 0, 0, lpbi->bmciHeader.bcWidth,
        lpbi->bmciHeader.bcHeight, 0, 0, 0,
        lpbi->bmciHeader.bcHeight,
        pBuf, (LPBITMAPINFO)lpbi,
        DIB_RGB_COLORS );
```

In this example, hDC identifies the device context of the target output device; **SetDIBitsToDevice** uses this information to identify the device surface and determine the correct color format for the device bitmap.

The next two parameters specify the point on the display surface where **SetDIBitsToDevice** will begin drawing the bitmap; in this case, it is the origin of the device context itself. The next two parameters supply the width and height of the bitmap.

The sixth and seventh parameters, both of which are set to zero in this example, specify the first pixel in the source bitmap to be set on the display device; again, since both are zero, **SetDIBitsToDevice** begins with the first pixel in the bitmap buffer.

The next two parameters are used for banding purposes. The first of these two parameters is set to zero, indicating that the beginning scan line should be the first in the buffer; the second of the two is set to the height of the bitmap. As a result, the entire source bitmap will be set on the display surface in a single band.

The actual bitmap bits are contained in the pBuf buffer, and the *lpbi* parameter supplies the **BITMAPINFO** data structure that describes the color format of the source bitmap.

The last parameter is a usage flag that indicates whether the bitmap color table contains actual RGB color values or indexes into the currently realized logical palette. DIB_RGB_COLORS specifies that the color table contains explicit color values.

11.3.5 Using a Bitmap as a Menu Item

You can use a bitmap as an item in a menu. To do so, replace the original menu item text, defined in the .RC file, with the bitmap. (You cannot specify a bitmap as a menu item in the .RC file.)

Chapter 7, "Menus," explains how to replace a menu item with a bitmap.

11.4 Adding Color to Monochrome Bitmaps

If your computer has a color display, you can add color to a monochrome bitmap by setting the foreground and background colors of the display context. The foreground and background colors specify which colors the white and black bits of the bitmap will have when displayed. You set the foreground and background colors by using the **SetTextColor** and **SetBkColor** functions. The following example shows how to set the foreground color to red and the background color to green:

```
SetTextColor(hDC, RGB(255,0,0));
SetBkColor(hDC, RGB(0,255,0));
```

The hDC variable holds the handle to the device context. The **SetTextColor** function sets the foreground color to red. The **SetBkColor** function sets the background color to green. The **RGB** utility creates an RGB color value by using the three specified values. Each value represents an intensity for each of the primary display colors—red, green, and blue—with the value 255 representing the highest intensity, and zero, the lowest. You can produce colors other than red and green by combining the color intensities. For example, the following statement creates a yellow RGB value:

```
RGB(255,255,0)
```

Once the foreground and background colors are set, no further action is required. You can display a bitmap (as described earlier) and Windows will automatically add the foreground and background colors. The foreground color is applied to the white bits (the bits set to 1) and the background color to the black bits (the bits set to zero). Note that the background mode, as specified by the **SetBkMode** function, does not apply to bitmaps. Also, the foreground and background colors do not apply to color bitmaps.

When displayed in color, the bitmap named "dog" will be red, the background will be green.

11.5 Deleting Bitmaps

A bitmap, like any resource, occupies memory while in use. After you have finished using a bitmap or before your application terminates, it is important that you delete the bitmaps you have created in order to make that memory available to other applications. To delete a bitmap, first remove it from any device context in which it is currently selected. Then, delete it by using the **DeleteObject** function.

The following example deletes the bitmap identified by the *hBitmap* parameter, after removing it as the currently selected bitmap in the memory device context identified by the *hMemoryDC* parameter:

```
SelectObject(hMemoryDC, hOldBitmap);
DeleteObject(hBitmap);
```

The **SelectObject** function removes the bitmap from selection by replacing it with a previous bitmap identified by the *hOldBitmap* parameter. The **DeleteObject** function deletes the bitmap. Thereafter, the bitmap handle in the *hBitmap* parameter is no longer valid and must not be used.

11.6 A Sample Application: Bitmap

This sample shows how to incorporate a variety of bitmap operations in an application. In particular, it shows how to do the following:

- Load and display a monochrome bitmap
- Create and display a color bitmap
- Stretch and compress a bitmap using the mouse
- Set the stretching mode
- Create and use a pattern brush
- Use a pattern brush for the window background

In this application, the user specifies (by using the mouse) where and how the bitmap will be displayed. If the user drags the mouse while holding down the left button, and then releases that button, the application uses the **StretchBlt** function to fill the selected rectangle with the current bitmap. If the user clicks the right button, the application uses the **BitBlt** function to display the bitmap.

To create the Bitmap application, copy and rename the source files for the Generic application, then make the following modifications:

1. Add constant definitions and a function declaration to the include file.
2. Add two monochrome bitmaps, created by using SDKPaint, to the resource script file.
3. Add Bitmap, Pattern, and Mode menus to the resource script file.
4. Add global and local variables.
5. Add the WM_CREATE case to the window function to create bitmaps and add bitmaps to the menus.
6. Modify the WM_DESTROY case in the window function to delete bitmaps.
7. Add the WM_LBUTTONUP, WM_MOUSEMOVE, and WM_LBUTTONDOWN cases to the window function to create a selection rectangle and display bitmaps.
8. Add the WM_RBUTTONUP case to the window function to display bitmaps.
9. Add the WM_ERASEBKGND case to the window function to erase the client area.
10. Modify the WM_COMMAND case to support the menus.
11. Modify the **LINK** command line in the make file to include the SELECT.LIB library file.
12. Compile and link the application.

NOTE Rather than typing the code presented in the following sections, you might find it more convenient to simply examine and compile the sample source files provided with the SDK.

The following sections explain each step in detail.

11.6.1 Modify the Include File

Add the following function declarations and constant definitions to the include file:

```
#define IDM_BITMAP1              200
#define IDM_BITMAP2              201
#define IDM_BITMAP3              202

#define IDM_PATTERN1             300
#define IDM_PATTERN2             301
#define IDM_PATTERN3             302
#define IDM_PATTERN4             303

#define IDM_BLACKONWHITE         400
#define IDM_WHITEONBLACK         401
#define IDM_COLORONCOLOR         402

#define PATORDEST        0x00FA0089L

HBITMAP MakeColorBitmap(HWND);
```

11.6.2 Add the Bitmap Resources

Add two **BITMAP** statements to your resource script file. The two statements add the bitmaps "dog" and "cat" to your application resources. Add the following statements:

```
dog BITMAP dog.bmp
cat BITMAP cat.bmp
```

The "dog" bitmap is the white outline of a dog on a black background. The "cat" bitmap is the black outline of a cat on a white background.

11.6.3 Add the Bitmap, Pattern, and Mode Menus

You need to add a **MENU** statement to your resource script file. This statement defines the Bitmap, Pattern, and Mode menus used to choose the various bitmaps and modes that are used in the application. Add the following **MENU** statement to the resource script file:

```
BitmapMenu MENU
BEGIN
    POPUP "&Bitmap"
    BEGIN
        MENUITEM "", IDM_BITMAP1
    END

    POPUP "&Pattern"
    BEGIN
        MENUITEM "", IDM_PATTERN1
    END

    POPUP "&Mode"
    BEGIN
        MENUITEM "&WhiteOnBlack", IDM_WHITEONBLACK, CHECKED
        MENUITEM "&BlackOnWhite", IDM_BLACKONWHITE
        MENUITEM "&ColorOnColor", IDM_COLORONCOLOR
    END
END
```

The Bitmap and Pattern menus each contain a single **MENUITEM** statement. This statement defines a command that serves as a placeholder only. The application will add the actual commands to use in the menu by using the **AppendMenu** function.

11.6.4 Add Global and Local Variables

You need to declare the pattern arrays, the bitmap handles and context handles, and other global variables used to create and display the bitmaps. To define these global variables, add the following statements to the beginning of your source file:

```
BYTE White[] =  { 0xFF, 0xFF, 0xFF, 0xFF, 0xFF, 0xFF, 0xFF, 0xFF };
BYTE Black[] =  { 0x00, 0x00, 0x00, 0x00, 0x00, 0x00, 0x00, 0x00 };
BYTE Zigzag[] = { 0xFF, 0xF7, 0xEB, 0xDD, 0xBE, 0x7F, 0xFF, 0xFF };
BYTE CrossHatch[] = { 0xEF, 0xEF, 0xEF, 0xEF, 0x00, 0xEF, 0xEF, 0xEF };

HBITMAP hPattern1;
HBITMAP hPattern2;
HBITMAP hPattern3;
HBITMAP hPattern4;
HBITMAP hBitmap1;
HBITMAP hBitmap2;
HBITMAP hBitmap3;
HBITMAP hMenuBitmap1;
HBITMAP hMenuBitmap2;
HBITMAP hMenuBitmap3;
HBITMAP hBitmap;
HBITMAP hOldBitmap;
```

```
HBRUSH hBrush;                /* brush handle                         */
WORD fStretchMode;             /* type of stretch mode to use         */

HDC hDC;                      /* handle to device context             */
HDC hMemoryDC;                /* handle to memory device context      */
BITMAP Bitmap;                /* bitmap structure                     */

BOOL bTrack = FALSE;          /* TRUE if user is selecting a region */
RECT Rect;

WORD wPrevBitmap = IDM_BITMAP1;
WORD wPrevPattern = IDM_PATTERN1;
WORD wPrevMode = IDM_WHITEONBLACK;
WORD wPrevItem;

int Shape = SL_BLOCK; /* shape to use for the selection rectangle */
```

The pattern arrays White, Black, Zigzag, and CrossHatch contain the bits defining the 8-by-8-pixel bitmap images. The variables hPattern1, hPattern2, hPattern3, and hPattern4 hold the bitmap handles of the brush patterns. The variables hBitmap1, hBitmap2, and hBitmap3 hold the bitmap handles of the bitmaps to be displayed. The variables hMenuBitmap1, hMenuBitmap2, and hMenuBitmap3 hold the bitmap handles of bitmaps to be displayed in the Bitmaps menu. The variables hBrush, hBitmap, and fStretchMode hold the current background brush, bitmap, and stretching mode. The variables hDC, hMemoryDC, and hOldBitmap hold handles used with the memory device context. The Bitmap structure holds the dimensions of the current bitmap. The bTrack variable is used to indicate a selection in progress. The Rect structure holds the current selection rectangle. The variables wPrevBitmap, wPrevPattern, wPrevMode, and wPrevItem hold the menu IDs of the previously chosen bitmap, pattern, and stretching mode. These are used to place and remove checkmarks in the menus.

Add the following local variables to the MainWndProc function:

```
HMENU   hMenu;
HBRUSH  hOldBrush;
HBITMAP hOurBitmap;
```

11.6.5 Add the WM_CREATE Case

You need a WM_CREATE case and supporting variable and function declarations to create or load the bitmaps and to set the menus. The WM_CREATE case creates four 8-by-8-pixel, monochrome bitmaps to be used as patterns in a pattern brush for the window background. It also creates or loads three 64-by-32-pixel bitmaps to be displayed in the window. To let the user choose a bitmap or pattern for viewing, the WM_CREATE case adds them to the Bitmap and Pattern menus by using the **AppendMenu** function. Finally, the case sets the initial values of the brush, bitmap, and stretching modes and creates the memory device context from which the bitmaps are copied.

The WM_CREATE case creates the four patterns by using the **CreateBitmap** function. It loads two bitmaps, "dog" and "cat", and creates a third by using the MakeColorBitmap function defined within the application. Once the patterns and bitmaps have been created, the WM_CREATE case creates pop-up menus, appends the patterns and bitmaps to the menus, and replaces the existing Bitmap and Pattern menus with the new pop-up menus. Next, the hBrush, hBitmap, and fStretchMode variables are set to the initial values for the background brush, bitmap, and stretching modes. Finally, the case creates the memory device context from which the bitmaps will be copied to the display. Add the following statements to your window function:

```
case WM_CREATE: /* message: create window */

    hPattern1 = CreateBitmap(8, 8, 1, 1, (LPSTR) White);
    hPattern2 = CreateBitmap(8, 8, 1, 1, (LPSTR) Black);
    hPattern3 = CreateBitmap(8, 8, 1, 1, (LPSTR) Zigzag);
    hPattern4 = CreateBitmap(8, 8, 1, 1, (LPSTR) CrossHatch);

    hBitmap1 = LoadBitmap(hInst, "dog");
    hBitmap2 = LoadBitmap(hInst, "cat");
    hBitmap3 = MakeColorBitmap(hWnd);

    hMenuBitmap1 = LoadBitmap(hInst, "dog");
    hMenuBitmap2 = LoadBitmap(hInst, "cat");
    hMenuBitmap3 = MakeColorBitmap(hWnd);

    hMenu = CreateMenu();
    AppendMenu(hMenu, MF_STRING | MF_CHECKED, IDM_PATTERN1, "&White");
    AppendMenu(hMenu, MF_STRING, IDM_PATTERN2, "&Black");
    AppendMenu(hMenu, MF_BITMAP, IDM_PATTERN3, (LPSTR) (LONG) hPattern3);
    AppendMenu(hMenu, MF_BITMAP, IDM_PATTERN4, (LPSTR) (LONG) hPattern4);
    ModifyMenu(GetMenu(hWnd), 1, MF_POPUP | MF_BYPOSITION, hMenu, "&Pattern");

    hMenu = CreateMenu();

    AppendMenu(hMenu, MF_BITMAP | MF_CHECKED, IDM_BITMAP1, (LPSTR) (LONG)
            hMenuBitmap1);
    AppendMenu(hMenu, MF_BITMAP, IDM_BITMAP2, (LPSTR) (LONG) hMenuBitmap2);
    AppendMenu(hMenu, MF_BITMAP, IDM_BITMAP3, (LPSTR) (LONG) hMenuBitmap3);

    ModifyMenu(GetMenu(hWnd), Ø, MF_POPUP | MF_BYPOSITION, "&Bitmap", hMenu);

    hBrush = CreatePatternBrush(hPattern1);
    fStretchMode = IDM_BLACKONWHITE;

    hDC = GetDC(hWnd);
    hMemoryDC = CreateCompatibleDC(hDC);
    ReleaseDC(hWnd, hDC);
    hOldBitmap = SelectObject(hMemoryDC, hBitmap1);
    GetObject(hBitmap1, 16, (LPSTR) &Bitmap);

    break;
```

The **CreateBitmap** and **LoadBitmap** functions work as described in earlier sections in this chapter. The MakeColorBitmap function is created for this application. It creates and draws a color bitmap, using the same method described in Section 11.2.2, "Creating and Filling a Blank Bitmap." The statements of this function are given later in this section. Notice that each bitmap is loaded or created twice. This is required since no single bitmap handle may be selected into two device contexts at the same time. To display in a menu requires a selection, and to display in the client area also requires a selection.

The **CreateMenu** function creates an empty menu and returns a handle to the menu. The **ChangeMenu** functions that specify the pattern handles add the patterns as menu items to the new menu. The MF_BITMAP option specifies that a bitmap will be added. The **CheckMenuItem** function places a checkmark next to the current menu item, and the last **ChangeMenu** function replaces the existing Pattern menu. The same steps are then repeated for the Bitmap menu.

The **CreateCompatibleDC** function creates a memory device context that is compatible with the display. The **SelectObject** function selects the current bitmap into the memory device context so that it is ready to be copied to the display. The **GetObject** function copies the dimensions of the bitmap into the Bitmap structure. The structure can then be used in subsequent **BitBlt** and **StretchBlt** functions to specify the width and height of the bitmap.

The following MakeColorBitmap function creates a color bitmap by creating a bitmap that is compatible with the display, then paints a plaid color pattern by using red, green, and blue brushes and the **PatBlt** function. Add the following function definition to the end of your source file:

```
HBITMAP MakeColorBitmap(hWnd)
HWND hWnd;
{
    HDC hDC;
    HDC hMemoryDC;
    HBITMAP hBitmap;
    HBITMAP hOldBitmap;
    HBRUSH hRedBrush;
    HBRUSH hGreenBrush;
    HBRUSH hBlueBrush;
    HBRUSH hOldBrush;

    hDC = GetDC(hWnd);
    hMemoryDC = CreateCompatibleDC(hDC);
    hBitmap = CreateCompatibleBitmap(hDC, 64, 32);
    hOldBitmap = SelectObject(hMemoryDC, hBitmap);
    hRedBrush = CreateSolidBrush(RGB(255,0,0));
    hGreenBrush = CreateSolidBrush(RGB(0,255,0));
    hBlueBrush = CreateSolidBrush(RGB(0,0,255));

    PatBlt(hMemoryDC, 0, 0, 64, 32, BLACKNESS);
    hOldBrush = SelectObject(hMemoryDC, hRedBrush);
    PatBlt(hMemoryDC, 0, 0, 24, 11, PATORDEST);
```

```
    PatBlt(hMemoryDC, 40, 10, 24, 12, PATORDEST);
    PatBlt(hMemoryDC, 20, 21, 24, 11, PATORDEST);
    SelectObject(hMemoryDC, hGreenBrush);
    PatBlt(hMemoryDC, 20, 0, 24, 11, PATORDEST);
    PatBlt(hMemoryDC, 0, 10, 24, 12, PATORDEST);
    PatBlt(hMemoryDC, 40, 21, 24, 11, PATORDEST);
    SelectObject(hMemoryDC, hBlueBrush);
    PatBlt(hMemoryDC, 40, 0, 24, 11, PATORDEST);
    PatBlt(hMemoryDC, 20, 10, 24, 12, PATORDEST);
    PatBlt(hMemoryDC, 0, 21, 24, 11, PATORDEST);

    SelectObject(hMemoryDC, hOldBrush);
    DeleteObject(hRedBrush);
    DeleteObject(hGreenBrush);
    DeleteObject(hBlueBrush);
    SelectObject(hMemoryDC, hOldBitmap);
    DeleteDC(hMemoryDC);
    ReleaseDC(hWnd, hDC);
    return (hBitmap);
}
```

This function carries out the same steps described at the end of Section 11.2.3, "Creating a Bitmap with Hard-Coded Bits."

11.6.6 Modify the WM_DESTROY Case

You need to delete the bitmaps, patterns, brushes, and memory device context you have created before terminating the application. You delete bitmaps, patterns, and brushes by using the **DeleteObject** function. You delete the memory device context by using the **DeleteDC** function. Modify the WM_DESTROY case so that it looks like this:

```
case WM_DESTROY: /* message: destroy window */
    SelectObject(hMemoryDC, hOldBitmap);
    DeleteDC(hMemoryDC);
    DeleteObject(hBrush);
    DeleteObject(hPattern1);
    DeleteObject(hPattern2);
    DeleteObject(hPattern3);
    DeleteObject(hPattern4);
    DeleteObject(hBitmap1);
    DeleteObject(hBitmap2);
    DeleteObject(hBitmap3);
    DeleteObject(hMenuBitmap1);
    DeleteObject(hMenuBitmap2);
    DeleteObject(hMenuBitmap3);

    PostQuitMessage(0);
    break;
```

11.6.7 Add WM_LBUTTONUP, WM_MOUSEMOVE, and WM_LBUTTONDOWN Cases

You need to add WM_LBUTTONUP, WM_MOUSEMOVE, and WM_LBUTTONDOWN cases to the window function to let the user select a rectangle in which to copy the current bitmap. These cases use the selection functions (described in Chapter 20, "Dynamic-Link Libraries") to create a selection rectangle and supply feedback to the user. The WM_LBUTTONUP case then uses the **StretchBlt** function to fill the rectangle. Add the following statements to your window function:

```
case WM_LBUTTONDOWN: /* message: left mouse button pressed */

    bTrack = TRUE;
    SetRectEmpty((LPRECT) &Rect);
    StartSelection(hWnd, MAKEPOINT(lParam), (LPRECT) &Rect,
        (wParam & MK_SHIFT) ? (SL_EXTEND | Shape) : Shape);
    break;

case WM_MOUSEMOVE: /* message: mouse movement */

    if (bTrack)
        UpdateSelection(hWnd, MAKEPOINT(lParam), (LPRECT) &Rect,
Shape);
    break;

case WM_LBUTTONUP: /* message: left mouse button released */

    bTrack = FALSE;
    EndSelection(MAKEPOINT(lParam), (LPRECT) &Rect);
    ClearSelection(hWnd, (LPRECT) &Rect, Shape);

    hDC = GetDC(hWnd);
    SetStretchBltMode(hDC, fStretchMode);
    StretchBlt(hDC, Rect.left, Rect.top,
        Rect.right - Rect.left, Rect.bottom - Rect.top,
        hMemoryDC, 0, 0,
        Bitmap.bmWidth, Bitmap.bmHeight,
        SRCCOPY);
    ReleaseDC(hWnd, hDC);
    break;
```

To use these functions, you also must include the SELECT.H file (defined in Chapter 20, "Dynamic-Link Libraries"). Add the following statement to the beginning of your source file:

```
#include "SELECT.H"
```

11.6.8 Add the WM_RBUTTONUP Case

You need to add a WM_RBUTTONUP case to display the current bitmap by using the **BitBlt** function. Add the following statements to your window function:

```
case WM_RBUTTONUP: /* message: right mouse button released */

    hDC = GetDC(hWnd);
    BitBlt(hDC, LOWORD(lParam), HIWORD(lParam),
        Bitmap.bmWidth, Bitmap.bmHeight,
        hMemoryDC, 0, 0, SRCCOPY);
    ReleaseDC(hWnd, hDC);
    break;
```

11.6.9 Add the WM_ERASEBKGND Case

You need to add a WM_ERASEBKGND case to make sure the selected background brush is used. Add the following statements to your window function:

```
case WM_ERASEBKGND: /* message: erase background */

    UnrealizeObject(hBrush);
    hOldBrush = SelectObject(wParam, hBrush);
    GetClientRect(hWnd, (LPRECT) &Rect);
    PatBlt(wParam, Rect.left, Rect.top,
        Rect.right-Rect.left, Rect.bottom-Rect.top,
        PATCOPY);
    SelectObject(wParam, hOldBrush);
    return TRUE;
```

The hOldBrush variable is declared as a local variable. The **UnrealizeObject** function sets the pattern alignment if the window has moved. The **SelectObject** function sets the background brush and the **GetClientRect** function determines which part of the client area needs to be erased. The **PatBlt** function copies the pattern to the update rectangle. The final **SelectObject** function restores the previous brush.

11.6.10 Modify the WM_COMMAND Case

You need to change the WM_COMMAND case to support the Bitmap, Pattern, and Mode menus. In the window function, replace the WM_COMMAND case with the following statements:

```
case WM_COMMAND: /* message: Windows command */
    switch (wParam) {
```

```
case IDM_ABOUT:
    lpProcAbout = MakeProcInstance (About, Inst);
    DialogBox (hInst,
          "AboutBox",
          hWnd,
          lpProcAbout);
     FreeProcInstance (lpProcAbout);
     break;

case IDM_BITMAP1:
    wPrevItem = wPrevBitmap;
    wPrevBitmap = wParam;
    GetObject(hBitmap1, 16, (LPSTR) &Bitmap);
    SelectObject(hMemoryDC, hBitmap1);
    break;

case IDM_BITMAP2:
    wPrevItem = wPrevBitmap;
    wPrevBitmap = wParam;
    GetObject(hBitmap2, 16, (LPSTR) &Bitmap);
    SelectObject(hMemoryDC, hBitmap2);
    break;

case IDM_BITMAP3:
    wPrevItem = wPrevBitmap;
    wPrevBitmap = wParam;
    GetObject(hBitmap3, 16, (LPSTR) &Bitmap);
    hOurBitmap = SelectObject(hMemoryDC, hBitmap3);
    break;

case IDM_PATTERN1:
    wPrevItem = wPrevPattern;
    wPrevPattern = wParam;
    DeleteObject(hBrush);
    hBrush = CreatePatternBrush(hPattern1);
    InvalidateRect(hWnd, (LPRECT) NULL, TRUE);
    UpdateWindow(hWnd);
    break;

case IDM_PATTERN2:
    wPrevItem = wPrevPattern;
    wPrevPattern = wParam;
    DeleteObject(hBrush);
    hBrush = CreatePatternBrush(hPattern2);
    InvalidateRect(hWnd, (LPRECT) NULL, TRUE);
    UpdateWindow(hWnd);
    break;

case IDM_PATTERN3:
    wPrevItem = wPrevPattern;
    wPrevPattern = wParam;
    DeleteObject(hBrush);
    hBrush = CreatePatternBrush(hPattern3);
```

```
                InvalidateRect(hWnd, (LPRECT) NULL, TRUE);
                UpdateWindow(hWnd);
                break;

            case IDM_PATTERN4:
                wPrevItem = wPrevPattern;
                wPrevPattern = wParam;
                DeleteObject(hBrush);
                hBrush = CreatePatternBrush(hPattern4);
                InvalidateRect(hWnd, (LPRECT) NULL, TRUE);
                UpdateWindow(hWnd);
                break;

            case IDM_BLACKONWHITE:
                wPrevItem = wPrevMode;
                wPrevMode = wParam;
                fStretchMode = BLACKONWHITE;
                break;

            case IDM_WHITEONBLACK:
                wPrevItem = wPrevMode;
                wPrevMode = wParam;
                fStretchMode = WHITEONBLACK;
                break;

            case IDM_COLORONCOLOR:
                wPrevItem = wPrevMode;
                wPrevMode = wParam;
                fStretchMode = COLORONCOLOR;
                break;
        }

        CheckMenuItem(GetMenu(hWnd), wPrevItem, MF_UNCHECKED);
        CheckMenuItem(GetMenu(hWnd), wParam, MF_CHECKED);
        break;
```

Note that this new WM_COMMAND case handles the IDM_ABOUT case using a **switch** statement rather than an **if** statement.

11.6.11 Modify the Make File

The resource file BITMAP.RES depends on the bitmap files DOG.BMP and CAT.BMP. To ensure that the Resource Compiler updates BITMAP.RES whenever DOG.BMP or CAT.BMP change, add the following to the make file:

```
BITMAP.RES: BITMAP.RC BITMAP.H DOG.BMP CAT.BMP
   RC -r BITMAP.RC
```

You need to modify the **LINK** command line in the make file to include the SELECT.LIB library file. This file contains the import declarations for the selection routines that are used with the WM_LBUTTONUP, WM_MOUSEMOVE, and WM_LBUTTONDOWN cases. You create the library as described in Chapter 20, "Dynamic-Link Libraries."

To include the SELECT.LIB library file, modify the **LINK** command line so that it looks like this:

```
LINK /NOD BITMAP, , , SLIBCEW LIBW SELECT.LIB, BITMAP.DEF
```

11.6.12 Compile and Link

After making the necessary changes, compile and link the Bitmap application. Start Windows, then start the Bitmap application.

To display the "dog" or "cat" bitmaps, depress the left mouse button, drag the mouse to form a rectangle, and release the button.

Use the menus to change the background and the stretching mode. Note the effect of the stretching mode on the "dog" and "cat" bitmaps.

11.7 Summary

This chapter explained how to create and use monochrome and color bitmaps. A bitmap is an image formed by a pattern of bits. In Windows, there are two kinds of bitmaps: device-dependent and device-independent. The simplest way to use a bitmap is to draw it using SDKPaint, then add it to your application's resources and load it using the **LoadBitmap** function. There are also several methods your application can use to create and display bitmaps during run time. The application can use GDI output to draw each bit. It can also initialize the bits in a bitmap by using an array of bits, or by using the image in an existing device-independent bitmap.

Windows provides several functions for displaying and manipulating bitmaps. You can also use a bitmap as a menu item, or as a menu checkmark.

For more information on topics related to bitmaps, see the following:

Topic	Reference
Selection functions	*Guide to Programming*: Chapter 6, "The Cursor, the Mouse, and the Keyboard"
	Guide to Programming: Chapter 20, "Dynamic-Link Libraries"
Using bitmaps in menus	*Guide to Programming*: Chapter 7, "Menus"

Topic	Reference
Bitmap functions	*Reference, Volume 1*: Chapter 2, "Graphics Device Interface Functions" and Chapter 4, "Functions Directory"
Using SDKPaint	*Tools*: Chapter 4, "Designing Images: SDKPaint"

Chapter 12 Printing

Most applications provide a way for users to get printed copies of their program data. In most environments, your application must deal with the varied capabilities and requirements of many different printers. In Microsoft Windows, your application need not provide any printer-specific code; it can simply print to the current printer. Windows, and the Windows printer drivers, translate your application's print request to information each printer can use.

This chapter covers the following topics:

- Printing in the Windows environment
- Getting information about the printer
- Printing a line of text
- Printing a bitmap
- Processing printing errors
- Canceling print operations
- Using banding to print graphics images

This chapter also explains how to create a sample application, PrntFile, that illustrates many of the concepts explained in the chapter.

12.1 Printing in the Windows Environment

In Windows, your application does not print by interacting directly with the printer. Instead, you print by sending output to a printer device context. This means that your application need not concern itself with each printer's specific capabilities or requirements.

Printing in Windows is handled by GDI. In general, the procedure for printing information is similar to that for displaying information; you get a handle to a device context, then send output to that device context. Normally, an application follows these steps in order to print to the current printer:

1. The application first retrieves information about the current printer, such as its type, device driver, and printer port, from the WIN.INI initialization file.

   This information is necessary in order to create a device context for the current printer.

2. When you send output to a printer device context, Windows activates the print spooler to manage your print request.
3. Your application uses printer escapes to communicate with the printer's device driver.

12.1.1 Using Printer Escapes

Your application uses escapes to communicate with the device driver associated with the printer. These sequences tell the device driver what to do, and also gather printer-specific information, such as page size, for the application. To send escape sequences to the device driver, the application uses the **Escape** function.

For example, to tell the printer device driver to start a print request, use the **Escape** function with the STARTDOC escape. The following example sends the STARTDOC escape to the printer device context identified by the variable hPrinterDC; it starts a print request named "My Print Request".

```
Escape(hPrinterDC, STARTDOC, 0, (LPSTR) "My Print Request", 0L);
```

When sending output to the printer, you follow the same general rules as for other types of GDI output. If you are printing text, or primitives such as rectangles, arcs, and circles, you can send them directly to the printer device context. You can also send text and primitives to a memory device context. This lets you create complex images before sending them to the printer.

12.2 Retrieving Information About the Current Printer

In order to create a printer device context, you need information about the printer, such as its type and the computer port to which it is connected. The Windows Control Panel application adds information about the current printer to the **device=** field in the **[windows]** section of the WIN.INI file. Any application can retrieve this information by using the **GetProfileString** function. You can then use the information with the **CreateDC** function to create a printer device context for a particular printer on a particular computer port.

Printer information from the WIN.INI file consists of three fields, separated by commas:

- The type of the current printer (for example, "EPSON")
- The device driver for the current printer (for example, "EPSON FX-80")
- The current printer port (for example, LPT1:)

The following example shows how to retrieve the printer information and divide the fields into separate strings:

```
char pPrintInfo[80];
LPSTR lpTemp;
LPSTR lpPrintType;
LPSTR lpPrintDriver;
LPSTR lpPrintPort;
     .
     .
     .
❶ GetProfileString("windows",
                   "device",
                    pPrintInfo,
                   (LPSTR) NULL, 80);
lpTemp = lpPrintType = pPrintInfo;
lpPrintDriver = lpPrintPort = 0;
❷ while (*lpTemp) {
    ❸ if (*lpTemp == ',') {
        *lpTemp++ = 0;
        ❹ while (*lpTemp == ' ')
            lpTemp++;
        if (!lpPrintDriver)
            lpPrintDriver = lpTemp;
        else {
            lpPrintPort = lpTemp;
            break;
        }
    }
    else
        lpTemp=AnsiNext(lpTemp);
}

❺ hPr = CreateDC(lpPrintDriver,
                 pPrinterType,
                 lpPrintPort,
                 (LPSTR) NULL);
     .
     .
     .
}
```

In this example:

❶ The **GetProfileString** function retrieves the **device=** field from the **[windows]** section of the WIN.INI file. The function then copies the line to the pPrintInfo array.

❷ A **while** statement divides the line into three separate fields: the printer type, the printer device-driver name, and the printer port.

❸ Because the fields are separated by commas, an **if** statement checks for a comma and, if necessary, replaces the comma with a zero in order to terminate the field.

❹ Another **while** statement skips any leading spaces in the next field.

Each pointer—lpPrintType, lpPrintDriver, and lpPrintPort—receives the address of the beginning of its respective field.

❺ These pointers are then used in the **CreateDC** function to create a printer device context for the current printer.

12.3 Printing a Line of Text

Printing a single line of text requires the following steps:

1. Create the device context for the printer.
2. Start the print request.
3. Print the line.
4. Start a new page.
5. End the print request.
6. Delete the device context.

The following example shows how to print a single line of text on an Epson FX-80 printer that is connected to the printer port, LPT1:

```
❶ hPr = CreateDC("EPSON",
                 "EPSON FX-80",
                 "LPT1:",
                 (LPSTR) NULL);

if (hPr != NULL) {
    ❷ Escape(hPr, STARTDOC, 5, (LPSTR) "Test", 0L);
    ❸ TextOut(hPr, 10, 10, "A single line of text.", 22);
    ❹ Escape(hPr, NEWFRAME, 0, 0L, 0L);
    ❺ Escape(hPr, ENDDOC, 0, 0L, 0L);
    ❻ DeleteDC(hPr);
}
```

In this example:

❶ The **CreateDC** function creates the device context for the printer, and returns a handle to the printer device context. This example stores the handle in the variable hPr. When calling **CreateDC**, an application must supply the first three parameters; the fourth parameter can be set to NULL. In this example, the application supplies the following parameters:

- The first parameter specifies the name of the device driver, "EPSON".

- The second parameter specifies the name of the printer device driver, "EPSON FX-80".
- The third parameter specifies the printer port, "LPT1:".
- The last parameter to **CreateDC** specifies how to initialize the printer. NULL specifies the default print settings. (Chapter 17, "Print Settings," explains how to specify print settings that differ from the default.)

❷ The **Escape** function starts the print request by sending the STARTDOC escape sequence to the device context. The name "Test" identifies the request; the third parameter is the length of the string "Test," plus a null terminator. Because the other parameter is not used, it is set to zero.

❸ **TextOut** copies the line of text to the printer. The line will be placed starting at the coordinates (10,10) on the printer paper (the printer coordinates are always relative to the upper-left corner of the paper). The default units are printer pixels.

❹ The NEWFRAME escape completes the page and signals the printer to advance to the next page. Because the other parameters are not used, they are set to zero.

❺ The ENDDOC escape signals the end of the print request. Because the other parameters are not used, they are set to zero.

❻ The **DeleteDC** function deletes the printer device context.

NOTE You should not expect the line of text to be printed immediately. The spooler collects all output for a print request before sending it to the printer, so actual printing does not begin until after the ENDDOC escape.

12.4 Printing a Bitmap

Printing a bitmap is similar to printing a line of text. To print a bitmap, follow these steps:

1. Create a memory device context that is compatible with the bitmap.
2. Load the bitmap and select it into the memory device context.
3. Start the print request.
4. Use the **BitBlt** function to copy the bitmap from the memory device context to the printer.
5. End the print request.
6. Remove the bitmap from the memory device context and delete the device context.

The following example shows how to print a bitmap named “dog” that has been added to the resource file:

```
HDC hDC;
HDC hMemoryDC;
HDC hPr;
BITMAP Bitmap;
        .
        .
        .

❶ hDC = GetDC(hWnd);
hMemoryDC = CreateCompatibleDC(hDC);
ReleaseDC(hWnd, hDC);

❷ hBitmap = LoadBitmap(hInstance, "dog");
❸ GetObject(hBitmap, sizeof(BITMAP), (LPSTR) &Bitmap);
❹ hOldBitmap = SelectObject(hMemoryDC, hBitmap);

❺ hPr = CreateDC("EPSON",
                "EPSON FX-80",
                "LPT1:",
                (LPSTR) NULL);

if (hPr != NULL) {
    Escape (hPr, STARTDOC, 4, (LPSTR) "Dog", 0L);
    ❻ BitBlt(hPr, 10, 30,
        Bitmap.bmWidth,
        Bitmap.bmHeight,
        hMemDC, 0, 0, SRCCOPY);
    ❼ Escape(hPr, NEWFRAME, 0, 0L, 0L);
    Escape(hPr, ENDDOC, 0, 0L, 0L);
    DeleteDC(hPr);
}

❽ SelectObject(hMemoryDC, hOldBitmap);
DeleteDC(hMemoryDC);
DeleteObject(hBitmap);
```

In this example:

❶ The application retrieves the current window’s display context using the **GetDC** function. The **CreateCompatibleDC** function then creates a memory device context that is compatible with that display context. After creating the memory device context, the application releases the window’s display context using the **ReleaseDC** function.

❷ The **LoadBitmap** function loads the bitmap “dog” from the application’s resources.

❸ The **GetObject** function retrieves information about the bitmap, such as its height and width. These values are used later in the **BitBlt** function.

❹ The **SelectObject** function selects the bitmap into the memory device context.

❺ The statements for creating the printer device context and starting the print request are identical to those used in the example that printed a line of text.

❻ To send the bitmap image to the printer, the application uses the **BitBlt** function. **BitBlt** copies the bitmap from the memory device context to the printer, placing the bitmap at the coordinates (10,30). (The **BitBlt** function takes the place of the **TextOut** function, used in the previous example to print a line of text.)

❼ The statements that send the NEWFRAME and ENDDOC escape sequences are identical to those used in the previous example.

❽ After the print request is complete, the **SelectObject** and **DeleteDC** functions remove the bitmap from selection and delete the memory device context. Since the bitmap is no longer needed, the **DeleteObject** function removes it from memory.

12.5 Processing Errors During Printing

Although GDI and the spooler attempt to report all printing errors to the user, your application must be prepared to report out-of-disk and out-of-memory conditions. When there is an error in processing a particular escape, such as STARTDOC or NEWFRAME, the **Escape** function returns a value less than zero. Out-of-disk and out-of-memory errors usually occur on a NEWFRAME escape. In this case, the return value includes an SP_NOTREPORTED bit. If the bit is clear, GDI has already notified the user. If the bit is set, the application needs to notify the user. The bit is typically set for general-failure, out-of-disk-space, and out-of-memory errors.

The following example shows how to process unreported errors during printing:

```
int status;
.
.
.

status = Escape(hPrDC, NEWFRAME, 0, 0L, 0L);

❶ if (status < 0) {   /* Any unreported errors? */
      if (status & SP_NOTREPORTED) {   /* Yes */
         ❷ switch (status) {
              case SP_OUTOFDISK:
                   /* inform user of situation
                      and perform any necessary processing */
                   break;
```

```
                case SP_OUTOFMEMORY:
                    /* inform user of situation
                       and perform any necessary processing */
                    break;
                default:
                    /* inform user of situation
                       and perform any necessary processing */
                    break;
            }
        }
    ❸ else   /* Reported, but may need further action */
            switch (status|SP_NOTREPORTED) {
                case SP_OUTOFDISK:
                    /* perform any necessary processing */
                    break;
                case SP_OUTOFMEMORY:
                    /* perform any necessary processing */
                    break;
            }
}
```

In this example:

❶ The first **if** statement checks to see if the value that the **Escape** function returns, status, is less than zero and the SP_NOTREPORTED bit is set. (When Windows sets the SP_NOTREPORTED bit, it indicates that this error has not been reported to the user.) If these two conditions are met, then the application must process the unreported error.

❷ In this example, the application uses a **switch** to provide special responses to the SP_OUTOFDISK error and the SP_OUTOFMEMORY error. For all other unreported errors, the application simply provides a general failure alert.

❸ If the status variable is less than zero but SP_NOTREPORTED is not set, then Windows has already reported the error to the user. However, the application can still process these reported errors.

In most cases, the correct response to an unreported error is to display a message box explaining the error and to terminate the print request. If the error has already been reported, you can terminate the request, then restart it after additional disk or memory space has been made available.

12.6 Canceling a Print Operation

Applications should always give the user a chance to cancel a lengthy printing operation. A common way to do this is to display a dialog box when the printing operation begins. During printing, the user can click the dialog's Cancel button to cancel the print operation.

To provide a dialog box that lets the user cancel a printing operation:

1. In your application's resource script (.RC) file, define a modeless AbortDlg dialog box that lets the user cancel a print operation.
2. In your application source code, provide a dialog function to drive the AbortDlg dialog box.
3. In your application source code, provide an Abort function that processes messages for the AbortDlg dialog box.
4. Modify your application's printing procedure so that it displays the AbortDlg dialog box and correctly processes messages.

The sections that follow describe each step in detail.

12.6.1 Defining an Abort Dialog Box

In your application's resource script file, provide a dialog-box template for the Abort dialog box. For example:

```
AbortDlg DIALOG 20,20,90, 64
STYLE DS_MODALFRAME | WS_CAPTION | WS_SYSMENU
CAPTION "PrntFile"
BEGIN
   DefPushButton "Cancel",         IDCANCEL,     29, 44, 32, 14, WS_GROUP
   Ctext     "Sending",           -1,            0,  8, 90,  8
   Ctext     "text",              IDC_FILENAME, 0, 18, 90,  8
   Ctext     "to print spooler.", -1,            0, 28, 90,  8
END
```

12.6.2 Defining an Abort Dialog Function

In your application source code, provide a dialog function for the Abort dialog box. The function should process the WM_INITDIALOG and WM_COMMAND messages. To let the user choose the Cancel button with the keyboard, the function takes control of the input focus when the dialog box is initialized. It then ignores all messages until a WM_COMMAND message appears. Command input causes the function to destroy the window and set the abort flag to TRUE. The following example shows the required statements for the dialog function:

```
BOOL bAbort=FALSE;      /* global variable */
.
.
.
int FAR PASCAL AbortDlg(hWnd, msg, wParam, lParam)
HWND hWnd;
unsigned msg;
WORD wParam;
```

```
LONG lParam;
{

/* Watch for Cancel button, RETURN key,
    ESCAPE key, or SPACE BAR */
    if (msg == WM_COMMAND) {

/* User has aborted operation */
        bAbort = TRUE;

/* Destroy Abort dialog box */
        DestroyWindow(hWnd);
        return (TRUE);
    }
    else if (msg == WM_INITDIALOG) {

/* Need input focus for user input */
        SetFocus(hWnd);
        return (TRUE);
    }
    return (FALSE);
}
```

12.6.3 Defining an Abort Function

In your application code, provide an abort function to process messages for the Abort dialog box.

An abort function retrieves messages from the application queue and dispatches them if they are intended for the Abort dialog box. The function continues to loop until it encounters the WM_DESTROY message or until the print operation is complete.

Applications that make lengthy print requests must pass an abort function to GDI to handle special situations during printing operations. The most common situation occurs when a printing operation fills the available disk space before the spooler can copy the data to the printer. Since the spooler can continue to print even though disk space is full, GDI calls the abort function to see if the application wants to cancel the print operation or simply wait until disk space is free.

To specify the abort function, first get the procedure-instance address for the function:

```
lpAbortProc = MakeProcInstance (AbortProc, hInst);
```

Then call the **Escape** function with the SETABORTPROC value and the Abort function's address:

```
Escape(hDC, SETABORTPROC, 0, lpAbortProc, 0L);
```

GDI will then call the abort function during spooling. An abort function must have the following form:

```
int FAR PASCAL AbortProc(hPr, Code)
➊ HDC hPr;
➋ int Code;
```

where:

➊ The hPr argument is a handle to the printer device context.

➋ The Code argument specifies the nature of the call. It can take one of two values:

Value	Meaning
SP_OUTOFDISK	Spooler has run out of disk space while spooling the data file. The printing operation will continue if the application waits for disk space to become free.
0	Spooler operation is continuing without error.

Once GDI has called the abort function, the function can return TRUE to continue the spooler operation immediately, or return FALSE to cancel the printing operation. Most abort functions call the **PeekMessage** function to temporarily yield control, then return TRUE to continue the print operation. Yielding control typically gives the spooler enough time to free some disk space.

If the abort function returns FALSE, the printing operation is canceled and an error value is returned by the application's next call to the **Escape** function.

IMPORTANT If your application encounters a printing error or a canceled print operation, it must not attempt to terminate the operation by using the **Escape** function with either the ENDDOC or ABORTDOC escape. GDI automatically terminates the operation before returning the error value.

The following example shows the statements required for the abort function:

```
int FAR PASCAL AbortProc(hPr, Code)
HDC hPr;    /* for multiple printer
               display contexts */
int Code;   /* for printing status */
{
    MSG msg;
```

```
/* Process messages intended
   for the abort dialog box */
    while (PeekMessage((LPMSG) &msg,
           NULL, NULL, NULL, PM_REMOVE))
        if (!IsDialogMessage(hAbortDlgWnd,
                             (LPMSG) &msg)) {
            TranslateMessage((LPMSG) &msg);
            DispatchMessage((LPMSG) &msg);
        }

/* bAbort is TRUE (return is FALSE)
   if the user has aborted */
    return (!bAbort);
}
```

12.6.4 Performing an Abortable Print Operation

Before beginning a print operation, your application should do the following in order to let the user cancel the operation:

1. Define an abort function as described in the preceding section.
2. Use the **MakeProcInstance** function to get the procedure-instance address for the abort function.

When your application begins a print operation, it should do the following:

1. Use the **Escape** function to specify the abort function the application will use during the print operation. When calling **Escape**, specify the SETABORT-PROC value and the procedure-instance address of the application's abort function.
2. Use the **CreateDialog**, **ShowWindow**, and **UpdateWindow** functions to create and display the Abort dialog box.
3. Use the **EnableWindow** function to disable your parent window.
4. Start the normal print operation, but check the return value from the **Escape** function after each NEWFRAME escape call. If the return value is less than zero, the user has canceled the operation or an error has occurred.
5. Use the **DestroyWindow** function to destroy the Abort dialog box, if necessary. (Windows destroys the box automatically if the user cancels the print operation.)
6. Use the **EnableWindow** function to reenable the parent window.

See the PrntFile sample application, included on the *Guide to Programming* sample disk, for an illustration of how an application performs these steps.

12.6.5 Canceling a Print Operation with the ABORTDOC Escape

You can use the ABORTDOC escape to cancel a print operation, even if you do not have an abort function or an Abort dialog box. Applications that do not have an abort function can use the ABORTDOC escape to cancel the operation at any time. Applications that do have abort functions can use the ABORTDOC escape only before the first NEWFRAME or NEXTBAND escape.

12.7 Using Banding to Print Images

Banding is a printing technique used to print full-page graphics on raster devices such as dot-matrix printers. In banding, an application prints an image by dividing the image into several bands (or slices) and sending each band to the printer separately. Banding lets you print complex graphics images without first creating the complete image in memory. This can reduce the memory requirements for printing and enhance system performance while printing operations are in effect. You can use banding with any printing device that has banding capability.

To use banding to print an image, follow these steps:

1. Use the **CreateDC** function to retrieve a device context for the printer.
2. Use the **GetDeviceCaps** function to make sure the printer is a banding device:

   ```
   if (GetDeviceCaps(hPrinterDC, RASTERCAPS) & RC_BANDING)
   ```

3. Use the **Escape** function and the NEXTBAND escape to retrieve the coordinates of a band:

   ```
   Escape(hPrinterDC, NEXTBAND, 0, (LPSTR) NULL, (LPRECT) &rcRect);
   ```

   The function sets the rcRect structure to the coordinates of the current band. Coordinates are in device units, and all subsequent GDI calls are clipped to this rectangle.
4. Check the rcRect structure to see if it is an empty rectangle. The empty rectangle marks the end of the banding operation. If it is empty, terminate the banding operation.
5. Use the **DPtoLP** function to translate the rcRect points from device units to logical units.

   ```
   DPtoLP(hPr, (LPRECT) &rcRect, 2);
   ```

6. Use GDI output and other functions to draw within the band. To save time, the application should carry out only those GDI calls that affect the current band. If an application does not need to save time, GDI will clip all output that does not appear in the band, so no special action is required.
7. Repeat steps 4 through 6.

Once the banding operation is complete, use the **DeleteDC** function to remove the printer device context.

The following example shows how to print using banding:

```
hPr = CreateDC("EPSON",
               "EPSON FX-80",
               "LPT1:",
               (LPSTR) NULL);

if (hPr != NULL) {
    if (GetDeviceCaps(hPr, RASTERCAPS) & RC_BANDING) {
        Escape(hPr, STARTDOC, 4, (LPSTR) "Dog", (LPSTR)NULL);
        Escape(hPr, NEXTBAND, 0, (LPSTR)NULL, (LPRECT) &rcRect);
        while (!IsRectEmpty(&rcRect)) {
            DPtoLP(hPr, (LPRECT) &rcRect, 2);

            /* Place your output function here.
             * To save time, use rcRect to determine
             * which functions need to be called for
             * this band.
            */

            Escape(hPr, NEXTBAND, 0, (LPSTR)NULL, (LPRECT) &rcRect);
        }
        Escape(hPr, NEWFRAME, 0, (LPSTR)NULL, (LPSTR)NULL);
        Escape(hPr, ENDDOC, 0, (LPSTR)NULL, (LPSTR)NULL);
    }
    DeleteDC(hPr);
}
```

12.8 A Sample Application: PrntFile

This section explains how to add printing capability to the EditFile application, described in Chapter 10, "File Input and Output," by copying the current text from the edit control and printing it by using the methods described in this chapter. To add printing capability, copy and rename the EditFile sources to PrntFile, then modify the sources as follows:

1. Add an AbortDlg dialog-box template to the resource script file.
2. Add new variables for printing.
3. Add the IDM_PRINT case to the WM_COMMAND case.
4. Create the AbortDlg dialog function and AbortProc function.
5. Add the GetPrinterDC function.
6. Export the AbortDlg dialog function and AbortProc function.
7. Compile and link the application.

This example shows how to print the contents of the edit control, including the statements required to support the abort function and the dialog function for the Abort dialog box.

NOTE Rather than typing the code provided in the following sections, you might find it more convenient to simply examine and compile the sample source files provided with the SDK.

12.8.1 Add an AbortDlg Dialog Box

You need a new dialog box to support printing. The AbortDlg dialog box permits the user to cancel a printing operation by choosing the Cancel button. Add the following **DIALOG** statement to the resource file:

```
AbortDlg DIALOG 20,20,90, 64
STYLE DS_MODALFRAME | WS_CAPTION | WS_SYSMENU
CAPTION "PrntFile"
BEGIN
   DefPushButton "Cancel",        IDCANCEL,    29, 44, 32, 14, WS_GROUP
   Ctext    "Sending",           -1,           0,  8, 90,  8
   Ctext    "text",              IDC_FILENAME, 0, 18, 90,  8
   Ctext    "to print spooler.", -1,           0, 28, 90,  8
END
```

12.8.2 Add Variables for Printing

You need to declare new variables to support printing. Add the following declarations to the beginning of your source file:

```
HDC hPr;                   /* handle for printer device context     */
int LineSpace;             /* spacing between lines                 */
int LinesPerPage;          /* lines per page                        */
int CurrentLine;           /* current line                          */
int LineLength;            /* line length                           */
DWORD dwLines;             /* number of lines to print              */
DWORD dwIndex;             /* index into lines to print             */
char pLine[128];           /* buffer to store lines before printing */
TEXTMETRIC TextMetric;     /* information about character size      */
POINT PhysPageSize;        /* information about the page            */
BOOL bAbort;               /* FALSE if user cancels printing        */
HWND hAbortDlgWnd;
FARPROC lpAbortDlg, lpAbortProc;
```

The hPr variable is the handle for the printer device context. It receives the return value from the **CreateDC** function call. The variables LineSpace and LinesPerPage hold the amount of spacing between lines and the number of lines that can be printed per page, respectively. The CurrentLine variable is a counter that keeps track of the current line on the current page. Lines of text are printed one line at a time. The dwLines variable holds the number of lines in the edit control. The TextMetric structure receives information about the font to be used to print the lines; this example uses only the TextMetric.tmHeight and TextMetric.tmExternalLeading fields. The PhysPageSize structure receives the physical width and height of the printer paper. The height is used to determine how many lines per page can be printed.

12.8.3 Add the IDM_PRINT Case

To carry out the printing operation, you need to add an IDM_PRINT case to the WM_COMMAND case of the main window function. Add the following statements:

```
case IDM_PRINT:
    hPr = GetPrinterDC();
    if (!hPr) {
        sprintf(str, "Cannot print %s", FileName);
        MessageBox(hWnd, str, NULL, MB_OK | MB_ICONHAND);
        break;
    }
    lpAbortDlg =  MakeProcInstance(AbortDlg, hInst);
    lpAbortProc = MakeProcInstance(AbortProc, hInst);
    Escape(hPr, SETABORTPROC, NULL,
        (LPSTR) (long) lpAbortProc, (LPSTR) NULL);
    if (Escape(hPr, STARTDOC, 14, (LPSTR) "PrntFile text",
       (LPSTR) NULL) < 0) {
        MessageBox(hWnd, "Unable to start print job",
            NULL, MB_OK | MB_ICONHAND);
        FreeProcInstance(AbortDlg);
        FreeProcInstance(AbortProc);
        DeleteDC(hPr);
        break;
    }

    bAbort = FALSE;                              /* Clears the abort flag */
    hAbortDlgWnd = CreateDialog(hInst, "AbortDlg", hWnd, lpAbortDlg);
    ShowWindow(hAbortDlgWnd, SW_NORMAL);
    UpdateWindow(hAbortDlgWnd);
    EnableWindow(hWnd, FALSE);
    GetTextMetrics(hPr, &TextMetric);
    LineSpace = TextMetric.tmHeight + TextMetric.tmExternalLeading;
    Escape(hPr, GETPHYSPAGESIZE, NULL, (LPSTR) NULL, (LPSTR) &PhysPageSize);
    LinesPerPage = PhysPageSize.y / LineSpace;
    dwLines = SendMessage(hEditWnd, EM_GETLINECOUNT, 0, 0L);
    CurrentLine = 1;
    for (dwIndex = IOStatus = 0; dwIndex < dwLines; dwIndex++) {
        pLine[0] = 128;                  /* Maximum buffer size */
        pLine[1] = 0;
        LineLength = SendMessage(hEditWnd, EM_GETLINE,
            (WORD) dwIndex, (LONG) ((LPSTR) pLine));
        TextOut(hPr, 0, CurrentLine*LineSpace, (LPSTR) pLine, LineLength);
```

```
        if (++CurrentLine > LinesPerPage ) {
            Escape(hPr, NEWFRAME, Ø, ØL, ØL);
            CurrentLine = 1;
            IOStatus = Escape(hPr, NEWFRAME, Ø, ØL, ØL);
            if (IOStatus < Ø || bAbort)
                break;
        }
    }

if (IOStatus >= Ø && !bAbort) {
    Escape(hPr, NEWFRAME, Ø, ØL, ØL);
    Escape(hPr, ENDDOC, Ø, ØL, ØL);
}
EnableWindow(hWnd, TRUE);
DestroyWindow(hAbortDlgWnd);
FreeProcInstance(AbortDlg);
FreeProcInstance(AbortProc);
DeleteDC(hPr);
break;
```

The locally-defined GetPrinterDC function checks the WIN.INI file for the current printer and creates a device context for that printer. If there is not a current printer or the device context cannot be created, the function returns NULL and processing ends with a warning. Otherwise, the **MakeProcInstance** function creates procedure instance addresses for the AbortDlg dialog function and the AbortProc function. The SETABORTPROC escape used with the **Escape** function sets the abort function. The STARTDOC escape starts the printing job and sets the printing title (shown in the Print Manager application). If the STARTDOC escape fails, the **FreeProcInstance** function frees the AbortDlg and AbortProc procedure instances and the **DeleteDC** function deletes the device context before processing ends.

The **CreateDialog** function creates the AbortDlg dialog box and the **EnableWindow** function disables the main window. This prevents users from attempting to work in the main window while printing. Users can, however, continue to work in some other application.

Since the edit control may contain more than one line, it is important to provide adequate spacing between lines. This keeps one line from overwriting or touching another. The **GetTextMetrics** function retrieves current font information, such as height and external leading, which can be used to compute adequate line spacing. The height is the maximum height of characters in the font. The external leading is the recommended amount of space, in addition to the height, that should be used to separate lines of text in this font. The line spacing, assigned to the LineSpace variable, is the sum of the height and external leading fields, TextMetric.tmHeight and TextMetric.tmExternalLeading.

Since the edit control might contain more lines than can fit on a single page, it is important to determine how many lines can fit on a page and to advance to the next page whenever this line limit is reached. The GETPHYSPAGESIZE escape retrieves the physical dimensions of the page and copies the dimensions to the

PhysPageSize structure. PhysPageSize contains both the width and height of the page. The lines per page, assigned to the LinesPerPage variable, is the quotient of the physical height of the page, PhysPageSize.y, and the line spacing, LineSpace.

The **TextOut** function can print only one line at a time, so a **for** statement provides the loop required to print more than one line of text. The EM_GETLINECOUNT message, sent to the edit control by using the **SendMessage** function, retrieves the number of lines to be printed and determines the number of times to loop. On each execution of the loop, the EM_GETLINE message copies the contents of a line from the edit control to the line buffer, pLine. The loop counter, dwIndex, is used with the EM_GETLINE message to specify which line to retrieve from the edit control. The EM_GETLINE message also causes **SendMessage** to return the length of the line. The length is assigned to the LineLength variable.

Once a line has been copied from the edit control, it is printed by using the **TextOut** function. The product of the variables CurrentLine and LineSpacing determines the *y*-coordinate of the line on the page. The *x*-coordinate is set to zero. After a line is printed, the value of the CurrentLine variable is increased by one. If CurrentLine is greater than LinesPerPage, it is time to advance to the next page. Any text printed beyond the physical bottom of a page is clipped. There is no automatic page advance, so it is important to keep track of the number of lines printed on a page and to use the NEWFRAME escape to advance to the next page when necessary. If there are any errors during printing, the NEWFRAME escape returns an error number and processing ends.

After all lines in the edit control have been printed, the NEWFRAME escape advances the final page and the ENDDOC escape terminates the print request. The **DeleteDC** function deletes the printer device context since it is no longer needed, and the **DestroyWindow** function destroys the AbortDlg dialog box.

12.8.4 Create the AbortDlg and AbortProc Functions

You need to create the AbortDlg and AbortProc functions to support the printing process. The AbortDlg dialog function provides support for the AbortDlg dialog box that appears while the printing is in progress. The dialog box lets the user cancel the printing operation if necessary. The AbortProc function processes messages intended for the AbortDlg dialog box and terminates the printing operation if the user has requested it.

The AbortDlg dialog function sets the input focus and sets the name of the file being printed. It also sets the bAbort variable to TRUE if the user chooses the Cancel button. Add the following statements to the C-language source file:

```
int FAR PASCAL AbortDlg(hDlg, msg, wParam, lParam)
HWND hDlg;
unsigned msg;
WORD wParam;
LONG lParam;
```

```
{
    switch(msg) {
        case WM_COMMAND:
            return (bAbort = TRUE);

        case WM_INITDIALOG:
            SetFocus(GetDlgItem(hDlg, IDCANCEL));
            SetDlgItemText(hDlg, IDC_FILENAME, FileName);
            return (TRUE);
        }
    return (FALSE);
}
```

The AbortProc function checks for messages in the application queue and dispatches them to the AbortDlg dialog function or to other windows in the application. If one of these messages causes the AbortDlg dialog function to set the bAbort variable to TRUE, the AbortProc function returns this value, directing Windows to stop the printing operation. Add the following statements to the C-language source file:

```
int FAR PASCAL AbortProc(hPr, Code)
HDC hPr;                    /* for multiple printer display contexts */
int Code;                   /* printing status                       */
{
    MSG msg;

    while (!bAbort && PeekMessage(&msg, NULL, NULL, NULL, TRUE))
        if (!IsDialogMessage(hAbortDlgWnd, &msg)) {
            TranslateMessage(&msg);
            DispatchMessage(&msg);
        }
    return (!bAbort);
}
```

12.8.5 Add the GetPrinterDC Function

You need to add a function to your C-language source file to support the printing operation. The GetPrinterDC function retrieves the **device=** field from the **[windows]** section of the WIN.INI file, divides the entry into its separate components, then creates a printer device context using the device name and printer port given in the entry. Add the following statements to the C-language source file:

```
HANDLE GetPrinterDC()
{
    char pPrintInfo[80];
    LPSTR lpTemp;
    LPSTR lpPrintType;
    LPSTR lpPrintDriver;
    LPSTR lpPrintPort;
```

```
    if (!GetProfileString("windows", "device",
            (LPSTR) "", pPrintInfo, 80))
        return (NULL);
    lpTemp = lpPrintType = pPrintInfo;
    lpPrintDriver = lpPrintPort = 0;
    while (*lpTemp) {
        if (*lpTemp == ',') {
            *lpTemp++ = 0;
            while (*lpTemp == ' ')
                lpTemp = AnsiNext(lpTemp);
            if (!lpPrintDriver)
                lpPrintDriver = lpTemp;
            else {
                lpPrintPort = lpTemp;
                break;
            }
        }
        else
            lpTemp = AnsiNext(lpTemp);
    }

    return (CreateDC(lpPrintDriver, lpPrintType, lpPrintPort, (LPSTR) NULL));
}
```

To separate the **device=** field into its three components, the **AnsiNext** function advances through the field one character at a time.

12.8.6 Export the AbortDlg and AbortProc Functions

You need to export the AbortDlg dialog function and the AbortProc function. Add the following lines to your module-definition file under the **EXPORTS** statement:

```
AbortDlg        @5  ; Called so user can cancel the print function
AbortProc       @6  ; Processes messages intended for the Abort dialog box
```

12.8.7 Compile and Link

No changes are required to the make file. Compile and link the PrntFile application, then start Windows and activate PrntFile; you will see that the Print command has been added to the File menu. You can print by opening a file or by entering text from the keyboard, then choosing the Print command.

12.9 Summary

This chapter explained how to print from a Windows application. In Windows, your application does not interact directly with the printer. Instead, you print by sending output to a device context for the printer. Your application communicates with the printer device driver using escape sequences.

For more information on topics related to printing, see the following:

Topic	Reference
Device contexts	*Guide to Programming*: Chapter 3, "Output to a Window"
Controlling printer settings	*Guide to Programming*: Chapter 17, "Print Settings"
Using fonts	*Guide to Programming*: Chapter 18, "Fonts"
Functions for working with device contexts	*Reference, Volume 1*: Chapter 2, "Graphics Device Interface Functions" and Chapter 4, "Functions Directory"

Chapter 13 The Clipboard

The clipboard is the main data-exchange feature of Microsoft Windows. It is a common area to store data handles through which applications can exchange formatted data. The clipboard holds any number of different data formats and corresponding data handles, all representing the same data, but in as many different formats as an application is willing to supply. For example, a pie chart might be held in the clipboard as both a metafile picture and a bitmap. An application pasting the pie chart would have to decide which representation it wanted. In general, the format that provides the most information is the most desirable, as long as the application understands that format.

This chapter covers the following topics:

- Copying text to the clipboard
- Pasting text from the clipboard
- Pasting a bitmap from the clipboard
- Using special clipboard features such as private data formats

This chapter also explains how to build a sample application, ClipText, that illustrates many of the concepts explained in the chapter.

13.1 Using the Clipboard

To copy data to the clipboard, you format the data using either a predefined or private format. For most formats, you allocate global memory and copy the data into it. You then use the **SetClipboardData** function to copy the memory handle to the clipboard.

In Windows applications, copying and pasting are carried out through Edit-menu commands. To add the Edit menu to an application, follow the steps described in Chapter 7, "Menus."

Windows provides several predefined data formats for use in data interchange. Following is a list of common formats and their contents:

Format	Contents
CF_TEXT	Null-terminated text
CF_OEMTEXT	Null-terminated text in the OEM character set
CF_METAFILEPICT	Metafile-picture structure
CF_BITMAP	A device-dependent bitmap
CF_DIB	A device-independent bitmap
CF_SYLK	SYLK standard data-interchange format
CF_DIF	DIF standard data-interchange format
CF_TIFF	TIFF standard data-interchange format

When you paste data from the clipboard using the **GetClipboardData** function, you specify the format you expect. The clipboard supplies the data only if it has been copied in that format.

Windows supports two formats for text, CF_TEXT and CF_OEMTEXT. CF_TEXT is the default Windows text clipboard format. Windows uses the CF_OEMTEXT format for text in non-Windows applications. If you call **GetClipboardData** to retrieve data in one text format and the other text format is the only available text format, Windows automatically converts the text to the requested format before supplying it to your application.

NOTE Clipboard data objects can be any size. Your application must be able to work with clipboard data objects larger than 64K. For more information on working with large data objects, see Chapter 16, "More Memory Management."

13.1.1 Copying Text to the Clipboard

To copy a short string of text to the clipboard, follow these steps:

1. Copy the string to global memory.
2. Open the clipboard.
3. Clear the clipboard.
4. Give the global memory handle to the clipboard.
5. Close the clipboard.

You copy text to the clipboard when the user chooses the Copy command from the Edit menu. To process the menu input and copy the text string to the clipboard, add a WM_COMMAND case to the window function. Add the following statements:

```
case WM_COMMAND:
   switch (wParam) {
      case IDM_COPY:
         if (!(hData = GlobalAlloc(GMEM_MOVEABLE, GlobalSize
(hText)))) {
             OutOfMemory();
             return (TRUE);
         }
         if (!(lpData = GlobalLock(hData))) {
             GlobalFree(hData);
             OutOfMemory();
             return (TRUE);
         }
         if (!(lpszText = GlobalLock (hText))) {
             OutOfMemory();
             return (TRUE);
         }
         lstrcpy(lpData, lpszText);
         GlobalUnlock(hData);
         GlobalUnlock (hText);

         /* Clear the current contents of the clipboard, and set
          * the data handle to the new string.
          */

         if (OpenClipboard(hWnd)) {
             EmptyClipboard();
             SetClipboardData(CF_TEXT, hData);
             CloseClipboard();
         }
         hData = NULL;
         break;
   }
```

The **GlobalAlloc** function allocates enough memory to hold the string. The GMEM_MOVEABLE flag specifies moveable memory. The clipboard can take either fixed or moveable memory, but should not be given discardable memory. Moveable memory is the most efficient.

NOTE You should always check the return value when allocating or locking memory; a NULL return value indicates an out-of-memory condition.

You must lock moveable memory in order to retrieve the memory address. Use the Windows **lstrcpy** function instead of the C run-time **strcpy** function, since **strcpy** cannot handle mixed pointers (string is a short pointer and lpData is a long pointer). The clipboard requires the string to have a terminating null character. Finally, the memory must be unlocked before it can be copied to the clipboard.

Each time you copy the string to the clipboard, this code allocates another global memory block. The reason is that once you have passed a data handle to the clipboard, the clipboard takes ownership of it. This means that you can no longer use the handle other than to view contents, and you must not attempt to free the handle or change its contents.

Copy the global memory handle to the clipboard by following these steps:

1. Open the clipboard.
2. Empty the clipboard.
3. Set the data handle.
4. Close the clipboard.

The following statements carry out these steps:

```
❶ if (OpenClipboard(hWnd)) {
    ❷ EmptyClipboard();
    ❸ SetClipboardData(CF_TEXT, hData);
    CloseClipboard();
}
❹ hData = NULL;
```

❶ The **OpenClipboard** function opens the clipboard for the specified window. **OpenClipboard** will fail if another window already has the clipboard open.

❷ The **EmptyClipboard** function clears all existing handles in the clipboard and assigns ownership of the clipboard to the window that has it open. An application must empty the clipboard before copying data to it.

❸ The **SetClipboardData** function copies the memory handle to the clipboard and identifies the data format, CF_TEXT. The clipboard is then closed by the **CloseClipboard** function.

❹ Since the clipboard now owns the global memory identified by hData, it is convenient to set this handle to zero to prevent attempts to free or change the memory.

13.1.2 Pasting Text from the Clipboard

You can paste text from the clipboard into your client area. That is, you can retrieve a text handle from the clipboard and display it in the client area by using the **TextOut** function. To do this you will need to do the following:

1. Open the clipboard.
2. Retrieve the data handle associated with CF_TEXT or CF_OEMTEXT.
3. Close the clipboard.

You should let the user paste only if there is text in the clipboard. To prevent attempts to paste when no text is present, check the clipboard before Windows displays the Edit menu by processing the WM_INITMENU message. If the clipboard is empty, disable the Paste command; if text is present, enable it. Add the following statements to the window function:

```
case WM_INITMENU:
➊    if (wParam == hEditMenu) {
    if (OpenClipboard(hWnd)) {
        ➋ if (IsClipboardFormatAvailable(CF_TEXT)
            || IsClipboardFormatAvailable(CF_OEMTEXT))
            ➌ EnableMenuItem(wParam, IDM_PASTE, MF_ENABLED);
        else
            EnableMenuItem(wParam, IDM_PASTE, MF_GRAYED);
        CloseClipboard();
        return (TRUE);
    }
    else                    /* Clipboard is not available */
        return (FALSE);

}
```

In this example:

➊ The first **if** statement checks the WM_INITMENU's *wParam* parameter against the menu handle returned by the **GetMenu** function. Since many applications have at least two menus, including a System menu, it is important to ensure that the message applies to the Edit menu.

➋ The two calls to the **IsClipboardFormatAvailable** function check for the CF_TEXT or CF_OEMTEXT format.

➌ The **EnableMenuItem** function enables or disables the Paste command based on whether the CF_TEXT or CF_OEMTEXT format is found.

You can paste from the clipboard when the user chooses the Paste command from the Edit menu. To process the menu input and retrieve the text from the clipboard, add an IDM_PASTE case to the WM_COMMAND case in the window function. Add the following statements immediately after the IDM_COPY case:

```
case IDM_PASTE:
    ➊ if (OpenClipboard(hWnd)) {

        /* get text from the clipboard */
```

```
    ❷ if (!(hClipData = GetClipboardData(CF_TEXT))) {
        CloseClipboard();
        break;
    }
    ❸ if (!(lpClipData = GlobalLock(hClipData))) {
        OutOfMemory();
        CloseClipboard();
        break;
    }

    ❹ hDC = GetDC(hWnd);
    TextOut(hDC, 10, 10, lpClipData);
    ReleaseDC(hWnd, hDC);
    GlobalUnlock(hClipData);
    CloseClipboard();
}
break;
```

In this example:

❶ The **OpenClipboard** function opens the clipboard for the specified window if it is not already open.

❷ The **GetClipboardData** function retrieves the data handle for the text; if there is no such data, the function retrieves zero. You should check this handle before using it.

❸ The **GetClipboardData** function returns a handle to global memory. Because the clipboard format is CF_TEXT, the global memory is assumed to contain a null-terminated ANSI string. This means the global memory can be locked by using the **GlobalLock** function, and the contents can be displayed in the client area by using the **TextOut** function.

❹ So that you will be able to see that your application has copied the contents of the clipboard, the **TextOut** function writes to the coordinates (10,10) in your client area. You will need a display context to use **TextOut**, so the **GetDC** function is required; and since you must release a display context immediately after using it, the **ReleaseDC** function is also required.

This method of displaying the text in the client area is for illustration only. Since the application does not save the content of the string, there is no way to repaint the text if the client-area background is erased, such as during processing of a WM_PAINT message. (The ClipText sample application, described later in this chapter, demonstrates one method of saving text so that the client-area display can be redrawn.)

You must not modify or delete the data you have retrieved from the clipboard. You can examine it or make a copy of it, but you must not change it. To examine the data, you might need to lock the handle, as in this example, but you must never leave a data handle locked. Unlock it immediately after using it.

Data handles returned by the **GetClipboardData** function are for temporary use only. Handles belong to the clipboard, not to the application requesting data. Accordingly, handles should not be freed and should be unlocked immediately after they are used. The application should not rely on the handle remaining valid indefinitely. In general, the application should copy the data associated with the handle, then release it without changes.

The **CloseClipboard** function closes the clipboard; you should always close the clipboard immediately after it has been used so that other applications can use it. Before closing the clipboard, be sure you unlock the data retrieved by **GetClipboardData**.

13.1.3 Pasting Bitmaps from the Clipboard

In addition to text, Windows lets you retrieve a bitmap from the clipboard and display it in your client area. To retrieve and display a bitmap, use the same technique as for pasting text, but make a few changes to accommodate bitmaps.

First, you must modify the WM_INITMENU case in the window function so that it recognizes the CF_BITMAP format. After you change it, the WM_INITMENU case should look like this:

```
case WM_INITMENU:
    if (wParam == GetMenu(hWnd)) {
        if (OpenClipboard(hWnd)) {
            if (IsClipboardFormatAvailable(CF_BITMAP))
                EnableMenuItem(wParam, IDM_PASTE, MF_ENABLED);
            else
                EnableMenuItem(wParam, IDM_PASTE, MF_GRAYED);
            CloseClipboard();
            return (TRUE);
        }
        else            /* Clipboard is not available */
            return (FALSE);

    }
```

Although retrieving a bitmap from the clipboard is as easy as retrieving text, displaying a bitmap requires more work than does displaying text. In general, you need to do the following:

1. Retrieve the bitmap data handle from the clipboard. Bitmap data handles from the clipboard are GDI bitmap handles (created by using functions such as **CreateBitmap**).
2. Create a compatible display context and select the data handle into it.

3. Use the **BitBlt** function to copy the bitmap to the client area.
4. Release the bitmap handle from the current selection.

After you have changed the IDM_PASTE case, it should look like this:

```
case IDM_PASTE:
    if (OpenClipboard(hWnd)) {

        /* get text from the clipboard */

        if (!(hClipData = GetClipboardData(CF_BITMAP))) {
            CloseClipboard();
            break;
        }
        if (!(lpClipData = GlobalLock(hClipData))) {
            OutOfMemory();
            CloseClipboard();
            break;
        }
        hDC = GetDC(hWnd);
      ❶ hMemoryDC = CreateCompatibleDC(hDC);
        if (hMemoryDC != NULL) {
          ❷ GetObject(hClipData, sizeof(BITMAP),
                &PasteBitmap);
          ❸ hOldBitmap = SelectObject(hMemoryDC,
                                      hClipData);
            if (!hOldBitmap) {
                BitBlt(hDC, 10, 10,
                    PasteBitmap.bmWidth,
                    PasteBitmap.bmHeight,
                    hMemoryDC, 0, 0, SRCCOPY);
                SelectObject(hMemoryDC, hOldBitmap);
            }
          ❹ DeleteDC(hMemoryDC);
        }
        ReleaseDC(hWnd, hDC);
        GlobalUnlock(hClipData);
        CloseClipboard();
        GlobalUnlock(hText);
    }
    break;
```

In this example:

❶ The **CreateCompatibleDC** function returns a handle to a display context, in memory, that is compatible with your computer's display. This means any bitmaps that you select for this display context can be copied directly to the client area. If **CreateCompatibleDC** fails (returns NULL), the bitmap cannot be displayed.

❷ The **GetObject** function retrieves the width and height of the bitmap, as well as a description of the bitmap format. It copies this information into the PasteBitmap structure, whose size is specified by the **sizeof** function. In this example, only the width and height are used and then only in the **BitBlt** function.

❸ The **SelectObject** function selects the bitmap into the compatible display context. If it fails (returns NULL), the bitmap cannot be displayed. **SelectObject** may fail if the bitmap has a different format than that of the compatible display context. This can happen, for example, if the bitmap was created for a display on some other computer.

❹ The **DeleteDC** function removes the compatible display context. Before a display context can be deleted, its original bitmap must be restored by using the **SelectObject** function.

13.1.4 The Windows Clipboard Application

The Windows Clipboard application, CLIPBRD.EXE, lets the user view the contents of the clipboard; for this reason, it is also known as the "clipboard viewer." It lists the names of all the formats for which handles (NULL or otherwise) exist in the clipboard, and displays the contents of the clipboard in one of these formats.

The clipboard viewer can display all the standard data formats. If there are handles for more than one standard data format, the clipboard viewer displays only one format, choosing from the following list, in decreasing order of priority: CF_TEXT, CF_OEMTEXT, CF_METAFILEPICT, CF_BITMAP, CF_SYLK, and CF_DIF.

For additional information on clipboard formats, see the *Reference, Volume 1*.

13.2 Using Special Clipboard Features

The clipboard provides several features that an application can use to improve the usability of the clipboard and save itself some work. These features are as follows:

- Applications can delay the formatting of data passed to the clipboard until the data is needed. If the data format is complex and no other application is likely to use that format, an application can save time by not formatting that data until necessary.
- Applications can draw within the Clipboard application's client area. This lets an application display data formats that Clipboard does not know how to display.

The following sections describe these features in more detail.

13.2.1 Rendering Data on Request

If an application uses many data formats, it can save formatting time by passing NULL data handles to the **SetClipboardData** function instead of generating all the data handles when a Cut or Copy command is used. The application does not actually have to generate a data handle until another application requests a handle by calling the **GetClipboardData** function.

When the application calls the **GetClipboardData** function with a request for a format for which a NULL data handle has been set, Windows sends a WM_RENDERFORMAT message to the clipboard owner. When an application receives this message, it can do the following:

1. Format the data last copied to the clipboard (the *wParam* parameter of WM_RENDERFORMAT specifies the format being requested).
2. Allocate a global memory block and copy the formatted data to it.
3. Pass the global memory handle and the format number to the clipboard by using the **SetClipboardData** function.

In order to accomplish these steps, the application needs to keep a record of the last data copied to the clipboard. The application may get rid of this data when it receives the WM_DESTROYCLIPBOARD message, which is sent to the clipboard owner whenever the clipboard is emptied by a call to the **EmptyClipboard** function.

13.2.2 Rendering Formats Before Termination

When an application is destroyed, it loses its knowledge of how to render data it has copied to the clipboard. Accordingly, when the application that owns the clipboard is being destroyed, Windows sends that application a special message, WM_RENDERALLFORMATS. Upon receiving a WM_RENDERALLFORMATS message, an application should follow the steps described in Section 13.2.1, "Rendering Data on Request," for all formats that the application is capable of generating.

13.2.3 Registering Private Formats

In addition, an application can create and use private formats, or even new public ones. To create and use a new data-interchange format, an application must do the following:

1. Call the **RegisterClipboardFormat** function to register the name of the new format.

2. Use the value returned by **RegisterClipboardFormat** as the code for the new format when calling the **SetClipboardData** function.

Registering the format name ensures that the application is using a unique format number. In addition, it allows the Clipboard application to display the correct name of the data being held in the clipboard. For more information about displaying private data types in Clipboard, see Section 13.2.4, "Controlling Data Display in the Clipboard."

If two or more applications register formats with the same name, they will all receive the same format code. This allows applications to create their own public data types. If two or more applications register a format called WORKSHEET, for example, they will all have the same format number when calling the **SetClipboardData** and **GetClipboardData** functions, and will have a common basis for transferring WORKSHEET data between them.

13.2.4 Controlling Data Display in the Clipboard

There are two reasons why an application might wish to control the display of information in the Clipboard application:

- The application may have a private data type that is difficult or impossible to display in a meaningful way.
- The application may have a private data type that requires special knowledge to display.

Using a Display Format for Private Data

You can use a display format to represent a private data format that would otherwise be difficult or impossible to display. The data associated with display formats are text, bitmaps, or metafile pictures that the clipboard viewer can display as substitutes for the corresponding private data. To use a display format, you copy both the private data and the display data to the clipboard. When the clipboard viewer chooses a format to display, it chooses the display format instead of the private data.

There are three display formats: CF_DSPTEXT, CF_DSPBITMAP, and CF_DSPMETAFILEPICT. The data associated with these formats are identical to the text, bitmap, and metafile-picture formats, respectively. Since text, bitmaps, and metafile pictures are also standard formats, the clipboard viewer can display them without help from the application.

The following description assumes that the application has already followed the steps described in Section 13.1.1, "Copying Text to the Clipboard," to take ownership of the clipboard and set data handles.

To force the display of a private data type in a standard data format, the application must take the following steps:

1. Open the clipboard for alteration by calling the **OpenClipboard** function.
2. Create a global handle that contains text, a bitmap, or a metafile picture, specifying the information that should be displayed in the clipboard viewer.
3. Set the handle to the clipboard by calling the **SetClipboardData** function. The format code passed should be CF_DSPTEXT if the handle is to text, CF_DSPBITMAP if the handle is for a bitmap, and CF_DSPMETAFILEPICT if it is for a metafile picture.
4. Signal that the application has finished altering the clipboard by calling the **CloseClipboard** function.

Taking Full Control of the Clipboard-Viewer Display

An application can take complete control of the display and scrolling of information in the clipboard viewer. This control is useful when the application has a sophisticated private data type that only it knows how to display. Microsoft Write uses this facility for displaying formatted text.

The following description assumes that the application has already followed the steps described in Section 13.1.1, "Copying Text to the Clipboard," to take ownership of the clipboard and set data handles.

To take control of the display of information in the clipboard viewer:

1. Open the clipboard for alteration by calling the **OpenClipboard** function.
2. Call the **SetClipboardData** function, using CF_OWNERDISPLAY as the data format, with a NULL handle.
3. Signal that the application has finished altering the clipboard by calling the **CloseClipboard** function.

The clipboard owner will then receive special messages associated with the display of information in the clipboard viewer:

Message	Action
WM_PAINTCLIPBOARD	Paint the specified portion of the window.
WM_SIZECLIPBOARD	Take note of the window size change.
WM_VSCROLLCLIPBOARD	Scroll the window vertically.

Message	Action
WM_HSCROLLCLIPBOARD	Scroll the window horizontally.
WM_ASKCBFORMATNAME	Supply the name of the displayed format.

For full descriptions of these messages, see the *Reference, Volume 1*.

Using the Clipboard-Viewer Chain

Chaining together clipboard-viewer windows provides a way for applications to be notified whenever a change is made to the clipboard. The notification, in the form of a WM_DRAWCLIPBOARD message, is passed down the viewer chain whenever the **CloseClipboard** function is called. The recipient of the WM_DRAWCLIPBOARD message must determine the nature of the change (Empty, Set, etc.) by calling the **EnumClipboardFormats** function, the **GetClipboardData** function, and other functions, as desired.

Any window that has made itself a link in the viewer chain must be prepared to do the following:

1. Remove itself from the chain before it is destroyed.
2. Pass along WM_DRAWCLIPBOARD messages to the next link in the chain.

The code for this action looks like this:

```
case WM_DESTROY:
    ChangeClipboardChain(hwnd, my_save_next);

    /* rest of processing for WM_DESTROY */

    break;
case WM_DRAWCLIPBOARD:
    if (my_save_next != NULL)
        SendMessage(my_save_next, WM_DRAWCLIPBOARD, wParam, lParam);

     /* rest of processing for WM_DRAWCLIPBOARD */

     break;
```

The my_save_next string is the value returned from the **SetClipboardViewer** function. These clipboard-viewer chain actions should be the first steps taken by the **switch**-statement branches that process the WM_DESTROY and WM_DRAWCLIPBOARD messages.

13.3 A Sample Application: ClipText

This sample application illustrates how to copy and paste from the clipboard. To create the ClipText application, copy and rename the source files of the EditMenu application, then make the following modifications:

1. Add new variables.
2. Modify the instance initialization code.
3. Add a WM_INITMENU case.
4. Modify the WM_COMMAND case to process the IDM_CUT, IDM_COPY, and IDM_PASTE cases.
5. Add a WM_PAINT case.
6. Add the OutOfMemory function.
7. Compile and link the application.

This sample uses global memory to store the text to be copied. For a full explanation of global memory, see Chapter 15, "Memory Management."

NOTE Rather than typing the code provided in the following sections, you might find it more convenient to simply examine and compile the sample source files provided with the SDK.

13.3.1 Add New Variables

You need to add new global variables to hold the handle of the client area text string and its initial data. Add the following to the beginning of your C-language source file:

```
HANDLE   hClientText = NULL; /* handle for current client-area text */
char     szInitialClientAreaText[] = "This program demonstrates..."
HANDLE   hData, hClipData;          /* handles to clip data */
LPSTR    lpData, lpClipData;        /* pointers to clip data */
```

You also need to add variables for painting and clipboard data manipulation. Add the following to the beginning of your MainWndProc main window function:

```
HDC hDC;
PAINTSTRUCT ps;
RECT rectClient;
LPSTR lpszText;
```

13.3.2 Modify the Instance Initialization Code

When an instance of ClipText is started, it must allocate a global memory object and fill it with an initial client-area text string. Add the following statements to the instance initialization code:

```
if (!(hText = GlobalAlloc(GMEM_MOVEABLE,
                          (DWORD)sizeof(szInitialClientAreaText)))) {
    OutOfMemory();
    return (FALSE);
}

if (!(lpszText = GlobalLock(hText))) {
    OutOfMemory();
    return (FALSE);
}

lstrcpy(lpszText, szInitialClientAreaText);
GlobalUnlock(hText);
```

13.3.3 Add a WM_INITMENU Case

You need to add a WM_INITMENU case to your window function to prepare the Edit menu for pasting. In general, the Paste command should not be available unless there is selected text in the clipboard to paste. Add the following statements to the window function:

```
case WM_INITMENU:
    if (wParam == GetMenu(hWnd)) {
        if (OpenClipboard(hWnd)) {
            if (IsClipboardFormatAvailable(CF_TEXT)
                                  || IsClipboardFormatAvailable(CF_OEMTEXT))
                EnableMenuItem(wParam, IDM_PASTE, MF_ENABLED);
            else
                EnableMenuItem(wParam, IDM_PASTE, MF_GRAYED);
            CloseClipboard();
            return (TRUE);
        }
        else                              /* Clipboard is not available */
            return (FALSE);
    }
```

These statements process the WM_INITMENU message only if the specified menu is the menu bar. The **IsClipboardFormatAvailable** function determines whether text data is present on the clipboard. If it is, the **EnableMenuItem** function enables the Paste command. Otherwise, the Paste command is disabled.

13.3.4 Modify the WM_COMMAND Case

You need to modify the IDM_CUT, IDM_COPY, and IDM_PASTE cases in the WM_COMMAND case to process the Edit menu commands. The IDM_CUT and IDM_COPY cases must create a global memory block, fill it with text, and copy the handle of the block to the clipboard, and the IDM_CUT case must also discard the current client-area text. The IDM_PASTE case must retrieve a handle from the clipboard, use its contents to replace the current client-area text, and request a client-area repaint.

Replace the existing IDM_CUT and IDM_COPY cases with the following statements:

```
case IDM_CUT:
case IDM_COPY:

    if (hText != NULL) {

        /* Allocate memory and copy the string to it */

        if (!(hData
             = GlobalAlloc(GMEM_MOVEABLE, GlobalSize (hText)))) {
            OutOfMemory();
            return (TRUE);
        }
        if (!(lpData = GlobalLock(hData))) {
            GlobalFree(hData);
                                    OutOfMemory();
            return (TRUE);
        }
        if (!(lpszText = GlobalLock (hText))) {
            OutOfMemory();
            return (TRUE);
        }
        lstrcpy(lpData, lpszText);
        GlobalUnlock(hData);
        GlobalUnlock (hText);

        /* Clear the current contents of the clipboard, and set
         * the data handle to the new string.
         */

        if (OpenClipboard(hWnd)) {
            EmptyClipboard();
            SetClipboardData(CF_TEXT, hData);
            CloseClipboard();
        }
        hData = NULL;
```

```
        if (wParam == IDM_CUT) {
            GlobalFree (hText);
            hText = NULL;
            EnableMenuItem(GetMenu (hWnd), IDM_CUT, MF_GRAYED);
            EnableMenuItem(GetMenu(hWnd), IDM_COPY, MF_GRAYED);
            InvalidateRect (hWnd, NULL, TRUE);
            UpdateWindow (hWnd);
        }
    }

    return (TRUE);
```

The **GlobalAlloc** function allocates the global memory block used to pass text data to the clipboard. The **lstrcpy** function copies the client-area text into the block after the handle has been locked by the **GlobalLock** function. The handle must be unlocked before copying the handle to the clipboard. The **EmptyClipboard** function is used to remove any existing data from the clipboard.

Replace the IDM_PASTE case with the following statements:

```
case IDM_PASTE:
    if (OpenClipboard(hWnd)) {

        /* get text from the clipboard */

        if (!(hClipData = GetClipboardData(CF_TEXT))) {
            CloseClipboard();
            break;
        }
        if (hText != NULL) {
            GlobalFree(hText);
        }
        if (!(hText = GlobalAlloc(GMEM_MOVEABLE
                                   , GlobalSize(hClipData)))) {
            OutOfMemory();
            CloseClipboard();
            break;
        }
        if (!(lpClipData = GlobalLock(hClipData))) {
            OutOfMemory();
            CloseClipboard();
            break;
        }
        if (!(lpszText = GlobalLock(hText))) {
            OutOfMemory();
            CloseClipboard();
            break;
        }
        lstrcpy(lpszText, lpClipData);
        GlobalUnlock(hClipData);
        CloseClipboard();
```

```
                GlobalUnlock(hText);
                EnableMenuItem(GetMenu(hWnd), IDM_CUT, MF_ENABLED);
                EnableMenuItem(GetMenu(hWnd), IDM_COPY, MF_ENABLED);

                /* copy text to the application window */

                InvalidateRect(hWnd, NULL, TRUE);
                UpdateWindow(hWnd);
                return (TRUE);
            }
            else
                return (FALSE);
        }
        break;
```

The **GetClipboardData** function returns a handle to a global memory block. The **GlobalLock** function locks this handle, returning the block address that is used to make a copy of the new client-area text.

13.3.5 Add a WM_PAINT Case

A WM_PAINT case is necessary in order to draw the current client-area text on the screen when the window has been minimized, resized, or overlaid. Add the following case to the window procedure:

```
case WM_PAINT:
    hDC = BeginPaint (hWnd, &ps);
    if (hText != NULL) {
        if (!(lpszText = GlobalLock (hText))) {
            OutOfMemory();
        } else {
            GetClientRect (hWnd, &rectClient);
            DrawText (hDC, lpszText, -1, &rectClient
                      , DT_EXTERNALLEADING | DT_NOPREFIX | DT_WORDBREAK);
            GlobalUnlock (hText);
        }
    }
    EndPaint (hWnd, &ps);
    break;
```

13.3.6 Add the OutOfMemory Function

You need to add a function that displays a message box when the application is out of memory. Add the following function to the application source file:

```
void OutOfMemory(void)
{
    MessageBox(
        GetFocus(),
        "Out of Memory",
        NULL,
        MB_ICONHAND | MB_SYSTEMMODAL);
    return;
}
```

In the application's include file, add a forward reference to the OutOfMemory function:

```
void OutOfMemory(void);
```

13.3.7 Compile and Link

No changes are required to the make file to recompile and link the ClipText application. After compiling and linking it, start Windows, the Clipboard application, and ClipText. Then, choose the Copy command in the Edit menu. You should see something like Figure 13.1:

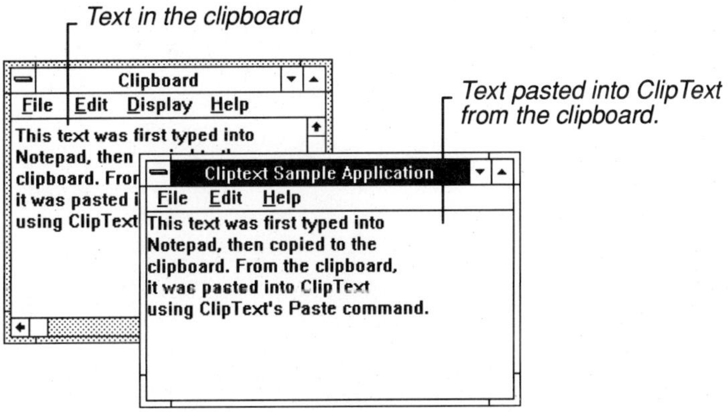

Figure 13.1 Pasting Text into ClipText from the Clipboard

13.4 Summary

This chapter explained how to use the clipboard to exchange data with other applications. The clipboard is an area in memory in which an application can store data handles; other applications can then retrieve the associated data. The application can provide the same data to the clipboard in several different formats at once; this helps to ensure that the data will be compatible with many different applications.

A simple use of the clipboard is to copy text or bitmaps to and from it. More advanced uses of the clipboard include controlling the clipboard data display and registering private data formats.

See the following for more information about topics related to the clipboard:

Topic	Reference
Display contexts	*Guide to Programming:* Chapter 3, "Output to a Window"
Working with bitmaps	*Guide to Programming:* Chapter 11, "Bitmaps"
Handling memory	*Guide to Programming:* Chapter 15, "Memory Management," and Chapter 16, "More Memory Management"
Exchanging data using the Windows DDE message-passing protocol instead of the clipboard	*Guide to Programming:* Chapter 22, "Dynamic Data Exchange"
Clipboard-management functions	*Reference, Volume 1*: Chapter 1, "Window Manager Interface Functions"
Clipboard formats	*Reference, Volume 2*: Chapter 4, "Functions Directory"
Clipboard file formats	*Reference, Volume 2*: Chapter 9, "File Formats"

Part 3 Advanced Programming Topics

The Microsoft Windows environment provides many standard features that make it easy to create an attractive, easy-to-use application. However, the difference between a good application and a great application is that, while a good application simply works, a great application works fast and efficiently, has additional user-interface features such as color and attractive fonts, and provides the power and flexibility for the user to accomplish large or complicated tasks.

The chapters in Part 2 provided a good foundation for you to get started with your own application development. Once you've been programming in Windows for a while, you will probably want to expand or refine your application—for example, use memory more efficiently, or provide more powerful printing capabilities.

Part 3 explores some more advanced Windows programming topics. It assumes that you've read Parts 1 and 2 of this guide, and are familiar with the Windows environment. Each chapter addresses a different topic. Because the sample applications for Part 3 are more complex than those in Part 2, the chapters do not include the complete code for each sample. You can find the complete source files for each sample application on the Sample Source Code disk provided with the SDK.

CHAPTERS

Chapter 14

C and Assembly Language

Parts 1 and 2 introduced the Microsoft Windows functions which you use in the context of a C- or assembly-language program to create a Windows application. The focus in these parts was on the Windows-specific elements of a Windows application.

A complete Windows application is not likely to rely exclusively on these Windows-specific functions, however. Instead, your application will probably use standard C run-time library routines and your own routines, which will be called back by Windows or by other modules in your application. It is important, therefore, for you to know how to incorporate these routines properly in your application.

This chapter covers the following topics:

- Choosing a memory model
- Using NULL
- Using command-line arguments and the DOS environment
- Writing exported functions
- Using C run-time functions
- Writing assembly-language code

14.1 Choosing a Memory Model

Like any DOS application, a Windows application can contain one or more code segments and one or more data segments, depending on the memory model you select when compiling the source-code modules of your application. Chapter 16, "More Memory Management," discusses in detail the memory-model options that are available to you.

The memory model you choose will affect how efficiently your application will run in the Windows environment. In most cases, the best model is the mixed model. When using the mixed model, you compile your modules to have default small- or medium-model settings and to name the data segments. You then override these default settings by using explicit **FAR** calls (in coded segments with the small-model settings) or explicit **NEAR** calls (in segments with the medium-model settings) to call functions in other segments.

The advantages of the mixed model are:

- Near calls reduce the amount of code generated by the compiler and make the function calls execute more quickly.
- Compiling the modules with named code segments partitions the code segments into smaller segments, which are easier for Windows to manage as it moves the code segments in memory.

To create an application using the mixed model (with the small-model default settings), follow these steps:

1. Provide prototypes for all functions in your source code that are called from outside the code segment that defines them. For the sake of convenience, you can place these prototypes in a header (.H) file. You must prototype all function calls made by one data segment to another as far calls using the **FAR** key word. The following is an example of a function prototype for a far call:

   ```
   int FAR MyCalculation(int,int);
   ```

2. Compile your C modules using the **–AS** switch to create the application using the small memory model.
3. Compile your C modules using the **–NT** switch to name the code segments of your application.

See *Tools* for more information on these and other compiler switches.

Creating an application using the mixed model with medium-model default settings is similar, except that you would explicitly declare as **NEAR** those functions which are called only within the data segment that defines them, and compile the modules using the **–AM** switch to produce the medium-model default settings.

14.2 Using NULL

The symbolic constant NULL has different definitions for Windows and the Microsoft C Compiler version 6.0. The WINDOWS.H header file defines NULL as:

```
#define NULL 0
```

On the other hand, C 6.0 library header files (such as STDDEF.H) define NULL as:

```
#ifndef NULL
#define NULL ((void *)0)
#endif
```

To avoid compiler warnings, you should use NULL only for pointers, such as the **LPSTR** parameters in Windows functions. You should not use NULL for variables that you declare as primary data types, such as **int**, **WORD**, **HANDLE**, and so on. WINDOWS.H defines **HANDLE** as a **WORD**.

You can avoid such compiler warnings by making sure that your program includes WINDOWS.H before any header file from the C run-time library that defines NULL, as shown in the following example:

```
#include <WINDOWS.H>
#include <STDDEF.H>
```

Because the header files in the C run-time library do not define NULL if it has already been defined, the preprocessor does not override the initial definition in WINDOWS.H.

14.3 Using Command-Line Arguments and the DOS Environment

Your application can obtain the command-line arguments used when the user started the application, as well as the current DOS environment.

When a Windows application executes, the Windows start-up routine copies the command-line arguments to the **_argc** and **_argv** variables. Like their counterparts in a standard C program, these variables represent the number of arguments and an array of strings containing the actual arguments. In addition, the **environ** variable receives a pointer to an array of strings that contain the current DOS environment when the application was started.

To use these variables, you must declare them as external to your application, as shown:

```
extern int      _argc;
extern char *   _argv[];
extern char *   _environ[];
```

If you want, you can also obtain the command-line parameters by parsing the *lpCommandLine* parameter, which Windows passes to your application's WinMain function.

If your application does not require access to the command-line arguments or the DOS environment, you can reduce the size of your heap, and code by eliminating C run-time initialization code. Section 14.5.10, "Eliminating C Run-Time Start-up Code," explains how to do this.

Dynamic-link libraries (DLLs) cannot access the **_argc**, **_argv**, and **environ** variables. Instead, to obtain the command-line arguments, the DLL must parse the *lpCommandLine* parameter, which Windows passes to the LibEntry routine. See Chapter 20, "Dynamic-Link Libraries," for more information on LibEntry.

Since a DLL does not have access to the _**environ** variable, it must call the **GetDOSEnvironment** function to retrieve the environment string.

14.4 Writing Exported Functions

Normally, the functions you define in your application do not require any special treatment. There are two exceptions to this rule, however:

- Functions in a DLL that are called outside of the library
- Callback functions

Refer to Chapter 20, "Dynamic-Link Libraries," for information on writing functions in a DLL.

Callback functions are functions in your application that are called by Windows, not your application. The following lists the common types of callback functions:

- WinMain. This is the entry point for your application.
- Application window procedures. These functions process messages sent to the window.
- Application dialog procedures. These functions process messages sent to the dialog box.
- Enumeration callback procedures. These functions handle the results of Windows enumeration functions.
- Memory-notification procedures. These functions are called by Windows to notify your application that a block of memory is about to be discarded.
- Window-hook procedures (filters). These functions process messages sent to the windows of other applications. Most window-hook callback functions must be in a library.

14.4.1 Creating a Callback Procedure

For all callback functions, you must follow these steps:

1. Define the callback procedure using the **PASCAL** key word. This causes the function parameters to be pushed onto the stack "from right to left," just like standard Windows functions.
2. Define the callback procedure using the **FAR** key word. This allows the function to be called outside the code segment that contains the function. This rule does not apply to the WinMain function.

3. Compile the module containing the callback procedure with the **–Gw** switch (not the **–GW** switch). This adds the proper Windows prolog and epilog code to the function, ensuring that the currect data segment is used by the function when it executes.

4. List the callback procedure in the **EXPORTS** statement of the application's module-definition (.DEF) file. This defines the ordinal value and attributes of the callback function.

With the exception of the WinMain function, your application passes the procedure-instance address of the callback procedure to a Windows function to tell Windows when it should execute the callback procedure. For example, when you create a dialog box, one of the parameters of the function that creates the dialog box is the procedure-instance address of the function that will handle the messages sent to the dialog box.

To create a procedure-instance address of a function, call the **MakeProcInstance** function. This function returns a procedure-instance address that points to prolog code that is executed before the function is executed. The prolog binds the data segment of the instance of your application to the callback function. Thus, when the function is executed, it has access to variables and data in the data segment of the application instance. You do not need to create a procedure-instance address for the WinMain function or any window procedure that your application registers with the **RegisterClass** function.

When your application no longer needs the callback procedure (that is, when you are certain Windows will no longer call it), you should call **FreeProcInstance** to free the function from the data segment.

14.4.2 Creating the WinMain Function

Every Windows application must have a WinMain function; like the main function of a standard C-language program, the WinMain function in effect serves as the entry point for your application. It contains statements and Windows function calls that create windows and read and dispatch input intended for the application. The function definition has the following form:

```
int PASCAL WinMain(hInst,hPrevInst,lpCmdLine,nCmdShow)
HANDLE hInst;
HANDLE hPrevInst;
LPSTR lpCmdLine;
int nCmdShow;
{
          .
          .
          .
}
```

Like all Windows functions, WinMain is declared with the **PASCAL** key word. As a result, your definition of WinMain must contain all four parameters, even if your application does not use them all.

Even though Windows calls it directly, WinMain must not be declared with the **FAR** key word or exported in the definition file because it is called from start-up code added by the linker to the same data segment. WinMain is implicitly declared **NEAR** or **FAR**, depending on the memory model that you use to compile the module that defines WinMain. This memory model must be consistent with the memory model of the C run-time link library containing the start-up code which calls WinMain.

14.5 Using C Run-Time Functions

The SDK contains special versions of the C-language run-time libraries that differ from the equivalent libraries supplied with the Microsoft C Optimizing Compiler. The following sections describe other ways in which the Windows C run-time libraries differ from those supplied with the C Compiler.

14.5.1 Using Windows C Libraries

You can use the Windows C run-time libraries with the Microsoft C Compiler, versions 5.1 and later. The Windows-specific versions of the C run-time libraries are adapted for the Windows environment. The Windows prolog and epilog have been added to all C run-time routines that require them. This prevents problems associated with code-segment movement in low-memory situations. Many C run-time routines have been rewritten to avoid the assumption that DS equals SS, which is not true for Windows DLLs. See Chapter 20, "Dynamic-Link Libraries," for information on calling C run-time library functions that assume DS equals SS from a DLL.

The Windows SDK contains two sets of run-time libraries. One set is linked with Windows applications, while the other set is linked with Windows DLLs. These libraries contain application- or DLL-start-up code as well as all C run-time routines, including memory model–dependent replacement routines. As a result, the SDK requires only one import library, LIBW.LIB. This import library is memory-model independent.

The SDK 3.0 **INSTALL** program always names the Windows versions of the C run-time libraries according to the following naming convention:

{S|M|C|L}{LIB|DLL}C{A|E}W.LIB

S, M, C, and L represent small, medium, compact, or large memory model libraries, respectively. LIB and DLL indicate libraries intended to be linked with application and DLL modules, respectively. A and E indicate alternate math or emulated math libraries. Because of this naming convention, you must explicitly name the Windows version of the C run-time library when linking your application. The following shows an example of using the **LINK** command to link an application module to a Windows C run-time library:

```
LINK GENERIC, , , /NOD SLIBCEW LIBW, GENERIC.DEF
```

The /**NOD** (no default directory search) option is recommended to prevent **LINK** from searching for a C run-time function in a DOS version of the C run-time library if it does not find the function in the Windows version of the library. When you use this option, your application will not compile if you inadvertently called a C run-time function that is not supported by the Windows C run-time libraries.

The SDK also contains Windows-specific versions of the C run-time header files. These files help you detect during compilation whether you have inadvertently called a C run-time routine that is not supported in the Windows environment. To perform this check, add the following directive to your module header file prior to any **#include** directives for the C run-time header files:

```
#define _WINDOWS
```

The set of C run-time routines that support calling from Windows applications includes a subset that support calling from Windows DLLs. The Windows-specific header files identify this subset. If you are creating a DLL, you should include both of these directives before any **#include** directives for the C run-time header files as shown:

```
#define _WINDOWS
#define _WINDLL
```

14.5.2 Allocating Memory

Although the Windows versions of the C run-time libraries supply replacements for such memory-allocation functions as **malloc** and **free**, you should instead use Windows-specific memory-allocation functions. For example, while **malloc** allocates a fixed memory object in the local heap, the Windows **LocalAlloc** function allows you to define the object as moveable in the local heap.

14.5.3 Manipulating Strings

You can use the C run-time string functions to manipulate strings. However, in the small and medium memory models, these functions do not handle strings declared as far pointers or arrays, such as a dynamically allocated global memory object created by the **GlobalAlloc** function. The C run-time buffer-manipulation routines (such as **memcpy** and **memset**) are subject to the same restrictions in the small and medium models.

Windows provides the following functions for manipulating far strings:

- **lstrcat**
- **lstrcmp**
- **lstrcmpi**
- **lstrcpy**
- **lstrlen**

To compare or test characters in the ANSI character set, use the following functions instead of the equivalent C run-time functions:

- **AnsiLower**
- **AnsiLowerBuff**
- **AnsiNext**
- **AnsiPrev**
- **AnsiUpperBuff**
- **IsCharAlpha**
- **IsCharAlphaNumeric**
- **IsCharLower**
- **IsCharUpper**

Windows uses a different collating sequence than do the C run-time functions.

Windows also provides the **wsprintf** and **wvsprintf** functions as replacements for the C run-time **sprintf** and **vsprintf** functions. The following are advantages of the Windows versions:

- The Windows versions use far buffers rather than near buffers.
- The Windows versions are much smaller.
- The Windows versions allow you to eliminate the C start-up code if your application does not need other C run-time functions. See Section 14.5.10, "Eliminating C Run-Time Start-up Code," for more information.

However, the Windows versions support only a subset of the string format specifications. In particular, floating-point formats, pointer format and octal base are not supported.

IMPORTANT If you replace a **sprintf** or **vsprintf** function call with the equivalent Windows function, be sure to type-cast any string passed as a **%s** argument to a far pointer:

```
char buffer[100];
char *strl; /* near pointer in small or medium model */
.
.
.
sprintf(buffer,"Strl=%s",strl);          /*  Valid  */
wsprintf(buffer,"Strl=%s",(LPSTR)strl); /*  Valid  */
wsprint(buffer,"Strl=%s",strl);          /* INVALID */
```

14.5.4 Using File Input and Output

Use the Windows **OpenFile** function to create, open, reopen, or delete a file. **OpenFile** returns a DOS file handle that you can use with such C run-time functions as **read**, **write**, **lseek**, and **close**. If you compile your C module using the small or medium memory model, the *buffer* parameter of **read** and **write** is a near pointer (**char near ***). If you want to read to or write from a buffer declared in your application as a far pointer or array, use the Windows functions **_lread** and **_lwrite**. There are particularly useful for reading into or writing out of dynamically allocated global memory objects. You can also use buffered file input and output C routines, such as **fopen**, **fread**, and **fwrite**.

You can also use the Windows functions **_lopen** and **_lcreat** to create or open a file.

Since Windows is a multitasking environment, other applications may attempt to access the same file that your application is reading or writing. You can control access by other applications when your application opens a file by setting the appropriate share bit in the *wStyle* parameter. You should leave files open only while you are actually reading and writing from them unless your application needs to control access to the file at other times.

NOTE If a DLL opens a file, the file handle belongs to the application that called the DLL. If the DLL opens more than one file on behalf of multiple applications, it is possible that the same file handle value will be assigned more than once by DOS.

14.5.5 Using Console Input and Output

Your application must share the system console with other applications. Consequently, the Windows versions of the C run-time libraries exclude the following C run-time console input and output functions:

- **cgets**
- **cprintf**
- **cputs**
- **getch**
- **getche**
- **kbhit**
- **putch**
- **ungetch**

Instead, your application should accept console input through the WM_KEYDOWN, WM_KEYUP, and WM_CHAR messages to your window and dialog procedures. If you require more advanced techniques, you can call the **PeekMessage** function to look ahead at keyboard input, or you can install a keyboard filter function in a DLL by calling the **SetWindowsHook** function.

14.5.6 Using Graphics Functions

The Windows graphics device interface (GDI) provides device-independent graphics functions. Consequently, the C run-time library functions are not included in the Windows versions of the C run-time libraries.

14.5.7 Using Floating-Point Arithmetic

If your application uses floating-point variables, you must link your application using the **-FPi**, **-FPc**, or **-FPa** options on the **LINK** command line.

An application compiled with the **-FPi** option will use an 80x87 math coprocessor if it is present at run time. Otherwise, the application will use a floating-point emulator.

An application compiled with the **-FPc** option compiles the same as an application compiled with the **-FPi** option, except that it can be linked with the alternate math library instead, if desired.

An application compiled with the **-FPa** option uses an alternative math library if no coprocessor is present at run time. This is the smallest and fastest option available without a coprocessor, but this option sacrifices some accuracy for speed, relative to the emulator library.

If you use the **-FPi** or **-FPc** option, you must include WIN87EM.LIB on the **LINK** command line, as shown:

```
LINK SAMPLE, , , SLIBCEW WIN87EM LIBW, SAMPLE.DEF
```

The Windows version 3.0 retail **SETUP** program automatically installs WIN87EM.DLL in the user's Windows system directory.

You can use the SIGFPE (signal floating-point error) option of the C run-time **signal** function to trap floating-point run-time errors, such as overflow and division by zero. To do so, you must prepare the address of your error-handling function by calling **MakeProcInstance**.

Non-Windows applications typically use the C run-time **setjmp** and **longjmp** functions to isolate floating-point exceptions. A Windows application should call the Windows **Catch** and **Throw** functions instead.

14.5.8 Executing Other Applications

Windows provides the **WinExec** and **LoadModule** functions to allow your application to execute another application. **LoadModule** executes Windows applications only, while **WinExec** executes both Windows and non-Windows applications. Your application should call these functions instead of the C run-time **exec** and **spawn** family of functions. Like the **spawn** function family, **WinExec** and **LoadModule** are nonpreemptive; that is, they allow your application to continue running while the spawned application executes.

WinExec provides a simple interface for spawning a child process. **LoadModule** is more difficult to use because it requires a parameter block for the application you are executing, but this also allows you greater control over the environment in which the application executes.

14.5.9 Using BIOS and MS-DOS Interface Functions

Do not use the C run-time BIOS interface routines with Windows.

You can use the C run-time INT 21H routines **intdos**, **intdosx** and some of the **_dos** functions such as **_dos_getdrive**. You can also use the **int86** and **int86x** routines to invoke interrupts other than INT 21H. However, you should use interrupts with extreme caution and only if necessary.

14.5.10 Eliminating C Run-Time Start-up Code

Normally when you link a Windows application or DLL, the linker adds C run-time start-up code to the _TEXT code segment. For Windows applications (but not DLLs), this start-up code in turn allocates memory for C run-time variables from the application's automatic data segment.

The Windows version 3.0 SDK allows you to eliminate this code and data overhead required by the C run-time libraries. You can eliminate this overhead if all of the following conditions are true:

- Your application or DLL does not explicitly call any C run-time routines.
- Your application does not use the **_argc** or **_argv** command-line arguments or the **_environ** variable. See Section 14.3, "Using Command-Line Arguments and the DOS Environment" for more information on how to retrieve the command line and the DOS environment. DLLs cannot use **_argc**, **_argv**, and **_environ** in any case.
- Your application or DLL does not implicitly call any C run-time routines, such as to perform stack checking or long division. Stack checking is enabled by default, but you can disable it use the C Compiler **–Gs** option.

Eliminating C Run-Time Start-Up Code from a Windows Application

To eliminate the C run-time start-up code from a Windows application, link the library named *x*NOCRT.LIB instead of the usual C run-time library *x*LIBCAW.LIB or *x*LIBCEW.LIB (the *x* placeholder stands for the memory-model specifier S, M, L, or C).

The following example shows the linker command line for an application named SAMPLE that does not make explicit or implicit calls to C run-time functions:

```
link /nod sample, , , snocrt libw, sample.def
```

The *x*NOCRT.LIB library includes the Windows start-up code that ultimately calls your application's WinMain function.

If you link your application using *x*NOCRT.LIB instead of *x*LIBCAW.LIB or *x*LIBCEW.LIB and the linker reports unresolved external symbols that do not belong to your application, your application is probably calling C run-time routines implicitly. In this case, you can still elminate C run-time start-up code and data required for explicit C run-time calls and for the use of the **_argc**, **_argv**, and **_environ** variables. To do this, include *x*NOCRT.LIB on your linker command line before (rather than instead of) *x*LIBCEW.LIB or *x*LIBCAW.LIB. You must also specify the linker **/NOE** option.

The following example shows the linker command line for Sample if it makes implicit C run-time calls, but not explicit C run-time calls:

```
link /nod /noe sample, ,., snocrt slibcew libw, sample.def
```

Eliminating C Run-Time Start-Up Code from a Windows DLL

To eliminate the C run-time start-up code from a Windows DLL, link the static library *x*NOCRTD.LIB in place of the usual C run-time library *x*DLLCAW.LIB or *x*DLLCEW.LIB.

The following example shows the linker command line for a DLL named SAMPDLL that does not make explicit or implicit calls to C run-time functions:

```
link /nod sampdll libentry, sampdll.dll, , snocrtd libw, sampdll.def
```

The *x*NOCRTD.LIB library includes the Windows start-up code that ultimately calls your DLL's LibMain routine.

As with an application, if the linker reports unresolved external references that do not belong to your DLL, the DLL is probably making implicit C run-time calls. In this case, you can eliminate the start-up code required for explicit C run-time calls by linking *x*NOCRTD.LIB along with *x*DLLCAW.LIB or *x*DLLCEW.LIB, as shown:

```
link /nod /noe sampdll libentry, sampdll.dll, , snocrtd sdllcew,
sampdll.def
```

Be sure to include the required /**NOE** option.

14.6 Writing Assembly-Language Code

Assembly-language Windows applications are highly structured assembly-language programs that use high-level-language calling conventions as well as Windows functions, data types, and programming conventions. Although you assemble assembly-language Windows programs using the Microsoft Macro Assembler, the goal is to generate object files that are similar to object files generated using the C Compiler. The following is a list of guidelines designed to help you meet this goal and create assembly-language Windows applications:

1. Include the CMACROS.INC file in the application source files. This file contains high-level-language macros that define the segments, programming models, function interfaces, and data types needed to create Windows applications. See the *Reference*, *Volume 2* for more information on Windows assembly-language macros.
2. Define the programming model, setting one of the options **memS**, **memM**, **memC**, or **memL** to 1. This option must be set before you specify the statement that includes the CMACROS.INC file.

3. Set the calling convention to Pascal by setting the **?PLM** option to 1. This option must be set before you specify the statement that includes the CMACROS.INC file. Pascal calling conventions are required only for functions that are called by Windows.

4. Set the Windows prolog and epilog option **?WIN** to 1. This option must be set before you specify the statement that includes the CMACROS.INC file. This option is required only for callback functions (or for exported functions in Windows libraries).

5. Create the application entry point, WinMain, and make sure that it is declared a public function. It should have the following form:

```
cProc WinMain, <PUBLIC>, <si,di>
             parmW hInstance
             parmW hPrevInstance
             parmD lpCmdLine
             parmW nCmdShow
cBegin WinMain
                  .
                  .
                  .
cEnd WinMain
```

   The WinMain function should be defined within the standard code segment **CODE**.

6. Make sure that your callback functions are declared:

```
cProc TestWndProc, <FAR,PUBLIC>, <si,di>
             parmW hWnd
             parmW message
             parmW wParam
             parmD lParam
cBegin TestWndProc
                  .
                  .
                  .
cEnd TestWndProc
```

   Callback functions must be defined within a code segment.

7. Link your application with the appropriate C-language library for Windows and C run-time libraries. To link properly, you might need to add an external definition for the absolute symbol **__acrtused** in your application source file.

NOTE All Windows functions destroy all registers except DI, SI, BP, and DS.

14.6.1 Modifying the Interrupt Flag

Windows in 386 enhanced mode runs at I/O Privilege Level 0 (IOPL0). At IOPL0, the **POPF** and **IRET** instructions will not change the state of the interrupt flag. (Other flags will still be saved and restored.) This means, for example, that the following code will leave interrupts disabled upon completion:

```
pushf   ; this is no longer valid code
cli
.
.
.
popf    ; will leave interrupts disabled
```

In this IOPL0 environment, **STI** and **CLI** are the only instructions that will change the interrupt flag. Upon exiting a critical section of code in which you require interrupts to be disabled, you cannot rely on the **POPF** instruction to restore the state of the interrupt flag. Instead, you should explicitly set the interrupt flag upon examination to its saved value (saved by a previous **PUSHF**). The following code illustrates the proper method for restoring the interrupt flag:

```
        pushf   ; this code illustrates the proper technique
        cli
        .
        .
        .
        pop ax
        test    ah,2
        jz SkipSTI
        sti
SkipSTI:
        .
        .
        .
```

If you have a software interrupt hook which calls the next interrupt handler in the chain, you similarly cannot rely on the **IRET** of the next interrupt handler to return the state of the interrupt flag. The following code is incorrect:

```
My_SW_Int_Hook: ; the following is incorrect
    sti
   .
   .
   .
   pushf ; simulate interrupt call with a pushf
   cli    ;   and a cli
```

```
    call  [Next_Handler_In_Chain]
           ; the IRET of the next interrupt handler will not restore the
           ; interrupt flag, so it may be left cleared (interrupts disabled)
    .
    .
    .
    iret
```

The proper technique is to place a **STI** instruction immediately after the call to the next interrupt handler, to once again enable interrupts in case the next interrupt handler left interrupts disabled. This proper technique is illustrated here:

```
My_SW_Int_Hook: ; the following is correct
    sti
    .
    .
    .
    pushf ; simulate interrupt call with a pushf
    cli    ;   and a cli
    call [Next_Handler_In_Chain]
    sti   ; enable interrupts again, in case next handler disabled them
    .
    .
    .
    iret
```

14.6.2 Writing Exported Functions in Assembly Language

When you write an exported function in assembly language, do not begin the function with the following code:

```
mov ax,xxxx
```

In this example, *xxxx* is any constant value.

This code at the beginning of an exported function is identical to the beginning of a library code segment that has been cached in extended memory by Windows running in real mode. When Windows attempts to reload the code segment, it assumes that the constant value is the address of the library's data segment and fixes up the constant value to the new address of the data segment.

To ensure that Windows does not treat your code segment as a cached library segment, simply precede the **MOV AX** instruction with a **NOP** instruction, as shown:

```
nop
mov ax,xxxx
```

14.6.3 Using the ES Register

You must take special care when using the ES register in an assembly-language program. Under certain circumstances, a selector that points to a discarded data object in the ES register can cause your application to produce a general-protection (GP) fault when running in standard mode or 386 enhanced mode. Also, a rare combination of circumstances can cause Windows to enter an infinite loop.

A GP fault occurs when a program pops the ES stack and the selector in the ES register refers to a segment that has been discarded.

For example, in the following code sample, ES refers to a globally allocated memory object. Freeing the object invalidates the selector that was temporarily pushed onto the stack.

```
push es
    .
    .
    .
cCall GlobalFree <es>
    .
    .
    .
pop es
```

Your program does not have to discard a segment explicitly for it to be discarded. The following sample shows how a segment can be indirectly discarded:

```
push es         ; ES refers to a discardable data segment
    .
    .
    .
call far Procl  ; Procl directly or indirectly causes the memory
    .          ; object pointed to by ES to be discarded
    .
    .
pop es
```

Windows handles code segment faults in standard and 386 enhanced modes. It does not handle data segment faults however, so this example would result in a GP fault.

An unusual situation can arise that puts Windows in an infinite loop when the ES register holds the selector to a discardable code segment. In such cases, you should clear it before making a call from one discardable segment to another.

The following sample shows how to make such a call:

```
mov es, _CODESEG1    ; CODESEG1 is discardable
    .
    .
    .
xor ax, ax            ; This sample clears the ES register before
mov es, ax            ; calling from a discardable segment to a
call far Procl        ; discardable segment
```

If you fail to clear the ES register in this situation, the Windows segment fault handler can enter an infinite loop discarding and reloading the three discardable code segments when memory is low. During this process, the ES stack is pushed and popped, forcing CODESEG1 to be unnecessarily reloaded when the "code fence" only has room for the other two segments.

14.7 Summary

This chapter discussed how to write a Windows application using the C and assembly programming languages. It explained how to choose the appropriate memory model for your application, how to use the NULL constant in your application, and how to make command-line arguments and DOS environment variables available to your application. This chapter also described how to write exported functions, and explained special considerations for writing applications using C run-time functions and assembly language.

For more information on topics related to creating Windows applications using the C and assembly languages, see the following:

Topic	Reference
Managing memory	*Guide to Programming*: Chapter 15, "Memory Management," and Chapter 16, "More Memory Management"
Creating dynamic-link libraries	*Guide to Programming*: Chapter 20, "Dynamic-Link Libraries"
Windows assembly-language macros	*Reference, Volume 2*: Chapter 13, "Assembly-Language Macros Overview," and Chapter 14, "Assembly-Language Macros Directory"
Compiling and linking applications	*Tools*: Chapter 1, "Compiling Applications: The C Compiler," and Chapter 2, "Linking Applications: The Linker"

Chapter 15 Memory Management

All applications must use memory in order to run. Because Microsoft Windows is a multitasking system, several applications may use memory simultaneously. Windows manages the available memory to make sure all applications have access to it, and to make the use of memory as efficient as possible.

This chapter provides a brief introduction to the Microsoft Windows memory-management system.

This chapter covers the following topics:

- Using memory in the Windows environment
- Using code and data segments efficiently

This chapter also explains how to build a sample application, Memory, that illustrates these concepts.

15.1 Using Memory

The Windows memory-management system lets your application allocate blocks of memory. You can allocate blocks of memory from either the global or the local heap. The global heap is a pool of free memory available to all applications. The local heap is a pool of free memory available to just your application. In managing the system memory, Windows also manages the code and data segments of your application.

In some memory-management systems, the memory you allocate remains fixed at a specific memory location until you free it. In Windows, allocated memory can be also be moveable and discardable. A moveable memory block does not have a fixed address; Windows can move it at any time to a new address. Moveable memory blocks let Windows make the best use of free memory. For example, if a moveable memory block separates two free blocks of memory, Windows can move the moveable block to combine the free blocks into one contiguous block. A discardable memory block is similar to moveable memory in that windows can move it, but Windows can also reallocate a discardable block to zero length if it needs the space to satisfy an allocation request. Reallocating a memory block to zero length destroys the data the block contains, but an application always has the option of reloading the discarded data whenever it is needed.

When you allocate a memory block, you receive a handle, rather than a pointer, to that memory block. The handle identifies the allocated block. You use it to retrieve the block's current address when you need to access the memory.

To access a memory block, you lock the memory handle. This temporarily fixes the memory block and returns a pointer to its beginning. While a memory handle is locked, Windows cannot move or discard the block. Therefore, after you have finished using the block, you should unlock the handle as soon as possible. Keeping a memory handle locked makes Windows' memory management less efficient and can cause subsequent allocation requests to fail.

Windows lets you compact memory. By squeezing the free memory from between allocated memory blocks, Windows collects the largest contiguous free-memory block possible, from which you may allocate additional blocks of memory. This squeezing is a process of moving and (if necessary) discarding memory blocks. Windows also lets you discard individual memory blocks if you temporarily have no need for them.

15.1.1 Using the Global Heap

The global heap contains all of system memory. Windows allocates the memory it needs for code and data from the global heap when it first starts. Any remaining free memory in the global heap is available to applications and Windows libraries.

Applications typically use the global heap for large memory allocations (greater than a kilobyte or so). Although you can allocate larger memory objects from the global heap than you can from the local heap, there is a tradeoff: because it's easier to manipulate local data than it is to manipulate global data, your application will be easier to write if you use only local data.

You can allocate any size of memory block from the global heap. Applications typically allocate large blocks from the global heap; these blocks can exceed 64K if the applications need that much contiguous space. Windows provides special services for accessing data past the first 64K segment. Chapter 16, "More Memory Management," explains how to use these services.

To allocate a block of global memory, use the **GlobalAlloc** function. You specify the size and type (fixed, moveable, or discardable); **GlobalAlloc** returns a handle to the memory block. Before you can use the memory block, you must lock it by using the **GlobalLock** function, which returns the full 32-bit address of the first byte in the memory block. You can then use this long pointer to access the bytes in the block.

In the following example, the **GlobalAlloc** function allocates 4096 bytes of moveable memory and the **GlobalLock** function locks it so that the first 256 bytes can be set to 0xFF:

```
HANDLE hMem;
LPSTR lpMem;
int i;

if ((hMem = GlobalAlloc(GMEM_MOVEABLE, 4096)) != NULL) {
    if ((lpMem = GlobalLock(hMem)) != (LPSTR) NULL) {
        for (i = 0; i < 256; i++)
            lpMem[i] = 0xFF;
        GlobalUnlock(hMem);
    }
}
```

In this example, the application unlocks the memory handle by using the **GlobalUnlock** function immediately after accessing the memory block. Once a moveable or discardable memory block is locked, Windows guarantees that the block will remain fixed in memory until it is unlocked. This means the address remains valid as long as the block remains locked, but this also keeps Windows from making the best use of memory if other allocation requests are made. Cooperative applications unlock memory.

The **GlobalAlloc** function returns NULL if an allocation request fails. You should always check the return value to ensure that it is a valid handle. If desired, you can check to see how much memory is available in the global heap by using the **GlobalCompact** function. This function returns the number of bytes in the largest contiguous free block of memory.

You should also check the address returned by the **GlobalLock** function. This function returns a null pointer if the memory handle was not valid or if the contents of the memory block have been discarded.

You can free any global memory you may no longer need by using the **GlobalFree** function. In general, you should free memory as soon as you no longer need it so that other applications can use the space. You should always free global memory before your application terminates.

15.1.2 Using the Local Heap

The local heap contains free memory that may be allocated for private use by the application. The local heap is located in the application's data segment and is therefore accessible only to a specific instance of the application. You can allocate memory from the local heap in blocks of up to 64K and the memory can be fixed, moveable, or discardable, as needed.

Windows does not automatically supply an application with a local heap. To request a local heap for your application, use the **HEAPSIZE** statement in the application's module-definition file. This statement sets the initial size, in bytes, of the local heap. (For more information on module-definition statements, see the *Reference, Volume 2*.) If the local heap is in a fixed data segment, you may allocate up to the specified heap size. If the local heap is in a moveable data segment, you may allocate beyond the initial heap size and up to 64K, since Windows will automatically allocate additional space for the local heap until the data segment reaches the 64K maximum. You should note, however, that if Windows allocates additional local memory to satisfy a local allocation, it may move the data segment, making invalid any long pointers to blocks in local memory.

The maximum size of any local heap depends on the size of the application's stack, static data, and global data. The local heap shares the data segment with the stack and this data. Since a data segment can be no larger than 64K, an application's local heap can be no larger than 64K minus the size of the application's stack, global data, and static data. The application's stack size is defined by the **STACKSIZE** statement in the application's module-definition file. (For more information, see the *Reference, Volume 2*.) The global and static data size depends on how many strings and global or static variables are declared in the application. Windows enforces a minimum stack size of 5K; if the module-definition file specifies a smaller stack size, Windows sets the stack size to 5K.

You can allocate local memory by using the **LocalAlloc** function. The function allocates a block of memory in the application's local heap and returns a handle to the memory. You lock the local memory block by using the **LocalLock** function. This returns a near address (a 16-bit offset) to the first byte in the memory block. The offset is relative to the beginning of your data segment. In the following example, the **LocalAlloc** function allocates 256 bytes of moveable memory and the **LocalLock** function locks it so that the first 256 bytes can be set to 0xFF:

```
HANDLE hMem;
PSTR pMem;
int i;

if ((hMem = LocalAlloc(LMEM_MOVEABLE, 256)) != NULL) {
    if ((pMem = LocalLock(hMem)) != NULL) {
        for (i = 0; i < 256; i++)
            pMem[i] = 0xFF;
        LocalUnlock(hMem);
    }
}
```

In this example, the application unlocks the memory handle by using the **Local-Unlock** function immediately after accessing the memory block. Once a moveable or discardable memory block is locked, Windows guarantees that the block will remain fixed in memory until it is unlocked. This means the address remains valid as long as the block remains locked, but this also keeps Windows from making the best use of memory if other allocation requests are made. If you want to ensure that you are getting the best performance from your application's local heap, make sure you unlock memory after using it.

The **LocalAlloc** returns NULL if an allocation request fails. You should always check the return value to ensure that a valid handle exists. If desired, you can check to see how much memory is available in the local heap by using the **LocalCompact** function. This function returns the number of bytes in the largest contiguous free block of memory in the local heap.

You should also check the address returned by the **LocalLock** function. This function returns NULL if the memory handle was not valid or if the contents of the memory block have been discarded.

15.1.3 Working with Discardable Memory

You create a discardable memory block by combining the GMEM_DISCARDABLE and GMEM_MOVEABLE options when allocating the block. The resulting block will be moved as necessary to make room for other allocation requests; or if there is not enough memory to satisfy the request, the block may be discarded. The following example allocates a discardable block from global memory:

```
hMem = GlobalAlloc(GMEM_MOVEABLE | GMEM_DISCARDABLE, 4096L);
```

When Windows discards a memory block, it empties the block by reallocating it, with zero bytes given as the new size. The contents of the block are lost, but the memory handle to this block remains valid. Any attempt to lock the handle and access the block will fail, however.

Windows determines which memory blocks to discard by using a least-recently-used (LRU) algorithm. It continues to discard memory blocks until there is enough memory to satisfy an allocation request. In general, if you have not accessed a discardable block in some time, it is a candidate for discarding. A locked block cannot be discarded.

You can discard your own memory blocks by using the **GlobalDiscard** function. This function empties the block but preserves the memory handle. You can also discard other applications' memory blocks by using the **GlobalCompact** function. This function moves and discards memory blocks until the specified or largest possible amount of memory is available. One way to discard all discardable blocks is to supply –1 as the argument. This is a request for every byte of memory. Although the request will fail, it will discard all discardable blocks and leave the largest possible block of free memory.

Since a discarded memory block's handle remains valid, you can still retrieve information about the block by using the **GlobalFlags** function. This is useful for verifying that the block has actually been discarded. **GlobalFlags** sets the GMEM_DISCARDED bit in its return value when the specified memory block has been discarded. Therefore, if you attempt to lock a discardable block and the lock fails, you can check the block's status by using **GlobalFlags**.

Once a discardable block has been discarded, its contents are lost. If you wish to use the block again, you need to reallocate it to its appropriate size and fill it with the data it previously contained. You can reallocate it by using the **GlobalReAlloc** function. The following example checks the block's status, then fills it with data if it has been discarded:

```
lpMem = GlobalLock(hMem);

if (lpMem == (LPSTR) NULL) {
    if (GlobalFlags(hMem) & GMEM_DISCARDED) {
        hMem = GlobalReAlloc(hMem, 4096L,
            GMEM_MOVEABLE | GMEM_DISCARDABLE);
        lpMem = GlobalLock(hMem);

        /* More program lines  */
        /* Fill with data */
        GlobalUnlock(hMem);
    }
}
```

You can make a discardable object nondiscardable (or vice versa) by using the **GlobalReAlloc** function and the GMEM_MODIFY flag. The following example changes a moveable block, identified by the hMem memory handle, to a moveable, discardable block:

```
hMem = GlobalReAlloc(hMem, 0, GMEM_MODIFY | GMEM_DISCARDABLE);
```

The following example changes a discardable block to a nondiscardable block:

```
hMem = GlobalReAlloc(hMem, 0, GMEM_MODIFY);
```

15.2 Using Segments

One of the principal features of Windows is that it lets the user run more than one application at a time. Since multiple applications place greater demands on memory than does a single application, Windows' ability to run more than one application at a time has a significant impact on how you write applications. Although many computers have at least 640K of memory, this memory rapidly becomes limited as the user loads and runs more applications. In Windows, you must be conscious of how your application uses memory and be prepared to minimize the amount of memory your application occupies at any given time.

To help you manage your application's use of memory, Windows uses the same memory-management system for your application's code and data segments that you use within your application to allocate and manage global memory blocks. When the user starts your application, Windows allocates space for the code and data segments in global memory, then copies the segments from the executable file into memory. These segments can be fixed, moveable, and even discardable. You specify their attributes in the application's module-definition file.

You can reduce the impact your application has on memory by using moveable code and data segments. Using moveable segments lets Windows take advantage of free memory as it becomes available.

You can minimize your application's impact on memory by using discardable code segments. If you make a code segment discardable, Windows discards it, if necessary, to satisfy requests for global memory. Unlike ordinary memory blocks that you may allocate, discarded code segments are monitored by Windows, which automatically reloads them if your application attempts to execute code within these segments. This means that your application's code segments are in memory only when they are needed.

Discarding a segment destroys its contents. Windows does not save the current contents of a discarded segment. Instead it assumes that the segment is no different than when originally loaded and will load the segment directly from the executable file when it is needed.

15.2.1 Using Code Segments

A code segment is one or more bytes of machine instructions. It represents all or part of an application's program instructions. A code segment is never larger than 64K.

IMPORTANT You must not store writeable data in code segments; writing to a code segment causes a general protection fault when your application runs in protected mode. Windows will, however, allow you to store read-only data, such as a jump table, in a code segment. For more information on protected mode, see Chapter 16, "More Memory Management."

Every application has at least one code segment. For example, the sample applications described in previous chapters have one and only one code segment. You can also create an application that has multiple code segments. In fact, most Windows applications have multiple code segments. Using multiple code segments lets you reduce the size of any given code segment to the number of instructions needed to carry out some task. If you also make these segments discardable, you effectively minimize the memory requirements of your application's code segments.

When you create medium- or large-model applications, you are creating applications that use multiple code segments. Medium- and large-model applications typically have one or more source files for each segment. Compile each source file separately and explicitly name the segment to which the compiled code will belong. Then link the application, defining the segments' attributes in the application's module-definition file.

To define a segment's attributes, use the **SEGMENTS** statement in the module-definition file. The following example shows definitions for three segments:

```
SEGMENTS
        PAINT_TEXT MOVEABLE DISCARDABLE
        INIT_TEXT MOVEABLE DISCARDABLE
        WNDPROC_TEXT MOVEABLE DISCARDABLE
```

You may also use the **CODE** statement in the module-definition file to define the default attributes for all code segments. The **CODE** statement also defines attributes for any segments that are not explicitly defined in the **SEGMENTS** statement. The following example shows how to make all segments not listed in the **SEGMENTS** statement discardable:

```
CODE MOVEABLE DISCARDABLE
```

If you use discardable code segments in your application, you need to balance discarding with the number of times the segment may be accessed. For example, the segment containing your main window function should probably not be discardable since Windows calls the function often. Since a discarded segment has to be loaded from disk when needed, the savings in memory you may realize by discarding the window function may be offset by the loss in performance that comes with accessing the disk often.

NOTE In a library, all code segments must be both moveable and discardable. If a library's module-definition file specifies that a code segment is moveable but not discardable, Windows will make that code segment discardable instead.

15.2.2 The DATA Segment

Every application has a **DATA** segment. The **DATA** segment contains the application's stack, local heap, and static and global data. Like a code segment, the **DATA** segment cannot be larger than 64K.

A **DATA** segment can be fixed or moveable, but not discardable. If the **DATA** segment is moveable, Windows automatically locks the segment when it passes control to the application. Otherwise, a moveable **DATA** segment may move if an application allocates global memory, or the application attempts to allocate more memory than is currently available in the local heap. For this reason, it is important not to keep long pointers to variables in the **DATA** segment.

You can define the attributes of the **DATA** segment by using the **DATA** statement in the module-definition file. The default attributes are **MOVEABLE** and **MULTIPLE**. The **MULTIPLE** attribute directs Windows to create one copy of an application's data segment for each instance of the application. This means the contents of the **DATA** segment are unique to each instance of the application.

A large-model application may have additional data segments, but only one **DATA** segment.

For more information on module-definition statements, see the *Reference, Volume 2*.

15.3 A Sample Application: Memory

This sample application illustrates how to create a medium-model Windows application that uses discardable code segments. To create the Memory application, copy and rename the source files of the Generic application, then make the following modifications:

1. Split the C-language source file into four separate files.
2. Modify the include file.
3. Add new segment definitions to the module-definition.
4. Modify the make file.
5. Compile and link the application.

The following sections describe each step in detail.

NOTE Rather than typing the code presented in the following sections, you might find it more convenient to simply examine and compile the sample source files provided with the SDK.

15.3.1 Split the C-Language Source File

You need to split the C-language source file into separate files so that the functions within the file are compiled as separate segments. For this application, you can split the source file into four parts, as described in the following list:

Source File	Content
MEMORY1.C	Contains the WinMain function. Since Windows executes WinMain fairly often, the segment created from this source file is not discardable. This prevents a situation in which the segment has to be loaded from the disk often. Since WinMain is relatively small anyway, keeping this segment in memory has very little impact on available global memory.
MEMORY2.C	Contains the MemoryInit function. Since the MemoryInit function is used only when the application first starts, the segment created from this source file can be discardable.

Source File	Content
MEMORY3.C	Contains the MemoryWndProc function. Although the segment created from this source file can be discardable, the MemoryWndProc function is likely to be called at least as often as the WinMain function receives control. In this case, the segment is moveable but not discardable.
MEMORY4.C	Contains the About function. Since the About function is seldom called (only when the About dialog box is displayed), the code segment created from this source file can be discardable.

You must include the WINDOWS.H and MEMORY.H files in each source file.

15.3.2 Modify the Include File

You need to move the declaration of the hInst variable into the MEMORY.H file. This ensures that the variable is accessible in all segments. The hInst variable is used in the WinMain and MemoryWndProc functions.

15.3.3 Add New Segment Definitions

You need to add segment definitions to the module-definition file to specify the attributes of each code segment. This means you need to add a **SEGMENTS** statement to the file and list each segment by name in the application. After making the changes, the module-definition file should look like the following:

```
NAME     Memory

DESCRIPTION 'Sample Microsoft Windows Application'

EXETYPE WINDOWS

STUB     'WINSTUB.EXE'

❶ SEGMENTS
    MEMORY_MAIN PRELOAD MOVEABLE
    MEMORY_INIT LOADONCALL MOVEABLE DISCARDABLE
    MEMORY_WNDPROC LOADONCALL MOVEABLE
    MEMORY_ABOUT LOADONCALL MOVEABLE DISCARDABLE

❷ CODE    MOVEABLE

DATA     MOVEABLE MULTIPLE

HEAPSIZE  1024
STACKSIZE 8192
```

```
EXPORTS
    MainWndProc       @1
    About             @2
```

In this module-definition file:

❶ The **SEGMENTS** statement defines the attributes of each segment:

- The MEMORY_MAIN segment contains WinMain.
- The MEMORY_INIT segment contains the initialization functions.
- The MEMORY_WNDPROC segment contains the window function.
- The MEMORY_ABOUT segment contains the dialog function.

Each segment has the **MOVEABLE** attribute, but only MEMORY_INIT and MEMORY_ABOUT have the **DISCARDABLE** attribute.

Also, only the MEMORY_MAIN segment is loaded when the application is started. The other segments have the **LOADONCALL** attribute, which means they are loaded when needed.

❷ Although each segment is explicitly defined, the **CODE** statement is still given. This statement specifies the attributes of any additional segments the linker may add to the application; for example, segments containing C run-time functions called in the application source files.

15.3.4 Modify the Make File

You need to modify the make file to separately compile the new C-language sources. Since this application is a medium-model application, you need to use the **–AM** option when compiling. For clarity, you should also name each segment by using the **–NT** option when compiling.

You will also need to change the **LINK** command line so that it refers to the medium-model library, MLIBCEW.LIB, rather than the small-model library SLIBCEW.LIB.

After changes, the make file should look like this:

```
MEMORY.RES: MEMORY.RC MEMORY.H
    RC -r MEMORY.RC

MEMORY1.OBJ: MEMORY1.C MEMORY.H
    CL -c -AM -Gsw -Zp -NT MEMORY_MAIN MEMORY1.C

MEMORY2.OBJ: MEMORY2.C MEMORY.H
    CL -c -AM -Gsw -Zp -NT MEMORY_INIT MEMORY2.C

MEMORY3.OBJ: MEMORY3.C MEMORY.H
    CL -c -AM -Gsw -Zp -NT MEMORY_WNDPROC MEMORY3.C
```

```
MEMORY4.OBJ: MEMORY4.C MEMORY.H
    CL -c -AM -Gsw -Zp -NT MEMORY_ABOUT MEMORY4.C

MEMORY.EXE: MEMORY1.OBJ MEMORY2.OBJ MEMORY3.OBJ MEMORY4.OBJ MEMORY.DEF
    LINK MEMORY1 MEMORY2 MEMORY3 MEMORY4,MEMORY.EXE,,MLIBCEW LIBW,MEMORY.DEF
    RC MEMORY.RES

MEMORY.EXE: MEMORY.RES
    RC MEMORY.RES
```

15.3.5 Compile and Link

After compiling and linking the Memory application, start Windows, the Heap Walker application (provided with the SDK), and Memory. Use Heap Walker to view the various segments of the Memory application.

15.4 Summary

This chapter explained how to allocate and use memory in the Windows environment. Because Windows is a multitasking system, your application should handle memory cooperatively.

This chapter also explained how to use code and data segments in your application.

For more information on topics related to memory management, see the following:

Topic	**Reference**
More about memory management	*Guide to Programming:* Chapter 16, "More Memory Management"
Memory-management functions	*Reference, Volume 1:* Chapter 4, "Functions Directory"
Module-definition statements	*Reference, Volume 2:* Chapter 10, "Module-Definition Statements"

Chapter 16 More Memory Management

Chapter 15, "Memory Management," presented the basic information you need to know about using memory in a Windows program. Some applications require more advanced memory-management techniques, however. This chapter provides more detailed information about Windows memory management and how you should write your application to make the best use of Windows' advanced memory features.

This chapter covers the following topics:

- Windows memory configurations
- Using data storage in Windows applications
- Using memory models
- Using huge data
- Managing program data
- Managing memory for program code

16.1 Windows Memory Configurations

You should expect that your application may run under any of several memory configurations; most often, the particular memory configuration depends on the type of the system CPU and the amount and configuration of memory. Windows supports four memory configurations:

- The basic (640K) memory configuration (Windows real mode)
- The Lotus-Intel-Microsoft (LIM) Expanded Memory Specification (EMS) 4.0 memory configuration (Windows real mode)
- The standard mode memory configuration
- The 386 enhanced mode memory configuration

The amount of memory available to Windows will be less than that installed in the system if the user started other programs before starting Windows.

Because Windows uses different memory configurations on different systems, your application should be able to run successfully with each memory configuration. The best way to ensure this is to write the application following all the Windows memory-management rules. See Section 16.5, "Traps to Avoid in Managing Program Data," for a list of these rules.

Wherever possible, your application should not contain code that is dependent upon a particular memory configuration. However, in some instances an application must be able to determine the memory configuration under which it is running.

To determine the current memory configuration, call the **GetWinFlags** function. This function returns a 32-bit value which contains flags indicating the memory configuration under which Windows is running and other information about the user's system.

The remainder of this section describes the four primary Windows memory configurations.

16.1.1 The Basic Memory Configuration

The basic Windows memory configuration assumes that the system has 640K of physical memory. Before the user starts Windows, the lowest portion of conventional memory has already been allocated by the system's BIOS and by DOS. The lowest portion of memory includes the following:

- The interrupt table
- RAM BIOS data
- DOS device drivers
- Any terminate-and-stay-resident (TSR) programs the user started before Windows

Windows, and applications running under Windows, can use only the remaining (upper) portion of conventional memory. This portion of memory is called the global heap.

Figure 16.1 illustrates the basic Windows memory configuration.

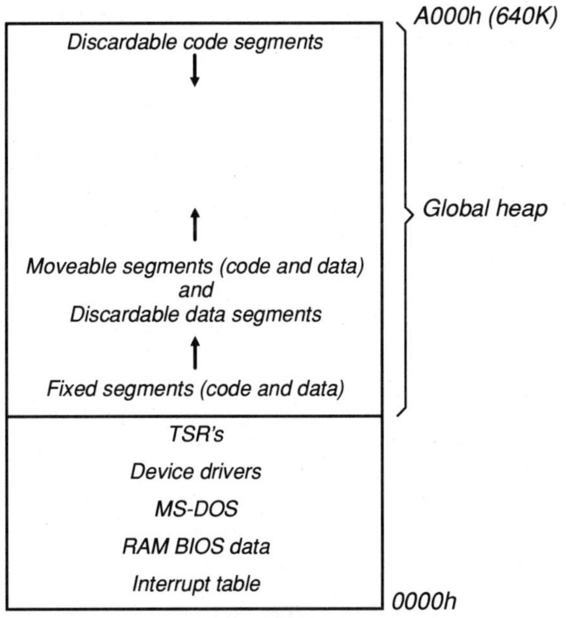

Figure 16.1 Windows Basic Memory Configuration

Chapter 15, "Memory Management," explains how Windows applications use the global heap. The data and code segments of all applications are located in the global heap; the position of each segment in the heap depends on whether that segment is fixed, moveable and discardable, or moveable but not discardable. Table 16.1 lists segment attributes and types, and indicates where Windows places each type in the global heap.

Table 16.1 Segment Positions in the Global Heap

Attribute	Segment Type	Position in Global Heap
Fixed	Code or data	Bottom of global heap
Discardable	Code	Top of global heap
Discardable	Data	Lower portion of global heap, but above fixed segments
Moveable (but not discardable)	Code or data	Above fixed segments

If an application allocates a fixed segment after moveable segments or discardable data segments have already been allocated, Windows tries to rearrange moveable segments and discardable data segments in order to place the new fixed segment as low in the heap as possible. Rearranging memory helps to reduce fragmentation of the heap but requires many more CPU cycles. Because of this, you should avoid declaring or allocating fixed segments.

With the basic memory configuration, if your application's module-definition (.DEF) file declares some code segments discardable, then the application can be larger than the physical memory that's available in the global heap. If physical memory is fully allocated and an application tries to call a code segment that is not currently in physical memory, Windows makes memory available for that code segment by discarding other code or data segments. Removing discardable code segments from memory is transparent to the application; if a discarded segment is needed again, Windows simply reloads it from the disk. On the other hand, removing discardable data segments can result in a loss of data. If your application declares a data segment as discardable, you should make sure that information in the segment can be reread from disk or re-created by some other method.

Under the basic memory configuration, Windows makes more memory available by simply removing discardable segments from memory; it does not perform true disk swapping (swapping code or data segments from memory to the disk and back). If your application requires a larger virtual data space than is available with the basic memory configuration, it can perform its own virtual memory management by swapping data to and from the disk.

16.1.2 The EMS 4.0 Memory Configuration

Windows can use the EMS 4.0 memory configuration if the user's system has EMS memory and an EMS 4.0 device driver. With the EMS configuration, the global heap is larger (from the application's perspective) than it is with the basic memory configuration: the physical address space of the global heap extends above the A000h (640K) line to F000h. Physical addresses F000h to FFFFh are reserved for the ROM BIOS. Some areas between A000h and F000h are also reserved for such hardware support as video memory and network cards. Therefore, the amount of physical memory available to Windows between A000h and F000h is less than 320K. This amount may be as much as 288K, but usually is less.

Figure 16.2 compares the basic memory and EMS 4.0 configurations.

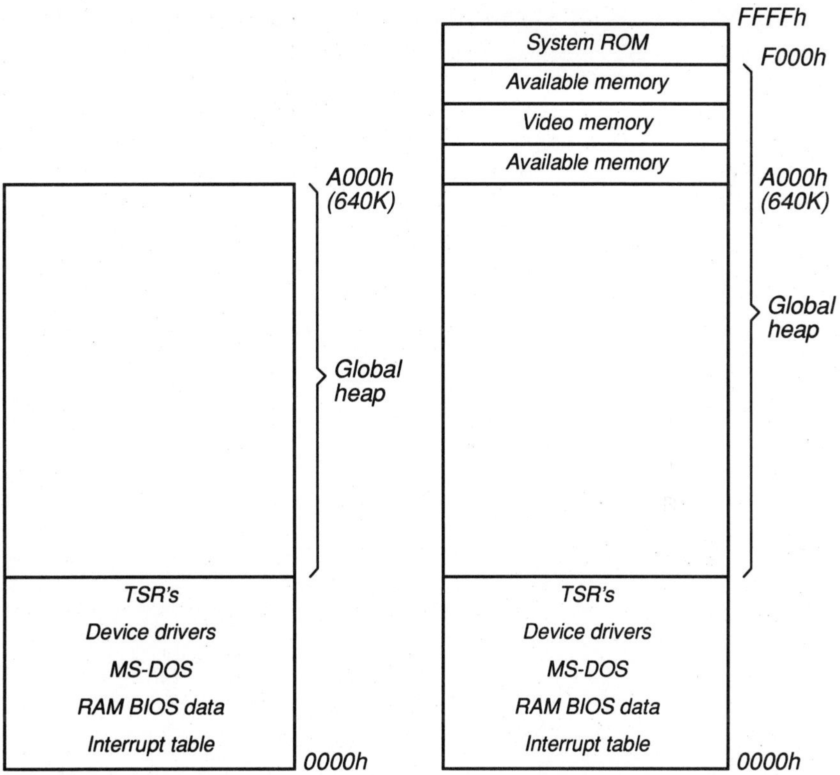

Figure 16.2 Comparison of Basic Memory and EMS 4.0 Configurations

EMS Memory and Banking

Windows can provide applications with more memory when using the EMS configuration. It does this by "banking" memory objects between expanded memory and part of the physical space of the global heap. Banking occurs when Windows resets certain EMS registers to change the mapping of the lower 1 megabyte address space to another area of expanded memory. Resetting the EMS registers is much faster than actually moving data. Figure 16.3 illustrates how Windows maps physical address space to expanded memory.

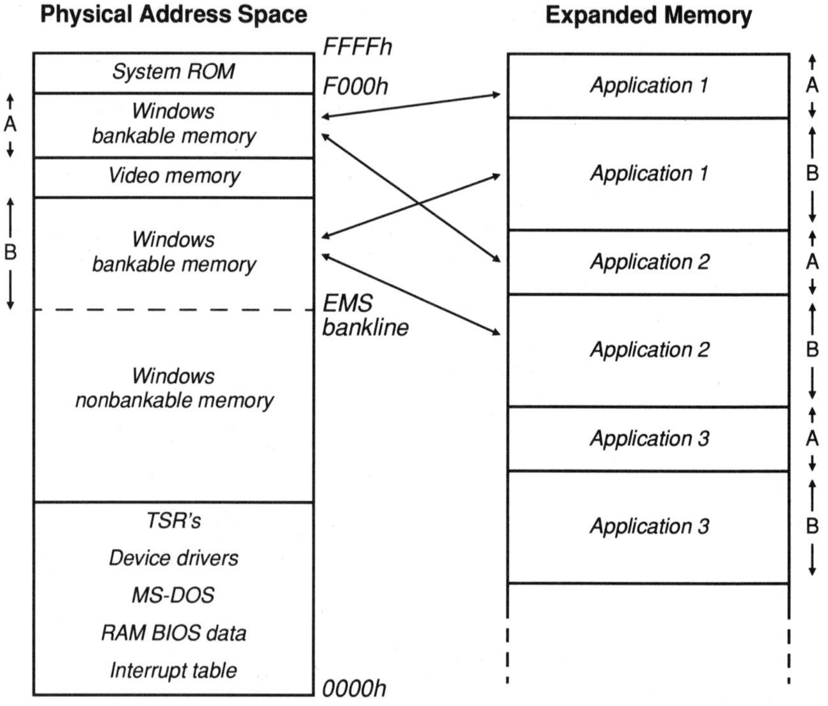

Figure 16.3 Mapping from a Physical Address Space to Expanded Memory

Windows banks code and data between the global heap and expanded memory during a "task context switch," which takes place when one application yields control to another application. Windows banks the first application's code and data from the bankable portion of the global heap to expanded memory; it then banks the second application's code and data into the global heap.

Banking of expanded memory takes place only at task context switches. Code and data are banked in and out for an entire application. Banking does not occur for individual memory blocks. As a result, the total memory available to a given application is not increased by adding to the total amount of expanded memory. Rather, the total memory available to an application depends on the usable portion of memory between A000h and F000h. This increase still significantly benefits an application. Also, the total amount of expanded memory influences how many applications can be banked out and, thus, how many applications the user can run simultaneously with Windows.

Bankable and Nonbankable Memory

When banking code and data between the global heap and expanded memory, Windows banks only certain types of objects. Such bankable code and data is said to be above the EMS bank line. Bankable information includes the following:

- Task (application) code that is fixed or moveable
- Task resources (resources added to an executable file by the Resource Compiler (**RC**))
- Private-library code and data segments. A library is declared private to the calling application when it is compiled with the Resource Compiler **–p** option
- Task module (.EXE) headers (in Windows version 3.0 and later)

Some kinds of memory objects are never banked. In particular, Windows never banks data that must always be available when needed by Windows or a dynamic-link library (DLL). Such nonbankable objects are said to be below the EMS bank line. Nonbankable information always includes the following:

- Task databases (task-specific data used by Windows to manage tasks)
- Library data segments
- Library fixed code
- Library module (.DLL) headers

Other kinds of code and data can reside either below or above the EMS bank line, depending upon where Windows sets the bank line. The location of the bank line depends on the size of the global heap.

If the global heap is smaller than a certain minimum size, then the EMS bank line is set at A000h (640K), resulting in a relatively small bankable area of memory. In this case, Windows is said to be running in small-frame EMS mode. In small-frame EMS mode, the following categories of code and data segments are nonbankable, and are placed below the EMS bank line:

- Library resources
- Discardable DLL code
- Task data segments
- Task global-memory allocations
- All module headers

If there is sufficient memory available, Windows may set the bank line so that there is a relatively large bankable area of memory. In this case, Windows runs in large-frame EMS mode. The bank line can be set as high as A000h in large-frame mode if there is more memory available above A000h than below.

Table 16.2 summarizes how different categories of code and data are placed above or below the EMS bank line, depending on whether Windows is running in small-frame or large-frame mode.

Table 16.2 Use of Expanded Memory

Object	Above or Below EMS Bank Line	
	Small-Frame	Large-Frame
Task database	Below	Below
Library data segment	Below	Below
Library code segment (fixed)	Below	Below
Library resource	Below	Above
Task code segment	Above/Below	Above
Task resource	Above/Below	Above
Task data segment	Below	Above
Library code segment (discardable)	Below	Above
Task module (.EXE) header	Below	Above
Library module (.DLL) header	Below	Below
Dynamically-allocated memory	Below	Above

If there is not enough memory above the bank line in small-frame EMS mode to accommodate the entire amount of bankable code and task resources, the remaining segments are located below the bank line.

Compiling a DLL with the Resource Compiler **–p** option will change how Windows loads DLL memory objects in the large-frame EMS mode. See Chapter 20, "Dynamic-Link Libraries," for more information.

Working Directly with Expanded Memory

Because Windows performs the banking automatically, your application does not have to do anything special to benefit from EMS memory. However, if you want, your application can manipulate expanded memory directly, through a 64K page frame. Using EMS directly gives your application an even larger address space, similar to DOS overlays, but faster. In order to do this:

- You must compile your application using the Resource Compiler's **–l** switch.
- Your application must follow the LIM EMS 3.2 specification.
- Your application must not use any EMS 4.0–specific functions (with the exception of reallocation function 17). Using these functions can conflict with Windows memory management.

When an application allocates expanded memory, it is competing with Windows (and thus with other applications). Therefore, your application should not allocate all of expanded memory for its private use.

16.1.3 The Windows Standard Mode Memory Configuration

Windows uses the standard mode memory configuration by default on systems that meet the following criteria:

- An 80286-based system with at least 1 megabyte of memory.
- An 80386-based system with at least 1 megabyte of memory, but less than 2 megabytes. On 80386-based systems with 2 megabytes or more, Windows uses the 386 enhanced mode memory configuration by default. Section 16.1.4, "The Windows 386 Enhanced Mode Memory Configuration," describes the memory configuration of the 386 enhanced mode.

When Windows is running in standard mode, the global heap is made up of at least two, usually three, distinct blocks of memory, depending on the amount of available memory.

The first block of memory that Windows uses for the global heap is in conventional memory, much like the basic memory configuration. This area begins above any TSR programs, device drivers, DOS, and so on, and extends to the top of conventional memory. This conventional memory is usually 640K, but can be less on some systems.

The second required block of memory for the Windows standard mode configuration is in extended memory. Windows allocates the block in extended memory through an extended-memory (XMS) driver and then accesses the block directly, without using the XMS driver. The size and location of this block can vary, depending on what the user loaded into extended memory before starting Windows.

Windows adds a third block of memory to the Windows standard mode global heap if it is available when Windows starts. This third block is the high memory area (HMA) and is controlled by the XMS driver. This block is not available if the user loaded software in the HMA before starting Windows. However, not much software is currently available that loads itself into this area, so it is likely that the HMA will be available to Windows in standard mode.

Windows links the two or three blocks of memory to form the Windows global heap. The start (bottom) of the conventional memory block is the start (bottom) of the global heap, and the end (top) of the extended memory block is the end (top) of the global heap. If Windows uses the HMA, Windows links the HMA block between the other two blocks.

Figure 16.4 shows a typical Windows standard mode memory configuration.

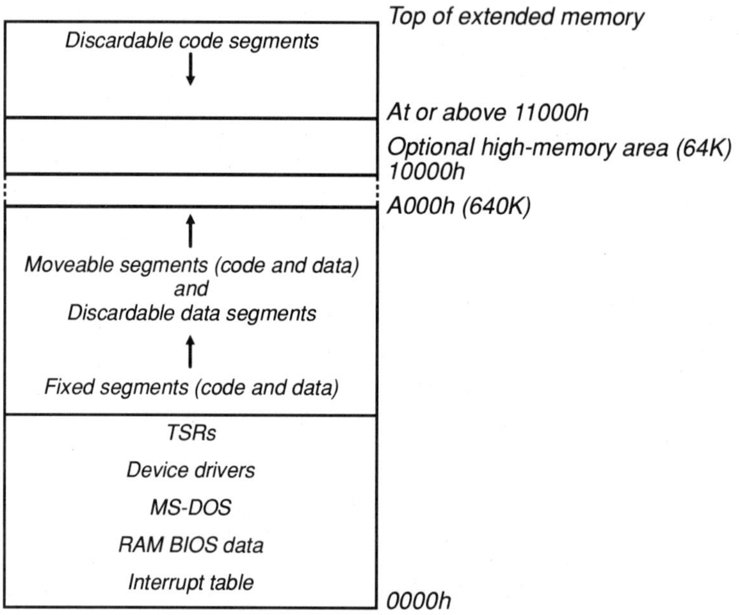

Figure 16.4 Typical Windows Standard Mode Configuration

As with other memory configurations, Windows allocates discardable code segments from the top of the heap, fixed segments from the bottom of the heap, and moveable code and data segments above fixed segments.

Some Windows data items must be allocated in the conventional memory block so they can be accessed when the processor is in real mode instead of protected mode. These items are program segment prefix (PSP) blocks and serial communications data queues.

Using Huge Memory Blocks in the Standard-Mode Memory Configuration

Under the standard mode memory configuration, Windows uses the protected mode of the 80286 or 80386 processor. In real mode, a far address is created from a 16-bit segment address and a 16-bit offset. The segment address points to paragraphs that are aligned on 16-byte increments in a 1-megabyte address space. The offset portion of the far address provides addressing within a range 0 to 64K relative to the segment paragraph address. In standard mode, the 16-bit segment address is a selector, similar to a Windows handle. The selector points to an entry in a local or global descriptor table (LDT or GDT). The table entry indicates whether the segment referred to by the selector currently resides in memory. If the segment resides in memory, then the table entry provides the linear address of the segment.

If you allocate a huge memory block (larger than 64K), the Microsoft C Compiler generates huge-pointer code that performs segment arithmetic to advance a far pointer across segment 64K boundaries. However, it does this only if the block is explicitly declared **huge** or if the module was compiled with the huge memory model. Do not directly change the segment address portion of a far pointer. Attempting to increment the segment address with the intent of advancing the physical paragraph address will only result in an invalid selector. When the invalid selector is subsequently used to read or write to the memory location, either Windows will report a general protection (GP) fault, or possibly worse, the invalid selector might inappropriately point to unintended data or code.

If you are programming in assembly language, the proper technique for incrementing a far pointer is to use the external variable **__ahincr**, defined in MACROS.INC. The value for the external variable **__ahincr** gets fixed up by Windows at load time to be 1000h in real mode, so adding it to the segment address portion of a far pointer will advance the pointer by 1000h paragraphs. In standard mode, Windows fixes up **__ahincr** with the correct constant to increment the segment selector. This is possible because when Windows allocates the huge memory block, it assigns related selector values to the related memory segments that are 64K (1000h paragraphs) in size. This is called "selector tiling." The following example illustrates the proper method for incrementing a far pointer by 64K (the only increment provided):

```
extrn    __ahincr:abs
          .
          .
          .
mov      ax, es          ; es is the segment address you
                         ; wish to increment
add      ax, __ahincr
mov      es, ax
```

Overall, the largest block of memory that you can allocate in standard mode is 1 megabyte in size. In standard mode, all parts of an application (code and data) are normally moveable in linear memory.

Using Global Selectors

To perform memory-mapped input and output, you can use the following global selector constants in an assembly-language program to access the corresponding locations in memory:

- __A000H
- __B000H
- __B800H
- __C000H
- __D000H

- _ _E000H
- _ _F000H

The following example illustrates how to use these selectors properly:

```
mov ax, _ _A000H
mov es,ax
```

Do not use these selectors except to support hardware devices that perform memory-mapped input and output.

Code-Segment and Data-Segment Aliasing

Normally you cannot execute code stored in a data segment. Under standard mode, an attempt to execute code in a data segment results in a general protection fault.

In rare cases, however, this may be necessary, and can be performed by aliasing the data segment in question. Aliasing involves copying a segment selector and then changing the TYPE field of the copy so that an operation that is not normally permitted can be performed on the segment.

Windows provides two functions which perform segment aliasing:

- **AllocDStoCSAlias**
- **ChangeSelector**

AllocDStoCSAlias accepts a data-segment selector and returns a code-segment selector. This permits you to write machine instructions on your data stack, create an alias for the stack segment, and then execute the code on the stack.

This function allocates a new selector; after calling **AllocDStoCSAlias**, you must call the **FreeSelector** function when you no longer need the selector.

You must be careful not to use a selector returned by **AllocDStoCSAlias** if it is possible that the segment has moved. The only way to prevent a segment from moving is by calling the **GlobalFix** function to fix it in linear address space before aliasing the segment.

You can also be sure that a segment has not moved if your application does not yield to another task and does not take any action that could result in memory being allocated. Normally this would require you to allocate and free a new selector each time your application yields or allocates memory. However, you can avoid allocating and freeing a selector so frequently by using a temporary selector. **ChangeSelector** provides a convenient method for aliasing a temporary selector. This function accepts two selectors: a temporary selector, and the selector you wish to alias. To alias this selector repeatedly, you would perform the following steps:

1. Call **AllocateSelector** to create a temporary selector.
2. As often as necessary, call **ChangeSelector**, passing it the temporary selector and the selector you want to alias. Since **ChangeSelector** uses a previously allocated selector, you do not have to free the selector each time you alias it. You only need to call **ChangeSelector** each time you need the aliased selector after the aliased segment might have moved.
3. When you no longer need to alias the selector, call **FreeSelector** to free the temporary selector.

16.1.4 The Windows 386 Enhanced Mode Memory Configuration

If the user's system has at least 2 megabytes of extended memory available and an Intel 80386 microprocessor, then Windows and Windows applications will run in 386 enhanced mode, a form of protected mode. In this mode, by taking advantage of certain features of the 80386 processor, Windows implements a virtual-memory management scheme using disk swapping. The result of this scheme is that the amount of memory available to all applications can be several times the amount of extended memory on the system. In this mode, Windows can theoretically address 4 gigabytes of memory, but is actually limited by the amount of RAM and disk space available for swapping. The largest object that can be allocated in 386 enhanced mode is 64 megabytes. In 386 enhanced mode, all parts of an application (code and data) are normally moveable as well as pageable in linear memory.

NOTE Because 386 enhanced mode uses the protected-mode features of the 80386 processor, the restrictions for using memory in standard mode also apply to using memory in 386 enhanced mode.

The following describes the memory configuration of 386 enhanced mode:

- The global heap is essentially one large virtual address space. Unlike the EMS 4.0 memory configuration, Windows does not bank code and data for individual applications between a 1-megabyte address space and secondary memory. Instead, all applications share the same virtual address space.
- The size of the global heap's virtual address space is not bounded by the amount of extended memory. The disk serves as a secondary memory medium that extends the virtual address space.

The 386 enhanced mode memory configuration is much more like the basic memory configuration than it is like the EMS 4.0 memory configuration or the standard mode memory configuration. Figure 16.5 compares the basic and 386 enhanced mode memory configurations.

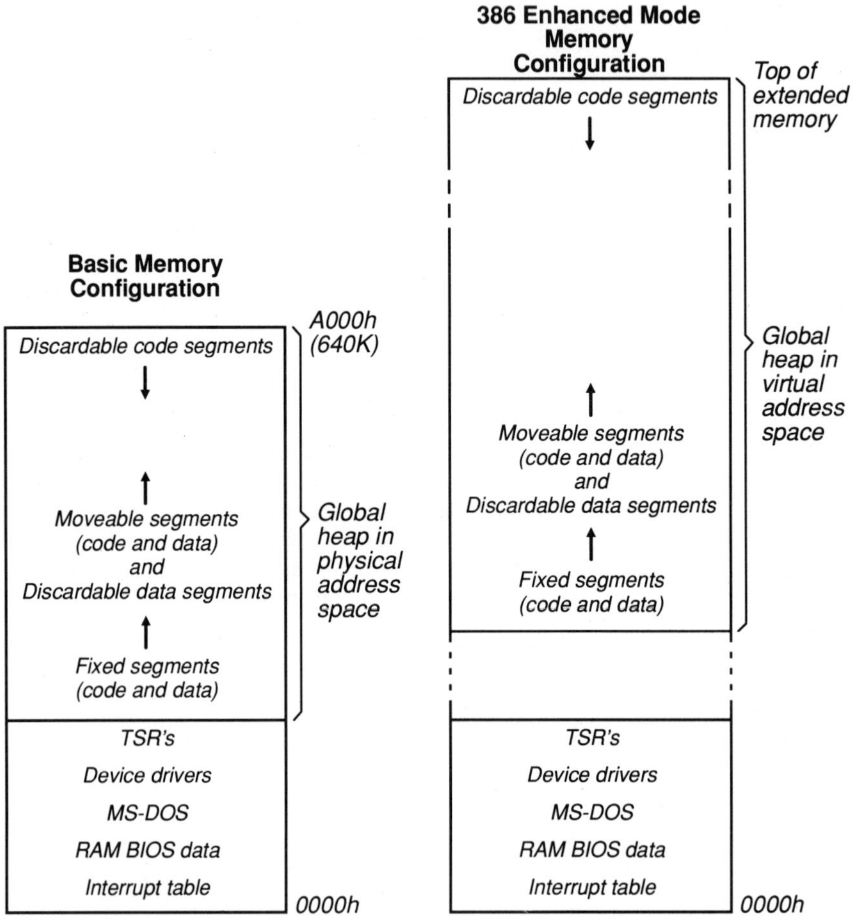

Figure 16.5 Comparison of Basic Memory and 386 Enhanced Mode Memory Configurations

In both the basic memory configuration and the 386 enhanced mode memory configuration, fixed code and data segments are located lower in memory. Non-discardable, moveable code and data segments, and discardable data segments are allocated above the fixed code and data segments. Discardable code segments are allocated from the top of memory. Windows minimizes memory fragmentation under the 386 enhanced mode memory configuration just as it does in the basic memory configuration.

The 386 enhanced mode memory configuration is distinct from the others because in this mode, Windows swaps code and data between physical memory and the disk. Under the other memory configurations, Windows may remove discardable data from memory, but it does not save the data to disk so that it may be read back into memory when needed.

With the 386 enhanced mode memory configuration, Windows continues allocating physical memory until it is used up. Windows then begins moving 4K pages of code and data from physical memory to disk in order to make additional physical memory available. Windows pages 4K blocks, rather than unequal-sized code and data segments. The swapped 4K block may be only part of a given code or data segment, or it may cross over two or more code or data segments.

This memory paging is transparent to the application. If the application attempts to access a code or data segment of which some part has been paged out to disk, the 80386 microprocessor issues an interrupt, called a "page fault," to Windows. Windows then swaps other pages out of memory and restores the pages that the application needs. Windows chooses the pages that it swaps to disk based on a least-recently-used (LRU) algorithm.

This virtual memory system provides as much additional memory as the size of the Windows swap file that is reserved on the user's disk. Windows determines the size of the swap file based on the total amount of physical memory on the system and the amount of disk space available. The user can modify the size of the swap file by changing an entry in the SYSTEM.INI file and can establish a permanent swap file using the **SWAPFILE** utility.

Windows' demand loading of code and data segments operates on top of Windows' virtual memory paging scheme. That is, Windows treats virtual memory as though it were basic 640K memory for purposes of determining what code and data segments to discard. However, Windows removes discardable code and data segments only when virtual memory is exhausted.

Preventing Memory from Being Paged to Disk

Occasionally, it is necessary to ensure that certain memory is always present in physical memory and is never paged to disk. For example, a DLL routine may be required to respond immediately to an interrupt instead of waiting for the system to generate a page fault and load the data from the disk. In such cases, a block of memory can be page locked to prevent it from being paged to disk.

To page-lock a block of memory, call the **GlobalPageLock** function, passing it the global selector of the segment that is to be locked. This function increments a page-lock count for the segment; as long as the page-lock count for a given segment is nonzero, the segment will remain at the same physical address and will not be paged out to disk. When you no longer require the memory to be locked, call the **GlobalPageUnlock** to decrement the page-lock count. In other modes, these functions have no effect.

NOTE You should page-lock memory only in critical situations. Do not routinely page-lock memory to lock down a spreadsheet, for example. Page-locking memory adversely affects the performance of all applications, including yours.

16.2 Using Data Storage in Windows Applications

Windows supports seven types of data storage, each of which is appropriate for different situations. The following list describes each type of data storage, and suggests how to decide which type to use.

Type	Description
Static data	Static data includes all C variables that the program source code implicitly or explicity declares using the **static** key word. Static data also includes all C variables declared as external, either explicitly (using the **extern** key word) or by default (by declaring it at the top of the source module before any function bodies).
Automatic data	Automatic data are variables allocated in the stack when a function is called. The variables include the function parameters and any locally declared variables. See Section 16.2.1, "Managing Automatic Data Segments," for more information.
Local dynamic data	Local dynamic data is data allocated using the **LocalAlloc** function. Local dynamic data is allocated out of a local heap in the automatic data segment to which an application's DS register is set. Allocating memory blocks from the local heap of a Windows application is similar to allocating memory with the **malloc** C run-time library function in a non-Windows application that uses the small or medium memory models. See Section 16.2.2, "Managing Local Dynamic-Data Blocks," for more information.
Global dynamic data	Global dynamic data is data allocated out of the Windows global heap using the **GlobalAlloc** function. The global heap is a system-wide memory resource. Allocating memory blocks from the global heap is roughly equivalent to allocating with **malloc** in a non-Windows application that uses the compact or large memory models. The difference is that in Windows, your application allocates memory objects out of a heap potentially shared by other applications, while a non-Windows application essentially has the whole heap to itself. See Section 16.2.3, "Managing Global Memory Blocks," for more information.

Type	Description
Window extra bytes	Your application can create a window so that extra bytes are allocated in the data structure that Windows maintains internally for that window. To do so, register the class for the window (by calling the **RegisterClass** function) and request that extra bytes be allocated for each window that is a member of the class. You request the extra bytes by specifying a nonzero value for the **cbWndExtra** field of the **WNDCLASS** data structure which you pass to **RegisterClass**. You can then store and retrieve data from this area by making calls to **SetWindowWord, SetWindowLong, GetWindowWord** and **GetWindowLong.** See Section 16.2.4, "Using Extra Bytes in Window and Class Data Structures," for more information.
Class extra bytes	A window class may be defined so that extra bytes are allocated at the end of the **WNDCLASS** structure created for the class. When you register the window class, you specify a nonzero value for the **cbClsExtra** field. You can then store and retrieve data from this area by making calls to **SetClassWord**, **SetClassLong**, **GetClassWord** and **GetClassLong**. See Section 16.2.4, "Using Extra Bytes in Window and Class Data Structures," for more information.
Resources	Resources are nonmodifiable collections of data stored in the resource portion of an executable file. This data can be loaded into memory where your application can use it conveniently. You can define private resources that contain whatever kind of read-only data you want to store. You compile a resource into your .EXE or .DLL file using the Resource Compiler. At run time, you can then access the resource data using various Windows library functions. See Section 16.2.5, "Managing Resources," for more information.

16.2.1 Managing Automatic Data Segments

Each application has one data segment called the "automatic data segment," which may contain up to 64K. The automatic data segment contains the following kinds of data:

Type	Description
Task header	Sixteen bytes of information that Windows maintains for each application. It is always located in the first 16 bytes of the automatic data segment.
Static data	All C variables that are declared as **static** or **extern**, either explicitly or by default.
Stack	The stack is used to store automatic data. The stack has a fixed size, but the active area within the stack grows and contracts as functions execute and return. Each time a function is called, the return address is pushed onto the active portion of the stack, along with the parameter values passed to the function.
Local heap	Contains all local dynamic data, which is data allocated using the **LocalAlloc** function.

Figure 16.6 shows the layout of the application's automatic data segment.

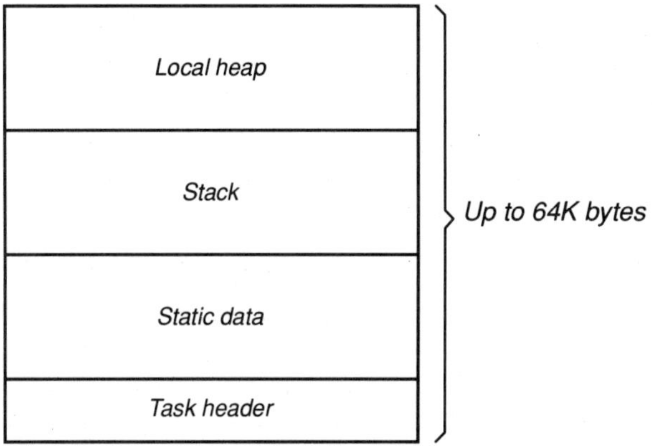

Figure 16.6 Automatic Data Segment

The size of the stack is always fixed for a given application. You specify the size (in bytes) of the stack using the **STACKSIZE** statement in the application's module-definition (.DEF) file. Windows enforces a minimum stack size of 5K. You should experiment with your application to determine an optimum stack size. The results of a stack overflow, however, are unpredictable.

The size of the local heap is set to an initial value for the application according to the **HEAPSIZE** statement in the .DEF file for the application. The local heap will grow as needed when you call **LocalAlloc**. For applications, the initial size of the local heap must be at least large enough to hold the current environment variables; a minimum heap size of 1K is recommended. If your application does not require access to environment information, you can link your application to an object file that will prevent this initialization information from being placed in the heap. For more information, see Chapter 14, "C and Assembly Language."

If your application's automatic data segment is not fixed or locked, it is possible that the data segment will move when your application calls **LocalAlloc**. If the local heap must grow, Windows may have to find another location in physical memory to accommodate the larger size of the local heap and, thus, the data segment. As long as your application uses near addresses for variables in the automatic data segment, this relocation of the automatic data segment will not present a problem. If necessary, you can temporarily prevent the application's automatic data segment from moving, even when it calls **LocalAlloc**, by calling **LockData**. However, locking the automatic data segment may cause **LocalAlloc** to fail if the data segment cannot be moved and a fixed segment is above the locked segment.

If your application requests memory from the local heap beyond what is available, the heap can grow until the total data segment reaches 64K. If some of the local heap objects are freed, however, the size of the heap does not automatically shrink. You can recover this area by calling **LocalShrink**. This function first compacts the local heap, then truncates the automatic data segment to the specified number of bytes. **LocalShrink** will neither truncate below the highest currently allocated memory object, nor below the originally specified heap size.

You can declare the automatic data segment to be fixed or moveable in the application's .DEF file, just as you can any data or code segment. Unless you have a good reason to do otherwise, the automatic data segment should be declared as moveable and multiple. The automatic data segment is always preloaded. The following example shows how to declare the automatic data segment in the .DEF file:

```
DATA MOVEABLE MULTIPLE
```

By declaring the application's automatic data segment as moveable, you allow Windows to relocate the data segment in memory as its size changes. If the automatic data segment is fixed, Windows increases the size of the local heap only if adjacent memory happens to be available. Consequently, if you declare the automatic data segment to be fixed, you should be careful to specify in the .DEF file an adequate initial **HEAPSIZE** value.

You should specify the **MULTIPLE** attribute for **DATA** to provide a separate automatic data segment for each instance of your application. Only dynamic-link libraries can be declared with the **SINGLE** attribute for **DATA**. In fact, dynamic-link libraries must be declared this way, since a DLL can have only one instance.

16.2.2 Managing Local Dynamic-Data Blocks

In Windows, a local heap can be set up in any data segment. The application's automatic data segment, however, is by far the most common place a local heap is used.

The **LocalInit** function establishes a specified area within any data segment as a local heap. Calls to **LocalAlloc** and other local-memory functions operate on the data segment currently referred to by the DS register. As long as this data segment was previously initialized by **LocalInit**, the local memory functions will work.

If you are developing a DLL that requires a local heap, then you should call **LocalInit** during the initialization of the library. Note that **LocalInit** leaves one outstanding lock on the data segment. After calling **LocalInit** in a DLL, you may want to call **UnlockData** to allow Windows to move the segment as needed.

If you are developing a Windows application, as opposed to a DLL, then you should not call **LocalInit** for the application's automatic data segment. Based on the location of other data in the automatic data segment (the task header, static data, and stack) and the heap size specified in the application's .DEF file, Windows itself calls **LocalInit** with the correct values for the location and size of the local heap.

The organization of a local heap is similar to that of a global heap:

- Fixed blocks are located at the bottom of the local heap.
- Nondiscardable, moveable blocks are allocated above the fixed blocks.
- Discardable blocks are allocated from the top of the local heap.

Figure 16.7 illustrates this organization.

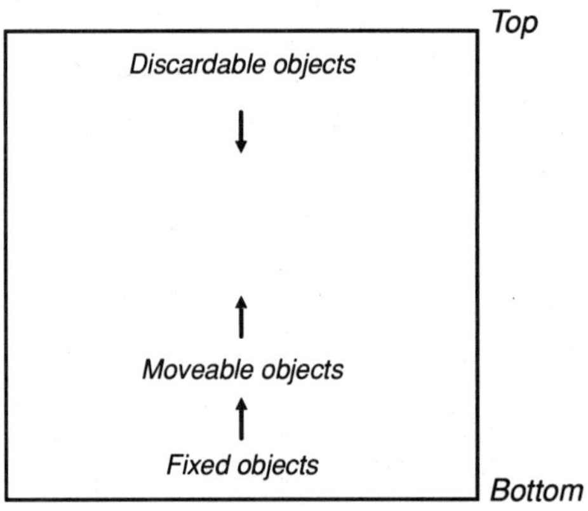

Figure 16.7 Organization of a Local Heap

As Windows adds new blocks to an application's local heap, moveable blocks may move as Windows compacts the heap. Also, Windows may discard blocks to make room for new blocks. Windows never moves fixed blocks when they are allocated in a local heap.

Allocating Memory in the Local Heap

The **LocalAlloc** function allocates a specified size block in a local heap and allows you to specify certain characteristics of the block. The most important characteristic is whether the block is fixed or moveable, and if moveable whether it is discardable. The valid combinations of the flags which set these attributes are:

- LMEM_FIXED
- LMEM_MOVEABLE
- LMEM_MOVEABLE and LMEM_DISCARDABLE

When you allocate a block in a local heap, other blocks may be moved or discarded. In certain cases, you may not want the local heap to be reorganized as the new block is added. You may want to guarantee that pointers previously set to moveable blocks remain unchanged. To guarantee that no blocks will be discarded from the local heap when you call **LocalAlloc**, set LMEM_NODISCARD in the *wFlags* parameter. To guarantee that no blocks in the local heap will be moved or discarded, specify LMEM_NOCOMPACT.

LocalAlloc returns a handle to the allocated local memory block. If memory in the local heap is not available, **LocalAlloc** returns NULL. In managing a block using all other Windows memory functions described below, you should use the handle returned by **LocalAlloc**.

Locking and Unlocking a Block of Local Memory

To many C programmers who are used to using the C run-time library function **malloc**, using memory handles may seem foreign at first. Because allocated objects in the local heap may move around as new objects are added, you cannot always expect a pointer to an allocated object to remain valid. The purpose of a local memory handle is to provide a constant reference to a moveable object.

Since a memory handle is an indirect reference, you must "dereference" the handle to obtain the near address of the local object. You do this by calling the Windows function **LocalLock**. **LocalLock** temporarily fixes the object at a constant location in the local heap. Therefore, the near address returned by **LocalLock** is guaranteed to remain valid until you subsequently call **LocalUnlock**. The following example shows how to use **LocalLock** to dereference the handle of a moveable object.

```
HANDLE hLocalObject;
char NEAR * pcLocalObject;  /*NEAR is not    */
        /* necessary in small and medium models*/

if (hLocalObject
 = LocalAlloc(LMEM_MOVEABLE, 32))
{
```

```
        if (pcLocalObject = LocalLock(hLocalObject))
        {
                /* Use pcLocalObject as the near  */
                /* address the locally allocated  */
                /* object                         */
                .
                .
                .
                LocalUnlock(hLocalObject);
        }
        else
        {
                /* The lock failed. React accordingly. */
        }
}
else
{
        /* The 32 bytes cannot be allocated. */
        /* React accordingly.                */
}
```

If you allocate a local memory block with the LMEM_FIXED attribute, it is already guaranteed not to move in memory. Consequently, you do not have to call **LocalLock** to lock the object temporarily at a fixed address. Also, you do not have to dereference the handle, as you normally do using **LocalLock** because the 16-bit handle is simply the 16-bit near address of the local memory block. The following example illustrates this:

```
char NEAR * pcLocalObject;  /* NEAR is not */
        /* necessary in small or medium models */

if (pcLocalObject = LocalAlloc(LMEM_FIXED,32))
{
        /* Use pcLocalObject as the near address */
        /* to the locally allocated object.            */
        /* It is not necessary to lock and unlock   */
        /* the fixed local object                   */
        .
        .
        .
}
else
{
        /* The 32 bytes cannot be allocated. */
        /* React accordingly.                */
}
```

You should avoid leaving a moveable block locked if your application needs to allocate other blocks in the local heap. Otherwise, Windows' memory management is less efficient. Windows has to work around the locked block as it tries to make room for another block in the moveable area of the local heap.

Changing a Block of Local Memory

You call **LocalReAlloc** to change the size of a block while preserving its contents. If you specify a smaller size, Windows truncates the block. If you specify a larger size, Windows fills the new area of the block with zeros if you specify LMEM_ZEROINIT; otherwise, the contents of the new area are undefined. Calling **LocalReAlloc** may cause blocks in the local heap to be discarded or moved, just as when you call **LocalAlloc**. To prevent Windows from discarding blocks, specify the LMEM_NODISCARD value; to prevent Windows from moving blocks, specify LMEM_NOCOMPACT.

You can also call **LocalReAlloc** to change the block's attribute from LMEM_MOVEABLE to LMEM_DISCARDABLE or vice versa. To do so, you must also specify LMEM_MODIFY, as follows.

```
hLocalObject
 = LocalAlloc (32, LMEM_MOVEABLE);
.
.
.
hLocalObject
= LocalReAlloc(hLocalObject,
              32,
              LMEM_MODIFY | LMEM_DISCARDABLE);
```

You cannot use LMEM_MODIFY with **LocalReAlloc** to change the attribute of the local memory block to or from LMEM_FIXED.

Freeing and Discarding Blocks of Local Memory

The Windows functions **LocalDiscard** and **LocalFree** discard and free local blocks, respectively.

There is a difference between freeing a local block and discarding it. When you discard a local block, its content is removed from the local heap, but its handle remains valid. When you free a local block, not only are its contents removed from the local heap, but its handle is removed from the table of valid local memory handles. A local memory block can be discarded or freed only if there are no outstanding locks on it.

You may want to discard a block rather than free it if you want to reuse its handle. To reuse the handle, call **LocalReAlloc** with the handle and a nonzero size value. By reusing the handle in this way, you save Windows the time required to free an old handle and create a new one. Reusing a handle allows you to determine how much local memory is available before attempting to allocate a local memory block.

Freezing Local Memory

You can call the **LocalFreeze** function to temporarily guarantee that no blocks will be relocated or discarded when you make subsequent calls to **LocalAlloc** and **LocalReAlloc.** You may call **LocalFreeze** as an alternative to specifying LMEM_NOCOMPACT in each subsequent call to **LocalAlloc** and **LocalReAlloc**.

You reverse the effect of **LocalFreeze** by calling the **LocalMelt** function.

Obtaining Information About a Local Memory Block

The **LocalSize** and **LocalFlags** functions provide you information about a local memory block. **LocalSize** returns the size of the block. **LocalFlags** indicates whether the memory block is discardable and, if so, whether the block has been discarded. **LocalFlags** also reports the lock count for the memory block.

16.2.3 Managing Global Memory Blocks

The global heap is the Windows system-wide memory resource that is shared among applications. An application may request Windows to allocate memory blocks out of the global heap by calling **GlobalAlloc**, the same function that Windows itself calls to allocate internally used memory blocks. By using the global memory functions described in this section, you can take advantage of the same memory management mechanisms Windows uses for its own purposes. In addition, these functions let your application compete or cooperate with the system itself with essentially the same privileges. Misusing these priveleges reduces your application's ability to cooperate with Windows and other applications.

The following considerations may help you determine whether to allocate memory for a given data block out of the global or the local heap:

- You should address a memory block allocated from the local heap with a near pointer (after you dereference the handle using **LocalLock**). On the other hand, you should address a memory block allocated from the global heap with a far pointer (after you dereference the handle using **GlobalLock**).
- An application's local heap is a relatively scarce memory resource, since it must fit in the application's automatic data segment (limited to 64K bytes) along with the stack and static data; the global heap is much larger.

If a memory object is in the current "working set" of your application, you should attempt to design it as a local object to take advantage of the more efficient near addressing. The current working set is data that you must frequently access during a fairly lengthy operation. Objects that are less frequently accessed belong in the global heap. In some applications, it might make sense to transfer data between the application's local heap and the global heap as the working set of data changes.

In designing the structure of global memory objects, you often have the choice of breaking them down into elementary objects, or consolidating them into larger objects. In making this choice, you should consider the following:

- Each global memory object carries an overhead of at least 20 bytes.
- Global memory objects are aligned on 32-byte boundaries. The first 16 bytes are reserved for certain overhead information. Under the Windows standard mode and 386 enhanced mode memory configurations, there is a system-wide limit of 8192 global memory handles, only some of which are available to any given application.

In general, you should avoid allocating small global memory objects. A small object (128 bytes or less) carries at least a 15-percent space overhead, plus the memory that is wasted if the object's size (plus 16 bytes) is not a multiple of 32 bytes. This overhead may be justifiable in some cases, but you should weigh carefully the overhead involved. You should especially avoid allocating a large number (many hundreds) of small global objects if they can be consolidated into fewer, larger global objects. This not only eliminates space overhead but also avoids unnecessary use of the limited number of global memory handles.

With these considerations in mind, the programming task of managing memory blocks in the global heap is very similar to that of managing memory blocks in a local heap. For information on managing local memory, see Section 16.2.2, "Managing Local Dynamic-Data Blocks."

The following sections discuss the functions that manage global memory.

Allocating Memory in the Global Heap

You call the **GlobalAlloc** function to allocate a specified size block in the global heap. Windows manages blocks of memory in the global heap according to the same classifications as those for blocks of memory in a local heap: fixed, moveable, and discardable. Thus, the analogous flags that may be specified in a call to **GlobalAlloc** are:

- GMEM_FIXED
- GMEM_MOVEABLE
- GMEM_MOVEABLE and GMEM_DISCARDABLE

The same mechanisms for compacting memory that are applied in the management of a local heap also apply to the global heap. Thus, you may specify GMEM_NODISCARD or GMEM_NOCOMPACT when you call **GlobalAlloc.** For details, see the discussion of LMEM_NODISCARD and LMEM_NOCOMPACT under the description of **LocalAlloc** in "Allocating Memory in the Local Heap" in Section 16.2.2.

GlobalAlloc returns a handle to the allocated global memory block. If memory in the global heap is not available, **GlobalAlloc** returns NULL. It is always important to check the return value from **GlobalAlloc**, since you have no guarantee that your allocation requests can be satisfied. Most of the functions that manage global memory described in the following sections require this handle to identify the memory block.

Allocating Global Memory in a Dynamic-Link Library Under the EMS Memory Configuration

By default, Windows satisfies **GlobalAlloc** requests by a DLL differently depending on how the library is loaded. If a library is loaded explicitly with a **LoadLibrary** call, Windows allocates global blocks from memory below the EMS bank line. For libraries that are loaded implicitly by an **IMPORTS** statement in the application's .DEF file, Windows allocates global blocks from memory above the EMS bank line in large-frame EMS mode. In small-frame EMS mode, all global memory blocks are allocated from below the EMS bank line.

Global memory objects allocated below the EMS bank line may be a hindrance for certain kinds of libraries, such as printer drivers, which typically need to buffer large amounts of data. If their data had to be allocated below the EMS bank line, this scarce system-wide memory resource would be poorly used. To avoid this problem, you can compile your DLL with the Resource Compiler using the **–e** option on the **RC** command line. This switch changes the default placement of global objects for libraries from below the EMS bank line to above the line.

A library that has been compiled with the Resource Compiler **–e** option must be written to compensate for the fact that global memory objects located above the EMS bank line will be banked out at a task context switch. The library may require that a particular global memory object reside below the EMS bank line so that the global handle remains valid, even as system control changes between applications. To accomplish this, the library can call **GlobalAlloc** with the GMEM_NOT_BANKED flag set.

Locking and Unlocking a Block of Global Memory

You can dereference the handle to a global memory object by calling the **GlobalLock** function. In real mode, this temporarily fixes the object at a constant location in the global heap. In all modes, **GlobalLock** returns a far pointer that is guaranteed to remain valid until you subsequently call **GlobalUnlock**.

In real mode, **GlobalLock** must lock the object by fixing it in memory to ensure that the pointer it returns will remain valid until you call **GlobalUnlock**. Because it has actually locked the object, **GlobalLock** increments a lock count for the object. This lock count helps prevent the object from being discarded or freed while it is still being used.

In protected (standard and 386 enhanced) mode, Windows does not have to fix the object in memory unless it is discardable. The pointer will always be valid whenever the object moves in linear memory. Because Windows does not actually lock the object in memory, **GlobalLock** does not increment the lock count for a nondiscardable object in protected mode. **GlobalUnlock** decrements the lock count of an object only if **GlobalLock** incremented it for the object.

However, you must still call **GlobalUnlock** in protected mode when you no longer need the pointer returned by **GlobalLock**.

In addition to **GlobalLock** and **GlobalUnlock**, several other functions affect the lock count for an object. The following lists these functions:

Increases Lock Count	Decreases Lock Count
GlobalFix	**GlobalUnfix**
GlobalWire	**GlobalUnWire**
LockSegment	**UnlockSegment**

See the descriptions of these functions in the *Reference, Volume 1* for more information about how they affect a global memory block and its lock count. The **GlobalFlags** function returns the lock count of a global memory block as set by these functions.

Earlier it was noted that it is not necessary to call **LocalLock** to dereference a local handle if the object is allocated as LMEM_FIXED. There is no similar capability for fixed global objects. Even fixed global objects must always be locked to dereference the handle.

The following example illustrates how to use **GlobalLock** to dereference the handle of a moveable global object:

```
HANDLE hGlobalObject;
LPSTR lpGlobalObject;

if (hGlobalObject
        = GlobalAlloc(GMEM_MOVEABLE,1024))
{
        if (lpGlobalObject
        = GlobalLock(hGlobalObject))
        {
                /* Use lpGlobalOBject as the far */
                /* address to the globally allocated */
                /* object.                          */
                .
                .
                .
                GlobalUnlock(hGlobalObject);
        }
        else
        {
                /* Lock failed. React accordingly. */
        }
}
```

```
else
{
        /* The 1024 bytes cannot be allocated. */
        /* React accordingly.                  */
}
```

If you allocate an object that is 64K or larger, you should cast and save the pointer returned by **GlobalLock** as a huge pointer. The following example illustrates the allocation of a 128K memory block:

```
HANDLE hGlobalObject;
char huge * hpGlobalObject;

if (hGlobalObject
= GlobalAlloc(GMEM_MOVEABLE,0x20000L))
{
        if (hpGlobalObject
        = (char huge * )GlobalLock(hGlobalObject))
        {
                /* Use hpGlobalOBject as the far  */
                /* address to the globally allocated */
                /* object.                        */
                .
                .
                .
                GlobalUnlock(hGlobalObject);
        }
        else
        {
                /* Lock failed. React accordingly. */
        }
}
else
{
        /* The 128K cannot be allocated. */
        /* React accordingly.            */
}
```

Changing a Block of Global Memory

You can change the size or attributes of a global block while preserving its contents by calling **GlobalReAlloc**. If you specify a smaller size, Windows truncates the block. If you specify a larger size and also specify GMEM_ZEROINIT, Windows fills the new area of the block with zeros. By specifying GMEM_DISCARD or GMEM_NOCOMPACT, you ensure that Windows will not discard or move blocks to satisfy the **GlobalReAlloc** request.

You can also call **GlobalReAlloc** to change the block's attribute from nondiscardable to discardable, or vice versa. Unlike **LocalReAlloc**, however, you also can change a GEM_FIXED block to GMEM_MOVEABLE or GMEM_DISCARDABLE. But you cannot change a moveable or discardable block to a fixed block. To change the attribute of a global block, you must also specify the

GMEM_MODIFY flag. See the example in "Changing a Block of Local Memory" in Section 16.2.2.

You must take care when you are changing the size of a global block if its size increases across a multiple of 64K. Windows may return a new global handle for the reallocated memory block. For example, this applies if you change the size of the block from 50K to 70K, or 120K to 130K. In standard mode, this applies if you change the size of the block across a multiple of 65,519 bytes (17 bytes less than 64K).

Because of the selector tiling technique employed by Windows when under the standard mode or 386 enhanced mode memory configuration, Windows might have to search for a larger set of related selectors when the size of a global block increases across a multiple of 64K. If so, Windows returns the first selector of the larger set as the global handle. "Using Huge Memory Blocks in the Standard Mode Memory Configuration" in Section 16.1.3 describes selector tiling.

The following code example shows how not to increase the size of a block of global memory. It is valid for the basic and EMS memory configurations, but is invalid for the standard mode and 386 enhanced mode memory configurations:

```
/* DON'T FOLLOW THIS EXAMPLE */
GlobalReAlloc(hHugeObject,
              0x20000L,
              GMEM_MOVEABLE);
```

In the preceding example, the handle hHugeObject might be invalidated, depending on how Windows satisfied the reallocation request. The following example shows how to reallocate a global memory block in any memory configuration.

```
/* FOLLOW THIS EXAMPLE */
if (hTempHugeObject = GlobalReAlloc(hHugeObject,
                                    0x20000L,
                                    GMEM_MOVEABLE))
{
        hHugeObject = hTempObject;
}
else
{
        /* Object could not be allocated. */
        /* React accordingly.             */
}
```

In this example, the temporary handle, hTempHugeObject, is employed to preserve the original handle in case **GlobalReAlloc** returns a NULL handle to indicate a failure to reallocate.

Freeing and Discarding Blocks of Global Memory

The **GlobalFree** and **GlobalDiscard** functions are identical to **LocalFree** and **LocalDiscard**, except that they operate on global rather than local memory objects. For more information, see the discussion on **LocalFree** and **LocalDiscard** in "Freeing and Discarding Blocks of Local Memory" in Section 16.2.2.

Obtaining Information About a Global Memory Block

The **GlobalSize** and **GlobalFlags** functions provide current information about a global memory block. **GlobalSize** returns the current size of the block. **GlobalFlags** indicates whether the memory block is discardable and, if so, whether the block has been discarded. It also indicates whether the block was allocated with the GMEM_DDESHARE or GMEM_NOT_BANKED flags.

Locking a Global Memory Block for Extended Periods

When you call **GlobalLock** to prevent a moveable object from moving as other objects are manipulated in the global heap, you can hinder the ability of Windows to manage these other objects efficiently. Locking the object for only a short time is acceptable. To lock an object for a long time, use **GlobalWire** instead of **GlobalLock.** This function relocates the moveable object to the lower area of the global heap reserved for fixed objects and then locks it. Moving the locked object to low memory allows Windows to compact upper memory more efficiently, but requires additional CPU cycles to move the object. Call **GlobalUnWire** to unlock the object. After the object is unlocked, it can migrate out of the fixed portion of the global heap.

Being Notified When a Global Block is To Be Discarded

If you want your application to be notified whenever Windows is about to discard a global block, call the **GlobalNotify** function. **GlobalNotify** is useful if you are writing a custom virtual-memory management system that swaps data to and from disk, for example. You specify the address of the notification callback function in your application.

Changing When a Global Block is Discarded

As Windows manages the global heap, it employs a least-recently-used (LRU) algorithm for determining which global objects should be discarded when memory must be freed. You can call the **GlobalLRUOldest** function to move an object to the oldest position in the LRU list. This means that this object will be the most likely object to be discarded if Windows subsequently needs more memory. Conversely, by calling **GlobalLRUNewest**, you ensure that an object is least likely to be discarded.

These functions are useful, for example, for discarding initialization code when it is no longer needed. You could also use these functions if you are writing a custom virtual-memory management system that swaps data to and from disk. With these functions, you can influence which objects are least or most likely to be discarded by Windows to minimize the amount of disk swapping.

Freeing Global Memory in Low-Memory Conditions

Global memory is a shared resource; the performance of all applications depends on the willingness of all applications to share that resource. When system memory is low, your application should be prepared to free global memory that it has allocated.

Windows sends the WM_COMPACTING message to all top-level windows when Windows detects that more than 15 percent of system time over a 30- to 60-second interval is being spent compacting memory. This indicates that system memory is low.

When your application receives this message, it should free as much memory as possible, taking into account the current level of activity of the application and the total number of applications running in Windows. The application can call the **GetNumTasks** function to determine how many applications are running.

16.2.4 Using Extra Bytes in Window and Class Data Structures

You can store extra, application-defined data with the data structures that describe the attributes of a window or a window class. This extra data is known as "window extra bytes" and "class extra bytes," respectively.

This private data resides at the end of a data structure that Windows maintains for the window. When you call **RegisterClass**, the **cbWndExtra** field of the **WNDCLASS** data structure specifies the number of extra bytes of information that will be maintained for each window member of that class.

The technique of using the private data area of a window is particularly useful in cases in which you have two or more windows that belong to the same class, and you want to associate different data with each window. Without the private data facility, you would have to maintain a list of private data structures for each window. Then, each time you needed to access the data for a particular window, you first would have to locate the corresponding entry in the list. However, by using the private data facility you can directly access the private data through the window handle rather than using a separate list.

An additional advantage of using the window's private area to store data is that you can encapsulate the data associated with each window better than if you were to store the same information as static data in the same module as the window procedure, for example.

To write to the window's private data area, call **SetWindowWord** and **SetWindowLong.** These two functions accept a byte offset within the area you set aside for private data. A zero offset refers to the first **WORD** or **LONG** in the private area. An offset of 2 (bytes) refers to the second **WORD** in the private area. An offset of 4 (bytes) refers to the third **WORD** or the second **LONG** in the private area. Note that **SetWindowWord** and **SetWindowLong** also accept constants such as GWW_STYLE and GWL_WNDPROC, which are defined in WINDOWS.H. These constants are negative offsets within the window's data structure. The length of the data structure (minus the private area) is thus added to the offset you provide in the call to **SetWindowWord** or **SetWindowLong** to determine the actual offset relative to the beginning of the data structure.

To read from the private data area of a window, call the **GetWindowWord** and **GetWindowLong** functions. The offsets you specify work the same way as for **SetWindowWord** and **SetWindowLong**.

In the EMS memory configuration, the data structure for a window is allocated in the relatively scarce memory area below the EMS bank line. If you wish to associate a large amount of data (more than 10 bytes) with the window, you should store a global handle in the window's private area instead of the actual data. The handle points to the actual data. This way, you increase the size of the window's data structure only by the two bytes needed for the global handle, rather than by the large size of the private data itself.

Just as you can associate private data with a particular window, you can also associate private data with a window class. The functions provided for this purpose are **SetClassWord, SetClassLong, GetClassWord,** and **GetClassLong.** There are probably fewer occasions for associating private data with a window class than with a window. Using the private area for the window class is appropriate for data that is logically related to the window class as a whole and that is common among multiple windows of the same class.

16.2.5 Managing Resources

A resource is read-only data stored in your application's .EXE or library's .DLL file that Windows reads from disk on demand. Certain types of resources have prescribed formats recognized by Windows. These include bitmaps, icons, cursors, dialog boxes, and fonts. You can create these resources using the Windows SDK resource editors **SDKPAINT**, **DIALOG**, and **FONTEDIT**. You link these resources into your .EXE or .DLL file using the Resource Compiler (**RC**). You take advantage of Windows' knowledge of these resource formats by calling associated functions such as **LoadIcon** and **CreateDialog**.

A resource is read into memory by Windows as a single data segment. The resource may be declared in the resource script to be fixed, moveable, or discardable. When determining whether a resource should be fixed, moveable, or discardable, you should take into account the same considerations as you do for a global memory block.

If you declare resource with the **PRELOAD** option, Windows loads it into memory during the start-up of your application. Otherwise, Windows loads it when it is needed (the **LOADONCALL** option). This option is particularly important when the application is running in the EMS small-frame configuration. See Section 16.6.4, "The Order of Code Segments in the .DEF File," for a discussion on loading resources in the EMS small-frame configuration.

In addition to resources whose formats are recognized by Windows, you can also develop resources recognized only by your application. The data may be in any format that you design, including ASCII text, binary data, or a mixture of these.

When deciding whether to maintain data as a resource or as a separate file, you should keep the following in mind:

- By compiling the resource into your application's .EXE file, you simplify the packaging of your application. You and your user do not need to worry about installing additional data files along with the application's .EXE file.
- On the other hand, maintaining the data as a resource means that you must recompile your application's .EXE file if you change the data. If you anticipate having several users to whom you may at some time distribute the updated data, it may be easier to distribute a new version of a data file than it is to distribute a new version of the .EXE file.

The steps for compiling a user-defined resource into an .EXE or .DLL file are described in *Tools*.

The following sections describe the Windows functions that access a custom resource.

Locating a Custom Resource

The **FindResource** function determines the location of the resource according to the name specified in your resource script. The function returns a handle which you can then use in a call to the **LoadResource** function to load the resource. The resource handle returned by **FindResource** refers to information that describes the resource type declared in the resource script, the position of the resource in the .EXE or .DLL file, and the size of the resource.

For example, suppose you wish to maintain an ASCII text file as a resource. The source text file is named MYTEXT.TXT. You name the resource "mytext," and you arbitrarily name the resource type "TEXT." The resource script for this resource is:

```
mytext TEXT mytext.txt
```

In your application, you obtain the resource handle by calling **FindResource** as shown:

```
HANDLE hMyTextResLoc;
        .
        .
        .
        hMyTextResLoc
                = FindResource(hInstance, "TEXT", "mytext");
```

Loading a Custom Resource

The call to **FindResource** does not load the resource from the .EXE or .DLL disk file to memory. Rather, it only finds the location of the resource and returns the result of the find as a handle that points to the resource location information. To actually load the resource into memory, you call **LoadResource**, as follows:

```
HANDLE hMyTextResLoc;
        HANDLE hMyTextRes;
        .
        .
        .
        hMyTextResLoc
                = FindResource(hInstance, "TEXT", "mytext");
        if (!hMyTextRes
                = LoadResource(hInstance, hMyTextResLoc))
        {
                /* Handle case that memory is not available */
                /* to load resource                         */
        }
```

LoadResource itself calls **GlobalAlloc** to allocate the memory block for the resource data, and then copies the data from disk to the memory block.

Locking and Unlocking a Custom Resource

To access the resource data now residing in a global memory block, you must call the **LockResource** function to lock the resource and obtain a far pointer to the data. This is equivalent to using **GlobalLock** to obtain the far pointer to a memory block allocated by **GlobalAlloc**. The following continues the previous example:

```
LPSTR lpstrMyText;
        .
        .
        .
        lpstrMyText = LockResource(hMyTextRes);
```

Once you have the far address to the resource, you can read it as you would from a global memory block locked by **GlobalLock**.

If you have defined the resource as discardable and it has been discarded, **LockResource** will first load the resource back from disk. Unlike **GlobalLock**, **LockResource** saves you the trouble of calling **LoadResource** again if the resource has been discarded.

You should call **UnlockResource** when you are not in the process of accessing the resource data. This function is equivalent to **GlobalUnlock**. If you declare the resource as moveable or discardable, this provides Windows the flexibility to move or discard the resource from memory as necessary to satisify other memory allocation requests.

Freeing a Custom Resource

The **FreeResource** function is similar to **GlobalFree**. It discards the memory used by the resource data as well as by the resource handle. If you need to load the resource again, you can call **LoadResource** using the resource location handle returned by your initial call to **FindResource**.

16.3 Using Memory Models

A Windows application, like a non-Windows DOS application, may have one or more code segments and one or more data segments. The memory model, which you specify when you compile your source code modules, determines whether compiler-generated instructions use near or far addresses. If you use a memory model that specifies only one code or data segment, the compiler generates instructions that employ near (16-bit) addresses for, respectively, code or data references. If you compile using a memory model that specifies multiple code or data segments, the compiler generates instructions that employ far (32-bit) addresses for code or data references. Figure 16.8 shows how the memory model affects the way the application addresses code and data.

		Number of code segments	
		One	Multiple
Number of data segments	One	*Small memory model*	*Medium memory model*
	Multiple	*Compact memory model*	*Large memory model*

Figure 16.8 Microsoft Language Memory Models

There are two memory models, large and huge, for compiling a module that generates far addresses for both code and data references. In the large memory model, far pointers can be incremented only within the 64K offset range of a segment. In the huge memory model, far pointers can be incremented across 64K boundaries, causing both the segment address and the offset to be incremented. Also, if a module is compiled with the large memory model, its data segments are always fixed in real mode, and in all modes Windows will be able to load only one instance of the module.

Generally, it is best to use the small or medium model for Windows applications. Under the basic and EMS memory configurations, using the compact, large or huge model requires far data segments to be fixed in memory; this constrains Windows' memory management. The far data segments must be fixed because Windows provides no mechanisms for redirecting references to far data segments as they move in memory. However, Windows does provide mechanisms for redirecting references to an application's automatic data segment and code segments as they move.

If you are using the Microsoft C Compiler, compile your Windows application's C-language source code modules using the **–AS** switch for the small model or the **–AM** switch for the medium model.

Windows also lets you use a "mixed" memory model. In the mixed model, you compile modules with the **–AS** switch, assign the same code segment name to those modules whose code segments you want to group together, and assign different code segment names to those modules for which you want to generate different code segments. To assign a code segment name to a module, use the C Compiler **–NT** switch. A function that is called from a different code segment must be declared as a far function in the module where the call is made, as follows:

```
WORD FAR PASCAL FuncInAnotherCodeSeg(WORD, LONG);
WORD wReturn;
          .
          .
          .
wReturn = FuncInAnotherCodeSeg(0,0L);
```

The advantage of using the mixed memory model is that you only need to define calls made between code segments as **far**. Functions that are declared **far** increase code size and require more machine cycles to be called.

In another form of the mixed memory model, you can compile modules with the **–AM** switch, which makes function calls far by default. Then, instead of declaring far functions, you prototype as near those functions that are called only within the same segment. The disadvantage of this method is that all C run-time library functions will also be far functions.

16.4 Using Huge Data

You can declare data as huge in C-language modules. The C Compiler will correctly perform the arithmetic required to increment the pointer across segment boundaries. You can pass a huge pointer to Windows library routines or to your own routines that expect a far pointer, but only if the routine is not expected to internally increment the far pointer to point to an object that straddles a 64K boundary. For example, the following code is acceptable because 16 is a factor of 64K (65,356):

```
char huge Record[10000][16];
int       i;

TextOut(hDC, x, y, (LPSTR)Record[i], 16);
```

The following example violates this limitation because the pointer passed to the **TextOut** function will eventually point to an object that straddles a 64K boundary:

```
char huge Record[10000][15];
int        i;

TextOut(hDC, x, y, (LPSTR)Record[i], 15);
/* DON'T DO THIS */
```

Since 15 is not a factor of 64K, the pointer would be incremented across a segment boundary.

16.5 Traps to Avoid in Managing Program Data

The previous sections of this chapter explained the basics of how Windows memory management works. They provided guidelines for choosing between methods for allocating program data and for effectively using a particular method.

This section focuses on common Windows programming errors that you should avoid in managing program data. If you understand how Windows manages memory, the following guidelines will be quite clear.

Do not assume the privilege level in which your application is running.

Future versions of Windows applications will change the privilege-level ring in which applications will run.

Avoid far pointers to static data in small and medium models.

Suppose a module contains the following declaration:

```
static LPSTR lpstrDlgName = "MyDlg";
                /* DON'T FOLLOW THIS EXAMPLE */
        .
        .
        .
        hDlg = CreateDialog(hInstance,
                        lpstrDlgName,
                        hWndParent,
                        lpDialogFunc);
```

The **LPSTR** (**char FAR ***) pointer initially set by the Windows loader will be made invalid if the automatic data segment that contains the literal "MyDlg" moves in memory (unless, of course, the automatic data segment is a fixed segment).

The proper way to write the preceding code is to declare the string with a near pointer, **PSTR (char NEAR *)**, and cast it to the **LPSTR** required by **CreateDialog**, as shown in the following example:

```
/* FOLLOW THIS EXAMPLE */
static PSTR pstrDlgName = "MyDlg";
    .
    .
    .
    hDlg = CreateDialog(hInstance,
(LPSTR)pstrDlgName,
                              hWndParent,
                              lpDialogFunc);
```

The cast to **LPSTR** dynamically pushes the current value of the DS register instead of the value of the DS register when the module was loaded.

Do not pass data to other applications via a global handle.

You may not use a global handle to share data with another application because you should assume that your application and other Windows applications have disjoint address spaces. For example, if your application is running in the large-frame EMS configuration, a global handle will dereference to an address in your EMS bank. If your application passes the global handle to another application which then attempts to dereference it (by calling **GlobalLock**), the resulting far address will be at the same position in the 1-megabyte physical address space. However, the handle will be pointing to the data currently banked in by the other application rather than to the data that was previously banked in for your application.

Consider the following bad example:

```
WORD wMyMsg;
           HANDLE hGlobalObject;
           .
           .
           .
           wMyMsg = RegisterWindowsMessage(
                                 (LPSTR)"MyMessage");
           hGlobalObject = GlobalAlloc(GMEM_FIXED, 100h);
           .
           .
           .
           PostMessage(-1, wMyMsg, hGlobalObject, 0L);
           /* DON'T FOLLOW THIS EXAMPLE */
```

This code broadcasts a specially registered message to all windows, including those of other applications. If another application has called **RegisterWindowsMessage** with the same message name, "MyMessage", the other application will detect this special message in one of its window procedures. If that other application then attempts to dereference the global handle hGlobalObject, the far pointer returned by **GlobalLock** will be invalid in large-frame EMS mode. Even though the global object was allocated with the GMEM_FIXED attribute, the global data owned by the first application will be banked out into EMS memory.

In addition, in future versons of Windows, the address spaces of applications will be disjoint in the standard and 386 enhanced mode memory configurations.

The only methods supported by Windows to pass data between applications are the clipboard and the Dynamic Data Exchange (DDE) protocol. If you pass a global handle through DDE to another application, the global object must have been allocated with the GMEM_DDESHARE flag. To share memory, you should always use DDE.

You can pass a global handle between applications by following the DDE protocol because Windows does some extra work when the other application dereferences the handle. When the second application calls **GlobalLock** for the handle, Windows reads the data from the EMS bank of the first application into a temporary global memory block of the currently banked-in second application. The far address returned by **GlobalLock** points to this temporary memory block. The currently banked-in application can only read this temporary memory block. When the application calls **GlobalUnlock,** Windows deletes the data from the global heap associated with the currently banked-in application.

Do not assume any relationship between a handle and a far pointer in any mode.

When using global memory blocks, you must always call the **GlobalLock** function to dereference a handle to a far pointer, regardless of the mode in which Windows is running.

Do not load a segment register with a value other than one provided by Windows or DOS.

Under the Windows standard mode and 386 enhanced mode memory configurations, segment registers are interpreted as selectors, not physical paragraph addresses. Therefore do not read the interrupt table by setting ES or DS to 0, for example. Use only the appropriate DOS call to hook an interrupt vector.

Do not perform segment arithmetic.

Do not increment the segment address of a far pointer in an attempt to increment the pointer. This technique is not supported under the Windows standard mode and 386 enhanced mode memory configurations. See "Locking and Unlocking a Block of Global Memory" in Section 16.2.3.

Do not compare segment addresses.

Do not compare the selector values that Windows assigns to memory objects to determine which object is lower in memory. This technique is not supported under the Windows standard mode and 386 enhanced mode memory configurations.

Do not read or write past the ends of memory objects.

Do not read or write past the ends of memory objects under any circumstances. Although this may go undetected in other memory configurations, this error will be reported by Windows as a general protection (GP) fault under the standard mode and 386 enhanced mode memory configurations.

16.6 Managing Memory for Program Code

You should plan how Windows will manage the code segments that make up the executable portion of your application or library. This planning should involve the following considerations:

- Whether your code segments should be fixed, moveable, or discardable
- Whether your application or library will contain one or more code segments
- How to maintain a balance of size and far calls between your code segments
- The order in which Windows loads the code segments

This section provides information on how Windows manages application and library code, and provides details and guidelines on how you should write your application with this information in mind.

16.6.1 Using Code-Segment Attributes

Windows uses the same memory management facilities for handling code segments as it does for handling data segments. You can, and generally should, partition your application into separate code segments. You can declare a particular code segment to be fixed, moveable, or discardable, just as you can for the application's automatic data segment and global objects.

In your application's .DEF file, you can use the **CODE** statement to specify whether the code segments are by default fixed, moveable or discardable. For example, the following statement declares that the default attribute of all code segments will be **MOVEABLE**.

```
CODE MOVEABLE;
```

You can override this default for specific code segments using the method described in Section 16.6.2, "Using Multiple Code Segments."

If you declare your code segments discardable, Windows can free memory held by those code segments when it needs to allocate additional memory. Because a code segment is always unmodifiable, there is no risk that information will be lost when it is discarded. When your application makes a call to a code segment that is not currently in memory, Windows will first load it from the .EXE file. However, if a discardable code segment is not in memory, it takes extra time for

Windows to load the segment from disk. On the other hand, this penalty is minimized because Windows uses a least-recently-used (LRU) algorithm for discarding segments, and so Windows does not discard frequently used segments.

16.6.2 Using Multiple Code Segments

Most Windows applications should be compiled using the mixed memory model. The code should be partitioned into relatively small (approximately 4K) segments. This allows Windows to move the code segments fluidly in memory. For more information on the mixed model, see Section 16.3, "Using Memory Models."

When you compile a C module, the code segment is assigned the name _TEXT by default. You can assign the code segment a different name, using the **–NT** option of the **cl** command. You partition the code by assigning different names to the code segments for different modules. The following compilation produces a code segment name CODESEG1.

```
cl -u -c -AS -Gsw -Oas -Zpe -NT CODESEG1 module1.c
```

You can assign attributes in the application's .DEF file that override the values you specified for the default **CODE**. For example, the following .DEF file excerpt declares all code segments to be moveable except the code segment named CODESEG1, which is discardable.

```
CODE LOADONCALL MOVEABLE

        SEGMENTS
                CODESEG1 MOVEABLE DISCARDABLE
```

16.6.3 Balancing Code Segments

Although it is desirable to keep code segments small, compare the cost of a far call between code segments to a near call within a code segment. A far call costs more for Windows applications than it does for non-Windows DOS applications. Each far call carries the overhead of extra instructions because Windows has to direct the call to a code segment that may have been moved or discarded.

The task of balancing code segments in an application is a matter of minimizing the frequency of far calls that must be made between segments, while maintaining roughly equal-sized segments that do not significantly exceed 4K. Functions that frequently call each other should be grouped in the same code segment, subject to the code size guideline.

16.6.4 The Order of Code Segments in the .DEF File

In EMS small-frame mode, code segments and resources are loaded above the EMS bank line according to the chronological order in which they are loaded into memory by Windows. Once a code segment is loaded above the EMS bank line, it will never be discarded.

To take maximum advantage of expanded memory in the small-frame configuration, you should declare frequently accessed code segments as **PRELOAD** and **MOVEABLE** in the application .DEF file. You should list the most frequently accessed code segments first since they will be preloaded first. If you do not, less important code segments are likely to be loaded into the EMS bank. For example, initialization code that is only needed once at program start-up could remain in the EMS bank for the entire life of the application. This means that other code segments that are more frequently accessed might still have to be discarded if not enough memory is available below the EMS bank line.

You can use Profiler to help determine which segments are most frequently used. For more information on Profiler, see *Tools*.

Declaring a code segment **MOVEABLE** or **DISCARDABLE** does not imply that it can be moved or discarded once it is loaded above the EMS bank line in the small-frame configuration. If you declare the code segment **FIXED**, it might still be loaded above the EMS bank line. You should not declare the code segment **FIXED**, however, if that is not what you would do for other memory configurations, such as the EMS large-frame configuration or the basic memory configuration.

Application resources may also be located above the EMS bank line. You can influence whether a resource is loaded above the line, just as you can a code segment. To do so, declare the resource with the **PRELOAD** option in the resource script, as follows:

```
mycursor CURSOR PRELOAD point.cur
```

Note that code segments are preloaded before resources.

16.7 Summary

Windows manages memory carefully to ensure the most efficient use of the available memory. There are four basic Windows memory configurations, which more or less correspond to the Windows operating modes. Windows manages memory differently for each configuration. Applications *must* follow certain memory-management guidelines in order to run successsfully with Windows in standard mode or 386 enhanced mode.

Topic	Reference
Using C and assembly language in a Windows application,	*Guide to Programming:* Chapter 14, "C and Assembly Language"

Topic	Reference
Memory-management functions	*Reference, Volume 1:* Chapter 4, "Functions Directory"
Module-definition statements	*Reference, Volume 2:* Chapter 10, "Module-Definition Statements"

Chapter 17

Print Settings

When a user prints from your application, the resulting output depends not only on the data your application sends to the printer; it also depends on the current print settings for that printer. Print settings can include information such as page size, print orientation, or which paper bin to use.

The simplest way to print (illustrated in Chapter 12, "Printing") uses the current print settings without validating or changing them. This approach works as long as the settings are appropriate for your application's needs. However, if not, your application's printed output could be less than ideal. For example, if your application prints a spreadsheet that requires a "landscape" print orientation on a printer that's set up for "portrait" orientation, your application's data will probably run off the right side of the paper.

Microsoft Windows version 3.0 lets your application change the print settings to fit its own needs (for example, change the print orientation to landscape, or specify a different paper bin). After your application has tailored the print settings, it can print using those settings.

Because print settings differ from printer to printer, an application must interact with a printer's device driver in order to change the settings for that printer. Most Windows printer drivers provide special functions that let your application manipulate print settings easily.

This chapter explains how to use these printer-driver functions to manipulate print settings.

This chapter covers the following topics:

- How Windows manages print settings
- Using device-driver functions
- Finding out the capabilities of a printer device driver
- Manipulating print settings
- Copying print settings from one driver to another
- Letting the user change the print settings
- Working with drivers written for previous versions of Windows

17.1 How Windows Manages Print Settings

When your application performs printing, it uses a printer device context that it created using the **CreateDC** function. When creating a device context for a printer, the application specifies the printer driver and name, the output port, and, optionally, print settings for that driver. These settings are device-specific; each collection of print settings applies to a specific printer and printer driver. Because the exact settings can differ from printer to printer, the application must be careful to supply the specific information each printer driver expects.

When an application calls **CreateDC** to create a printer device context in preparation for printing, Windows creates the device context using the first print settings it can find. It looks for print settings in the following order:

1. Windows first tries to use the print settings (if any) that the application passed using the *lpInitData* parameter of the **CreateDC** function.
2. If the application did not pass any print settings when calling **CreateDC**, Windows looks for the print settings that the printer driver most recently stored in memory using the **SetEnvironment** function.
3. If the printer driver has not yet stored any print settings in memory using **SetEnvironment**, Windows looks for the print settings in WIN.INI.
4. If the WIN.INI file does not contain complete print settings for this printer and port, the printer driver fills any gaps using its own built-in default settings.

Your application has the most control over print settings if you specify settings when calling **CreateDC**. If you specify print settings using **CreateDC**, Windows uses those settings instead of other settings that may be available from the driver or WIN.INI.

17.1.1 Print Settings and the DEVMODE Structure

Usually, print settings come in the form of a **DEVMODE** structure. For example, when you pass print settings to **CreateDC**, you are actually passing a pointer to a **DEVMODE** structure. (A notable exception is the WIN.INI file, which contains print settings in the form of strings.) Normally, your application does not create the **DEVMODE** structure itself; instead, it gets a complete structure from the printer driver, and modifies it as necessary. This method ensures that the structure is complete and correct.

The **DEVMODE** structure includes three types of information:

Information	Description
Header information	The first five fields in the **DEVMODE** structure make up the structure's header information. This information includes the printer name (for example, "PCL/HP Laserjet"), version information, and information about the size of the **DEVMODE** structure. You should always provide complete header information.
Device-independent settings	Most of the fields in the **DEVMODE** structure are device-independent settings, such as print orientation, paper size, and number of copies. Although a complete **DEVMODE** structure always includes all the device-independent settings, some printers do not support all the settings. For example, many printers can print only on one side of the paper; printer drivers for those printers would therefore ignore the **DEVMODE** structure's **dmDuplex** field, which specifies two-sided printing.
Device-specific data	The **DEVMODE** structure's **dmDriverData** field contains device-specific data that is defined by each device driver. Normally, an application would simply pass this data on without modifying it in any way.

The best way to supply a complete **DEVMODE** structure when calling **CreateDC** is to first use the **ExtDeviceMode** function (included in printer drivers written for Windows version 3.0). This function tells the printer driver to create a **DEVMODE** structure using its current print settings. Because the driver itself creates the **DEVMODE** structure and includes its device-specific data, your application can assume that the structure is complete and correct. Your application can then pass the resulting **DEVMODE** structure when calling the **CreateDC** function.

For details on the **DEVMODE** data structure, see the *Reference, Volume 2*. For details on the **CreateDC** function, see the *Reference, Volume 1*.

17.1.2 Print Settings and the Printer Environment

A "printer environment" is a collection of print settings in memory. There can be one printer environment for each printer port. The current printer driver (whatever the user has installed for that port) is responsible for creating and maintaining the port's printer environment.

The settings in each port's environment are the same as those in the WIN.INI file, except that the WIN.INI information consists of character strings in a file, while the environment is the same information in the form of a **DEVMODE** structure in memory. Having the information in memory speeds up the process of creating a printer device context for that port.

When an application creates a printer device context without specifying its own customized print settings, Windows uses the settings in the printer environment.

Because the printer environment is associated with a printer port, changes to the settings in a printer environment affect any application that does not provide its own print settings when creating a printer device context for that port.

When using printer drivers written for Windows version 3.0, an application can manipulate the print settings to suit its own needs; the changes need not affect other applications that are using the same port. (When using printer drivers written for earlier versions of Windows, applications can change the print settings only by changing the WIN.INI file and the printer environment; this affects all applications that use that port without providing their own print settings.)

17.2 Using Device-Driver Functions

Most printer drivers include special functions that an application can use to manipulate print settings for that driver and printer port.

- Older printer drivers provide the **DeviceMode** function. This function displays a dialog box that lets the user select print settings, such as page orientation and paper size, for the printer. The user's changes affect the WIN.INI file and the print environment.
- Windows version 3.0 printer drivers provide the **ExtDeviceMode** function, which provides many ways for the application to manipulate print settings without affecting other applications. This function also lets an application get a copy of the settings in a driver's **DEVMODE** structure; the application can then modify those settings, rather than creating a **DEVMODE** structure from scratch. (**ExtDeviceMode** also includes the functionality that **DeviceMode** provides in older drivers.)
- Windows version 3.0 drivers also provide the **DeviceCapabilities** function. This function lets the application find out which **DEVMODE** fields a particular driver supports.

Device-driver functions are actually part of the device driver, and not regular Windows functions. Because of this, you must use the following procedure to call a device-driver function:

1. Load the device driver into memory by calling the **LoadLibrary** function.
2. Use the **GetProcAddress** function to retrieve the address of the function you want. (If **GetProcAddress** returns a null pointer, then that device driver does not provide the function you requested.)

3. Use the pointer returned by **GetProcAddress** to call the device-driver function.

4. After you have finished using the device-driver function, call the Windows **FreeLibrary** function to unload the device driver from the system.

The following example shows the code necessary to call the **ExtDeviceMode** function of the PSCRIPT.DRV printer driver:

```
FARPROC lpfnExtDeviceMode;
FARPROC lpfnDeviceMode;
HANDLE hDriver;

hDriver = LoadLibrary("PSCRIPT.DRV");
lpfnExtDeviceMode = GetProcAddress(hDriver, "ExtDeviceMode");

if (lpfnExtDeviceMode != NULL)
       {
       /*  If the driver supports ExtDeviceMode, call the *
        *  driver's ExtDeviceMode function using the      *
        *  procedure address in lpfnExtDeviceMode. */
       }
else
       {
       /*  The driver is not a Version 3.0 driver and     *
        *  does not support the newer functions;          *
        *  use the DeviceMode function instead. */

       lpfnDeviceMode = GetProcAddress(hDriver, "DeviceMode");

       if (lpfnDeviceMode != NULL)
              {
              /* If the driver supports DeviceMode, call    *
               * the driver's DeviceMode function using     *
               * the procedure address in lpfnDeviceMode. */
              }
       }
}
FreeLibrary(hDriver);  /* When finished, unload driver from memory. */
```

17.3 Finding Out the Capabilities of the Printer Driver

The **DeviceCapabilities** device-driver function lets you find out the capabilities of a particular printer, including the **DEVMODE** fields that the driver supports. For example, if your application depends on printing in landscape orientation, it might call **DeviceCapabilities** to find out if the current printer supports landscape orientation.

The *Reference, Volume 1,* provides detailed information on the **DeviceCapabilities** function.

17.4 Working with Print Settings

The **ExtDeviceMode** device-driver function lets you perform one or more actions at a time. You can use **ExtDeviceMode** to:

- Retrieve a **DEVMODE** structure containing the driver's current print settings
- Change one or more of the driver's current print settings
- Prompt the user for print settings
- Reset the print environment and the information in WIN.INI

Because **ExtDeviceMode** provides so many different features, you will probably find that your application calls **ExtDeviceMode** repeatedly during the process of retrieving, altering, and maintaining print settings.

When calling the **ExtDeviceMode** function, you specify:

- The module handle of the printer driver you want (returned by the **LoadLibrary** or **GetModuleHandle** function).
- The name of the printer device (for example, "PCL/HP LaserJet").
- The name of the port to which the printer is connected (for example, "LPT2:").
- The operation(s) that you want the device driver to perform.

  You request different operations by setting the values that make up the *wMode* parameter. To request several operations at once, you can combine two or more values using the OR (|) operator.
- The input buffer (if any).

  The application can supply a partial or complete **DEVMODE** data structure as input. (Unlike other functions that use a **DEVMODE** structure, **ExtDeviceMode** does not require that the input **DEVMODE** structure be complete.)
- The output buffer (if any).

  At the application's request, the driver writes a complete **DEVMODE** structure to the output buffer.

NOTE The ***ExtDeviceMode*** function actually requires eight parameters in all; the list above includes only parameters that are directly relevant to this discussion. See the *Reference, Volume 1,* for a complete list of parameters for the **ExtDeviceMode** function.

17.4.1 Specifying ExtDeviceMode Input and Output

By setting the *wMode* parameter, you specify how a driver's **ExtDeviceMode** function will receive input, and where it will send output. The driver's response differs depending on the value(s) you use.

If you set *wMode* to zero, **ExtDeviceMode** simply returns the size of the output **DEVMODE** data structure in bytes. This is often the first call you'll make to **ExtDeviceMode**, since it lets you know how large to make the output buffer.

You can set *wMode* to one or more values other than zero. Table 17.1 lists these values. The table shows the following for each value:

- The name of the value
- Whether the value controls input or output
- A brief description of what each value does

Table 17.1 Values for the *wMode* Parameter

Value	Input/Output	Description
DM_IN_BUF	Input	Tells the driver to change its current print settings to match those the application supplied as a **DEVMODE** structure in the input buffer.
DM_IN_PROMPT	Input	Tells the driver to display its Print Setup dialog box, then change its current print settings to match those the user specifies.
DM_OUT_BUF	Output	Writes the driver's current print settings to the output buffer in the form of a **DEVMODE** structure.
DM_OUT_DEFAULT	Output	Writes the driver's current print settings to the printer environment and the WIN.INI file.

You can use a combination of *wMode* values to let both your application and the user manipulate the print settings.

IMPORTANT In order to change the settings, you must specify at least one input value and one output value. For example, you could use a combination of the input value DM_IN_PROMPT and the output value DM_OUT_DEFAULT to tell the driver to take input from the user and write the resulting settings to the current print environment and WIN.INI.

If you specify only output values (DM_OUT_BUF or DM_OUT_DEFAULT), the driver provides its current settings, and ignores any input you provide. If you specify only input values (DM_IN_PROMPT or DM_IN_BUF), calling **ExtDeviceMode** generates no output, so your input has no real effect.

17.4.2 Getting a Copy of the Print Settings

It is often useful, when working with print settings, to find out a particular printer driver's current settings. This lets your application determine whether the settings are appropriate for its own printing needs.

To get a copy of a driver's print settings:

1. Determine how much space the output **DEVMODE** structure will require. To do this, call **ExtDeviceMode** with *wMode* set to zero.

   ExtDeviceMode returns the size in bytes of the output **DEVMODE** structure (the one the driver would create if you set *wMode* to DM_OUT_BUF).
2. Allocate a buffer of this size.
3. Call **ExtDeviceMode** again. The parameters you specify should include the following information:

Parameter	Value
lpDEVMODEOutput	A pointer to the output buffer you just allocated
wMode	DM_OUT_BUF

The printer driver then puts a **DEVMODE** structure containing its current print settings into the buffer you specified.

Because the output buffer contains a complete **DEVMODE** structure, you can easily pass that data to the **CreateDC** or **SetEnvironment** function, since both of these functions accept the **DEVMODE** structure as input.

NOTE Calling **ExtDeviceMode** using only the DM_OUT_BUF value for the *wMode* parameter is similar to calling **GetEnvironment**, since both return the default print settings. The difference between the two is that **ExtDeviceMode** always works because it gets the settings directly from the driver; **GetEnvironment**, on the other hand, retrieves valid settings only if the device driver has previously called **SetEnvironment**.

17.4.3 Changing the Print Settings

Often, when printing information, your application may need to change the print settings to suit its own printing needs.

To change the print settings, set *wMode* to both an input value (DM_IN_BUF or DM_IN_PROMPT) and an output value (DM_OUT_BUF or DM_OUT_DEFAULT). You can specify multiple values, as long as you use at least one input and one output value. (To change the settings without affecting other applications, do not specify the DM_OUT_DEFAULT output value; that value causes the driver to change the default printer settings to those you specify.)

There are several different ways to provide new print settings as input. For each method, you set *wMode* to a different combination of values. The input methods are:

- Provide a partial **DEVMODE** structure with the new settings you want. (When calling **ExtDeviceMode**, specify the value DM_IN_BUF.)
- Display the driver's Printer Setup dialog box so that the user can change the settings. (When calling **ExtDeviceMode**, specify the value DM_IN_PROMPT.)
- Provide a partial **DEVMODE** structure and, in addition, display the driver's Printer Setup dialog box. This method lets both your application and the user change the settings. (When calling **ExtDeviceMode**, specify both the DM_IN_BUF and DM_IN_PROMPT values.)

When changing the print settings, you not only provide new print settings as input; you also specify where you want the driver to place the updated print settings. The driver provides as output a complete, valid **DEVMODE** structure that reflects the changes your application and/or the user has just made to the print settings. Your instructions tell the driver where to put this output structure. You determine the driver's output by specifying one or more output values for the *wMode* parameter of the **ExtDeviceMode** function.

You can direct the driver to do one of the following:

- Place the updated **DEVMODE** structure in the output buffer. Your application can then pass this output structure to **CreateDC** and other Windows functions. (When calling **ExtDeviceMode**, specify the value DM_OUT_BUF.)
- Write the updated **DEVMODE** structure to memory using **SetEnvironment**. When the printer driver does this, it resets the print environment for that printer port and changes the relevant entries in WIN.INI. The new settings

affect any application that uses that port and does not provide its own print settings. (When calling **ExtDeviceMode**, specify the value DM_OUT_DEFAULT.)

- Place the updated **DEVMODE** structure in the output buffer, reset the print environment, and update WIN.INI. (When calling **ExtDeviceMode**, specify both the DM_OUT_BUF and DM_OUT_DEFAULT values.)

The rest of this section describes some common ways to use and combine **ExtDeviceMode** features.

17.4.4 Tailoring Print Settings for Use with CreateDC

In order to use a printer, your application must first create a printer device context using the **CreateDC** function. This function has an optional parameter, *lpInitData*, which specifies the print settings to use when creating the printer device context. The simplest way to print is to set *lpInitData* to NULL; Windows then creates the device context using the current print settings for that printer port.

To print using your own print settings instead of the current default settings, you can pass the print settings you want to **CreateDC**. Windows then creates the device context using your customized print settings instead.

To pass print settings to **CreateDC**, provide a complete **DEVMODE** structure that contains the print settings you want.

When calling the **CreateDC** function, you should provide only **DEVMODE** structures that you have received directly from the printer driver. Although it is possible to simply edit a **DEVMODE** structure and then immediately pass it to **CreateDC**, it's not a good idea to do so. **CreateDC** requires a perfectly correct and complete **DEVMODE** structure. Therefore, any minor inconsistencies in the structure can result in an invalid device context. To ensure that a **DEVMODE** structure is valid, you pass it to the printer driver as input. The driver then provides a complete, correct **DEVMODE** structure that incorporates your changes; you can safely pass this output structure to **CreateDC**.

To use particular print settings, provide, as input to the **ExtDeviceMode** function, a partial **DEVMODE** structure that contains the settings you want. The driver changes only those settings for which you supply a new value. This means that you can use this method to change a single print setting—for example, to change from portrait to landscape orientation—without affecting the driver's other print settings. In response to the **ExtDeviceMode** function, the driver provides as output a complete **DEVMODE** structure that includes your changes.

To change the print settings, follow these steps:

1. Set up a partial or complete **DEVMODE** structure that contains the fields you want to change.

If you are supplying a partial structure:

- Be sure to include all five header fields (**dmDeviceName**, **dmSpecVersion**, **dmDriverVersion**, **dmSize**, and **dmDriverExtra**). Set the **dmDriverVersion** and **dmDriverExtra** fields to zero if you are not passing any driver-specific information.
- Set the **dmFields** field to indicate which of the device-independent settings you are providing.

For example, to request that a printer driver use landscape orientation with letter-sized paper, you could set up the following **DEVMODE** structure:

```
DEVMODE dm;
lstrcpy(dm.dmDeviceName,szDeviceName);
/* Header information */
dm.dmVersion = DM_SPECVERSION;
dm.dmDriverVersion = 0;
dm.dmSize = sizeof(DEVMODE);
dm.dmDriverExtra = 0;
/* Device-independent settings */
dm.dmFields = DM_ORIENTATION | DM_PAPERSIZE;
dm.dmOrientation = DMORIENT_LANDSCAPE;
dm.dmPaperSize = DMPAPER_LETTER;
```

The first five fields make up the structure's header information. The szDeviceName value is a string that contains the name of the device, such as "PCL/HP Laserjet". Chapter 12, "Printing," explains how to retrieve this value from the WIN.INI initialization file.

2. Call **ExtDeviceMode**.

   The parameters you specify should include the following information:

Parameter	**Value**
lpDevModeInput	A pointer to the buffer that contains the partial or complete **DEVMODE** structure you are supplying
lpDevModeOutput	A pointer to the output buffer
wMode	DM_IN_BUF | DM_OUT_BUF

   The driver then changes its settings to match those in your input structure, and writes the resulting settings to the output buffer as a complete **DEVMODE** structure.

3. Pass the output **DEVMODE** structure to **CreateDC** to create a printer device context that uses the new settings.

After modifying its **DEVMODE** structure, the driver copies the modified **DEVMODE** structure to the output buffer. The output **DEVMODE** structure will be a complete structure, and will include the changes you specified in your partial structure. Because the driver has just "validated" your changes, it is safe to pass this output structure to the **CreateDC** function.

17.4.5 Changing the Print Settings Without Affecting Other Applications

Your application can manipulate the print settings without affecting other applications. To do so, follow these steps:

1. Call **ExtDeviceMode**.

   The parameters you specify should include the following information:

Parameter	Value
lpDevModeInput	A pointer to the buffer that contains the partial or complete **DEVMODE** structure you are supplying
lpDevModeOutput	A pointer to the output buffer
wMode	DM_IN_BUF | DM_OUT_BUF or DM_IN_PROMPT | DM_OUT_BUF or DM_IN_BUF | DM_IN_PROMPT | DM_OUT_BUF

   Note that you can specify either or both input values (DM_IN_PROMPT and DM_IN_BUF). This call to **ExtDeviceMode** saves a private copy of the print settings in a buffer that your application maintains. Since the call omits the DM_OUT_DEFAULT output value, the driver does not copy the new print settings to the printer environment and WIN.INI. Therefore, other applications will not be affected by your private print settings.

2. Pass the output **DEVMODE** structure to **CreateDC** to create a printer device context that uses the new settings.

NOTE You can save the output **DEVMODE** structure to a permanent location such as a reserved area in your application's document file. Then, in a later session, your application can

can read the **DEVMODE** structure from the document file, and pass it directly to **CreateDC** without having to first call **ExtDeviceMode**.

17.4.6 Prompting the User for Changes to the Print Settings

Your application can tell the printer driver to display its Printer Setup dialog box. This dialog box lets the user specify changes to the print settings. The driver changes its current settings to reflect the user's selections. The driver's output **DEVMODE** structure (if any) then includes the user's changes.

To prompt the user for print settings, follow these steps:

1. Call **ExtDeviceMode**.

   The parameters you specify can include the following information:

Parameter	Value
lpDevModeOutput	A pointer to the output buffer
wMode	DM_IN_PROMPT | DM_OUT_BUF

   The driver then displays its Printer Setup dialog box, which lets the user select new print settings.

   If the user clicks the OK button after changing the print settings, the **ExtDeviceMode** function returns the value IDOK, and the driver places a **DEVMODE** structure in the output buffer. This output structure includes the user's changes. If the user clicks the Cancel button instead, the function returns the value IDCANCEL, and the driver's output structure will not include any of the user's selections.

2. To set up a printer device context that includes the user's changes, pass the output **DEVMODE** structure to **CreateDC**.

Setting the Values in the Printer Setup Dialog Box

To preset the values that appear in the driver's Printer Setup dialog box, your application can supply a **DEVMODE** structure with its own settings, and tell the driver to display its dialog box. The driver's Printer Setup dialog box would then appear with the settings you specified in the input **DEVMODE** structure. The user can then change some or all of the settings. After the user clicks the OK button, the driver provides an output **DEVMODE** structure that reflects the settings as they appeared when the user clicked OK. The output structure includes settings your application passed as input, with any changes the user made.

To prompt the user with a dialog box that reflects your application's print settings, follow these steps:

1. Set up a partial or complete **DEVMODE** structure that contains any settings you want to change. (See Section 17.4.4, "Tailoring Print Settings for Use with CreateDC," for information on providing a partial **DEVMODE** structure.)

2. Call **ExtDeviceMode**.

   The parameters you specify should include the following information:

Parameter	Value
lpDevModeInput	A pointer to the buffer that contains the partial or complete **DEVMODE** structure you are supplying
lpDevModeOutput	A pointer to the output buffer
wMode	DM_IN_BUF | DM_IN_PROMPT | DM_OUT_BUF

   The driver first changes its current settings to reflect the settings you provided. It then displays its Printer Setup dialog box with the new settings; the user can change some or all of the settings in the dialog box.

   If the user clicks the OK button after changing the print settings, the **ExtDeviceMode** function returns the value IDOK, and the driver places in the output buffer a **DEVMODE** structure that includes your changes as updated by the user. If the user clicks the Cancel button instead, the function returns the value IDCANCEL, and the driver's output **DEVMODE** structure includes only the changes your application provided.

3. To set up a printer device context that includes the new settings, pass the output **DEVMODE** structure to **CreateDC**.

17.5 Copying Print Settings Between Drivers

To copy print settings from one driver to another, follow these steps:

1. Copy the first driver's **DEVMODE** structure using the steps outlined in Section 17.4.2, "Getting a Copy of the Print Settings."

2. Delete the device-specific information in the output **DEVMODE** structure by setting the **dmDriverVersion** and **dmDriverExtra** fields to zero.

3. Change the **dmDeviceName** field to the name of the second device.

4. Call the second driver's **ExtDeviceMode** function.

   The parameters you specify should include the following information:

Parameter	Value
lpDevModeInput	A pointer to the buffer that contains the altered **DEVMODE** structure
lpDevModeOutput	A pointer to the output buffer
wMode	DM_IN_BUF | DM_OUT_BUF

The second driver then places a valid, complete **DEVMODE** structure in the output buffer. The output structure reflects the device-independent settings your application copied from the first driver, but contains the second driver's device-specific information.

17.6 Maintaining Your Own Print Settings

Windows version 3.0 lets your application maintain application-specific default print settings, or even settings specific to a particular document. To do this, store the **DEVMODE** structure containing the settings you want to use as defaults. You can store the structure in an application setup file to provide application-wide defaults, or as part of a document, for document-specific setups.

17.7 Working with Older Printer Drivers

Printer drivers written for previous versions of Windows provide only the **DeviceMode** function, which displays a dialog box that lets the user specify print settings, such as page orientation and paper size, for the printer. Changes made to the print settings affect the entire system, not just the calling application.

Like other device-driver functions, the **DeviceMode** function is part of the driver, not part of GDI. (Section 17.2, "Using Device-Driver Functions," explains how to call device-driver functions.) When you call a driver's **DeviceMode** function, the driver displays its Printer Setup dialog box. The user can then change the print settings for that printer and printer port.

The following example shows how to use the function's procedure address, lpfnDeviceMode, to call the **DeviceMode** function:

```
if (lpfnDeviceMode != NULL) /* if driver supports this function */
{
(*lpfnDeviceMode)(
        (HWND)hWnd,             /* handle to parent window */
        (HANDLE)hDriver,        /* handle to driver module */
        (LPSTR)"PSCRIPT",       /* printer name            */
        (LPSTR)"LPT1:");        /* port name               */
}
```

17.8 Summary

This chapter explains how to use device-driver functions to manipulate print settings. The main reason to change print settings is so that your application can pass its own tailored settings to the **CreateDC** function when preparing to print. Windows then sets up the printer device context using the application's settings instead of the printer driver's default settings, the settings in the print environment, or the settings in WIN.INI. In addition, device-driver functions let your application change print settings without affecting other applications that are using the same printer driver.

For more information on topics related to print settings, see the following:

Topic	Reference
Printing from a Windows application	*Guide to Programming*: Chapter 12, "Printing"
The **ExtDeviceMode**, **Device-Capabilities**, **DeviceMode**, and **CreateDC** functions	*Reference, Volume 1*: Chapter 2, "Graphics Device Interface Functions" and Chapter 4, "Functions Directory"
The **DEVMODE** structure	*Reference, Volume 2*: Chapter 7, "Data Types and Structures"
An example of simple printer initialization	The sample application MULTIPAD.EXE, included on the SDK Sample Source Code disk
Writing printer device drivers	Microsoft Windows Device Development Kit

Chapter 18

Fonts

Microsoft Windows offers a rich array of text-writing capabilities that goes far beyond simple terminal-based text output. In particular, Windows lets you choose the font to be used for text output.

A font is a collection of characters that have a unique combination of height, width, typeface, character set, and other attributes. An application uses fonts to display or print text of various faces and sizes. For example, a word-processing application uses fonts to give the user a "what you see is what you get" interface.

This chapter covers the following topics:

- Using fonts in your applications
- Creating font resources that your application and others can use

This chapter also explains how to create a sample application, ShowFont, that illustrates these concepts.

18.1 Writing Text

You can write text in a given font by selecting the font and using the **TextOut** function to write it. **TextOut** writes the characters of the string by using the font that is currently selected in the device context. The following example shows how to write the string "This is a sample string":

```
hDC = GetDC(hWnd);
TextOut(hDC, 10, 10, "This is a sample string", 23);
ReleaseDC(hWnd, hDC);
```

In this example, **TextOut** starts the string at the coordinates (10,10) and prints all 23 characters of the string.

The default font for a device context is the system font. This is a variable-width font representing characters in the ANSI character set. Its font name is "System". Windows uses the system font for menus, window captions, and other text.

18.2 Using Color when Writing Text

You can add color to the text you write by setting the text and background colors of the device context. The text color determines the color of the character to be written; the background color determines the color of everything in the character cell except the character. GDI writes the entire character cell (the rectangle enclosing the character) when it writes text. A character cell usually has the same width and height as the character.

You can set the text and background colors by using the **SetTextColor** and **SetBkColor** functions. The following example sets the text color to red and the background color to green:

```
SetTextColor(hDC, RGB(255,0,0));
SetBkColor(hDC, RGB(0,255,0));
```

When you first create a device context, the text color is black and the background color is white. You can change these colors at any time.

NOTE If you are using a common display context obtained with **GetDC** or **BeginPaint**, your colors are lost each time you release the context, so you need to set them each time you retrieve the display context.

The background color applies only when the background mode is opaque. The background mode determines whether the background color in the character cell has any effect on what is already on the display surface. If the mode is opaque, the background color overwrites anything already on the display surface; if it is transparent, anything on the display surface that would otherwise be overwritten by the background is preserved. You can set the background mode by using the **SetBkMode** function, or you can retrieve the current mode by using the **GetBkMode** function. Similarly, you can retrieve the current text and background color by using the **GetTextColor** and **GetBkColor** functions.

18.3 Using Stock Fonts

You are not limited to using the system font in your application. GDI offers a variety of stock fonts that you can retrieve and use as desired. To use stock fonts in your application, you must specify the type of font you want in the **GetStockObject** function. **GetStockObject** creates the font you request and returns a handle to the font that you can use to select into a device context. GDI offers the following stock fonts:

Font	Description
ANSI_FIXED_FONT	Specifies a fixed-pitch font based on the ANSI character set. For example, a Courier font is typically used, if one is available.
ANSI_VAR_FONT	Specifies a variable-width font based on the ANSI character set. For example, a Helv font is typically used, if it is available.
DEVICEDEFAULT_FONT	Specifies a font preferred by the given device. This font depends on how the GDI font mapper interprets font requests, so the font may vary widely from device to device.
OEM_FIXED_FONT	Specifies a fixed-pitch font based on an OEM character set. OEM character sets vary from system to system. For IBM computers and compatibles, the OEM font is based on the IBM PC character set.
SYSTEM_FONT	Specifies the system font. This is a variable-pitch font based on the ANSI character set, and is used by the system to display window captions, menu names, and text in dialog boxes. The system font is always available. Other fonts are available only if they have been installed.

To use a stock font, create it by using the **GetStockObject** function, then select the font handle into the device context by using the **SelectObject** function. Any subsequent calls to **TextOut** will use the selected font. The following example shows how to use the variable-width ANSI font:

```
HFONT hFont;
HFONT hOldFont;
    .
    .
    .

hFont = GetStockObject(ANSI_VAR_FONT);
if (hOldFont = SelectObject(hDC, hFont)) {
    TextOut(hDC, 10, 10, "This is a sample string", 23);
    SelectObject(hDC, hOldFont);
}
```

As you would with any other GDI object, you must select a font before it can be used in an output operation. The **SelectObject** function selects the font you have created and returns a handle to the previous font. The system stock font is always available, even if no other stock font is. If no other stock fonts are available, **GetStockObject** returns a handle to the system font.

18.4 Creating a Logical Font

A logical font is a list of font attributes, such as height, width, character set, and typeface, that you want GDI to consider when choosing a font for writing text. You can create a logical font by using the **CreateFont** function. **CreateFont** returns a handle to the logical font. You can use this handle in the **SelectObject** function to select the font for the device context. When you select a logical font, GDI chooses a physical font, based on your request, to write subsequent text. GDI attempts to choose a physical font that matches your logical font exactly, but if it cannot find an exact match in its internal pool of fonts, it chooses the closest matching font.

In the following example, the **CreateFont** function creates a logical font:

```
hFont = CreateFont(
    10,                                     /* lfHeight          */
    8,                                      /* lfWidth           */
    0,                                      /* lfEscapement      */
    0,                                      /* lfOrientation     */
    FW_NORMAL,                              /* lfWeight          */
    FALSE,                                  /* lfItalic          */
    FALSE,                                  /* lfUnderline       */
    FALSE,                                  /* lfStrikeOut       */
    ANSI_CHARSET,                           /* lfCharSet         */
    OUT_DEFAULT_PRECIS,                     /* lfOutPrecision    */
    CLIP_DEFAULT_PRECIS,                    /* lfClipPrecision   */
    DEFAULT_QUALITY,                        /* lfQuality         */
    FIXED_PITCH | FF_MODERN,                /* lfPitchAndFamily  */
    "System"                                /* lfFaceName        */
    );
```

This logical font asks for a fixed-pitch font in which each character is 10 pixels high and 8 pixels wide. Font dimensions are always described in pixels. The requested escapement and orientation are zero, which means the baseline along which the characters are displayed is horizontal and none of the characters will be rotated. FW_NORMAL is the requested weight. Other typical weights are FW_BOLD (for darker, heavier characters) and FW_LIGHT (for lighter characters). Italic, underlined, or strikethrough characters are not desired in this example. The requested character set is ANSI, the standard character set of Windows. Default output precision, clipping precision, and quality are requested. These attributes affect the way the characters are displayed. Setting these attributes to default values lets the display device take advantage of its own capabilities to display characters. The requested font family is FF_MODERN. The font name is "System".

When you supply a logical font to **SelectObject**, the function examines the pool of available fonts to find a font that satisfies the requested attributes. If it finds an exact match, it returns a handle to that font. If it fails to find an exact match, it chooses the closest possible font and returns that handle. In some cases, **SelectObject** might not find an exact match but nevertheless can synthesize the requested font by using an existing font that is close. For example, if the only available system font were 5 pixels high and your logical font specified a height of 10 pixels, **SelectObject** could synthesize the requested font by doubling the height. In such cases, **SelectObject** returns the synthesized font for writing text.

18.5 Using Multiple Fonts in a Line

If you are developing an application that uses a variety of fonts—a word processor, for instance—you will probably want to use more than one font in a line of text. To do so, you will need to write the text in each font separately. The **TextOut** function cannot change fonts for you.

The main difficulty with using more than one font in a line of text is that you need to keep track of how far each call to **TextOut** advances the line of text, so that you can supply the appropriate starting location for the next part of the line. If you are using variable-width fonts, keeping track of the length of a written string can be difficult. However, Windows provides the **GetTextExtent** function, which computes the length of a given string by using the widths of characters in the current font.

One way to write a line of text that contains multiple fonts is to use the **GetTextExtent** function after each call to **TextOut** and add the length to a current position. The following example shows how to write the line "This is a sample string.", using italic characters for the word "sample", and bold characters for all others:

```
X = 10;
SelectObject(hDC, hBoldFont);
TextOut(hDC, X, 10, "This is a ", 10);

X = X + LOWORD(GetTextExtent(hDC, "This is a ", 10));
SelectObject(hDC, hItalicFont);
TextOut(hDC, X, 10, "sample ", 7);

X = X + LOWORD(GetTextExtent(hDC, "sample ", 7));
SelectObject(hDC, hBoldFont);
TextOut(hDC, X, 10, "string.", 7);
```

In this example, the **SelectObject** function sets the font to be used in the subsequent **TextOut** function. The hBoldFont and hItalicFont font handles are assumed to have been previously created using the **CreateFont** function. Each

TextOut function writes a part of the line, then the **GetTextExtent** function computes the length of that part. **GetTextExtent** returns a double-word value containing both the length and height. You need to use the **LOWORD** utility to retrieve the length. This length is added to the current position to determine the starting location of the next part of the line.

Another way to write a line with multiple fonts is to create a function that consolidates all the required actions into a single call. The following example shows such a function:

```
WORD StringOut(hDC, X, Y, lpString, hFont)
HDC hDC;
short X;
short Y;
LPSTR lpString;
HANDLE hFont;
{
    HANDLE hPrevFont;

    hPrevFont = SelectObject(hDC, hFont);
    TextOut(hDC, X, Y, lpString, lstrlen(lpString));
    SelectObject(hDC, hPrevFont);
    return (LOWORD(GetTextExtent(hDC, lpString, lstrlen(lpString)));
}
```

This function writes the string in the given font, then resets the font to its previous setting and returns the length of the written string. The following example shows how to write the line, "This is a sample string.":

```
X = 10;
X = X + StringOut(hDC, X, 10, "This is a ", hBoldFont);
X = X + StringOut(hDC, X, 10, "sample  ", hItalicFont);
StringOut(hDC, X, 10, "string.", hBoldFont);
```

18.6 Getting Information About the Selected Font

You can retrieve information about the selected font from a device context by using the **GetTextMetrics** and **GetTextFace** functions.

The **GetTextMetrics** function copies a **TEXTMETRIC** structure into a buffer that you supply. The structure contains a description of the font, including the average dimensions of the character cells within the font, the number of characters in the font, and the character set on which the font is based. You can use the text metrics to determine how much space you'll need between lines of text, or which character values have corresponding characters and which are represented by the font's default character.

The text metrics are most often used to determine how much space you need between lines of text to prevent one line from overwriting another. For example, to compute an appropriate value for single-line spacing, you add the values of the

tmHeight and **tmExternalLeading** fields of the **TEXTMETRIC** structure. The **tmHeight** field specifies the height of each character cell and **tmExternal-Leading** specifies the font designer's recommended spacing between the bottom of one character cell and the top of the next. The following example shows how to write several lines with single-spacing:

```
TEXTMETRIC TextMetric;
int nLineSpacing;
int i;
    .
    .
    .
GetTextMetrics(hDC, &TextMetric);
nLineSpace = TextMetric.tmHeight + TextMetric.tmExternalLeading;

Y = 0;
for (i = 0; i < 4; i++) {
    TextOut(hDC, 0, Y, "Single-line spacing", 19);
    Y += nLineSpace;
}
```

You can also use the text metrics to verify that the selected font has the characteristics you need, such as weight, character set, pitch, and family. This is useful if you did not prepare the device context; for example, if you received it as part of a window message from a child window or control. For more information about the fields of the **TEXTMETRIC** structure, see the *Reference, Volume 2*.

The **GetTextFace** function copies a name identifying the typeface of the selected font into a buffer that you supply. The name of the typeface together with the text metrics let you fully specify the font. The following example copies the name of the current font into the character array FaceName.

```
char FaceName[32];
    .
    .
    .
GetTextFace(hDC, 32, FaceName);
```

18.7 Getting Information About a Logical Font

You can retrieve information about a font from the font handle by using the **GetObject** function. The **GetObject** function copies logical-font information, such as the height, width, weight, and character set, to a structure that you supply. You can use the logical-font information to see if the given font meets your needs. **GetObject** is often used after creating a font with the **CreateFont** function to see how closely the font matches the requested font. In the following example, **GetObject** retrieves logical-font information for a newly created font and compares the character-set values and facenames:

```
HFONT hFont;
LOGFONT LogFont;
    .
    .
    .
hFont = CreateFont(
    10,                                         /*         Height */
    10,                                         /*          Width */
    0,                                          /*     Escapement */
    0,                                          /*    Orientation */
    FW_NORMAL,                                  /*         Weight */
    FALSE,                                      /*         Italic */
    FALSE,                                      /*      Underline */
    FALSE,                                      /*      StrikeOut */
    OEM_CHARSET,                                /*        CharSet */
    OUT_DEFAULT_PRECIS,                         /*   OutPrecision */
    CLIP_DEFAULT_PRECIS,                        /*  ClipPrecision */
    DEFAULT_QUALITY,                            /*        Quality */
    FIXED_PITCH | FF_MODERN,                    /* PitchAndFamily */
    "Courier",                                  /*       Typeface */
        );

GetObject(hFont, sizeof(LogFont), (LPSTR) &LogFont);

if (LogFont.lfCharSet != OEM_CHARSET) {
    .
    .
    .
}
if (strcmp(LogFont.lfFaceName, "Courier")) {
    .
    .
    .
}
```

The font that GDI uses when you actually select a font by using the **SelectObject** function may vary widely from system to system. The selected font, which depends on the fonts available at the time of the selection, may or may not closely match your request. The only way to guarantee a request is to determine which fonts are actually available and request only those fonts, or add the appropriate font resource to the system font table before making the request, or change the method the font mapper uses to choose a font.

18.8 Enumerating Fonts

You can find out which fonts are available for a given device by using the **EnumFonts** function. This function sends information about the available fonts to a callback function that you supply. The callback function receives both logical-font and text-metric information. From this information you can determine which fonts you want to use and create appropriate font handles for them. If you create font handles by using the supplied information, you are guaranteed to get an exact match for the font when you select it for writing text.

The **EnumFonts** function usually provides font information about all the fonts that have a specific typeface name. You can supply the name when you call **EnumFonts**. If you do not supply a name, **EnumFonts** supplies information about arbitrarily selected fonts, each representing a typeface currently available. The way to examine all available fonts is to get a list of the available typefaces, then examine each font in each typeface.

The following example shows how to use **EnumFonts** to find out how many fonts having the Courier typeface are available. The callback function, EnumFunc, receives the font information and creates handles for each font:

```
FARPROC lpEnumFunc;
     .
     .
     .

int FAR PASCAL EnumFunc( )
{
}

hDC = GetDC(hWnd);
lpEnumFunc = MakeProcInstance(EnumFunc, hInst);
EnumFonts(hDC, "Courier", lpEnumFunc, NULL);
FreeProcInstance(lpEnumFunc);
```

To use the **EnumFonts** function, you must supply a callback function. As with all callback functions, EnumFunc must be explicitly named in the **EXPORTS** statement in your module-definition file and must be declared with the **FAR** and **PASCAL** attributes. For each font to be enumerated, the EnumFunc callback function receives a pointer to a logical-font structure, a pointer to a text-metrics structure, a pointer to any data you may have passed in the **EnumFonts** function call, and an integer specifying the font type. The following example shows a simple callback function that creates a list of all the sizes (in terms of height) of a given set of raster fonts:

```
short SizeList[10];
short SizeCnt = 0;
     .
     .
     .

int FAR PASCAL EnumFunc(lpLogFont, lpTextMetric, FontType, lpData)
LPLOGFONT lpLogFont;
LPTEXTMETRIC lpTextMetric;
short FontType;
LPSTR lpData;
```

```
{
    if (FontType & RASTER_FONTTYPE) {
        SizeList[SizeCnt++] = lpLogFont->lfHeight;
        if (SizeCnt >= 10)
            return (0);
    }
    return (1);
}
```

This example first checks the font to make sure it is a raster font. If the RASTER_FONTTYPE bit is 1, the font is a raster font; otherwise, it is a vector font. The next step is to save the value of the lfHeight field in the SizeList array. The callback function saves the first 10 sizes, then returns zero to stop the enumeration.

You can also use the DEVICE_FONTTYPE bit of the FontType parameter to distinguish GDI-supplied fonts from device-supplied fonts. This is useful if you want GDI to simulate bold, italic, underline, and strikeout attributes. GDI can simulate these attributes for GDI-supplied fonts, but not for device-supplied fonts.

18.9 Checking a Device's Text Capabilities

You can determine the extent of a device's text-writing capabilities by using the **GetDeviceCaps** function and the TEXTCAPS index. This index directs the function to return a bit flag identifying the text capabilities of the device. For example, you can use the text-capability flag to determine if the given device can use vector fonts, rotate characters, or simulate font attributes such as underlining and italicizing. GDI can simulate vector fonts on a device that does not directly support them by drawing lines.

Most of the text capabilities apply to fonts that are supplied by the device as opposed to those supplied by GDI. Typically, GDI can scale fonts and simulate attributes for the fonts it supplies, but it cannot do so for device-supplied fonts. You can determine how many device fonts there are by using the **GetDeviceCaps** function with the NUMFONTS index. You can retrieve information about the device fonts by using the **EnumFonts** function and checking the DEVICE_FONTTYPE bit in the *nFontType* parameter each time your **EnumFonts** callback function is called.

The following example shows how to make a list of device-supplied fonts. The **GetDeviceCaps** function returns the number of device-supplied fonts and **EnumFonts** creates font handles for each font:

```
HDC hDC;
HANDLE hDevFonts;
FARPROC lpEnumFunc;
short NumFonts;
    .
    .
```

```
int FAR PASCAL EnumFunc(lpLogFont, lpTextMetric, FontType, Data)
LPLOGFONT lpLogFont;
LPTEXTMETRIC lpTextMetric;
short FontType;
LONG Data;
{
    PSTR pDevFonts;
    short index;
    int code = 1;

    if (FontType & DEVICE_FONTTYPE) {
        pDevFonts = LocalLock(LOWORD(Data));
        if (pDevFonts != NULL) {
            index = ++pDevFonts[Ø];
            if (index < HIWORD(Data))
                pDevFonts[index] = CreateFontIndirect(lpLogFont);
            else
                code = Ø;
        }
        LocalUnlock(LOWORD(Data));
    }
    return (code);
}

    .
    .
    .
hDC = GetDC(hWnd);
NumFonts = GetDeviceCaps(hDC, NUMFONTS);
hDevFonts = LocalAlloc(LMEM_FIXED | LMEM_ZEROINIT,
    sizeof(HANDLE)*(NumFonts + 1));
lpEnumFunc = MakeProcInstance(EnumFunc, hInst);
EnumFonts(hDC, NULL, lpEnumFunc, MAKELONG(hDevFonts, NumFonts));
FreeProcInstance(lpEnumFunc);
```

18.10 Adding a Font Resource

GDI keeps a system font table that contains all the fonts that applications can use. GDI chooses a font from this table when an application makes a request for a font by using the **CreateFont** function.

A font resource is a group of individual fonts representing characters in a given character set that have various combinations of heights, widths, and pitches. For example, the system font resource contains a collection of fonts representing different sizes of characters in the ANSI character set. Similarly, the OEM font resource contains a collection of fonts representing different sizes of characters in an OEM character set.

An application can have up to 253 entries in the system font table.

Applications can load font resources and add the fonts in the resource to the system font table by using the **AddFontResource** function. Once a font resource is added, the individual fonts in the resource are accessible to the application. In other words, the **CreateFont** function considers the fonts when it tries to match a physical font with the specified logical font. (Fonts in the system font table are never directly accessible to an application. They are available only through the **CreateFontIndirect** and **CreateFont** functions, which return handles to the fonts, not memory addresses.)

You can add a font resource to the system font table by using the **AddFontResource** function. Similarly, to make room for other font resources, you can remove a font resource from the system font table by using the **RemoveFontResource** function.

Whenever an application adds or removes a font resource, it should inform all other applications of the change by sending a WM_FONTCHANGE message to them. You can use the following call to the **SendMessage** function to send the message to all windows:

```
SendMessage(-1, WM_FONTCHANGE, 0, 0L);
```

If the user has installed fonts by using the Control Panel application, you can retrieve a list of those fonts by using the **GetProfileString** function to search the **[fonts]** section of the WIN.INI file.

18.11 Setting the Text Alignment

The **TextOut** function uses a device context's current text alignment to determine how to position text relative to a given location. For example, the default text alignment is top-left, so **TextOut** places the upper-left corner of the character cell of the first character in the string at the specified location. That is, a function call such as the following places the upper-left corner of the letter "A" at the coordinates (10,10):

```
TextOut(hDC, 10, 10, "ABCDEF", 6);
```

You can change the text alignment for a device context by using the **SetTextAlign** function. If you think of **TextOut** as filling a rectangle with a text string, then you can think of the text alignment as specifying what part of the rectangle to place the specified point of the string in. **SetTextAlign** recognizes the left end, the center, and the right end of the rectangle, as well as the rectangle's top and bottom and the baseline within it. You can combine any one horizontal position with one vertical position to specify several combinations of alignment. For example, the following function sets the text alignment to right-bottom:

```
SetTextAlign(hDC, TA_RIGHT | TA_BOTTOM);
TextOut(hDC, 10, 10, "ABCDEF", 6);
```

This example places the lower-right corner of the letter "F" at the coordinates (10,10).

You can always determine the current text alignment by using the **GetTextAlign** function.

18.12 Creating Font-Resource Files

You can create your own font resources for your application and others by creating font files and adding them as resources to a font-resource file. To create a font-resource file, you must follow these steps:

1. Create the font files.
2. Create a font-resource script.
3. Create a dummy code module.
4. Create a module-definition file that describes the fonts and the devices that use the fonts.
5. Compile and link the sources.

A font-resource file is actually an empty Windows library; it contains no code or data, but does contain resources. Once you have font files, you can add them to the empty library by using the Resource Compiler. You can also add other resources to the library, such as icons, cursors, and menus.

The following sections explain how to create font-resource files.

18.12.1 Creating Font Files

Before creating a font resource, you need one or more font files. You can create font files by using the Font Editor, described in *Tools*. You are free to determine the number, size, and type of font files in a font resource. In most cases, you should include enough fonts to reasonably satisfy most logical-font requests for the device the fonts are to be used with.

When planning font sizes, remember that GDI can scale device-independent raster fonts by 1 to 8 times vertically and 1 to 5 times horizontally. GDI can also simulate bold, underlined, strikethrough, and italic fonts.

18.12.2 Creating the Font-Resource Script

You add the resources to the file by adding one or more **FONT** statements to your resource script file. The resource script can, alternatively, add .FNT files to a Windows library, a device driver, or a resource-only file that contains only icons, cursor, fonts, and other resources. Because font resources are available to all applications, you should not add them to application modules.

The **FONT** statement has the following form:

number **FONT** *filename*

One statement is required for each font file to be placed in the resource. The *number* must be unique since it is used to identify the font later. The following is a typical resource script file for a font resource:

```
1  FONT FntFil01.FNT
2  FONT FntFil02.FNT
3  FONT FntFil03.FNT
4  FONT FntFil04.FNT
5  FONT FntFil05.FNT
6  FONT FntFil06.FNT
```

Fonts can be added to modules that contain other resources by adding them to the existing resource script. This means you can have icon, menu, cursor, and dialog-box definitions in the resource script file, as well as in **FONT** statements.

18.12.3 Creating the Dummy Code Module

The dummy code module provides the object file from which the font-resource file is made. You create the dummy code module by using the assembler and the Cmacros. The module's source file should like like this:

```
TITLE   FONTRES - Stub file to build a .FON resource file

.xlist
include cmacros.inc
.list

sBegin  CODE
sEnd    CODE
end
```

Assemble this source file by using the **masm** command. It will create an object file that contains no code and no data, but which can be linked to an empty Windows library to which you can add the font resources.

18.12.4 Creating the Module-Definition File

You need to create a module-definition file for the font resource. The file must contain a **LIBRARY** statement defining the resource name, a **DESCRIPTION** statement that describes the font-resource characteristics, and a **DATA** statement. The module-definition file for a font resource should look like this:

```
LIBRARY FontRes

DESCRIPTION 'FONTRES 133,96,72 : System, Terminal (Set #3)'

STUB 'WINSTUB.EXE'
DATA NONE
```

The **DESCRIPTION** statement provides device-specific information about the font that is used to match a font with a given display or printer. The following are the three possible formats for the **DESCRIPTION** statement in a font resource:

DESCRIPTION 'FONTRES *Aspect*, *LogPixelsX*, *LogPixelsY*: *Cmt*'

DESCRIPTION 'FONTRES CONTINUOUSSCALING: *Cmt*'

DESCRIPTION 'FONTRES DEVICESPECIFIC *DeviceTypeGroup*: *Cmt*'

The first format specifies a font that was designed for a specific aspect ratio and logical pixel width and height, and can be used with any device having the same aspect and logical pixel dimensions. *Aspect* is the value (100**AspectY*)/*AspectX* rounded to an integer. The *AspectX*, *AspectY*, *LogPixelsX*, and *LogPixelsY* values are the same as given in the corresponding device's **GDIINFO** structure (the values of which are accessible by using the **GetDeviceCaps** function). You can give more than one set of *Aspect*, *LogPixelX*, and *LogPixelY* values, if desired. The *Cmt* value is a comment. The following statements are examples:

```
DESCRIPTION 'FONTRES 133,96,72: System, Terminal (Set #3)'
DESCRIPTION 'FONTRES 200,96,48; 133,96,72; 83,60,72; 167,120,72: Helv'
```

The second format specifies a continuous scaling font. This typically corresponds to vector fonts that can be drawn to any size and that do not depend on the aspect or logical pixel width of the output device. The following statement is an example:

```
DESCRIPTION 'FONTRES CONTINUOUSSCALING : Modern, Roman, Script'
```

The third format specifies a font that is specific to a particular device or group of devices. The *DeviceTypeList* can be **DISPLAY** or a list of device-type names, the same names you would specify as the second parameter in a call to the **CreateDC** function. For example:

```
DESCRIPTION 'FONTRES DISPLAY: HP 7470 plotters'
DESCRIPTION 'FONTRES DEVICESPECIFIC HP 7470A, HP 7475A: HP 7470 plotters'
```

NOTE The maximum length of a **DESCRIPTION** line is 127 characters.

Because Windows is capable of synthesizing attributes, such as bold, italic, and underline, you do not need to create separate .FNT files for fonts with these attributes. However, you are free to do so if you want.

Windows may use other fonts that do not correspond to the user's display aspect ratio. These are generic raster fonts that are intended for output devices such as bitmap printers, which rely on the display driver to draw their text.

18.12.5 Compiling and Linking the Font-Resource File

The following **MAKE** file lists the commands required to compile and link the font-resource file:

```
fontres.obj: fontres.asm
    masm fontres;

fontres.exe: fontres.def fontres.obj fontres.rc fontres.exe \
             FntFil01.FNT FntFil02.FNT FntFil03.FNT \
             FntFil04.FNT FntFil05.FNT FntFil06.FNT
    link4 fontres.obj, fontres.exe, NUL, /NOD, fontres.def
    rc fontres.rc
    rename fontres.exe fontres.fon
```

By convention, all font-resource files have the .FON filename extension. The last line in the make file renames the executable file to FONTRES.FON.

18.13 A Sample Application: ShowFont

This sample application illustrates how to use fonts in a Windows application. Although the ShowFont application has the same basic structure as any application described in this guide, it contains considerably more statements, in a far greater variety, than any other sample application. For this reason, a full description of the application is given in the application source files found on the SDK Sample Source Code disk.

The ShowFont application illustrates more than how to use fonts. It also shows how to modify many of the tasks previously described in this guide in order to carry out slightly different tasks. For example, it shows how to create and use modeless dialog boxes, how to use list boxes with your own strings (instead of the current directory), and how to use Windows' direct-access method for group boxes and radio buttons in a dialog box.

18.14 Summary

A font is a set of characters that have common attributes such as height, width, typeface, and so on. Applications use fonts to display or print text. Windows offers several stock fonts you can use in your application. You can also define your own fonts using the Font Editor, and then include them as application resources.

For more information on topics related to fonts, see the following:

Topic	Reference
Using the Font Editor	*Tools*: Chapter 6, "Designing Fonts: The Font Editor"
Printing	*Guide to Programming*: Chapter 12, "Printing"
Displaying text	*Guide to Programming*: Chapter 3, "Output to a Window"

Chapter 19 Color Palettes

Windows color palettes provide an interface between an application and a color output device (such as a display device). This interface allows the application to take full advantage of the color capabilities of the output device without severely interfering with the colors displayed by other applications. Windows takes color information contained in an application's logical palette (a GDI object that is essentially a list of colors needed by the application) and applies it to a system palette (the list of colors that is actually available on the system and that is shared by all Windows applications). When more than one application displays colors from a logical palette, Windows intervenes, controlling which application has primary access to the system palette and maintaining a high-level of color quality for the remaining applications.

This chapter covers the following topics:

- Creating a logical palette for your application and preparing it for use
- Using colors in the palette for painting in a window's client area
- Making changes in your logical palette and controlling when Windows displays those changes
- Responding to changes in the system palette made by other applications

Where indicated, C-language program-code examples in this chapter are extracted from the source code for the ShowDIB sample application, which can be found on the Sample Source Code disk supplied with the SDK. This application demonstrates how to display device-independent bitmaps with colors controlled by a color palette.

19.1 What a Color Palette Does

Many color graphics displays are capable of displaying a wide range of colors. In most cases, however, the actual number of colors that the display can render at any given time is more limited. For example, a display that is potentially able to produce 26,000 different colors may be able to show only 256 of those colors simultaneously because of hardware limitations. When such a limitation exists, the display device often maintains a palette of colors. When an application requests a color that is not currently displayed, the display device adds the requested color to the palette. However, when the number of requested colors exceeds the maximum number for the device, it replaces an existing color with the requested color, and so the actual colors displayed are incorrect.

Windows color palettes provide a buffer between a color-intensive application and the system. A color palette allows an application to use as many colors as needed without interfering with colors displayed by other windows. When a window uses a color palette and has input focus, Windows ensures that it will display all the colors it requests, up to the maximum number available simultaneously on the display, and displays additional colors by matching them to available colors. In addition, Windows matches the colors requested by inactive windows as closely as possible to the available colors. This reduces undesirable changes in the color display in inactive windows.

19.2 How Color Palettes Work

Windows provides a device-independent method for accessing the color capabilities of a display device by managing the device's system palette, if the device has one.

As noted previously, your application employs the system palette by creating and using one or more logical palettes. A logical palette is a GDI object that specifies the colors to be drawn in the device context. Each entry in the palette contains a specific color. Then, when performing graphics operations, the application does not indicate which color is to be displayed by supplying an explicit RGB value. Instead, you access the palette either directly or indirectly. Using the direct method, you indicate which color to use in your logical palette by specifying an index into the palette entries. Using the indirect method, you specify a palette-relative RGB value similar to an explicit RGB value. Sections 19.4.1, "Directly Specifying Palette Colors," and 19.4.2, "Indirectly Specifying Palette Colors," describe these two methods more completely.

When a window requests that the system use the colors in the window's logical palette (a process known as "realizing" the window's palette), Windows first exactly matches entries in the logical palette to current entries of the system palette.

If an exact match for a given logical-palette entry is not possible, Windows sets the entry in the logical palette into an unused entry in the system palette.

Finally, when all entries in the system palette have been used, Windows matches logical-palette entries as closely as possible to entries in the system palette. Windows sets aside 20 static colors (called the default palette) in the system palette to aid this color matching.

Windows always satisfies the color requests of the foreground window first; this ensures that the active window will have the best color display. For the remaining windows, Windows satisfies the color requests of the window which most recently received input focus, and so on. Figure 19.1 illustrates this process.

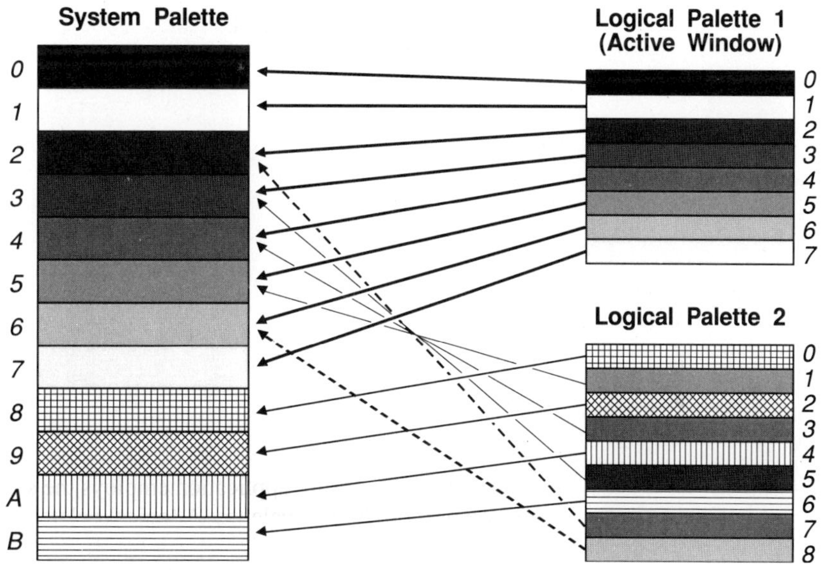

Figure 19.1 Logical Palettes and the System Palette

In Figure 19.1, a hypothetical display has a system palette capable of containing 12 colors. The application that created Logical Palette 1 owns the active window and was the first to realize its logical palette. Logical Palette 1 consists of eight colors. Logical Palette 2 is owned by a window which realized its logical palette while it was inactive. Logical Pallette 2 contains nine colors.

Because the active window was active when it realized its palette, Windows mapped all of the colors in Logical Palette 1 directly to the system palette.

Three of the colors (1, 3, and 5) in Logical Palette 2 are identical to colors in the system palette. When the second application realized its logical palette, Windows simply matched those colors to the existing system colors to save space in the palette. Colors 0, 2, 4, and 6 of Logical Palette 2 were not already in the system palette, however, and so Windows mapped those colors into the system palette.

Colors 7 and 8 in Logical Palette 2 do not exactly match colors in the system palette. Because the system palette is now full, Windows could not map these two colors into the system palette. Instead, it matched them to the closest colors in the system palette.

19.3 Creating and Using a Logical Palette

In order to use a logical palette, your application must first perform four steps:

1. Create a **LOGPALETTE** data structure that describes the palette.
2. Create the palette itself.
3. Select the palette into a device context.
4. Realize the palette.

The following sections describe how to perform each of these steps.

19.3.1 Creating a LOGPALETTE Data Structure

The **LOGPALETTE** data structure describes the logical palette you plan to use. It contains:

- A Windows version number (for Windows 3.0, it is 300H)
- The number of entries in the palette
- An array of **PALETTEENTRY** data structures, each of which contains one-byte values for red, green, and blue, and a flags field. The flags field can be set to either of the following values:
  - PC_EXPLICIT
  - PC_RESERVED

Setting the PC_EXPLICIT flag informs Windows that the palette entry does not contain color values; instead, the low-order word of the entry specifies an index into the system palette. For example, the SDK sample application MyPal shows the current state of the system palette. MyPal does this by setting the PC_EXPLICIT flag in all the entries in its own logical palette, specifying a system-palette index in each logical palette entry, and then drawing in its client area using the entries in its logical palette.

An application sets PC_RESERVED in a palette entry when it is going to animate the entry (that is, change it dynamically using the **AnimatePalette** function). Setting this flag prevents Windows from attempting to match colors from other logical palettes to this color while the entry is mapped to the system palette.

The ShowDIB sample application creates its **LOGPALETTE** structure as shown:

```
#define PALETTESIZE     256
        .
        .
        .
/* make space for our logical palette */
pLogPal = (NPLOGPALETTE) LocalAlloc(LMEM_FIXED,
               (sizeof(LOGPALETTE) +
               (sizeof(PALETTEENTRY)*(PALETTESIZE))));
```

ShowDIB initializes the palette structure with 256 entries; however, you can make a palette any size you need.

ShowDIB fills in the palette entries by opening a bitmap (.BMP) file and copying the color values in the **BITMAPINFO** data structure color table to the corresponding palette entries:

```
HPALETTE CreateBIPalette (lpbi)
LPBITMAPINFOHEADER lpbi;
{
    LOGPALETTE          *pPal;
    HPALETTE            hpal = NULL;
    WORD                nNumColors;
    BYTE                red;
    BYTE                green;
    BYTE                blue;
    int                 i;
    RGBQUAD         FAR *pRgb;

    if (!lpbi)
        return NULL;

    if (lpbi->biSize != sizeof(BITMAPINFOHEADER))
        return NULL;

    /* Get a pointer to the color table and the number of colors in it */
    pRgb = (RGBQUAD FAR *)((LPSTR)lpbi + (WORD)lpbi->biSize);
    nNumColors = DibNumColors(lpbi);

    if (nNumColors){
        /* Allocate for the logical palette structure */
        pPal = (LOGPALETTE*)LocalAlloc(LPTR,sizeof(LOGPALETTE) + nNumColors *
sizeof(PALETTEENTRY));
        if (!pPal)
            return NULL;

        pPal->palNumEntries = nNumColors;
        pPal->palVersion    = 0x300;
```

```
        /* Fill in the palette entries from the DIB color table and
         * create a logical color palette.
         */
        for (i = 0; i < nNumColors; i++){
            pPal->palPalEntry[i].peRed   = pRgb[i].rgbRed;
            pPal->palPalEntry[i].peGreen = pRgb[i].rgbGreen;
            pPal->palPalEntry[i].peBlue  = pRgb[i].rgbBlue;
            pPal->palPalEntry[i].peFlags = (BYTE)0;
        }
        hpal = CreatePalette(pPal);
        LocalFree((HANDLE)pPal);
    }
    else if (lpbi->biBitCount == 24){
        /* A 24 bitcount DIB has no color table entries so, set the number of
         * to the maximum value (256).
         */
        nNumColors = MAXPALETTE;
        pPal = (LOGPALETTE*)LocalAlloc(LPTR,sizeof(LOGPALETTE) + nNumColors *
sizeof(PALETTEENTRY));
        if (!pPal)
            return NULL;

        pPal->palNumEntries = nNumColors;
        pPal->palVersion    = 0x300;

        red = green = blue = 0;

        /* Generate 256 (= 8*8*4) RGB combinations to fill the palette
         * entries.
         */
        for (i = 0; i < pPal->palNumEntries; i++){
            pPal->palPalEntry[i].peRed   = red;
            pPal->palPalEntry[i].peGreen = green;
            pPal->palPalEntry[i].peBlue  = blue;
            pPal->palPalEntry[i].peFlags = (BYTE)0;

            if (!(red += 32))
                if (!(green += 32))
                    blue += 64;
        }
        hpal = CreatePalette(pPal);
        LocalFree((HANDLE)pPal);
    }
    return hpal;
}
```

ShowDIB first calls the DibNumColors function to determine the number of colors in the color table. If there is a color table (that is, the **biClrUsed** field is not 0 and the **biBitCount** field is not 24), it copies the **RGBQUAD** values in each **bmiColors** field in the **BITMAPINFO** structure to the corresponding palette entry. If there is no color table, ShowDIB creates a palette of 256 entries containing a "spread" of colors. When ShowDIB displays the bitmap, Windows matches the colors in the bitmap to the colors in this palette.

19.3.2 Creating a Logical Palette

Once the application has created the **LOGPALETTE** data structure, the next step is to create a logical palette by calling the **CreatePalette** function:

```
hPal = CreatePalette((LPSTR)pLogPal)
```

CreatePalette accepts a long pointer to the **LOGPALETTE** structure as its only parameter and returns a handle to the palette (**HPALETTE**).

19.3.3 Selecting the Palette Into a Device Context

As you would any other GDI object, you must select the palette into the device context in which it is to be used. The usual way of selecting an object into a device context is by calling the **SelectObject** function. However, because **Select-Object** does not recognize a palette object, you must instead call **SelectPalette** to select the palette into the device context:

```
hDC = GetDC(hWnd);
SelectPalette (hDC, hPal, 0);
```

This associates the palette with the device context so that any reference to a palette (such as a palette index passed to a GDI function instead of a color) will be to the selected palette.

To delete a logical-palette object, you use the **DeleteObject** function.

Since the palette is independent of any particular device context, it can be shared by several windows. However, Windows does not make a copy of the palette object when an application selects the palette into a device context; consequently, any change to the palette affects all device contexts using the same palette. Also, if an application selects a palette object into more than one device context, the device contexts must all belong to the same physical device (such as a display or printer). In other respects, however, a palette object is like other Windows objects.

19.3.4 Realizing the Palette

After your application has selected its palette into a device context, it must realize the palette before using it:

```
RealizePalette(hDC);
```

When your application calls the **RealizePalette** function, Windows compares the system palette with your logical palette and matches identical colors. If there is room in the system palette, Windows then maps unmatched colors in the logical palette to the system palette. Finally, if there are unmatched colors that could not be mapped to the system palette, Windows matches the remaining colors to the nearest color in the system palette.

19.4 Drawing With Palette Colors

Once your application has created a logical palette, selected it into a device context, and realized it, you can use the palette to control the colors used by GDI functions that draw within the client area of the device. For functions that require a color (such as **CreatePen** and **CreateSolidBrush**), you specify which palette color you wish to use either directly or indirectly.

19.4.1 Directly Specifying Palette Colors

Use the direct method to specify a palette color by supplying an index into your logical palette instead of an explicit RGB value to functions that expect a color. The **PALETTEINDEX** macro accepts an integer representing an index into your logical palette and returns a palette-index **COLORREF** value which you would use as the color specifier for such functions. For example, to fill a region bounded by pure green with a solid brush consisting of pure red, you could use a sequence similar to the following:

```
pLogPal->palPalEntry[5].pRed = 0xFF;
pLogPal->palPalEntry[5].pGreen = 0x00;
pLogPal->palPalEntry[5].pBlue = 0x00;
pLogPal->palPalEntry[5].pFlags = (BYTE) 0;
pLogPal->palPalEntry[6].pRed = 0x00;
pLogPal->palPalEntry[6].pGreen = 0xFF;
pLogPal->palPalEntry[6].pBlue = 0x00;
pLogPal->palPalEntry[6].pFlags = (BYTE) 0;
        .
        .
        .
hPal = CreatePalette((LPSTR)pLogPal);
hDC = GetDC(hWnd);
SelectPalette(hDC, hPal, 0);
RealizePalette(hDC);
lSolidBrushColor = PALETTEINDEX(5);
lBoundaryColor = PALETTEINDEX(6);
hSolidBrush = CreateSolidBrush(lSolidBrushColor);
hOldSolidBrush = SelectObject(hDC,hSolidBrush);
hPen = CreatePen(lBoundaryColor);
hOldPen = SelectObject(hDC,hPen);
Rectangle(hDC, x1, y1, x2, y2);
```

This code fragment informs Windows that it should draw a rectangle bounded by the color in the palette entry at index 6 (green) and filled with the color located in the entry at index 5 (red).

It is important to note that the brush created by **CreateSolidBrush** is independent of any device context. As a result, the color specified by the lSolidBrushColor parameter is whatever color is located in the sixth entry of the palette that is currently selected when the brush is selected into the device context, not when the application creates the brush. Selecting and realizing a different palette and selecting the brush again would change the color drawn by the brush. Thus, when using a logical palette, you need only create a brush for each type needed (such as solid or vertical hatch). You can then change the color of the brush by using different palettes or by changing the color in the palette entry to which the brush refers.

19.4.2 Indirectly Specifying Palette Colors

Using an index into a logical palette allows your application greater control over the actual colors displayed. However, this method becomes impractical when dealing with a device that has 2^{24} colors with no system palette. On a device capable of supporting full 24-bit color, this limits the colors that your application can display to the colors in your logical palette. Specifying palette colors indirectly allows you to avoid this limitation.

You specify a palette color indirectly by using a palette-relative RGB **COLORREF** value instead of a palette index. A palette-relative RGB is a 32-bit value that has the second bit in the high-order byte set to 1 and one-byte values for red, green, and blue in the remaining bytes. The **PALETTERGB** macro accepts three values indicating relative intensities of red, green, and blue, and returns a palette-relative RGB **COLORREF** value which, like a palette-index **COLORREF** value, you can use in place of an explicit RGB **COLORREF** value for functions that require a color.

By specifying a palette-relative RGB instead of a palette index, your application can draw to an output device using palette colors without having to determine first whether the device supports a system palette. The following shows how Windows interprets a palette-relative RGB value.

Device Supports a System Palette?	How Windows Uses a Palette-Relative RGB Value
Yes	Windows matches the RGB information to the nearest color in the currently selected logical palette and uses that palette entry as though the application had directly specified the entry.
No	Windows uses the RGB information as though the palette-relative RGB were an explicit RGB value.

For example, assume your application does the following:

```
pLogPal->palPalEntry[5].pRed = 0xFF;
pLogPal->palPalEntry[5].pGreen = 0x00;
pLogPal->palPalEntry[5].pBlue = 0x00;
CreatePalette((LPSTR)&pa);
crRed = PALETTERGB(0xFF,0x00,0x00);
```

If the target output device supports a system palette, then crRed would be equivalent to:

```
crRed = PALETTEINDEX(5);
```

However, if the output device does not support a system palette, then crRed would be equivalent to:

```
crRed = RGB(0xFF,0x00,0x00);
```

Even when using a logical palette, an application can use an explicit RGB value to specify color. In such cases, Windows displays the color as it would for an application that does not use a color palette by displaying the nearest color in the default palette. If an application creates a solid brush with an explicit RGB value, Windows simulates the color by "dithering," that is, producing a pattern of pixels made up of colors in the default palette.

19.4.3 Using a Palette When Drawing Bitmaps

As shown in Section 19.3.1, "Creating a LOGPALETTE Data Structure," a device-independent bitmap can directly access the colors in the currently selected logical palette by filling the bitmap color table with indexes into the palette instead of explicit RGB values. Then, when an application creates the bitmap by calling **CreateDIBitmap**, retrieves bits from a bitmap with **GetDIBits**, sets bits in the bitmap using **SetDIBits**, or sets bitmap bits directly on a device surface with **SetDIBitsToDevice**, the application passes a flag parameter to the function indicating that the color table contains palette indices. The following shows how ShowDIB sets bits in a previously created memory bitmap:

```
SetDIBits(hMemDC, hBitmap, 0,
       pBitmapInfo->bmciHeader.bcHeight,
       pBuf, (LPBITMAPINFO) pBitmapInfo,
       ((pBitmapInfo->bmciHeader.bcBitCount == 24) ?
       DIB_RGB_COLORS :
       DIB_PAL_COLORS));
```

Depending on whether the original DIB used 24-bit pixels, ShowDIB sets the *wUsage* parameter of **SetDIBits** to DIB_RGB_COLORS (for a 24-bit bitmap) or DIB_PAL_COLORS (for all other bitmaps). DIB_RGB_COLORS instructs

Windows to use the color values in the **BITMAPINFO** color table when setting the bits in the device-dependent memory bitmap. If the *wUsage* parameter is set to DIB_PAL_COLORS, however, Windows interprets the color table as 16-bit indexes into a logical palette and sets the bits in the memory bitmap using the indicated color values in the logical palette of the current device context.

If, instead of palette indexes, the **BITMAPINFO** color table contains explicit RGB values, Windows matches those values to the nearest colors in the currently selected logical palette, as though they were palette-relative RGBs.

NOTE If the source and destination device contexts have selected and realized different palettes, the **BitBlt** function does not properly move bitmap bits to or from a memory device context. In this case, you must call the **GetDIBits** with the *wUsage* parameter set to DIB_RGB_COLORS to retrieve the bitmap bits from the source bitmap in a device-independent format. You then use the **SetDIBits** function to set the retrieved bits in the destination bitmap. This ensures that Windows will properly match colors between the two device contexts.

BitBlt can successfully move bitmap bits between two screen display contexts, even if they have selected and realized different palettes. The **StretchBlt** function properly moves bitmap bits between device contexts whether or not they use different palettes.

19.5 Changing a Logical Palette

You can change one or more entries in a logical palette by calling the **SetPaletteEntries** function. This function accepts the following parameters:

- The handle of the palette to be changed, an integer specifying the first palette entry to be changed
- An integer specifying the number of entries to be changed
- An array of **PALETTEENTRY** data structures, each of which contains the red, green, and blue intensities and flags for each entry

Windows does not map changes made to the palette until the application calls **RealizePalette** for any device context in which the palette is selected. Because this changes the system palette, colors displayed in the client area will likewise change. Section 19.6, "Responding to Changes in the System Palette," explains how to respond when Windows changes the system palette.

A second method of updating a logical palette is by animating it. In most cases, an application animates its logical palette when it wants to change the palette rapidly and to make those changes immediately apparent.

To animate a palette, the application must first set the flags in the affected palette entries to PC_RESERVED. This flag has two functions:

- It enables animation for the palette entry.
- It prevents Windows from matching colors displayed in other device contexts to the corresponding color in the system palette.

The following example illustrates how ShowDIB sets the PC_RESERVED flag in all the entries in an existing logical palette:

```
/* create a palette for animation purposes */
for (i = 0; i < pLogPal->palNumEntries; i++) {
        pLogPal->palPalEntry[i].peFlags =
                (BYTE)(PC_RESERVED);
}

SetPaletteEntries(hPal, 0, pLogPal->palNumEntries,
       (LPSTR) &(pLogPal->palPalEntry[0]));
```

The **AnimatePalette** function accepts the same parameters as **SetPaletteEntries**. However, unlike **SetPaletteEntries**, **AnimatePalette** changes only those palette entries with the PC_RESERVED flag set.

When an application calls **AnimatePalette**, Windows immediately maps the changed entries to the system palette, but it does not rematch the colors displayed in the device contexts using the palette for which the application called **AnimatePalette**. In other words, if a pixel was displaying the color in the fifth entry in the system palette before the application called **AnimatePalette**, it will continue to display the color in that entry after **AnimatePalette** is called, even if the fifth entry now contains a different color.

To demonstrate palette animation, ShowDIB sets a system timer and then calls **AnimatePalette** to shift each entry in the palette each time its window receives a WM_TIMER message:

```
case WM_TIMER:
   /* Signal for palette animation */
   hDC = GetDC(hWnd);
   hOldPal = SelectPalette(hDC, hpalCurrent, 0);
   {
       PALETTEENTRY peTemp;

       /* Shift all palette entries left by one position and wrap
        * around the first entry
        */
       peTemp = pLogPal->palPalEntry[0];
       for (i = 0; i < (pLogPal->palNumEntries - 1); i++)
          pLogPal->palPalEntry[i] = pLogPal->palPalEntry[i+1];
       pLogPal->palPalEntry[i] = peTemp;
   }
```

```
/* Replace entries in logical palette with new entries*/
AnimatePalette(hpalCurrent, 0, pLogPal->palNumEntries, pLogPal->palPalEntry);

SelectPalette(hDC, hOldPal, 0);
ReleaseDC(hWnd, hDC);

/* Decrement animation count and terminate animation
 * if it reaches zero
 */
if (!(--nAnimating))
    PostMessage(hWnd,WM_COMMAND,IDM_ANIMATE0,0L);
break;
```

Animating an entire logical palette will degrade colors displayed by other applications' windows if the active window is using the animated palette, particularly if the animated palette is large enough to "take over" the system palette. For this reason, your application should animate no more entries than it requires.

19.6 Responding to Changes in the System Palette

Whenever an application realizes a logical palette for a particular device context, Windows maps colors in that logical palette into the system palette if the system palette does not already contain those colors and if there are available entries in the system palette. Because the system palette has changed, many or all of the colors displayed in the client areas of all windows using palettes likewise change. To allow applications to respond appropriately to these changes, Windows sends two messages to overlapped and pop-up windows to deal with the changes. These messages are:

- WM_QUERYNEWPALETTE
- WM_PALETTECHANGED

19.6.1 Responding to WM_QUERYNEWPALETTE

Windows sends the WM_QUERYNEWPALETTE message to the window that is about to become active. When a window receives this message, the application that owns the window should realize its logical palette, invalidate the contents of the window's client area, and then return TRUE to inform Windows that it has changed the system palette.

ShowDIB responds to the WM_QUERYNEWPALETTE message as follows:

```
case WM_QUERYNEWPALETTE:

                /* if palette realization causes a palette
                   change, we need to do a full redraw. */
```

```
if (bLegitDraw) {
        hDC = GetDC(hWnd);
        hOldPal = SelectPalette (hDC, hPal, 0);

        i = RealizePalette(hDC);

        ReleaseDC(hWnd, hDC);

        if (i) {
                InvalidateRect(hWnd,
                                (LPRECT) (NULL), 1);
                UpdateCount = 0;
                return(1);
        } else
                return(0);
} else
        return(0);

break;
```

19.6.2 Responding to WM_PALETTECHANGED

Windows sends the WM_PALETTECHANGED message to all overlapped and pop-up windows when the active window changes the system palette by realizing its logical palette. The *wParam* parameter of this message contains the handle of the window that realized its palette. If your window responds to this message by realizing its own palette, you should first determine that this handle is not the handle of your window to avoid creating a loop.

When an inactive window receives the WM_PALETTECHANGED message, it has three options:

- It can do nothing. In this case, the colors displayed in the window's client area will potentially be incorrect until the window updates its client area. You should consider this option only if color quality is unimportant to your application when its windows are inactive or if your application does not use a palette.
- It can realize its logical palette and redraw its client area. This option ensures that the colors displayed in the window's client area will be as correct as possible because Windows updates the colors in the client area using the window's logical palette. This accuracy is at the cost of the time required to redraw the client area, however. If the quality of the colors displayed by your inactive window is crucial to your application, or if the image contained in your window's client area can be redrawn quickly, then you should choose this option.

- It can realize its logical palette and directly update the colors in its client area. This option provides a reasonable compromise between performance and color quality. A window directly updates the colors in its client area by realizing its palette and then calling **UpdateColors**. When an application calls **UpdateColors**, Windows quickly updates the client area by matching the current colors in the client area to the system palette on a pixel-by-pixel basis. Since the match is made based on the color of the pixel before the system palette changed rather than on the contents of the window's logical palette, the accuracy of the match decreases each time the window calls **UpdateColors**. Consequently, if color accuracy is of any importance to your application when your windows are inactive, your application should limit the number of times it calls **UpdateColors** for a window before repainting the window's client area.

The following demonstrates how ShowDIB updates its client area in response to the WM_PALETTECHANGED message:

```
case WM_PALETTECHANGED:
if (wParam != hWnd) {
        if (bLegitDraw) {
                hDC = GetDC(hWnd);
                hOldPal = SelectPalette (hDC, hPal, 0);

                i = RealizePalette(hDC);

                if (i && bUpdateColors) {
                        UpdateColors(hDC);
                        UpdateCount++;
                } else if (i)
                        InvalidateRect(hWnd,
                                (LPRECT) (NULL), 1);
        ReleaseDC(hWnd, hDC);
        }
}
break;
```

When ShowDIB receives the WM_PALETTECHANGED message, it first determines whether the *wParam* message parameter contains its own window handle. This would indicate that it was the window which had realized its logical palette and so no response is needed. Then, after selecting and realizing its logical palette, it determines whether a flag was set indicating that the user had selected Update Colors from the Options menu. If this is true, it calls **UpdateColors** to update its client area and sets a flag to indicate that it has directly updated its colors. Otherwise, it invalidates its client area to force redrawing of the client area.

19.7 Summary

By using a color palette, your application can display as many colors as possible on a given display device. Instead of specifying explicit color values when performing graphics operations, your application creates a palette of colors from which it selects when drawing on the display. It can select the color directly by specifying an index into the palette or indirectly by specifying a palette-relative color which Windows matches to your color palette. When your window has input focus, Windows guarantees that the colors specified in its palette will be displayed (up to the maximum available) and will match remaining colors as closely as possible to available colors. Even when your window is in the background, Windows continues to display the window's colors as correctly as possible by matching its colors to the colors currently available on the display.

For more information on topics related to Windows color palettes, see the following:

Topic	Reference
Displaying color bitmaps	*Guide to Programming*: Chapter 11, "Bitmaps"
Color-palette and GDI functions	*Reference, Volume 1*: Chapter 2, "Graphics Device Interface Functions" and Chapter 4, "Functions Directory"
Data types and structures used by logical palettes	*Reference, Volume 2*: Chapter 7, "Data Types and Structures"

Chapter 20 Dynamic-Link Libraries

Microsoft Windows provides special libraries, called "dynamic-link libraries," (DLLs) that let applications share code and resources. Windows uses DLLs to provide code and resources that all Windows applications can use. In addition, you can create your own DLLs to share code and resources among your applications.

This chapter covers the following topics:

- What is a DLL?
- When to use a DLL
- Building a DLL

This chapter also explains how to build a sample library, SELECT.DLL, that illustrates the concepts this chapter covers.

20.1 What is a DLL?

A DLL is an executable module containing functions that Windows applications can call in order to perform useful tasks. DLLs exist primarily to provide services to application modules. DLLs play an important role in the Windows environment; Windows uses them to make Windows functions and resources available to Windows applications.

DLLs are similar to run-time libraries, such as the C run-time libraries. The main difference is that DLLs are linked with the application at run time, not when you link the application files using the linker (**LINK**). Linking a library with an application at run time is called "dynamic linking"; linking a library with an application using the linker is called "static linking."

One way to understand DLLs is to compare them to static-link libraries. An example of a static-link library is MLIBCEW.LIB, the medium-model Windows C run-time library. MLIBCEW.LIB contains the executable code for C run-time routines such as **strcpy** and **strlenr**. You use C run-time routines in your application without having to include the source code for those routines. When you link your C application, the linker incorporates information from the appropriate static-link library. Wherever the application's code uses a C run-time routine, the linker copies that routine to the application's .EXE file.

The primary advantage of static-link libraries is that they make a standard set of routines available to applications, and do not require the applications to include the original source code for those routines.

However, static-link libraries can be inefficient in a multitasking environment like Windows. If two applications are running simultaneously, and they use the same static-library routine, there will be two copies of that routine present in the system. This is an inefficient use of memory. It would be more efficient for both applications to share a single copy of the routine; however, static-link libraries provide no facility for sharing code between applications.

DLLs, on the other hand, allow several applications to share a single copy of a routine. Every standard Windows function, such as **GetMessage**, **Create-Window** and **TextOut**, resides in one of three DLLs: KERNEL.EXE, USER.EXE, and GDI.EXE. If two Windows applications are running at the same time, and both use a particular Windows function, both share a single copy of the source code for that function.

In addition to letting applications share code, DLLs can be used to share other resources, such as data and hardware. For example, Windows fonts are actually text-drawing data that applications can share via DLLs. Likewise, Windows device drivers are actually DLLs that allow applications to share hardware resources.

All Windows libraries are DLLs. For example, the GDI.EXE, USER.EXE, and KERNEL.EXE files that comprise the major part of Windows are DLLs. You can develop your own custom DLLs to share code, data, or hardware among your applications.

20.1.1 Import Libraries and DLLs

Thus far, we have described two types of libraries: static link libraries and DLLs. There is a third type of library that is important when working with DLLs: import libraries. An import library contains information which helps Windows locate code in a DLL.

During linking, the linker uses static-link libraries and import libraries to resolve references to external routines. When an application uses a routine from a static-link library, the linker copies the code for that routine into the application's .EXE file. However, when the application uses a routine from a DLL, the linker does not copy any code. Instead, it copies information from the import library which indicates where to find the desired code in the DLL at run time. During application execution, this relocation information creates a "dynamic link" between the executing application and the DLL.

Table 20.1 summarizes the uses of each of the three types of libraries.

Table 20.1 Uses of the Three Library Types

Library Type	Linked at Link Time	Linked at Run Time	Example Library	Example Routine
Static	Yes	No	MLIB-CEW.LIB	**strcpy**
Import	Yes	No	LIBW.LIB	**TextOut**
Dynamic	No	Yes	GDI.EXE	**TextOut**

As this table indicates, when an application calls the **strcpy** function in the C run-time library, the linker links the application to the library by copying the code of the routine from the MLIBCEW.LIB run-time library into the application's .EXE file. But when the application calls the **TextOut** Windows GDI function, the linker copies location information for **TextOut** from the LIBW.LIB import library into the .EXE file. It does not copy the code of the function itself. Then, at run time, when the application makes the call to **TextOut**, Windows uses the location information in the .EXE file to locate **TextOut** in the dynamic-link library GDI.EXE. It then executes the actual **TextOut** function in GDI.EXE. In other words, import libraries provide the connection between application modules and DLL modules.

20.1.2 DLL and Application Modules

Modules are a fundamental structural unit in Windows. There are two types of modules: application modules and DLL modules. You should already be familiar with application modules; the .EXE file for every Windows application is considered a module. Examples of dynamic-link modules include any Windows system file with an extension of .DLL, .DRV, or .FON. (Some Windows system modules have a filename extension of .EXE instead of .DLL.)

Application and library modules have the same file format. (In fact, OS/2 shares this file format for OS/2 applications and OS/2 DLLs.) This file format, which is sometimes called the "New EXE Header Format," allows dynamic linking to take place. You can use the **EXEHDR** utility to read the header of a module file. **EXEHDR** provides information about the functions that the module imports or exports. **EXEHDR** is included with the Microsoft C Optimizing Compiler; see the C Compiler documentation for information about how to run **EXEHDR**.

A module exports a function in order to make the function available to other modules. Thus, DLLs export functions for use by applications and other DLLs. For example, the Windows dynamic-link library GDI.EXE exports all the graphics device interface (GDI) functions. Unlike DLLs, however, application modules cannot export functions for use by other applications.

A module imports a function contained in another module if it needs to use that function. Importing a function creates a dynamic link to the code for that function.

There are two ways to import a function into a module:

- By linking the module with an import library that contains information for that function
- By listing the individual function in the **IMPORTS** section of the module's .DEF file

While both application and DLL modules can import and export functions, they differ in one important respect: unlike applications modules, DLL modules are not tasks.

20.1.3 DLLs and Tasks

One of the basic differences between an application module and a dynamic-link module is reflected in the notion of the "task." A task is the fundamental unit of scheduling in Windows. An application module is said to be a "tasked executable" module. When an application module is loaded, a call is made to its entry point, the WinMain function, which typically contains the message loop. As the application module creates windows and begins to interact with the user, the message loop connects the application module to the Windows scheduler. As long as the user is interacting with the application's windows, messages are fed to the application module, and the module retains control of the processor.

A DLL is sometimes said to be a "nontasked executable" module. Like the application module, a dynamic-link module may contain an entry point. When it is loaded, the entry point for the library is called, but typically, it performs only minor initialization. Unlike the application module, a DLL does not interact with the Windows scheduler via a message loop; instead, the DLL waits for tasks to request its services.

Application modules are the active components of Windows. They receive system- and user-generated messages, and, when necessary, call library modules for specific data and services. Library modules exist to provide services to application modules.

NOTE Some DLLs are not completely passive. For example, some DLLs are device drivers for interrupt-driven devices like the keyboard, mouse, and communication ports. However, the interaction of such libraries is carefully controlled to avoid disrupting the Windows scheduler. DLLs that require such an active role should be written according to the guidelines described in Section 20.2.4, "Device Drivers."

20.1.4 DLLs and Stacks

Unlike a task module, a DLL module does not have its own stack. Instead, it uses the stack segment of the task that called the DLL. This can create problems when a DLL calls a function that assumes the DS register and the SS register hold the same address. This problem is most likely to occur in small- and medium-model DLLs, since pointers in these models are, by default, near pointers.

Many C run-time library routines, for example, assume that DS and SS are equal. You must take care when you call these functions from within your DLL.

Your DLL can also encounter difficulties when calling user-written functions. Consider, for example, a DLL that contains a function that declares a variable within the body of the function. The address of this function will be relative to the stack of the task which called the DLL. If this function passes that variable to a second function that expects a near pointer, the second function will assume that the address it receives is relative to the DLL's data segment rather than to the stack segment of the task which called the DLL.

The following code fragment shows a function in a DLL passing a variable from the stack, rather than from its data segment:

```
void DLLFunction(WORD wMyWord)
   WORD myWord
   {
                char szMyString[10];
   .
   .
   .
       AnotherFunction(szMyString);
   }
```

If AnotherFunction was declared as accepting a near pointer to a character array (**char NEAR ***), it will interpret the address it receives as being an offset of the data segment, rather than of the stack segment of the task that called the DLL.

To ensure that your DLL does not attempt to pass stack variables to functions that expect near pointers, you should compile your DLL modules using the C Compiler **–Aw** option. This will produce warning messages that indicate when the DLL is making a call to a function that assumes that DS and SS are equal. When you receive a warning for a particular function, you can either remove that function call from your DLL, or rewrite the DLL source module so that it does not pass a stack variable to that function.

20.1.5 How Windows Locates DLLs

Windows locates a DLL by searching the same directories it searches to find an application module. To be found by Windows, the DLL must be in one of the following directories:

1. The current directory
2. The Windows directory (the directory containing WIN.COM); the **GetWindowsDirectory** function obtains the pathname of this directory

3. The Windows system directory (the directory containing such system files as KERNEL.EXE); the **GetSystemDirectory** function obtains the pathname of this directory
4. Any of the directories listed in the PATH environment variable
5. Any directory in the list of directories mapped in a network

Windows searches the directories in the listed order.

Implicitly loaded libraries must be named with the .DLL extension.

This section explained what a DLL does in the context of the Windows environment. The next section explains what a custom DLL can do for your application.

20.2 When to Use a Custom DLL

Although DLLs are central to the architecture of Windows, they are not necessary components of most Windows applications. Your application does not have to use a DLL simply to maximize Windows' management of memory. If you split your application into multiple code segments, Windows provides a type of dynamic linking between code segments that allows for optimal memory usage. See Chapter 16, "More Memory Management," for more information on using multiple code segments.

However, among other purposes, DLLs are useful for:

- Sharing code and resources among applications.
- Easily customizing your application for different markets.
- Filtering messages on a system-wide basis.
- Creating device drivers.
- Allowing the Dialog Editor (**DIALOG**) to support your custom-designed controls.
- Facilitating the development of a complex application.

In this section, we discuss some criteria for deciding when to develop a custom DLL.

20.2.1 Sharing Between Applications

DLLs can be used to share objects between applications. Certain types of objects, including code and resources, can be freely shared using a DLL. The sharing of other types of objects, including data and file handles, is much more limited. This is because file handles and data are created in an application's private address space. Attempts to share file handles, or to share data (outside of DDE, the clipboard, and the library's data segment) will lead to unpredictable results, and could be incompatible with future versions of Windows.

This section describes how to use a DLL so applications can share code and resources.

Sharing Code

If you are developing a family of applications, you may want to consider using one or more DLLs. A DLL saves memory when two or more applications that use a common set of DLL routines are running at the same time. DLLs allow multiple applications to share common routines that would be duplicated for each application if static-link libraries were used.

Suppose, for example, that you are creating two graphics applications, one a vector (draw) program and the other a bitmap (paint) application. A common requirement of both programs is the ability to import drawings created by other applications. You could create DLLs for each supported "foreign" file format that would convert it into an intermediate format. Your paint and draw applications could then convert this intermediate data into their own formats. The applications themselves would be required to contain only the code to convert from a single format to their own format. To support the importing of a new file type, you would simply develop a new DLL and distribute it to the user, instead of modifying, recompiling, and distributing the application modules themselves.

Sharing Resources

Resources are read-only data objects that are bound into an executable file by the Resource Compiler. Resources can be bound into an application's .EXE file, as well as into a library's .DLL file. Windows has built-in support for eight resource types:

- Accelerator tables
- Bitmaps
- Cursors
- Dialog box templates
- Fonts
- Icons
- Menu templates
- String tables

In addition to using the standard Windows resources, you can create custom resources and install them into an executable file. See Chapter 16, "More Memory Management," for more information on resources.

A DLL's resources can be shared between applications; this saves memory when multiple applications are running.

Resources that reside in a DLL can be freely used by any application. However, it is important for each application to explicitly request each resource object it needs. For example, if an application uses a menu resource called MainMenu in a library named MENULIB.DLL, it would have to contain code like the following:

```
HANDLE hLibrary;
HMENU  hMenu;

hLibrary = LoadLibrary ("MENULIB.DLL");

hMenu = LoadMenu (hLibrary, "MainMenu");
```

20.2.2 Customizing an Application for Different Markets

You can use DLLs for customizing your application for different markets. For each market, you would create a DLL for which would contain code, data, and resources which would make your application more appropriate for that market. You don't have to design and compile a completely separate application module for each market. Instead, you can create a general-purpose application which would draw upon the market-specific information contained in the DLL.

DLLs are often used to customize applications for international markets. DLLs can supply language- and culture-specific data for applications that are to be marketed in different countries. For example, an application could be shipped with its application module, APPFILE.EXE, and with three language-specific DLLs: ENGLISH.DLL, FRENCH.DLL, and GERMAN.DLL.

When the product is installed, the correct language library could be selected and used for all dialog box templates, menus, string information, and other language-specific information.

You use an instance handle of the library to identify the library when you use the resources of the library. You obtain the library instance handle by calling the **LoadLibrary** function:

```
HANDLE hLibrary;

hLibrary = LoadLibrary ("FRENCH.DLL");
```

The hLibrary value could be used anywhere that an hInstance value is requested for normal resource loading. For example, if the FRENCH.DLL library contains a menu template named "MAINMENU", the application loads the library and then accesses the menu with the following call:

```
HANDLE hMenu;

hMenu = LoadMenu (hLibrary, "MAINMENU");
```

20.2.3 Windows Hooks

Windows lets applications use "hooks" to filter messages on a system-wide basis. A Windows hook is a function that receives and processes events before they are sent to an application's message loop. For example, a function that provides special-purpose processing of key strokes before passing them to an application is a Windows hook function.

There are seven types of Windows hooks, which are explained more fully in the *Reference, Volume 1*.

System-wide Windows hooks must be implemented using DLLs, and must reside in fixed code segments. This is because, as a system-wide resource, the code associated with a hook must be available at all times. Certain EMS memory configurations place all code except fixed library code segments in application-specific EMS memory. This location is sometimes referred to as "above the EMS line." When a code segment is above the EMS line, its availability is limited to the application that owns the EMS memory. Furthermore, this code is not called within the context of the application that sets the hook. In protected mode, Windows treats fixed library code as a special case so that this code can still be called. The only Windows hook that does not have to reside in a DLL is the WH_MSGFILTER hook, which is application specific. In addition, Windows in protected (standard or 386 enhanced) mode assumes that system hooks are located in fixed DLL code segments.

20.2.4 Device Drivers

The standard Windows device drivers are implemented as DLLs. The following lists the default name for many of the standard Windows device drivers:

Device Driver	Purpose
COMM.DRV	Serial communication
DISPLAY.DRV	Video display
KEYBOARD.DRV	Keyboard input
MOUSE.DRV	Mouse input
SOUND.DRV	Sound output
SYSTEM.DRV	Timer

The SYSTEM.INI file identifies the drivers that are to be installed when Windows boots.

Device drivers for nonstandard devices also must be implemented using custom DLLs. Different applications can then access the device; the device driver provides the necessary synchronization to prevent conflict between the applications.

Because interrupts can occur at any time, not just during the execution of the application that is using the device, device interrupt-handling code must reside in a fixed code segment. In the large-frame EMS memory configuration, the only type of code that is guaranteed to be available at all times to service such an interrupt is the code in a DLL's fixed code segment. The protected mode memory configuration requires that interrupt code be in such a DLL code segment. For more information about memory configurations, see Chapter 16, "More Memory Management."

Interrupt-handling code in a device driver should not call client applications directly. In addition, such device drivers must not call application code using the **SendMessage** routine, because there is no mechanism to synchronize such calls with an application's normal message processing. Such calls can lead to race conditions, data corruption, and indeterminate results.

Instead, interrupt-handling code must wait to be polled by the client applications, in much the same way that the communication driver must be polled by its client applications. Alternatively, a device driver can use the **PostMessage** routine to place a message on the application's message queue.

20.2.5 Custom Controls

If you have developed custom controls, you can place the code for the controls in a DLL. As detailed in *Tools*, the Dialog Editor (**DIALOG**) can then access the DLL to display your custom control during a dialog-box editing session.

For your control library to be used by the Dialog Editor and other applications, you will need to define and export the functions described in this section. The Rainbow example on the Sample Source Disk illustrates how to write a custom control DLL.

In the following function descriptions, *Class* is used as a placeholder for the class name of your control. The name of your custom control is the same name the Dialog Editor user employs to identify the control. The name of the control is typically the same as the module name of the DLL, but not necessarily.

Structure definitions, such as for **CTLINFO**, and constants that define the interface of a custom control with the Dialog Editor, are provided in CUSTCNTL.H.

This section describes six functions that your custom-control DLL must export. The DLL should export these functions by ordinal value, as shown in the following list:

Exported Function	**Ordinal Value**
WEP	Any number except 2–6
*Class*Init or LibMain	Not required
*Class*Info	2
*Class*Style	3
*Class*Flags	4
*Class*WndFn	5
*Class*DlgFn	6

For example, the functions exported by the example Rainbow custom control are declared in the RAINBOW.DEF file as shown in the following example:

```
EXPORTS
   WEP             @1 RESIDENTNAME
   RAINBOWINFO     @2
   RAINBOWSTYLE    @3
   RAINBOWFLAGS    @4
   RAINBOWWNDFN    @5
   RAINBOWDLGFN    @6
```

For more information on the LibMain function, see "Initiating a DLL" in Section 20.3.1. For more information on the WEP function, see "Terminating a DLL." in Section 20.3.1.

The *Class*Init Function

Syntax

HANDLE FAR PASCAL *Class***Init**(*hInstance*, *wDataSegment*, *wHeapSize*, *lpszCmdLine*)

The *Class***Init** function is responsible for all the initialization necessary to use the dynamic-link control library. Your assembly-language entry point to the library normally calls this function. In addition to saving the library instance handle with a global static variable, this function should register the control window class and initialize the local heap by calling the **LocalInit** function if your assembly-language entry routine does not initialize the local heap.

If you link the custom-control DLL with LIBENTRY.OBJ instead of providing your own assembly-language entry point, this function is named LibMain. See "Initializing a DLL" in Section 20.3.1 for more information about DLL entry points and initialization.

Parameter	Type/Description
hInstance	**HANDLE** Identifies the instance of the library.
wDataSegment	**WORD** Specifies the library data segment.
wHeapSize	**WORD** Specifies the default library heap size.
lpszCmdLine	**LPSTR** Specifies the initial command line arguments.

Return Value

The return value is a library-instance handle if the control class has been registered and if initialization has succeeded. The return value is NULL if the initialization process failed.

The *Class*Info Function

Syntax

HANDLE FAR PASCAL *Class***Info( )**

The *Class***Info** function provides the calling process with basic information about the control library. Based on the information returned, the application can create instances of the control using one of the supported styles. For example, the Dialog Editor calls this function to query a library about the different control styles it can display.

This function has no parameters.

The return value identifies a **CTLINFO** data structure. This information becomes the property of the caller. The caller must explicitly release it using the **GlobalFree** function when the data structure is no longer needed. If memory was insufficient to allocate and define this structure, the return value is a NULL handle.

The **CTLINFO** structure defines the class name and version number. The **CTLINFO** data structure also contains an array of **CTLTYPE** data structures that lists commonly used combinations of control styles (called "variants") with a short description and suggested size information.

The following shows the definition of these structures and related values:

```
/* general style & size definitions */
#define      CTLTYPES   12
#define      CTLDESCR   22
#define      CTLCLASS   20
#define      CTLTITLE   94

/* control information structure */
typedef struct {
      WORD        wType;
      WORD        wWidth;
      WORD        wHeight;
      DWORD       dwStyle;
      char        szDescr[CTLDESCR];
} CTLTYPE;

typedef struct {
      WORD        wVersion;
      WORD        wCtlTypes;
      char        szClass[CTLCLASS];
      char        szTitle[CTLTITLE];
      char        szReserved[10];
      CTLTYPE     Type[CTLTYPES];
} CTLINFO;

typedef CTLINFO *   PCTLINFO;
typedef CTLINFO FAR *LPCTLINFO;
```

The **CTLTYPE** structure has the following fields:

Field	Description
wType	Is reserved for future implementation. This field should be set to zero.
wWidth	Specifies the suggested width of the control when created with the Dialog Editor. If the most significant bit of this field is zero, then the lower byte is the default width in Resource Compiler coordinates. If the most significant bit is 1, then the remaining bits specify the default width in pixels.
wHeight	Specifies the suggested height of the control when created using the Dialog Editor. If the most significant bit of this field is zero, then the lower byte is the default height in Resource Compiler coordinates. If the most significant bit is 1, then the remaining bits specify the default height in pixels.

Field	Description
dwStyle	Specifies the initial style bits used to obtain this control type. This value includes both the control-defined flags in the high-order word and the Windows-defined flags in the low-order word.
szDescr	Defines the name to be used by other development tools when referring to this particular variant of the base control class. The Dialog Editor does not refer to this information.

The **CTLINFO** structure has the following fields:

Field	Description
wVersion	Specifies the control version number. Although you can start your numbering scheme from one, most implementations use the lower two digits to represent minor releases.
wCtlTypes	Specifies the number of control types supported by this class. This value should always be greater than zero and less than or equal to **CTLTYPES**.
szClass	Specifies a null-terminated string that contains the control class name supported by the DLL.
szTitle	Specifies a null-terminated string that contains various copyright or author information relating to the control library.
Type[ ]	Specifies an array of **CTLTYPE** data structures which contain information relating to each of the control types supported by the class.

The *Class*Style Function

Syntax

BOOL FAR PASCAL *Class***Style**(*hWnd*, *hCtlStyle*, *lpfnStrTold*, *lpfnIdToStr*)

The Dialog Editor calls the *Class***Style** function to display a dialog box to edit the style of the selected control. When this function is called, it should display a modal dialog box that enables the user to edit the **CTLSTYLE** parameters. The user interface of this dialog box should be consistent with that of the predefined controls supported by the Dialog Editor.

Parameter	Type/Description
hWnd	**HWND** Identifies the parent window of the dialog box.
hCtlStyle	**HANDLE** Identifies the **CTLSTYLE** data structure.
lpfnStrToId	**LPFNSTRTOID** Points to a function supplied by the Dialog Editor that converts a string to a numerical ID value. See the following "Comments" section for more information.
lpfnIdToStr	**LPFNIDTOSTR** Points to a function supplied by the Dialog Editor that converts a numerical ID value to a string. See the following "Comments" section for more information.

Return Value

The return value is TRUE if the **CTLSTYLE** data structure was changed. If the user canceled the operation or an error occurred, the return value is FALSE.

Comments

The **CTLSTYLE** structure specifies the attributes of the selected control, including the current style flags, location, dimensions, and associated text. The following shows the definition of the **CTLSTYLE** data structure:

```
/* control style structure */
typedef struct {
      WORD      wX;
      WORD      wY;
      WORD      wCx;
      WORD      wCy,
      WORD      wId;
      DWORD     dwStyle;
      char      szClass[CTLCLASS];
      char      szTitle[CTLTITLE];
} CTLSTYLE;

typedef CTLSTYLE *   PCTLSTYLE;
typedef CTLSTYLE FAR *   LPCTLSTYLE;
```

The **CTLSTYLE** structure has the following fields:

Field	Description
wX	Specifies in screen coordinates the *x*-origin of the control relative to the client region of the parent window.

Field	Description
wY	Specifies in screen coordinates the *y*-origin of the control relative to the client region of the parent window.
wCx	Specifies the current width of the control in screen coordinates.
wCy	Specifies the current height of the control in screen coordinates.
wId	Specifies the current ID number of the control. In most cases you should not allow the user to change this value as it is automatically coordinated by the Dialog Editor with an include file.
dwStyle	Specifies the current style of the control. The high-order word contains the control-specific flags, while the low-order word contains the Windows-specific flags. You may let the user change these flags to any values supported by your control library.
szClass	Specifies a null-terminated string representing the name of the current control class. You should not allow the user to edit this field, as it is provided for informational purposes only.
szTitle	Specifies with a null-terminated string the text associated with the control. This text is usually displayed inside the control or may be used to store other associated information required by the control.

The Dialog Editor keeps track of user-specified control ID names and their corresponding symbolic-constant names, maintaining them in a header file which is included when the application is compiled. The control style function accesses this information by using the *lpfnStrToId* and *lpfnIdToStr* functions.

The *lpfnStrToId* and *lpfnIdToStr* parameters point to two function entry points within the Dialog Editor itself. To call these functions, you should prototype them as shown:

```
/* ID to string translation function prototypes */
typedef WORD   (FAR PASCAL *LPFNIDTOSTR)(WORD, LPSTR, WORD);
typedef DWORD  (FAR PASCAL *LPFNSTRTOID)(LPSTR);
```

The *lpfnIdToStr* entry point into the Dialog Editor allows you to translate the numeric ID provided in the **CTLSTYLE** data structure into a text string containing the symbolic-constant name defined in the include file. This text string can then be displayed in place of a numeric value in your custom control's style dialog box. The first parameter is the control ID. The second parameter is a long pointer to a buffer that receives the string, and the third parameter is the maximum length of that buffer. The *lpfnIdToStr* function returns the number of characters copied to the string. If the function returns zero, the function call failed.

The *lpfnStrToId* function works in reverse, translating a string to a numeric ID value. The function accepts the string containing a symbolic-constant name and returns the corresponding control ID value. If the low-order word of the return value is nonzero, the high-order word contains the control ID value which you can use to update the **wID** field of the **CTLSTYLE** data structure. If the low-order word of the return value is zero, the constant name was undefined and *Class***Style** should generate an error message.

Typically, whenever *Class***Style** is called, it will call *lpfnIdToStr*, passing it the value contained in the **CTLSTYLE.wID** field. If *lpfnIdToStr* returns a value greater than zero, then *Class***Style** displays the resulting string in an edit field so the user can change it. Otherwise, it displays the numerical value of the control ID. If the user changes the edit field, *Class***Style** calls *lpfnStrToId* to verify that the string does, in fact, contain a valid symbolic-constant name and replaces the **CTLSTYLE.wID** field with the high-order word of the return value.

The *Class*DlgFn Function

Syntax

BOOL FAR PASCAL *Class***DlgFn**(*hDlg*, *wMessage*, *wParam*, *lParam*)

The *Class***DlgFn** function is the dialog procedure responsible for processing all the messages sent to the style dialog box. The style dialog box is invoked when the *Class***Style** function is called. The *Class***DlgFn** function should enable the user to edit selected portions of the **CTLSTYLE** data structure passed to the *Class***Style** function.

Parameter	Type/Description	
hDlg	**HWND**	Identifies the window receiving the message.
wMessage	**WORD**	Specifies the message.
wParam	**WORD**	Specifies the 16-bit message parameter.
lParam	**LONG**	Specifies the 32-bit message parameter.

Return Value

The return value is TRUE if the dialog procedure processed the message. Otherwise, it is FALSE.

The Class**Flags** *Function*

Syntax

WORD FAR PASCAL *Class***Flags**(*dwFlags*, *lpStyle*, *wMaxString*)

The *Class***Flags** function translates the class style flags provided into a corresponding text string for output to a resource script (.RC) file. This function should not interpret the flags contained in the high-order word since these are managed by Dialog Editor. Note that you should use the same control style definitions specified in your control include file.

Parameter	Type/Description
dwFlags	**DWORD** Specifies the current control flags.
lpStyle	**LPSTR** Points to a buffer to receive the style string.
wMaxString	**WORD** Specifies the maximum length of the style ring.

Return Value

The return value is the number of characters copied to the buffer identified by the *lpStyle* parameter. If an error occurred, the return value is zero.

The Class**WndFn** *Function*

Syntax

LONG FAR PASCAL *Class***WndFn**(*hWnd*, *wMessage*, *wParam*, *lParam*)

The *Class***WndFn** function is the window procedure responsible for processing all the messages sent to the control.

Parameter	Type/Description
hWnd	**HWND** Identifies the window receiving the message.
wMessage	**WORD** Specifies the message.
wParam	**WORD** Specifies the 16-bit message parameter.
lParam	**LONG** Specifies the 32-bit message parameter.

Return Value

The return value indicates the result of message processing and depends on the actual message sent.

20.2.6 Project Management

If you are developing a large or complex application, you can use DLLs to facilitate application development. Splitting an application into clearly defined subsystems can provide a logical way to divide work between different groups of developers. Each subsystem can then be developed as a separate DLL.

One of the challenges in such a project is defining the interface between each subsystem. Since DLL code can freely call routines in other DLLs, Windows imposes no constraints on subsystem definitions. In addition, Windows manages the movement and discarding of code segments to minimize the problems that memory limitations often cause for DOS development projects. To take advantage of this feature, code segments should be defined as **MOVEABLE**, or **MOVEABLE** and **DISCARDABLE**, in the module-definition (.DEF) file.

One benefit in using multiple DLLs is that, because each DLL has its own data segment, data contamination between subsystems is minimized. This type of encapsulation is useful in developing large applications.

There is another type of encapsulation, however, that might cause problems in large projects that require multiple applications to run simultaneously. Due to the fact that each application is treated as if it has its own private address space, applications can move global data to other applications only by using Dynamic Data Exchange (DDE). See Chapter 22, “Dynamic Data Exchange,” for more information on using DDE.

20.3 Creating a DLL

This section provides sample code that can be used as a basis for creating a DLL.

To create a DLL, you must have at least three files:

- A C-language source file
- A module-definition (.DEF) file
- A make file

Once you have created these files, you run the **MAKE** utility to compile and link the source file. The remainder of this section explains how to create these files.

20.3.1 Creating the C-Language Source File

This section provides C source code as a template for creating a DLL. Like any other type of C program, DLLs can contain multiple functions. Each function that other applications or DLLs will use must be declared as **FAR**, and must be listed in the **EXPORTS** section of the library's module-definition (.DEF) file. The module-definition file for this sample library is discussed further in Section 20.3.2, "Creating the Module-Definition File."

```
/*  MINDLL.C -- Sample DLL code to demonstrate minimum code needed
to create a dynamic-link library. */

#include WINDOWS.H

int FAR PASCAL LibMain (HANDLE hInstance,
                         WORD   wDataSeg,
                         WORD   cbHeapSize,
                         LPSTR  lpszCmdLine)
{

   .
   .
   /*  Perform DLL initialization. */
   .
   .


if (cbHeapSize != Ø)     /*  If DLL data seg is MOVEABLE */
    UnlockData(Ø);

return (1);             /* Initialization successful. */
}

VOID FAR PASCAL MinRoutine (int iParam1,
                            LPSTR lpszParam2)
{
char  cLocalVariable;  /* Local variables on stack. */

   .
   .
   /*  MinRoutine Code goes here. */
   .
   .
}

VOID FAR PASCAL WEP (int nParameter)
{
if (nParameter == WEP_SYSTEMEXIT)
    {
     /*  System shutdown in progress. Respond accordingly.*/
        return (1);
    }
```

```
else
    {if (nParameter == WEP_FREE_DLL)
      {
          /*  DLL use count is zero. Every application that had
loaded the DLL has freed it. */
          return (1);
      }
     else      {
         /*  Undefined value. Ignore. */
          return (1);
       }
    }

}
```

DLL source code uses WINDOWS.H in the same way as does application source code. WINDOWS.H contains data-type definitions, API entry-point definitions, and other useful parameter information.

The **PASCAL** declaration defines the parameter-passing and stack-cleanup convention for this routine. This is not required for DLL routines, but its use results in slightly smaller and faster code, and therefore its use is strongly recommended. The Pascal calling convention cannot be used for routines with a variable number of parameters, or for calling C run-time routines. In such cases, the CDECL calling convention is required.

There are two parameters shown on the MinRoutine parameter list, but DLL routines can have as few or as many parameters as are required. The only requirement is that pointers passed from outside the DLL module must be long pointers.

Initializing a DLL

You must include an automatic initialization function in a DLL. The initialization function performs one-time start-up processing. Windows calls the initialization function once, when the library is initially loaded. When subsequent applications that use the library load the library, Windows does not call the initialization function. Instead, Windows simply increments the DLL's use count.

Windows maintains a library in memory as long as its use count is greater than zero. If a library's use count becomes zero, it is removed from memory. When an application causes the library to be reloaded into memory, the initialization function will again be called.

Following are some typical tasks a DLL's initialization function might perform:

- Registering window classes for window procedures contained in the DLL
- Initializing the DLL's local heap
- Setting initial values for the DLL's global variables

The library initialization procedure is required in order to allocate the local heap of your DLL. The local heap must be created before the DLL calls any local heap functions, such as **LocalAlloc**. While Windows automatically initializes the local heap for Windows applications, DLLs must explicitly initialize the local heap by calling the **LocalInit** function.

In addition, you should include the following declaration in the initialization procedure:

```
extrn __acrtused:abs
```

This ensures that the DLL will be linked with the DLL start-up code in the Windows DLL C run-time libraries (xDLLCyW.LIB) if the DLL does not call any C run-time routines.

Initialization information is passed in hardware registers to a library when it is loaded. Since hardware registers are not accessible from the C language, you must provide an assembly language routine to obtain these values. The location and value of the heap information are as follows:

Register	Value
DI	The DLL's instance handle
DS	The DLL's data segment, if any
CX	The heap size specified in the DLL's .DEF file
ES:SI	The command line (in the *lpCmdLine* field of the **LoadModule** function's *lpParameterBlock* parameter)

The SDK disks contain an assembly language file, LIBENTRY.ASM, that can be used to create a DLL initialization function. (You can find this file in the SELECT directory of the Sample Source Code disk.) The **LibEntry** function in this file is defined as follows:

```
;;;;;;;;;;;;;;;;;;;;;;;;;;;;;;;;;;;;;;;;;;;;;;;;;;;;;;;;;;;;;;;;;;;;;;;;;;;;;;;;;
;
;       LIBENTRY.ASM
;
;       Windows dynamic link library entry routine
;
;   This module generates a code segment called INIT_TEXT.
;   It initialises the local heap if one exists and then calls
;   the C routine LibMain() which should have the form:
;   BOOL FAR PASCAL LibMain(HANDLE hInstance,
;                           WORD   wDataSeg,
;                           WORD   cbHeapSize,
;                           LPSTR  lpszCmdLine);
;
;   The result of the call to LibMain is returned to Windows.
```

```
;   The C routine should return TRUE if it completes initialisation
;   successfully, FALSE if some error occurs.
;
;;;;;;;;;;;;;;;;;;;;;;;;;;;;;;;;;;;;;;;;;;;;;;;;;;;;;;;;;;;;;;;;;;;;;;;;;;;;;

   extrn LibMain:far          ; the C routine to be called
   extrn LocalInit:far        ; Windows heap init routine
        extrn __acrtused:abs       ; ensures that Win DLL startup code is linked

        public LibEntry       ; entry point for the DLL

INIT_TEXT segment byte public 'CODE'
        assume cs:INIT_TEXT

LibEntry proc far

   push   di         ; handle of the library instance
        push   ds         ; library data segment   push   cx        ; heap size
   push   es         ; command line segment
   push   si         ; command line offset

   ; if we have some heap then initialize it
   jcxz   callc        ; jump if no heap specified

   ; call the Windows function LocalInit() to set up the heap
   ; LocalInit((LPSTR)start, WORD cbHeap);

   push   ds         ; Heap segment
        xor     ax,ax
   push   ax         ; Heap start offset in segment
   push   cx         ; Heap end offset in segment
   call   LocalInit    ; try to initialise it
   or   ax,ax        ; did it do it ok ?
   jz   exit         ; quit if it failed

   ; invoke the C routine to do any special initialisation

callc:
   call   LibMain       ; invoke the 'C' routine (result in AX)

exit:
   ret          ; return the result

LibEntry endp

INIT_TEXT       ends

        end LibEntry
```

The SDK disks also contain an assembled copy of this function in the file LIBENTRY.OBJ. (You can find this file in the SELECT directory of the Sample Source Code disk.) The LibEntry function allows a C language initialization function to be created. To use the LibEntry function unchanged, just add its filename, LIBENTRY.OBJ, to your **LINK** command line as follows:

```
LINK MINDLL.OBJ LIBENTRY.OBJ, MINDLL.DLL,MINDLL.MAP/map,
        MDLLCEW.LIB LIBW.LIB/NOE/NOD,MINDLL.DEF
```

LibEntry calls a **FAR PASCAL** function named LibMain. Your DLL must contain the LibMain function if you link the DLL with the file LIBENTRY.OBJ.

The following is a sample LibMain function:

```
int FAR PASCAL LibMain (HANDLE hInstance,
                        WORD   wDataSeg,
                        WORD   cbHeapSize,
                        LPSTR  lpszCmdLine)
{

   .
   .
   /*  Perform DLL initialization. */
   .
   .


if (cbHeapSize != Ø)    /*  If DLL data seg is MOVEABLE
*/
    UnlockData(Ø);

return (1);    /*  Successful installation. Otherwise,
return(Ø); */
}
```

LibMain takes four parameters: *hInstance*, *wDataSeg*, *cbHeapSize*, and *lpszCmdLine*. The first parameter, *hInstance*, is the instance handle of the DLL. The *wDataSeg* parameter is the value of the data-segment (DS) register. The *cbHeapSize* parameter is the size of the heap defined in the module-definition file. LibEntry uses this value to initialize the local heap. The *lpszCmdLine* parameter contains command line information and is rarely used by DLLs.

If you do not want the DLL data segment to be locked, the call to **UnlockData** is necessary because the **LocalInit** function leaves the data segment locked. **UnlockData** restores the data segment to its normal unlocked state.

If the DLL initialization has been successful, the DLL should return a value of 1. A value of zero indicates that initialization was not successful, and the DLL is unloaded from system memory.

NOTE If you are writing the DLL entirely in assembly language, you must reserve the first 16 bytes of the DLL data segment and initialize the area with zeros. However, if the DLL module contains any C-language code, the C Compiler automatically reserves and initializes this area.

Terminating a DLL

Windows DLLs must include a termination function. A termination function, sometimes called an exit procedure, performs cleanup for a DLL before it is unloaded.

DLLs that contain window procedures that have been registered (using **Register-Class**) are not required to remove the class registration (using **UnRegisterClass**); Windows does this automatically when the DLL terminates.

A sample termination function is shown next. The termination function should be defined as shown here. A single argument is passed, *nParameter*, which indicates whether all of Windows is shutting down (nParameter==WEP_SYSTEMEXIT), or just the single DLL (WEP_FREE_DLL). It always returns 1 to indicate success.

```
VOID FAR PASCAL WEP (int nParameter)
{
if (nParameter == WEP_SYSTEMEXIT)
    {
     /*  System shutdown in progress. Respond accordingly.*/
             return (1);
    }
else
    {if (nParameter == WEP_FREE_DLL)
                {
                /*  DLL use count is zero. Every application that had
                loaded the DLL has freed it. */
               return (1);
                }
          else          {
                        /*  Undefined value. Ignore. */
               return (1);
        }
         }

}
```

The name of the termination function must be WEP, and it must be included in the **EXPORTS** section of the DLL's module-definition file. It is strongly recommended, for performance reasons, that the ordinal entry value and the **RESIDENTNAME** key word be used, to minimize the time used to find this function. Since the use of the **RESIDENTNAME** key word causes the export information for this routine to stay in memory at all times, it is not recommended for use with other exported functions.

See the following section for more information.

20.3.2 Creating the Module-Definition File

This section contains the module-definition file for the minimum DLL. This file provides input to the linker (**LINK**) to define various attributes of the DLL. Note that there is no **STACKSIZE** statement, since DLLs make use of the calling application's stack. For a more complete discussion of module-definition files, see the *Reference, Volume 2.*

```
LIBRARY MinDLL

DESCRIPTION 'MinDLL — Minimum Code Required for DLL.'

EXETYPE WINDOWS

STUB   'WINSTUB.EXE'

CODE   MOVEABLE DISCARDABLE

DATA   MOVEABLE SINGLE

HEAPSIZE 0

EXPORTS
    MinRoutine @1
    WEP        @2 RESIDENTNAME
```

The **LIBRARY** key word identifies this module as a DLL. The name of the library, MinDLL, follows this key word and must be the same as the name of the library's .DLL file.

The **EXETYPE WINDOWS** statement is required for every Windows application and DLL.

The **DESCRIPTION** statement takes a string that can be up to 128 characters in length. It is typically used to hold module description information, and perhaps a copyright notice. This statement is optional in a DLL.

The **STUB** statement defines a DOS 2.x program that is copied into the body of the library's executable (.DLL) file. The purpose of the stub is to provide information to users who attempt to run Windows modules from the DOS command prompt. If no **STUB** statement is provided, the linker inserts one automatically.

The **CODE** statement is used to define the default memory attributes of the library's code segments. Moveable and discardable code segments allow the most freedom to the Windows memory manager, which will make sure that the proper code segment is available when it is needed. The **SEGMENTS** statement, which is not included in this example, can also be used to define the attributes for individual code segments.

The **DATA** statement is required. It defines memory attributes of the library's data segment. The **MOVEABLE** key word allows the memory manager to move the segment if needed. The **SINGLE** key word is required for DLLs. The reason is that DLLs always have a single data segment, regardless of the number of applications that access it.

The **HEAPSIZE** statement is used to define the initial (and minimum) size of a DLL's local heap. DLLs that perform local memory allocation (using **LocalAlloc**) must initialize the heap at library start-up time. The heap size is passed to the DLL's LibEntry routine, which, in turn, can call **LocalInit** to initialize the DLL's local heap using that heap size. See "Initializing a DLL" in Section 20.3.1 for more information. In our example, the heap size is set to zero since the local heap is not used.

The **EXPORTS** statement defines the routines that will be used as entry points from applications or from other DLLs. This information is used by Windows to establish the proper data segment to be used by each DLL routine. Each routine should have a unqiue ordinal entry value, which in this example is specified after the "@" as the value 1. The ordinal entry value is an optimization that allows the dynamic-link mechanism to operate faster and to use less memory.

20.3.3 Creating the Make File

The **MAKE** utility is used to control the creation of executable files to insure that only the minimum required processing is performed. Four utilities are used in the creation of the DLL:

- The C Compiler (**CL**)
- The linker (**LINK**)
- The import library creation utility (**IMPLIB**)
- The Resource Compiler (**RC**)

The make file to create the sample DLL is as follows.

```
MINDLL.OBJ: MINDLL.C
   CL -ASw -c -Gsw -Os -W2 MINDLL.C

MINDLL.DLL: MINDLL.OBJ
   LINK MINDLL.OBJ LIBENTRY.OBJ, MINDLL.DLL,MINDLL.MAP/map,
         MDLLCEW.LIB LIBW.LIB/NOE/NOD,MINDLL.DEF
   MAPSYM MINDLL.MAP
   IMPLIB MINDLL.LIB MINDLL.DEF
   RC MINDLL.DLL
```

More information on **MAKE** is provided in the Microsoft C Compiler documentation.

C Compiler Switches

The C Compiler uses five sets of switches, which are briefly described below. For more information, please consult the Microsoft C Compiler reference set, version 4.0 or later. The following example shows the switches used to compile the sample DLL:

```
CL -ASw -c -Gsw -Os -W2 MINDLL.C
```

The **–ASw** switch controls the default addressing to be created by the compiler. The **S** option specifies the small model, which uses short data pointers and near code pointers. The **w** option tells the compiler that the stack is not part of the default data segment, or, to put it another way, SS != DS. This causes the compiler to generate an error message when it detects the improper creation of a near pointer to an automatic variable.

The **–c** switch requests compile-only operation. This is required if your DLL has multiple C source code modules.

The **–Gsw** switch consists of two parts. The **s** option disables normal C Compiler stack checking. This is required since the stack checking is incompatible with Windows. The **w** option requests that Windows prolog and epilog code be attached to every **FAR** routine. This code is used for two purposes: to assist in the establishment of the correct data segment, and to allow the memory manager to move code segments at any time during system operation.

The **–Os** switch tells the C Compiler to optimize for size rather than for speed. This switch is optional, but recommended.

The **–W2** switch sets the warning level to "2" (the highest warning level is "3"). It's a good idea to use this switch during development to allow the C Compiler to perform various checks on data types and routine prototypes, among others. The use of this switch is optional, but recommended.

Linker Command Line

The **LINK** command takes five arguments, each separated by a comma:

```
LINK MINDLL.OBJ LIBENTRY.OBJ, MINDLL.DLL,MINDLL.MAP/map,
        MDLLCEW.LIB LIBW.LIB/NOE/NOD,MINDLL.DEF
```

The first argument lists the object (.OBJ) files that are to be used to create the DLL. If you use the standard DLL initialization routine, include LIBENTRY.OBJ as an object.

The second argument specifies the name of the final DLL executable file. The linker uses the .DLL extension for dynamic-link libraries. Implicitly loaded libraries must be named with the .DLL extension. An implictly loaded library is imported in the application's module-definition file rather than explicitly loaded with the **LoadLibrary** function. See Section 20.4, "Application Access to DLL Code," for more information on loading a DLL.

The third argument is the name of the .MAP file, which is created when the **/map** switch is used. This file contains symbol information for the global variables and functions. It is used as input to the **MAPSYM** utility, which is described later.

The fourth argument lists the import libraries and the static-link libraries required to create the DLL. There are two listed in this example: MDLLCEW.LIB and LIBW.LIB. MDLLCEW.LIB is a C run-time library which contains some DLL start-up code and C run-time library routines and math support. LIBW.LIB contains import information for KERNEL.EXE library routines. The fourth argument also includes two linker switches, **/NOD** and **/NOE.** The **/NOD** switch is used to disable default library searches based on memory model selection. If C run-time routines are used, the appropriate C run-time library would have to be included in this library list. The **/NOE** switch is used to disable extended library searches. This inhibits the error messages created by the linker when a symbol is identified in multiple libraries.

The fifth argument is the name of the module-definition file, described in Section 20.3.2 "Creating the Module-Definition File."

MAPSYM

The **MAPSYM** utility reads the .MAP file created by the linker, and creates a symbol file having the .SYM extension. The symbol file is used by the Symbolic Debugger (**SYMDEB**), and is also used by the debugging version of Windows to create stack trace information when a fatal error occurs.

IMPLIB

The **IMPLIB** utility creates an import library with the .LIB extension from a DLL's module-definition file. An import library is listed on the linker command line of applications that wish to use the routines in the DLL. In this way, references to DLL routines in an application can be properly resolved.

For more information on **IMPLIB**, see *Tools*.

The Resource Compiler

All DLLs must be compiled with the Resource Compiler to mark them as compatible with Windows version 3.0.

You can compile a DLL with the Resource Compiler **–p** option. This marks the library as private to the calling application; no other applications should attempt to use the library. In the large-frame EMS memory configuration, Windows places the code and data segments of a private library above the EMS bank line. In the small-frame EMS memory configuration, Windows loads all library objects below the bank line, even if the library is private.) See Chapter 16, "More Memory Management," for more information on Windows memory configurations.

The following list summarizes the difference between private and nonprivate libraries in the two EMS memory configurations.

	Nonprivate Library		Private Library	
Library Memory Object	**Small Frame**	**Large Frame**	**Small Frame**	**Large Frame**
Data segment	Below	Below	Below	Above
Fixed code segment	Below	Below	Below	Above
Resource	Below	Above	Below	Above
Discardable code segment	Below	Above	Below	Above

20.4 Application Access to DLL Code

This section describes the three steps necessary to allow an application to access a routine in a DLL:

1. Create a prototype for the library function.
2. Call the library function.
3. Import the library function.

20.4.1 Creating a Prototype for the Library Function

A prototype statement should be used to define each DLL routine in each application source file. The prototype statement for our sample DLL routine is as follows:

```
VOID FAR PASCAL MinRoutine (int, LPSTR);
```

The purpose of a prototype statement is to define a routine's parameters and return value to the compiler. The compiler is then able to create the proper code for the library routine. In addition, the compiler is able to issue warning messages when a routine's prototype differs from its usage and when the **–W2** compiler switch has been selected. It is strongly recommended that prototypes be created for application routines as well, to minimize the problems that can occur from errors of this type. For example, a warning message would be generated if MinRoutine, as defined previously, were to be used with the wrong number of parameters, as shown next:

```
MinRoutine (5);
```

Calling the Library Function

The call to a DLL function is indistinguishable from a call to a static-link library function, or to other routines in the application itself. Once the proper prototype definition has been made, the exported DLL functions can be called using normal C syntax.

20.4.2 Importing the Library Function

There are three ways an application can import DLL functions:

- Import implicitly at link time
- Import explicitly at link time
- Import dynamically at run time

In each case, dynamic-link information contained in the application identifies the name of the library and the function name or function's ordinal entry value. The implicit import is the most commonly used method, and it is discussed first.

Implicit Link-Time Import

An implicit import is performed by listing the import library for the DLL on the linker command line for an application. The import library is created using the **IMPLIB** utility, as discussed in section 20.3.3, "Creating the Make File"

The SDK contains a set of import libraries to allow linking to Windows DLLs. Table 20.2 lists these files and the purpose of each.

Table 20.2 Windows SDK Import Libraries

Filename	Purpose
LIBW.LIB	Import information for USER.EXE, KERNEL.EXE, and GDI.EXE.
SDLLCEW.LIB	Start-up code for Windows DLLs, C run-time library routines, and emulated math packages for small-model DLLs.
MDLLCEW.LIB	Start-up code for Windows DLLs, C run-time library routines, and emulated math packages for medium-model DLLs.
CDLLCEW.LIB	Start-up code for Windows DLLs, C run-time library routines, and emulated math packages for compact-model DLLs.

Table 20.2 Windows SDK Import Libraries *(continued)*

Filename	Purpose
LDLLCEW.LIB	Start-up code for Windows DLLs, C run-time library routines, and emulated math packages for large-model DLLs.
SDLLCAW.LIB	Start-up code for Windows DLLs, C run-time library routines, and alternate math packages for small-model DLLs.
MDLLCAW.LIB	Start-up code for Windows DLLs, C run-time library routines, and alternate math packages for medium-model DLLs.
CDLLCAW.LIB	Start-up code for Windows DLLs, C run-time library routines, and alternate math packages for compact-model DLLs.
LDLLCAW.LIB	Start-up code for Windows DLLs, C run-time library routines, and alternate math packages for large-model DLLs.
SLIBCEW.LIB	Start-up code for Windows applications, C run-time library routines, and emulated math packages for small-model applications.
MLIBCEW.LIB	Start-up code for Windows applications, C run-time library routines, and emulated math packages for medium-model applications.
CLIBCEW.LIB	Start-up code for Windows applications, C run-time library routines, and emulated math packages for compact-model applications.
LLIBCEW.LIB	Start-up code for Windows applications, C run-time library routines, and emulated math packages for large-model applications.
SLIBCAW.LIB	Start-up code for Windows applications, C run-time library routines, and alternate math packages for small-model applications.
MLIBCAW.LIB	Start-up code for Windows applications, C run-time library routines, and alternate math packages for medium-model applications.
CLIBCAW.LIB	Start-up code for Windows applications, C run-time library routines, and alternate math packages for compact-model applications.
LLIBCAW.LIB	Start-up code for Windows applications, C run-time library routines, and alternate math packages for large-model applications.
WIN87EM.LIB	Import information for Windows' floating- point DLL.

Explicit Link-Time Import

Like an implicit import, an explicit import is perfomed at link time. An explicit import is performed by listing each routine in the **IMPORTS** section of the application's module definition file. In the following example, there are three parts: the imported routine name (MinRoutine), the DLL name (MinDLL), and the ordinal entry value of the function in the library (1).

```
IMPORTS
   MinRoutine=MinDLL.1
```

Due to performance and size considerations, it is strongly advised that application developers define ordinal entry values for all exported DLL routines. However, if you do not assign an ordinal entry value, you perform the explicit import as shown in the following example:

```
IMPORTS
   MinDLL.MinRoutine
```

Dynamic Run-Time Import

In dynamic run-time imports, the application must first load the library and explicitly ask for the address of the desired function. Once this is done, the application can call the function. In the following example, an application links dynamically with the CreateInfo function in the Windows library INFO.DLL.

```
HANDLE hLibrary;
FARPROC lpFunc;

hLibrary = LoadLibrary ("INFO.DLL");
if (hLibrary >= 32)
    {
    lpFunc = GetProcAddress (hLibrary, "CreateInfo");
    if (lpFunc != (FARPROC) NULL)
        (*lpFunc) ((LPSTR) Buffer, 512);

    FreeLibrary (hLibrary);
    }
```

In this example, the **LoadLibrary** function loads the desired Windows library and returns a module handle to the library. The **GetProcAddress** function retrieves the address of the CreateInfo function by using the function's name, "CreateInfo". The function address can then be used to call the function. The following statement is an indirect function call that passes two arguments (Buffer and the integer 512) to the function:

```
*(lpFunc) ((LPSTR) Buffer, 512);
```

Finally, the **FreeLibrary** function decrements the library's use count. When the use count becomes zero (that is, no application is using the library), the Windows library is removed from memory.

Slightly better performance would be obtained if the CreateInfo function had an ordinal value assigned in the library's module-definition file. The following is an example of such a .DEF file entry:

```
EXPORTS
    CreateInfo @27
```

This statement defines the ordinal value of CreateInfo as 27. Using this value involves changing the call to **GetProcAddress** to the following:

```
GetProcAddress (hLibrary, MAKEINTRESOURCE(27));
```

20.5 Rules for Windows Object Ownership

Windows memory "objects" can be in global or local memory. Windows objects include:

- Bitmaps
- Metafiles
- Application code segments
- Resources (except fonts)

Windows treats memory objects as follows:

- An application that allocates memory owns that memory.
- When a DLL allocates a global object, the application that called the DLL owns that object.
- When an application or DLL terminates, Windows purges the system of all objects and window classes owned by that application or DLL.
- Data sharing should be performed using the clipboard or dynamic data exchange (DDE), although you can also share data using the data segment of a DLL. When using the clipboard or DDE, the Windows copies the data into the private address space of the receiving application.
- GDI objects (pens, brushes, device contexts, and regions) are not typical Windows objects in that they are not purged when the owning application terminates. For this reason, an application or DLL must explicitly destroy any GDI objects it created before it terminates.

20.6 A Sample Library: Select

This sample library contains functions that you can use to carry out selections by using the mouse. The functions are based on the graphics selection method described in Chapter 6, "The Cursor, the Mouse, and the Keyboard." These functions provide two kinds of selection feedback: a box that shows the outline of the selection, and a block that shows the entire selection inverted. The library exports the following functions:

Function	Action
StartSelection	Starts the selection and initializes the selection rectangle. When selecting with the mouse, you call this function when you receive a WM_LBUTTONDOWN message.
UpdateSelection	Updates the selection box or block. When selecting with the mouse, you call this function when you receive a WM_MOUSEMOVE message.
EndSelection	Ends the selection and fills in the selection rectangle with the final selection dimensions. When selecting with the mouse, you call this function when you receive a WM_LBUTTONUP message.
ClearSelection	Clears the selection box or block from the screen and empties the selection rectangle.

The selection rectangle is a **RECT** structure that the application supplies and the library functions fill in. The coordinates given in the rectangle are client coordinates.

To create this library you need to create several files:

File	Contents
SELECT.C	The C-language source for selection functions
SELECT.DEF	The module-definition file for the Select library
SELECT.H	The include file for the Select library
SELECT	The make file for the Select library
SELECT.LIB	The import library for the Select library

The Select library does not have an initialization file because the functions do not use a local heap and because no other initialization is necessary.

NOTE Rather than typing the code presented in the following sections, you might find it more convient simply to examine and compile the sample source files provided with the SDK.

20.6.1 Create the Functions

You can create the library functions by following the description given in Chapter 6, "The Cursor, the Mouse, and the Keyboard." Simply copy the statements used to make the graphics selection into the corresponding functions. Also, to make the selection functions more flexible, add the additional block capability.

After you change it, the StartSelection function should look like this:

```
int FAR PASCAL StartSelection(hWnd, ptCurrent, lpSelectRect, fFlags)
HWND hWnd;
POINT ptCurrent;
LPRECT lpSelectRect;
int fFlags;
{
    if (!IsEmptyRect(lpSelectRect))
        ClearSelection(hWnd, lpSelectRect, fFlags);
    if (!fFlags & SL_EXTEND) {
        lpSelectRect->left = ptCurrent.x;
        lpSelectRect->top = ptCurrent.y;
    }
    lpSelectRect->right = ptCurrent.x;
    lpSelectRect->bottom = ptCurrent.y;
    SetCapture(hWnd);
}
```

This function receives four parameters: a window handle, *hWnd*; the current mouse location, *ptCurrent*; a long pointer to the selection rectangle, *lpSelectRect*; and the selection flags, *fFlags*.

The first step is to clear the selection if the selection rectangle is not empty. The **IsRectEmpty** function returns TRUE if the rectangle is empty. The StartSelection function clears the selection by calling the ClearSelection function, which is also in this library.

The next step is to initialize the selection rectangle. The StartSelection function extends the selection (it leaves the upper-left corner of the selection unchanged), if the SS_EXTEND bit in the *fFlags* argument is set. Otherwise, it sets the upper-left and lower-right corners of the selection rectangle to the current mouse location. The **SetCapture** function directs all subsequent mouse input to the window even if the cursor moves outside of the window. This is to ensure that the selection process continues uninterrupted. To call this function, an application would use the following statements:

```
case WM_LBUTTONDOWN:
    bTrack = TRUE;
    StartSelection(hWnd, MAKEPOINT(lParam), &SelectRect,
        (wParam & MK_SHIFT) ? SL_EXTEND : NULL);
    break;
```

After you change it, the UpdateSelection function should look like this:

```
int FAR PASCAL UpdateSelection(hWnd, ptCurrent, lpSelectRect, fFlags)
HWND hWnd;
POINT ptCurrent;
LPRECT lpSelectRect;
int fFlags;

{
    HDC hDC;
    short OldROP;

    hDC = GetDC(hWnd);
    switch (fFlags & SL_TYPE) {
        case SL_BOX:
            OldROP = SetROP2(hDC, R2_XORPEN);
            MoveTo(hDC, lpSelectRect->left,
                lpSelectRect->top);
            LineTo(hDC, lpSelectRect->right,
                lpSelectRect->top);
            LineTo(hDC, lpSelectRect->right,
                lpSelectRect->bottom);
            LineTo(hDC, lpSelectRect->left,
                lpSelectRect->bottom);
            LineTo(hDC, lpSelectRect->left,
                lpSelectRect->top);
            LineTo(hDC, ptCurrent.x, lpSelectRect->top);
            LineTo(hDC, ptCurrent.x, ptCurrent.y);
            LineTo(hDC, lpSelectRect->left, ptCurrent.y);
            LineTo(hDC, lpSelectRect->left, lpSelectRect->top);
            SetROP2(hDC, OldROP);
        break;

        case SL_BLOCK:
            PatBlt(hDC,
                lpSelectRect->left, lpSelectRect->bottom,
                lpSelectRect->right - lpSelectRect->left,
                ptCurrent.y - lpSelectRect->bottom,
                DSTINVERT);
            PatBlt(hDC, PrevX, OrgY,
                lpSelectRect->right, lpSelectRect->top,
                ptCurrent.x - lpSelectRect->right,
                ptCurrent.y - lpSelectRect->top, DSTINVERT);
        break;
    }
    lpSelectRect->right = ptCurrent.x;
    lpSelectRect->bottom = ptCurrent.y;
    ReleaseDC(hWnd, hDC);
}
```

As the user makes the selection, the UpdateSelection function provides feedback about the user's progress. For the box selection, the function first clears the current box by drawing over it, then draws the new box. This requires eight calls to the **LineTo** function.

To update a block selection, the UpdateSelection function inverts the rectangle by using the **PatBlt** function. To avoid flicker while the user selects, UpdateSelection inverts only the portions of the rectangle that are different from the previous selection rectangle. This means the function inverts two separate pieces of the screen. It assumes that the only area that needs inverting is the area between the previous and current mouse locations. Figure 20.1 shows the typical coordinates for describing the areas being inverted:

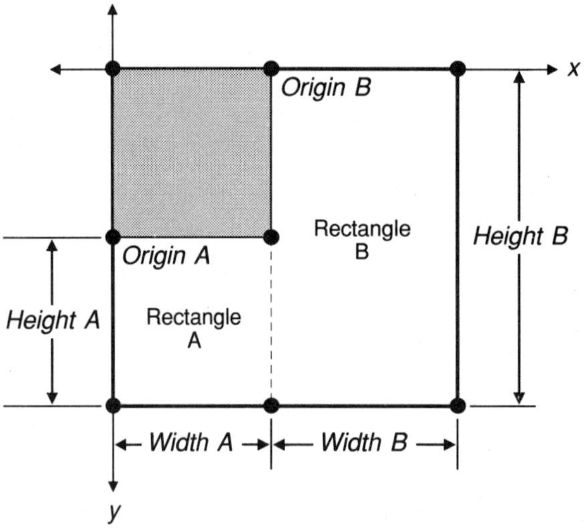

Figure 20.1 Inverting a Rectangle

The first **PatBlt** call inverts the left-most rectangle by using lpSelectRect->left, the original location on the *x*-coordinate of the mouse button when first pressed, and lpSelectRect->bottom, the most recent update of the location of the mouse on the *y*-coordinate, to set the origin of the area to be inverted. The width of the first area is determined by subtracting lpSelectRect->left from lpSelectRect->right, the most recent update of the location of the mouse on the *x*-coordinate. The height of this area is determined by subtracting lpSelectRect->bottom from ptCurrent.y, the current location of the mouse on the *y*-coordinate.

The second **PatBlt** call inverts the right-most rectangle by using lpSelectRect->right, the most recent location on the *x*-coordinate of the mouse button, and lpSelectRect->top, the original location on the *y*-coordinate of the mouse, to set the origin of the area to be inverted. The width of this second area is determined by subtracting lpSelectRect->bottom, the most recent update of the location of the mouse on the *x*-coordinate, from ptCurrent.x, the current location of the mouse on the *x*-coordinate. The height of this area is determined by subtracting lpSelectRect->top from ptCurrent.y, the current location of the mouse on the *y*-coordinate.

When the selection updating is complete, the values lpSelectRect->right and lpSelectRect->bottom are updated by assigning them the current values contained in ptCurrent.

To update a box selection, the application should call the UpdateSelection function as follows:

```
case WM_MOUSEMOVE:
    if (bTrack)
        UpdateSelection(hWnd, MAKEPOINT(lParam), &SelectRect,
SL_BOX);
    break;
```

After you change it, the EndSelection function should look like this:

```
int FAR PASCAL EndSelection(ptCurrent, lpSelectRect)
POINT ptCurrent;
LPRECT lpSelectRect;
{
    if (ptCurrent.x < lpSelectRect->left) {
        lpSelectRect->right = lpSelectRect->left;
        lpSelectRect->left = ptCurrent.x;
    }
    else
        lpSelectRect->right = ptCurrent.x;
    if (ptCurrent.y < lpSelectRect->top) {
        lpSelectRect->bottom = lpSelectRect->top;
        lpSelectRect->top = ptCurrent.y;
    }
    else
        lpSelectRect->bottom = ptCurrent.y;
    ReleaseCapture();
}
```

The EndSelection function saves the current mouse position in the selection rectangle. For convenience, the final mouse position is checked to make sure it represents a point to the lower right of the original point. Rectangles typically are described by upper-left and lower-right corners. If the final position is not to the lower right (that is, if either the *x*- or *y*-coordinate of the position is less than the original *x*- and *y*-coordinates), the values of the original point and the final point are swapped as necessary. The **ReleaseCapture** function is required since a corresponding **SetCapture** function was called. In general, you should release the mouse immediately after mouse capture is no longer needed.

Finally, when the user releases the left button, the application should call the EndSelection function to save the final point:

```
case WM_LBUTTONUP:
    bTrack = FALSE;
    EndSelection(MAKEPOINT(lParam), &SelectRect);
    break;
```

After you change it, the ClearSelection function should look like this:

```
int FAR PASCAL ClearSelection(hWnd, lpSelectRect, fFlags)
HWND hWnd;
LPRECT lpSelectRect;
int fFlags;
{
    HDC hDC;
    short OldROP;

    hDC = GetDC(hWnd);
    switch (fFlags & SL_TYPE) {
        case SL_BOX:
            OldROP = SetROP2(hDC, R2_XORPEN);
            MoveTo(hDC, lpSelectRect->left, lpSelectRect->top);
            LineTo(hDC, lpSelectRect->right, lpSelectRect->top);
            LineTo(hDC, lpSelectRect->right, lpSelectRect->bottom);
            LineTo(hDC, lpSelectRect->left, lpSelectRect->bottom);
            LineTo(hDC, lpSelectRect->left, lpSelectRect->top);
            SetROP2(hDC, OldROP);
        break;

        case SL_BLOCK:
            PatBlt(hDC,
                lpSelectRect->left, lpSelectRect->top,
                lpSelectRect->right - lpSelectRect->left,
                lpSelectRect->bottom - lpSelectRect->top,
                DSTINVERT);
        break;
    }
    ReleaseDC(hWnd, hDC);
}
```

Clearing a box selection means removing it from the screen. You can remove the outline by drawing over it with the XOR pen. Clearing a block selection means restoring the inverted screen to its previous state. You can restore the inverted screen by inverting the entire selection.

20.6.2 Create the Initialization Routine

Select uses the standard LibEntry function contained in the LIBENTRY.OBJ file. This function in turn calls a function named LibMain, which is expected to be defined in the source code of the DLL and which performs library-specific initialization. Since Select does not require initialization beyond that provided by LibEntry, it simply returns a value of 1 to indicate success. The LibMain routine of the Select DLL is defined as follows:

```
int FAR PASCAL LibMain(hInstance, wDataSeg, cbHeapSize, lpszCmdLine)
WORD   wDataSeg,
HANDLE hInstance;
WORD   cbHeapSize;
```

```
LPSTR  lpszCmdLine;

{
        return 1;
}
```

20.6.3 Create the Exit Routine

Like every DLL, Select must include the standard exit routine, WEP. Again, since Select does not require any cleanup tasks, the WEP routine simply returns:

```
VOID FAR PASCAL WEP(nParameter)
int nParameter;
{
   return;
}
```

20.6.4 Create the Module-Definition File

To link the Select library, you need to create a module-definition file containing the following:

```
LIBRARY Select

CODE MOVEABLE DISCARDABLE
DATA SINGLE
HEAPSIZE 1024

EXPORTS
    WEP                 @1 RESIDENTNAME
    StartSelection      @2
    UpdateSelection     @3
    EndSelection        @4
    ClearSelection      @5
```

Since the selection functions do not use global or static variables and there is no local heap, the **DATA** statement is used to specify no data segment, and the **HEAPSIZE** statement is used to set the heap size to zero.

20.6.5 Create the Include File

You need to create the SELECT.H include file for the Select library. This file contains the definitions for the constants used in the functions, as well as function definitions. The include file should look like this:

```
int FAR PASCAL StartSelection(HWND, POINT, LPRECT, int);
int FAR PASCAL UpdateSelection(HWND, POINT, LPRECT, int);
int FAR PASCAL EndSelection(POINT, LPRECT);
int FAR PASCAL ClearSelection(HWND, LPRECT, int);
```

You should also use the include file in applications that use the selection functions. This will ensure that proper parameter and return types are used with the functions.

20.6.6 Compile and Link

To compile and link the Select library you need to create the make file as follows:

```
select.obj: select.c select.h
        cl -c -Asnw -Gsw -Os -Zp select.c

select.dll: select.obj
        link select libentry, select.dll, , /NOE /NOD sdllcew libw,
        select.def
   rc select.dll   implib select.lib select.def
```

Once you have compiled and linked the Select library, you can create a small test application to confirm that it is working properly. For a description of an application that uses the selection functions, see Chapter 11, "Bitmaps" or Chapter 13, "The Clipboard."

20.7 Summary

This chapter described dynamic-link libraries (DLLs), a special type of library that permits applications to share code and resources. DLLs exist primarily to provide services to applications. For example, the Windows DLLs make Windows functions available to applications; therefore, the applications need not contain the code that defines each function. You can create your own DLLs in order to share code and resources among your own applications.

With a static-link library, such as MLIBCEW.LIB, the linker copies the code for a particular routine to the application's executable file. In contrast, with a dynamic-link library, two or more applications can share a single copy of the source code for a routine. Applications link to DLL routines at run time, rather than at build time.

A typical use of a DLL is for defining custom controls. Your applications can then use those controls, and you can include the controls in your dialog boxes using the Dialog Editor.

For more information on topics related to dynamic-link libraries, see the following:

Topic	**Reference**
Special considerations when creating DLLs using the C language	*Guide to Programming:* Chapter 14, "C and Assembly Language"
Managing memory in a DLL	*Guide to Programming:* Chapter 16, "More Memory Management"
Linking and importing DLLs	*Tools:* Chapter 2, "Linking Applications: The Linker"
Installing a custom control using the Dialog Editor	*Tools:* Chapter 5, "Designing Dialog Boxes: The Dialog Editor"

Chapter 21 Multiple Document Interface

The multiple document interface (MDI) is a user interface standard for presenting and manipulating multiple documents within a single application. An MDI application has one main window, within which the user can open and work with several documents. Each document appears in its own separate child window within the main application window. Because each child window has a frame, system menu, maximize and minimize buttons, and icon; the user can manipulate it just as if it were a normal, independent window. The difference is that the child windows cannot move outside the main application window.

This chapter covers the following topics:

- The structure of an MDI application
- Writing procedures for an MDI application
- Controlling an MDI application's child windows

This chapter uses as its example a simple text editor called Multipad, supplied on the SDK Sample Source Code disk. Multipad is an MDI variation of the Windows Notepad desktop application. (Multipad actually serves as a sample application for several of the chapters in this manual. This chapter will discuss in detail only the parts of Multipad that are relevant to the MDI interface.)

21.1 The Structure of an MDI Application

Like most Windows applications, an MDI application contains a message loop for dispatching messages to the application's various windows. The MDI message loop is similar to normal message loops, except for the way it handles menu accelerators.

The main window of an MDI application is similar to that of most Windows applications. In an MDI application, the main window is called the "frame window." The frame window differs from a normal main window in that its client area is filled by a special child window called the "client window." Because Windows maintains the MDI client window and controls the MDI interface, the application needs to store very little information about the MDI user interface. (In this sense, the MDI client window is similar to a standard control, such as a radio button; it has a standard behavior that Windows provides automatically. The application can use the client window, but need not provide code that defines how the window appears or behaves.)

Visually, an MDI client window is simply a large monochromatic rectangle. To the user, the client window is part of the main window; it provides a background upon which the child windows appear. The application defines the child windows; normally, there is one child window per document. The MDI child windows look much like the main window: they have window frames, system menus, and minimize and maximize buttons. The main difference to the user is that each child window contains a separate document; also, the child windows cannot move outside the client window.

Figure 21.1 shows the sample application Multipad, which is a typical MDI application.

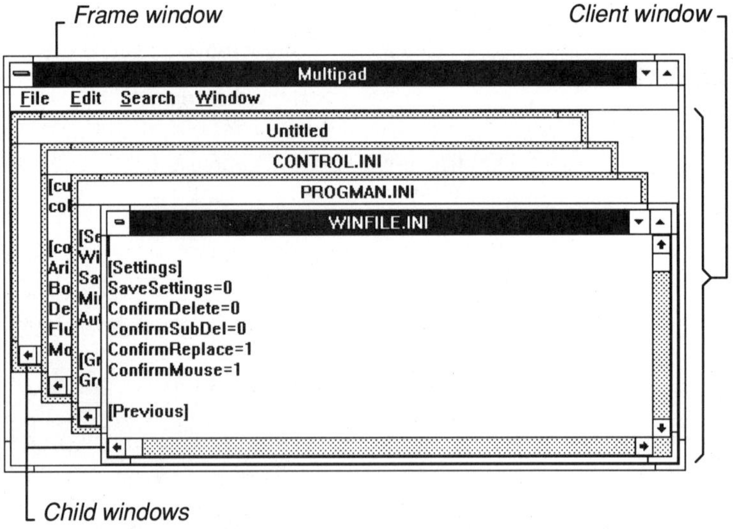

Figure 21.1 Multipad: A Sample MDI Application

In general, an application controls the MDI interface by passing messages up and down the hierarchy of MDI windows. The MDI client window, which Windows controls, carries out many operations on behalf of the application.

The rest of this chapter explains how to write an MDI application, and how to use messages to control the MDI child windows.

21.2 Initializing an MDI Application

The first place in which an MDI application differs from a normal Windows application is in the initialization process. Although the overall process is the same, an MDI application requires that you set certain values in the window class structure.

To initialize an MDI application, you first register its window classes (if there is no previous instance of the application) just as you would for a normal application. You then create and display any windows that will be initially visible.

21.2.1 Registering the Window Classes

In general, a typical MDI application needs to register two window classes:

- A window class for the application's MDI frame window. The class structure for the frame window is similar to the class structure for the main window in non-MDI applications.
- A window class for the application's MDI child windows. The class structure for the MDI child windows is slightly different from the structure for child windows in non-MDI applications.

  An application may have more than one window class for its MDI child windows, if there is more than one type of document available in the application.

Note that the application does not register a class for the MDI client window, which is defined by Windows.

The class structure for MDI child windows differs from that for normal child windows in the following ways:

- The class structure should have an icon, because the user can minimize an MDI child window as if it were a normal application window.
- The menu name should be NULL, because MDI child windows cannot have their own menus.
- The class structure should reserve extra space in the window structure. This lets the application associate data, such as a filename, with a particular child window.

In the Multipad application, the locally-defined function InitializeApplication registers Multipad's MDI window classes.

21.2.2 Creating the Windows

After registering its window classes, your MDI application can create its windows. It first creates its frame window using the **CreateWindow** function. (The *System Application Architecture, Common User Access: Advanced*

Interface Design Guide describes how an MDI application's frame window should look.)

After creating its frame window, the application can then create its client window using the **CreateWindow** function. It should specify MDICLIENT as the client window's class name. MDICLIENT is a preregistered window class, defined by Windows. The *lParam* parameter to the **CreateWindow** function should point to a **CLIENTCREATESTRUCT** data structure. A **CLIENTCREATESTRUCT** structure contains the following fields:

Field	Description
hWindowMenu	A handle to a pop-up menu used for controlling MDI child windows. As child windows are created, the application adds their titles to the pop-up menu as menu items. The user can then activate a child window by selecting its title from the window menu. Multipad places this pop-up menu in its "Window" menu, and obtains a handle to the pop-up menu with the **GetSubMenu** function.
idFirstChild	The window ID of the first MDI child window. The first MDI child window created will be assigned this ID. Additional windows will be created with subsequent window IDs; when a child window is destroyed, Windows immediately reassigns the window IDs to keep the range of IDs continuous.

When a child window's title is added to the window menu, the menu item is assigned the child window's ID, which means that the frame window will receive WM_COMMAND messages with these IDs in the *wParam* parameter. Thus, the value for the **idFirstChild** field should be chosen so as not to conflict with menu-item IDs in the frame window's menu.

The MDI client window is created with WS_CLIPCHILDREN style bit, since the window must not paint over its child windows.

The Multipad's locally-defined InitializeInstance function creates Multipad's frame window. However, Multipad does not create its client window at this point. Instead, it does this as part of the frame window's WM_CREATE message processing. Multipad handles the WM_CREATE message in its MPFrameWndProc function. After creating the frame window and the client window, Multipad performs additional initialization, such as loading the accelerator table and checking a printer driver.

Multipad then creates its first MDI child window, either empty or containing a file appearing on the command line. (For information on creating MDI child windows, see Section 21.7.1, "Creating Child Windows.")

21.3 Writing the Main Message Loop

The main message loop for an MDI application is similar to a normal message loop, except that the MDI application uses the **TranslateMDISysAccel** function to translate child-window accelerators.

The system-menu accelerators for an MDI child window are similar to accelerators for a normal window's system menu. The difference is that child window accelerators respond to the CONTROL key rather than the ALT (Menu) key.

A typical MDI application's message loop looks like this:

```
while (GetMessage(&msg,NULL,0,0))
{
if (!TranslateMDISysAccel(hwndMDIClient,&msg)
 && !TranslateAccelerator(hwndFrame,hAccel,&msg))
        {
        TranslateMessage(&msg);
        DispatchMessage(&msg);
        }
}
```

This example MDI message loop is similar to a normal message loop that handles accelerators. The difference is that the MDI message loop calls **TranslateMDISysAccel** before checking for application-defined accelerators or dispatching the message normally.

The **TranslateMDISysAccel** function translates WM_KEYDOWN messages into WM_SYSCOMMAND messages to the active MDI child window. It returns FALSE if the message is not an MDI accelerator message; in that case, the application uses the **TranslateAccelerator** function to see if any of the application-defined accelerators were invoked. If not, the loop dispatches the message to the appropriate window function.

21.4 Writing the Frame Window Function

The frame window function for an MDI application is very similar to a normal application's main window function. However, there are a few differences:

- Normally, a window function passes all messages it does not handle to the **DefWindowProc** function. The window function for an MDI frame window passes messages to the **DefFrameProc** function instead.
- The frame window function passes **DefFrameProc** all messages it does not handle; in addition, it also passes some messages that the application does handle. See the *Reference, Volume 1,* for a list of messages your application must pass to **DefFrameProc**.

DefFrameProc also handles WM_SIZE messages by resizing the MDI client to fit into the new client area. The application can calculate a smaller area for the MDI client if it chooses (for example, to allow room for status or ribbon windows).

DefFrameProc will also set the focus to the client window when it sees a WM_SETFOCUS message. The client window sets the focus to the active child window, if there is one. As noted previously, the WM_CREATE message causes the frame window to create its MDI client window.

Multipad's frame window procedure is called MPFrameWndProc. The handling of other messages by Multipad's MPFrameWndProc function is similar to that of non-MDI applications. WM_COMMAND messages in Multipad are handled by Multipad's locally-defined CommandHandler function, which calls the **DefFrameProc** function for command messages Multipad does not handle. If Multipad did not do this, then the user would not be able to activate a child window from the Window menu, since the WM_COMMAND message sent by selecting the window's item would be lost.

21.5 Writing the Child Window Function

Like the frame window function, MDI child window functions use a special function for processing messages by default. All messages the child window function does not handle must be passed to the **DefMDIChildProc** function rather than the **DefWindowProc** function. In addition, some window-management messages (such as WM_SIZE, WM_MOVE, WM_GETMINMAXINFO) must be passed to **DefMDIChildProc** even if the application handles the message, in order for the MDI interface to function correctly. See the *Reference, Volume 1,* for a complete list of messages the application must pass to **DefMDIChildProc**.

Multipad's child-window function is named MPChildWndProc.

21.6 Associating Data with Child Windows

Since the number of child windows varies depending on how many documents the user opens, the MDI application must be able to associate data (for example, the name of the current file) with each child window. There are two ways to do this:

- Storing data in the window structure
- Using window properties

The rest of this section explains how to use these data-storage techniques.

21.6.1 Storing Data in the Window Structure

When the application registers the class of a window, it may reserve extra space in the window structure for application data specific to this particular class of windows. To store and retrieve data in this extra space, the application uses the functions **GetWindowWord**, **SetWindowWord**, **GetWindowLong**, and **SetWindowLong**.

If the application needs to maintain a large amount of data for a document window, the application can allocate memory for a data structure, then store the handle to the data structure in the extra space of the window structure.

Multipad uses this technique. For example, the WM_CREATE message processing in Multipad's MPChildWndProc function creates a multiple-line edit control used as the text-editor window. Multipad stores the handle to this control in its child window structure using the **SetWindowWord** function. Whenever Multipad needs to manipulate the edit control, it uses the **GetWindowWord** function to retrieve the handle to the edit control. Multipad maintains several per-document variables this way.

21.6.2 Using Window Properties

Your application can also store per-document data using window properties. Properties are different from extra space in the window structure in that no extra space needs to be allocated when the window class is registered. A window can have any number of properties. Also, where offsets are used to access the extra space in window structures, properties are referred to by string names.

Associated with each property is a handle. For example, Multipad could have used a property called "EditControl" to store the edit control window handle discussed previously. The handle could actually be any two-byte value, and could be a handle to a data structure. Properties are often more convenient than extra space in the window structure. This is because, when using properties, the application does not need to reserve extra space in advance or calculate offsets to variables. On the other hand, accessing extra space by offset is generally faster than accessing properties.

21.7 Controlling Child Windows

To control its child windows, the MDI application sends messages to its MDI client window. This includes creating, destroying, activating or changing the state of a child window.

Generally, an application will only be concerned with the current active child window. For example, in Multipad, most of the File menu commands and all of the Edit and Search menu commands refer to the current active window. Thus,

Multipad maintains the hwndActive and hwndActiveEdit variables, since only those two windows will receive messages.

There are exceptions. For example, the application might send messages to all child windows in order to inquire about the window's state. Multipad does this when closing, to ensure that all files have been saved.

Since MDI child windows may be iconic, the application must be careful to avoid manipulating icon title windows as if they were normal MDI child windows. Icon title windows will show up when the application enumerates child windows of the MDI client, but icon titles differ from other child windows in that they are owned by an MDI child window. Thus, the **GetWindow** function with the GW_OWNER index can be used to detect when a child window is an icon title. Non-title windows will return NULL. Note that this test is insufficient for top-level windows since pop-ups and dialog boxes are owned windows as well.

The rest of this section explains how to create, destroy, activate or deactivate, and rearrange MDI child windows.

21.7.1 Creating Child Windows

To create an MDI child window, the application sends a WM_MDICREATE message to the MDI client. (The application must not use the **CreateWindow** function to create MDI child windows.) The *lParam* parameter of a WM_MDICREATE message is a far pointer to a structure called an **MDICREATESTRUCT**, which contains fields similar to **CreateWindow** function parameters.

Multipad creates its MDI child windows using its locally-defined AddFile function (located in the source file MPFILE.C). The AddFile function sets the title of the child window by assigning the szTitle field of the window's **MDICREATESTRUCT** structure to either the name of the file being edited or to "Untitled." The szClass field is set to the name of the MDI child window class registered in Multipad's InitializeApplication function. The owner field, hOwner, is set to the application's instance handle.

The **MDICREATESTRUCT** contains four dimension fields: **x** and **y**, which are the position of the window, and **cx** and **cy**, the horizontal and vertical extents of the window. Any of these may be either explicitly assigned by the application or may be set to CW_USEDEFAULT, in which case Windows picks a position and/or size according to a cascading algorithm. All four fields must be initialized in all cases. Multipad uses CW_USEDEFAULT for all dimensions.

The last field is the **style** field, which may contain style bits for the window. Windows requires certain style bits for MDI child windows, and allows certain others, masking off inappropriate bits.

The bits WS_MINIMIZE or WS_MAXIMIZE may be used to set the original state of the window.

The pointer passed in the *lParam* parameter of the WM_MDICREATE message is passed to create window and appears as the first field in the **CREATE-STRUCT** passed in the WM_CREATE message. In Multipad, the child window initializes itself during WM_CREATE message processing by initializing document variables in its extra data and by creating the edit control child window.

21.7.2 Destroying Child Windows

To destroy an MDI child window, use the WM_MDIDESTROY message. Pass the child window's window handle in the message's *wParam* parameter.

21.7.3 Activating and Deactivating Child Windows

Activation may be changed using the WM_MDINEXT and WM_MDIACTIVATE messages. WM_MDINEXT activates the next MDI child window in the window list, and WM_MDIACTIVATE activates the child window specified by the message's *wParam* parameter. Activation is usually controlled by the user through the use of the MDI user interface. Multipad does not use either of these messages directly.

A more common use of WM_MDIACTIVATE is following activation changes. WM_MDIACTIVATE is also sent to the MDI child windows losing and gaining the MDI activation, so by watching WM_MDIACTIVATE messages sent to child windows, the application can follow the active window.

Multipad maintains two global variables, hwndActive and hwndActiveEdit, which are the windows handles of the current active MDI child and its edit control, respectively. Keeping these variables makes sending messages to these windows simple.

At any time, the active MDI child can be retrieved using the WM_MDIGETACTIVE message, which returns the active child in its low-order word. The application could then use the **GetWindowWord** function to get a window handle to the document's edit control. To explicitly maximize and restore a child window, the application could use the WM_MDIMAXIMIZE and WM_MDIRESTORE messages, with the *wParam* parameter of each message set to the handle of the child window the application wants to change. Again, these are messages that an application will not normally use, since Windows manages the MDI user interface on behalf of the application.

21.7.4 Arranging Child Windows on the Screen

Windows also provides three utility messages you can use to arrange MDI child windows:

Message	Description
WM_MDICASCADE	Arranges all the noniconic child windows in order, diagonally from upper-left to lower-right. (This message also arranges child icons.)
WM_MDIICONARRANGE	Arranges all iconic child windows along the bottom of the MDI client window.
WM_MDITILE	Arranges all noniconic child windows so that they are tiled within the MDI client window. (This message also arranges child icons.)

21.8 Summary

This chapter introduced the Windows multiple document interface, and explained the structure of an MDI application. It also explained how to write an MDI application.

For more information on topics related to MDI, see the following:

Topic	Reference
Creating and managing windows	*Reference, Volume 1*: Chapter 1, "Window Manager Interface Functions"
The window class structure	*Reference, Volume 1*: Chapter 1, "Window Manager Interface Functions"
MDI functions	*Reference, Volume 1*: Chapter 1, "Window Manager Interface Functions" and Chapter 4, "Functions Directory"
A sample MDI application	The sample application Multipad, supplied on the SDK Sample Source Code disk

Chapter 22 Dynamic Data Exchange

Microsoft Windows provides several methods for transferring data between applications. One way to transfer data is to use Windows Dynamic Data Exchange (DDE). DDE is a message protocol for data exchange between Windows programs. It allows software developers to share data among applications, and thereby provides the user a more integrated Windows environment.

This chapter provides a guide to implementing Dynamic Data Exchange in your Windows application. The *Reference, Volume 2*, provides details of the protocol.

This chapter covers the following topics:

- Data exchange in Windows
- DDE concepts
- DDE messages
- DDE message flow

This chapter also explains how to use two sample applications, Client and Server, that illustrate these concepts.

22.1 Data Exchange in Windows

In general, the Windows environment supports three mechanisms that applications can use to exchange data with one another:

- Clipboard transfers
- Dynamic link libraries
- Dynamic Data Exchange

Windows *does not* support sharing global memory handles directly. Due to expanded memory considerations, as well as compatibility with future versions of Windows, you should not dereference (using **GlobalUnlock**), or otherwise manipulate, global memory handles created by another application. DDE is the only Windows mechanism that supports passing of global memory handles between applications.

22.1.1 Clipboard Transfers

The clipboard lets a user transfer data between applications in the system. The user issues a command in an application to copy selected data to the clipboard. Then, in another application the user issues a command to paste the data from the clipboard into the second application's workspace. In general, the clipboard is a temporary repository of information that requires direct involvement of the user to initiate and complete the transfer.

22.1.2 Dynamic Link Libraries

A dynamic-link library (DLL) can be designed to serve as a repository for data shared between applications. The DLL offers an application interface for storing and retrieving data. The actual data is stored in the DLL's local heap, or in the static data area of its data segment. Handles or addresses to this data can be passed to applications only as logical identifications, never to be deferenced by the applications themselves. Only the DLL can dereference its handles or address, using **GlobalUnlock**, **LocalUnlock**, or address indirection. In general, you can use only the DLL's data segment for data exchange.

22.1.3 Dynamic Data Exchange

The Windows DDE protocol is a standard for cooperating applications that allows them to exchange data and invoke remote commands by means of Windows messages.

Because Windows is based on a message-based architecture, message passing is the most appropriate method for automatically transferring information between applications. However, Windows messages contain only two parameters (*wParam* and *lParam*) for passing data. As a result, these parameters must refer indirectly to other pieces of data if more than a few words of information is to be passed between applications.

The DDE protocol defines exactly how the *wParam* and *lParam* message parameters are used to pass larger pieces of data by means of global atoms and global shared-memory handles.

A global atom is a reference to a character string. In the DDE protocol, atoms are used to identify the applications exchanging data, the nature of the data being exchanged, and the data items themselves.

A global shared-memory handle is a handle to a block of memory allocated with **GlobalAlloc**, using the GMEM_DDESHARE option. In the DDE protocol, global shared-memory objects store data items passed between applications, protocol options, and remote command execution strings.

The DDE protocol has very specific rules for assigning responsibility to the applications involved in a DDE exchange for allocating and deleting global atoms and shared memory objects. Chapter 15 in the *Reference, Volume 2*, provides these rules in detail for each message.

22.1.4 Uses for Windows DDE

DDE is most appropriate for data exchanges that do not require ongoing user interaction. Normally an application provides a method for the user to establish the link between the applications exchanging data. But once that link is established, the applications exchange data without further user involvement.

DDE can be used to implement a broad range of application features, including:

- Linking to real-time data, such as to stock market updates, scientific instruments, or process control.
- Creating compound documents, such as a word-processing document that includes a chart produced by a graphics program. Using DDE, the chart will change when the source data is changed, while the rest of the document remains the same.
- Performing data queries between applications, such as a spreadsheet querying a database application for accounts past due.

22.1.5 DDE from the User's Point of View

The following example illustrates two cooperating Windows DDE applications, as seen from the user's point of view.

A Microsoft Excel spreadsheet user wishes to track the price of a particular stock on the New York Stock Exchange. The user has a Windows application called Quote that in turn has access to NYSE data. The DDE conversation between Excel and Quote takes place as follows:

- The user initiates the conversation by supplying the name of the application (Quote) that will supply the data and the particular topic of interest (NYSE). The resulting DDE conversation is used to request quotes on specific stocks.
- Excel broadcasts the application and topic names to all DDE applications currently running in the system. Quote responds, establishing a conversation with Excel about the NYSE topic.
- The user can then request that the spreadsheet be automatically updated whenever a particular stock quotation changes by entering a spreadsheet formula in a cell. For example, the user could request an automatic update whenever a change in the selling price of IBM stock occurs, by specifying the following Excel formula:

  ```
  ='Quote'|'NYSE'!IBM
  ```

- The user can terminate the automatic updating of the IBM stock quotation at any time. Other data links that were established separately (such as for quotations for other stocks) still will remain active under the same NYSE conversation.
- The user can also terminate the entire conversation between Excel and Quote on the NYSE topic, so that no specific data links may be subsequently established on that topic without initiating a new conversation.

22.2 DDE Concepts

Certain concepts and terminology are key to understanding Dynamic Data Exchange. The following sections explain the most important of these.

22.2.1 Client, Server, and Conversation

Two applications participating in dynamic data exchange are engaged in a DDE "conversation." The application that initiates the conversation is the "client" application; the application responding to the client is the "server" application. An application can be engaged in several conversations at the same time, acting as the client in some and as the server in others.

A DDE conversation takes place between two windows, one for each of the participating applications. The window may be the main window of the application, a window associated with a specific document (as in a multiple document interface (MDI) application), or a hidden (invisible) window whose only purpose is to process DDE messages.

Since a DDE conversation is identified by the pair of handles of the windows engaged in the conversation, no window should be engaged in more than one conversation with another window. Either the client application or the server application must provide a different window for each of its conversations with a particular server or client application.

An application can ensure that a pair of client and server windows is never involved in more than one conversation by creating a hidden window for each conversation. The sole purpose of this window is to process DDE messages.

22.2.2 Application, Topic, and Item

DDE identifies the units of data passed between the client and server with a three-level hierarchy of item, topic, and application name.

Each DDE conversation is uniquely defined by the application name and topic. At the beginning of a DDE conversation, the client and server agree upon the application name and topic. The application is normally the name of the server application. For example, in a conversation in which Microsoft Excel acts as the server, the conversation application name is "Excel".

The DDE topic is a general classification of data within which multiple data items may be discussed (exchanged) during the conversation. For applications that operate on file-based documents, the topic is usually a file name. For other applications, the topic is an application-specific name.

Because the client and server window handles together identify a DDE conversation, the application name and topic that define a conversation cannot be changed during the course of the conversation.

A DDE data item is the actual information related to the conversation topic that is exchanged between the applications. Values for the data item can be passed from the server to the client, or from the client to the server. The format of the data item may be any of several clipboard formats defined for DDE (see the *Reference, Volume 1*).

22.2.3 Permanent ("Hot" or "Warm") Data Link

Once a DDE conversation has begun, the client can establish one or more permanent data links with the server. A data link is a communication mechanism by which the server notifies the client whenever the value of a given data item changes. The data link is permanent in the sense that this notification process continues until the data link or the DDE conversation itself is terminated.

There are two kinds of permanent DDE data links: "hot" and "warm." In a warm data link, the server notifies the client that the value of the data item has changed, but the server does not actually send the data value to the client until the client requests it. In a hot data link, the server immediately sends the changed data value to the client.

Applications that support hot or warm links typically provide a Copy or Paste Link command in their Edit menu to permit the user to establish links between applications. See "Initiating a Data Link With the Paste Link Command," in Section 22.4.3 for more information.

22.3 DDE Messages

Because DDE is a message-based protocol, DDE employs no special Windows functions or libraries. All DDE transactions are conducted by passing certain defined DDE messages between the client and server windows.

There are nine DDE messages; the symbolic constants for these messages are defined in the SDK header file DDE.H, not WINDOWS.H. Certain data structures for the various DDE messages are also defined in DDE.H.

The nine DDE messages are summarized as follows. A detailed description of each DDE message is provided in the *Reference, Volume 2*.

Message	Description
WM_DDE_ACK	Sent in response to a received message. Provides a positive or negative acknowledgement of the message receipt.
WM_DDE_ADVISE	Requests the server application to supply an update or notification for a data item whenever it changes. This establishes a permanent data link.
WM_DDE_DATA	Sends a data-item value to the client application.
WM_DDE_EXECUTE	Sends a string to the server application, which is expected to process it as a series of commands.
WM_DDE_INITIATE	Initiates a conversation between the client and server applications.
WM_DDE_POKE	Sends a data-item value to the server application.
WM_DDE_REQUEST	Requests the server application to provide the value of a data item.
WM_DDE_TERMINATE	Terminates a conversation.
WM_DDE_UNADVISE	Terminates a permanent data link.

22.4 DDE Message Flow

A typical DDE conversation consists of the following events:

1. The client application initiates the conversation, and the server application responds.
2. The applications exchange data by any or all of the following methods:
   - The server application sends data to the client at the client's request.
   - The client application sends unsolicited data to the server application.
   - The client application requests the server application to send data whenever the data changes (hot link).

- The client application requests the server application to notify the client whenever a data item changes (warm link).
- The server application executes a command at the client's request.

3. Either the client or server application terminates the conversation.

The following sections describe the normal flow of DDE messages between the client and server applications.

22.4.1 Initiating a Conversation

To initiate a DDE conversation, the client sends a WM_DDE_INITIATE message. Usually, the client broadcasts this message by calling the **SendMessage** with –1 as the first parameter. If the application already has the window handle of the server application, however, it can send the message directly to that window. The client prepares atoms for the application and topic names by calling **GlobalAddAtom.** The client may request conversations with any potential server application and for any potential topic by supplying null (wildcard) atoms for, respectively, the application and topic.

The following example illustrates how the client initiates a conversation, where both the application and topic are specified.

```
❶ atomApplication = GlobalAddAtom("Server");
atomTopic = GlobalAddAtom(szTopic);
❷ SendMessage(-1,
          WM_DDE_INITIATE,
          hwndClientDDE,
          MAKELONG(atomApplication, atomTopic));
❸ GlobalDeleteAtom(atomApplication);
GlobalDeleteAtom(atomTopic);
```

In this example:

❶ The client application creates two global atoms containing the name of the server and the name of the topic, respectively.

❷ The client application sends a WM_DDE_INITIATE message with the application-name and topic-name atoms in the *lParam* parameter of the message. The special window handle –1 in the **SendMesage** call instructs Windows to send this message to all other active applications. The **SendMessage** function does not return to the client application until all applications that receive the message have, in turn, returned control to Windows. This means that all WM_DDE_ACK messages sent in reply by the server applications are guaranteed to have been processed by the client by the time the **SendMessage** call has returned.

❸ After **SendMessage** returns, the client application deletes the global atoms.

Server applications respond according to the logic shown in Figure 22.1.

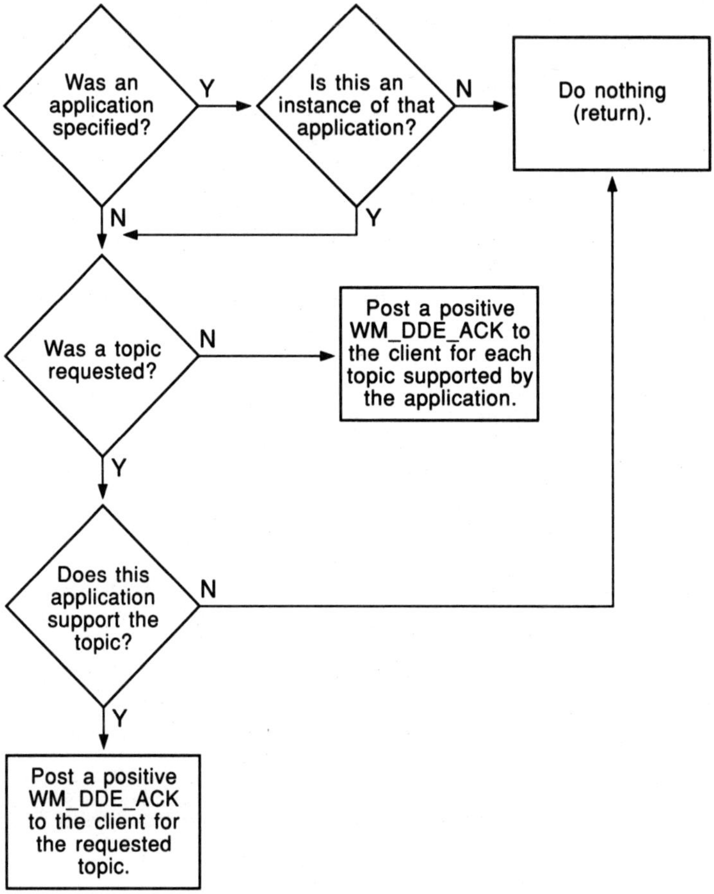

Figure 22.1 Responding to WM_DDE_INITIATE

To acknowledge one or more topics, the server must create atoms for each conversation (requiring duplicate application-name atoms if there are multiple topics) and send a WM_DDE_ACK message for each conversation, as follows:

```
atomApplication = GlobalAddAtom("Server");
atomTopic = GlobalAddAtom(szTopic);
if (!SendMessage(hwndClientDDE,
            WM_DDE_ACK,
            hwndServerDDE,
            MAKELONG(atomApplication, atomTopic)))
```

```
{
        GlobalDeleteAtom(atomApplication);
        GlobalDeleteAtom(atomTopic);
}
```

When a server responds with a WM_DDE_ACK message, the client application should save the handle of the server window. The client application receives this handle as the *wParam* parameter of the WM_DDE_ACK message. The client application then sends all subsequent DDE messages to the server window identified by this handle.

If the client appliction uses null (wildcard) atoms for the application or topic, the client should expect to receive acknowledgments from more than one server application. As stated in Section 22.2.1, "Client, Server, and Conversation," creating a unique, hidden window for each DDE conversation ensures that a pair of client and server windows is never involved in more than one conversation. To follow this practice, however, the client application must terminate conversations with all but one of the server applications that respond to the same WM_DDE_INITIATE message from the client.

22.4.2 Transfering a Single Item

Once a DDE conversation has been established, the client can obtain the value of a data item from the server by issuing the WM_DDE_REQUEST message, or the client can submit a data item value to the server by issuing the WM_DDE_POKE message.

Obtaining an Item from the Server

To obtain an item from the server, the client sends the server a WM_DDE_REQUEST message specifying the desired item and format, as follows:

```
atomItem = GlobalAddAtom(szItemName);
if (!PostMessage(hwndServerDDE,
                WM_DDE_REQUEST,
                hwndClientDDE,
                MAKELONG(CF_TEXT, atomItem)))
        GlobalDeleteAtom(atomItem);
```

In this example, the client specifies the clipboard format CF_TEXT as the desired format for the requested data item.

The receiver (server) of the WM_DDE_REQUEST message is normally responsible for deleting the item atom; but if the **PostMessage** call itself fails, then the client must delete the atom.

If the server has access to the requested item and can render it in the requested format, the server copies the item value as a global shared memory object and sends the client a WM_DDE_DATA message, as follows:

```
/* Allocate size of DDE data header, plus the data: a string,    */
/* <CR><LF><NULL>. The byte for the string null terminator       */
/* is counted by DDEDATA.Value[1]. */

❶ if (!(hData = GlobalAlloc(GMEM_MOVEABLE | GMEM_DDESHARE,
                (LONG)sizeof(DDEDATA)+strlen(szItemValue)+2)))
        return;
❷ if (!(lpData = (DDEDATA FAR *)GlobalLock(hData)))
{   GlobalFree(hData);
        return;
}
    .
    .
    .
❸ lpData->cfFormat = CF_TEXT;
❹ lstrcpy((LPSTR)lpData->Value, (LPSTR)szItemValue);
/* each line of CF_TEXT data is terminated by CR/LF */
lstrcat((LPSTR)lpData->Value, (LPSTR)"\r\n");
❺ GlobalUnlock(hData);
❻ atomItem = GlobalAddAtom((LPSTR)szItemName);
❼ if (!PostMessage(hwndClientDDE,
                WM_DDE_DATA,
                hwndServerDDE,
                MAKELONG(hData, atomItem)))
{
        GlobalFree(hData);
        GlobalDeleteAtom(atomItem);
}
```

In this example:

❶ The server application allocates a block of memory to contain the data item. The memory is allocated with the GMEM_DDESHARE; this allows the memory to be shared by the server and client applications.

❷ Next, the server application locks the block of memory so it can obtain its address. The data block is initialized as a **DDEDATA** data structure.

❸ The server application sets the **cfFormat** field of the data block to CF_TEXT to inform the client application that the data is in text format.

❹ The client copies the value of the requested data into the **Value** field of the **DDEDATA** structure.

❺ Now that the server has filled the data block, the server unlocks the data.

❻ Next, the server creates a global atom containing the name of the data item.

❼ Finally, the server issues the WM_DDE_DATA message by calling the **PostMessage** function. The handle of the data block and the atom containing the item name are contained in the *lParam* parameter of the message.

If the server is unable to satisfy the request, it sends the client a negative WM_DDE_ACK message, as follows:

```
/* negative acknowledgement */
PostMessage(hwndClientDDE,
            WM_DDE_ACK,
            hwndServerDDE,
            MAKELONG(0, atomItem));
```

Upon receiving a WM_DDE_DATA message, the client processes the data item value as appropriate. Then, if the **fAckReq** bit specified in the WM_DDE_DATA message is 1, the client is expected to send the server a positive WM_DDE_ACK message, as illustrated:

```
hData = LOWORD(lParam);   /* of WM_DDE_DATA message */
atomItem = HIWORD(lParam);
❶ if (!(lpDDEData = (DDEDATA FAR*)GlobalLock(hData))
        || (lpDDEData->cfFormat != CF_TEXT))
{
        PostMessage(hwndServerDDE,
                WM_DDE_ACK,
                hwndClientDDE,
                MAKELONG(0, atomItem)); /* negative ACK */
}

/* copy data from lpDDEData here */

❷ if (lpDDEData->fAckReq)
{
        PostMessage(hwndServerDDE,
                WM_DDE_ACK,
                hwndClientDDE,
                MAKELONG(0x8000, atomItem)); /* positive ACK */
}
❸ bRelease = lpDDEData->fRelease;
GlobalUnlock(hData);
if (bRelease)
        GlobalFree(hData);
```

In this example:

❶ The client examines the format of the data; if it is not CF_TEXT (or if the client cannot lock the memory for the data), the client sends a negative WM_DDE_ACK message to indicate that it could not process the data.

❷ If it can process the data, the client examines the **fAckReq** flag of the **DDE-DATA** structure to determine if the server requested that it be informed that the client received and processed the data successfully. If so, the client sends a positive WM_DDE_ACK message to the server.

❸ The client saves the **fRelease** flag before unlocking the block of data, since unlocking the data invalidates the pointer to the data. Then it examines the value of the flag to determine whether the server application requested the client to free the global memory containing the data and acts accordingly.

Upon receiving a negative WM_DDE_ACK message, the client may ask for the same item value again, specifying a different clipboard format. Typically, a client will first ask for the most complex format it can support, then step down if necessary through progressively simpler formats until it finds one the server can provide.

If the server supports the Formats item of the System topic, the client can determine once what clipboard formats the server supports, instead of determining them each time the client requests an item. See the *Reference, Volume 2* for more information on the System topic.

Submitting an Item to the Server

The client may send an item value to server by using the WM_DDE_POKE message. The client renders the item to be sent and sends the WM_DDE_POKE message, as illustrated:

```
if (!(hPokeData
      = GlobalAlloc(GMEM_MOVEABLE | GMEM_DDESHARE,
                    (LONG)sizeof(DDEPOKE) + lstrlen(szValue) + 2)))
    return;
if (!(lpPokeData
      = (DDEPOKE FAR*)GlobalLock(hPokeData)))
{
    GlobalFree(hPokeData);
    return;
}
lpPokeData->fRelease = TRUE;
lpPokeData->cfFormat = CF_TEXT;
lstrcpy((LPSTR)lpPokeData->Value, (LPSTR)szValue);
/* each line of CF_TEXT data is terminated by CR/LF */
lstrcat((LPSTR)lpPokeData->Value, (LPSTR)"\r\n");
GlobalUnlock(hPokeData);
atomItem = GlobalAddAtom((LPSTR)szItem);
    .
    .
    .
if (!PostMessage(hwndServerDDE,
        WM_DDE_POKE,
        hwndClientDDE,
        MAKELONG(hPokeData, atomItem)))
{
    GlobalDeleteAtom(atomItem);
    GlobalFree(hPokeData);
}
```

Note that sending data with a WM_DDE_POKE message is essentially the same as sending it with a WM_DDE_DATA message except that WM_DDE_POKE is sent from the client to the server.

If the server is able to accept the data item value in the format in which it was rendered by the client, the server processes the item value as appropriate, and sends a positive WM_DDE_ACK message. If it is unable to process the item value, due to format or other reasons, the server sends a negative WM_DDE_ACK message.

```
hPokeData = LOWORD(lParam);
atomItem = HIWORD(lParam);
❶ GlobalGetAtomName(atomItem, szItemName, ITEM_NAME_MAX_SIZE);
❷ if (!(lpPokeData = (DDEPOKE FAR *)GlobalLock(hPokeData))
        || lpPokeData->cfFormat != CF_TEXT
        || !IsItemSupportedByServer(szItemName)))
{
        PostMessage(hwndClientDDE,
                WM_DDE_ACK,
                hwndServerDDE,
                MAKELONG(0, atomItem));  /* negative
                                            acknowledgement */
}
lstrcpy(szItemValue, lpPokeData->Value); /* copy the value*/
bRelease = lpPokeData->fRelease;
GlobalUnlock(hPokeData);
if (bRelease)
{
        GlobalFree(hPokeData);
        GlobalDeleteAtom(atomItem);
}
PostMessage(hwndClientDDE,
                WM_DDE_ACK,
                hwndServerDDE,
                MAKELONG(0x8000, atomItem)); /* positive ACK */
```

In this example:

❶ The server calls **GlobalGetAtomName** to retrieve the name of the item sent by the client.

❷ The server then determines whether it supports the item and whether the item is rendered in the correct format (CF_TEXT). If not, or if the server cannot lock the memory for the data, it sends a negative acknowledgment back to the client application.

22.4.3 Establishing a Permanent Data Link

A client application can use DDE to establish a link to an item in a server application. When such a link is established, the server sends periodic updates of the linked item to the client (typically, whenever the value of the item changes). Thus, a permanent data stream is established between the two applications and remains in place until it is explicitly disconnected.

Initiating the Data Link

The client initiates a data link by sending a WM_DDE_ADVISE message, as illustrated:

```
if (!hOptions = GlobalAlloc(GMEM_MOVEABLE | GMEM_DDESHARE,
                         sizeof(DDEADVISE))))
        return;
if (!(lpOptions = (DDEADVISE FAR *)GlobalLock(hOptions)))
{
    GlobalFree(hOptions);
    return;
}
lpOptions->cfFormat = CF_TEXT;
lpOptions->fAckReq = TRUE;
❶ lpOptions->fDeferUpd = FALSE;
GlobalUnlock(hOptions);
atomItem = GlobalAddAtom(szItemName);
if (!(PostMessage(hwndServerDDE,
                WM_DDE_ADVISE,
                hwndClientDDE,
                MAKELONG(hOptions, atomItem)))
{
        GlobalDeleteAtom(atomItem);
        GlobalFree(hOptions);
}
```

In this example:

❶ The client application sets the *fDeferUpd* flag of the WM_DDE_ADVISE message to FALSE. This informs the server application that the server application should send the actual data to the client whenever the data changes.

If the server has access to the requested item and can render it in the desired format, the server notes the new link (remembering the flags specified in hOptions), and sends the client a positive WM_DDE_ACK message. From then on, until the client issues a matching WM_DDE_UNADVISE message, the server sends the new data to the client every time the value of the item changes in the server application.

If the server is unable to service the WM_DDE_ADVISE request, it sends the client a negative WM_DDE_ACK message.

Initiating a Data Link With the Paste Link Command

Applications that support hot or warm links typically support a registered clipboard format named "Link". When associated with the application's Copy and Paste Link commands, this clipboard format allows the user to establish DDE conversations between applications simply by copying a data item in the server application and pasting it into the client application.

A server application supports the Link clipboard format by placing in the clipboard a string containing the application, topic, and item names when the user selects the Edit Copy command. The following shows the standard Link format:

application\0*topic*\0*item*\0\0

A single null character separates the names and two null characters terminate the entire string.

Both the client and server applications must register the Link clipboard format, as shown:

```
cfLink = RegisterClipboardFormat("Link");
```

A client application supports the Link clipboard format by offering a Paste Link command in its Edit menu. When the user selects this command, the client application parses the application, topic, and item names from the Link-format clipboard data. Using these names, the client application initiates a conversation for the application and topic if such a conversation does not already exist. The client application then sends a WM_DDE_ADVISE message to the server application, specifying the item name contained in the Link-format clipboard data. The following shows an example of a client application's response to the Paste Link command:

```
void DoPasteLink(hwndClientDDE)
   HWND hwndClientDDE;
{

    HANDLE hData;
    LPSTR  lpData;
    HWND   hwndServerDDE;
    char   szApplication[APP_MAX_SIZE+1];
    char   szTopic[TOPIC_MAX_SIZE+1];
    char   szItem[ITEM_MAX_SIZE+1];
    int    nBufLen;

❶   if (OpenClipboard(hwndClientDDE))
    {
       if (!(hData = GetClipboardData(cfLink)) ||
           !(lpData = GlobalLock(hData)))
       {
          CloseClipboard();
          return;
       }
```

```
❷       /* Parse clipboard data */
        if ((nBufLen = lstrlen(lpData)) >= APP_MAX_SIZE)
        {
            CloseClipboard();
            GlobalUnlock(hData);
            return;
        }
        lstrcpy(szApplication, lpData);
        lpData += (nBufLen+1); /* skip over null */
        if ((nBufLen = lstrlen(lpData)) >= TOPIC_MAX_SIZE)
        {
            CloseClipboard();
            GlobalUnlock(hData);
            return;
        }
        lstrcpy(szTopic, lpData);
        lpData += (nBufLen+1); /* skip over null */
        if ((nBufLen = lstrlen(lpData)) >= ITEM_MAX_SIZE)
        {
            CloseClipboard();
            GlobalUnlock(hData);
            return;
        }
        lstrcpy(szItem, lpData);

        GlobalUnlock(hData);
        CloseClipboard();

❸       if (hwndServerDDE = FindServerGivenAppTopic(szApplication, szTopic))
        {   /* app/topic conversation already started */
            if (DoesAdviseAlreadyExist(hwndServerDDE, szItem))
                MessageBox(hwndMain,"Advisory already established",
                    "Client", MB_ICONEXCLAMATION | MB_OK);
            else
                SendAdvise(hwndClientDDE, hwndServerDDE, szItem);
        }
❹       else
        {   /* must initiate new conversation first */
            SendInitiate(szApplication, szTopic);
            if (hwndServerDDE = FindServerGivenAppTopic(szApplication, szTopic))
            {
               SendAdvise(hwndServerDDE, szItem);
            }
        }
    }

    return;
}
```

In this example:

❶ The client application opens the clipboard and checks whether the clipboard contains data in the Link format (cfLink) which it had previously registered. If not, or if it cannot lock the data in the clipboard, it returns.

❷ Once the client application has obtained a pointer to the clipboard data, it parses the data to extract the application, topic, and item names.

❸ The client application determines whether a conversation already exists between it and the server application on the topic. If it does, the client application checks whether a link already exists for the item. If such a link exists, the application displays a message box to the user; otherwise, it calls its own SendAdvise routine to send a WM_DDE_ADVISE message to the server for the item.

❹ If a conversation does not already exists between the client and server for the topic, the client calls its own SendInitiate routine to broadcast the WM_DDE_INITIATE message to request a conversation and then calls its own FindServerGivenAppTopic function to establish the conversation with the window that responds on behalf of the server application. Once the conversation has begun, the client application calls SendAdvise to request the link.

Notifying the Client that the Data Has Changed

When the client establishes a link with the WM_DDE_ADVISE *fDeferUpd* flag not set (that is, equal to zero), the client has requested the server to send the data item each time the item value changes. In such cases, the server renders the new value of the data item in the previously specified format, and sends the client a WM_DDE_DATA message, as illustrated:

```
/* Allocate size of DDE data header, plus data (a string), plus */
a <CR><LF><NULL>
if (!(hData = GlobalAlloc(GMEM_MOVEABLE | GMEM_DDESHARE),
                          sizeof(DDEDATA)+strlen(szItemValue)+3)))
        return;
if (!(lpData = (DDEDATA FAR *)GlobalLock(hData)))
   {
       GlobalFree(hData);
        return;
   }
lpData->fAckReq = bAckRequest; /* as specified in original
                                  WM_DDE_ADVISE message */
lpData->cfFormat = CF_TEXT;
lstrcpy(lpData->Value, szItemValue); /* copy value to be sent */
lstrcat(lpData->Value, "\r\n"); /* CR/LF for CF_TEXT format */
GlobalUnlock(hData);
atomItem = GlobalAddAtom(szItemName);
```

```
if (!PostMessage(hwndClientDDE,
                WM_DDE_DATA,
                hwndServerDDE,
                MAKELONG(hData, atomItem)))
{
        GlobalFree(hData);
        GlobalDeleteAtom(atomItem);
}
```

The client processes the item value as appropriate. If the *fAckReq* bit for the item is set, the client sends the server a positive WM_DDE_ACK message.

When the client establishes the link with a *fDeferUpd* flag set (that is, equal to 1), the client has requested that only a notification, not the data itself, be sent each time the data changes. In such cases, when the item value changes, the server does not render the value, but simply sends the client a WM_DDE_DATA message with a null data handle, as illustrated:

```
if (bDeferUpd)  /* checking the flag originally set
                        in the WM_DDE_ADVISE message */
{
        atomItem = GlobalAddAtom(szItemName);
        if (!PostMessage(hwndClientDDE,
                        WM_DDE_DATA,
                        hwndServerDDE,
                        MAKELONG(Ø, atomItem)))
                                /* notify client with null data */
        {
                GlobalDeleteAtom(atomItem);
        }
}
```

At its discretion, the client can then request the latest value of the data item by issuing a normal WM_DDE_REQUEST message, or it can simply ignore the notice from the server that the data has changed. In either case, if *fAckReq* is equal to 1, the client is expected to send a positive WM_DDE_ACK message to the server.

Terminating the Data Link

If the client wishes to terminate a specific data link, the client sends the server a WM_DDE_UNADVISE message, as illustrated:

```
atomItem = GlobalAddAtom(szItemName);
if (!PostMessage(hwndServerDDE,
                WM_DDE_UNADVISE,
                hwndClientDDE,
                MAKELONG(Ø, atomItem)))
{
        GlobalDeleteAtom(atomItem);
}
```

The server checks whether the client currently has a link to the specific item in this conversation. If so, the server sends the client a positive WM_DDE_ACK message; it is then no longer responsible for sending updates about the item. If the server has no such link, it sends a negative WM_DDE_ACK message.

To terminate all links for a conversation, the client sends the server a WM_DDE_UNADVISE message with a null item atom. The server checks whether the conversation has at least one link currently established. If so, the server sends a positive WM_DDE_ACK message; it is then no longer responsible for sending any updates in the conversation. The server sends a negative WM_DDE_ACK message if the server has no links in the conversation.

22.4.4 Executing Commands in a Remote Application

A Windows application can use the WM_DDE_EXECUTE message to cause a certain command or series of commands to be executed in another application. The client sends the server a WM_DDE_EXECUTE message containing a handle to a command string, as follows:

```
if (!(hCommand = GlobalAlloc(GMEM_MOVEABLE | GMEM_DDESHARE,
                       sizeof(szCommandString)+1)))
        return;
if (!(lpCommand = GlobalLock(hCommand)))
   {
       GlobalFree(hCommand);
        return;
   }
lstrcpy(lpCommand, szCommandString);
GlobalUnlock(hCommand);
if (!PostMessage(hwndServerDDE,
                WM_DDE_EXECUTE,
                hwndClientDDE,
                MAKELONG(0, hCommand)))
{
        GlobalFree(hCommand);
}
```

The server attempts to execute the specified command string. If successful, the server sends the client a positive WM_DDE_ACK message; if unsuccessful, a negative WM_DDE_ACK message. This WM_DDE_ACK message reuses the hCommand handle passed in the original WM_DDE_EXECUTE message.

Program Manager DDE Command Set

Windows Program Manager features a DDE command-string interface that allows other applications to create, display, and delete groups; add items to groups; and to close Program Manager. The following commands perform these actions:

- **CreateGroup**
- **AddItem**
- **DeleteGroup**
- **ShowGroup**
- **ExitProgman**

Your application's setup program can use these commands to instruct Program Manager to install your application's icon in a group, for example.

NOTE The user can configure Windows to use a default shell other than Program Manager. As a result, your application should not assume that Program Manager will be available for a DDE conversation.

To use these commands, your application must first initiate a conversation with Program Manager. The application and topic names for the conversation are both "PROGMAN". Your application then sends the WM_DDE_EXECUTE message, specifying the appropriate command and its parameters. For example, the following set of commands would add WINAPP.EXE to the Windows Applications group:

```
[CreateGroup(Windows Applications)]
[ShowGroup(1)]
[AddItem(winapp.exe,Win App,winapp.exe,2)]
```

The following paragraphs describe the Program Manager DDE command strings in detail.

CreateGroup

The following is the syntax for the **CreateGroup** command:

CreateGroup(*GroupName*[[,*GroupPath*]]**)**

The **CreateGroup** command instructs Program Manager to create a new group or activate the window of an existing group.

The required *GroupName* parameter is a string that names the group to be created. If a group already exists with the name specified by *GroupName*, **CreateGroup** activates the group window.

The optional *GroupPath* parameter is a string that contains the pathname of the group file. If you do not supply this parameter, Windows will use a default filename for the group in the Windows directory.

AddItem

The following is the syntax for the **AddItem** command:

AddItem(*CmdLine*⟦, *Name*⟦,*IconPath*⟦,*IconIndex*⟦,*xPos*,*yPos*] ⟧ ⟧ ⟧)

The **AddItem** command adds an icon to an existing group.

The required *CmdLine* parameter is a string that contains the full command line required to execute the application. At a minimum, this is the name of the application's executable file. It can also include the full pathname of the application and any parameters required by the application.

The optional *Name* parameter is a string that supplies the title displayed below the icon in the group window.

The optional *IconPath* parameter is a string that contains the name of the file containing the icon to be displayed in the group window. This file can be either a Windows executable file or an icon file created by SDKPaint. If you do not supply *IconPath*, Program Manger uses the first icon in the file specified by *CmdLine*; if that file does not contain an icon, then Program Manager uses a default icon.

The optional *IconIndex* parameter is an integer that specifies the index of the icon in the *IconPath* file which Program Manager is to display. PROGMAN.EXE contains five built-in icons which you can use for non-Windows programs.

The optional *xPos* and *yPos* parameters are integers that specify the horizontal and vertical position of the icon in the group window. You must use both parameters to specify the icon's position. If you do not specify the position, Program Manager places the icon in the next available space.

DeleteGroup

The following is the syntax for the **DeleteGroup** command:

DeleteGroup(*GroupName*)

The **DeleteGroup** command deletes the group specified by the *GroupName* parameter.

ShowGroup

The following is the syntax for the **ShowGroup** command:

ShowGroup(*GroupName*,*ShowCommand*)

The **ShowGroup** command minimizes, maximizes, or restores the window of the group specified by the *GroupName* parameter.

The required *ShowCommand* parameter is an integer that specifies the action that Program Manager is to perform on the group window, and must be one of the following values:

Value	Meaning
1	Activates and displays the group window. If the window is minimized or maximized, Windows restores it to its original size and position.
2	Activates the group window and displays it as iconic.
3	Activates the group window and displays it as a maximized window.
4	Displays the group window in its most recent size and position. The window that is currently active remains active.
5	Activates the group window and displays it in its current size and position.
6	Minimizes the group window.
7	Displays the group window as iconic. The window that is currently active remains active.
8	Displays the group window in its current state. The window that is currently active remains active.

ExitProgman

The following is the syntax for the **ExitProgman** command:

ExitProgman(*bSaveState*)

The **ExitProgman** instructs Program Manager to exit and optionally save its state. The *bSaveState* parameter is a Boolean value which, if TRUE, instructs Program Manager to save its state before closing. If *bSaveState* is FALSE, Program Manager does not save its state.

22.4.5 Terminating a Conversation

Either the client or server can issue a WM_DDE_TERMINATE message to terminate a conversation at any time. Similarly, both the client and server applications should be prepared to receive this message at any time. An application must terminate all of its conversations before shutting down.

The application terminating the conversation sends a WM_DDE_TERMINATE message, as follows:

```
PostMessage(hwndServerDDE, WM_DDE_TERMINATE, hwndClientDDE, 0L);
```

This informs the other application that the sending application will send no further messages and that the recipient can close its window. The recipient is expected in all cases to send a WM_DDE_TERMINATE message promptly in response. It is not permissible to send a negative, busy, or positive WM_DDE_ACK message.

Once an application has sent the WM_DDE_TERMINATE message to the partner of a DDE conversation, it must not respond to any messages from that partner, since the partner might already have destroyed the window to which the response would be sent.

When an application is about to terminate, it should end all active DDE conversations before completing processing of the WM_DESTROY message. Your application should include time-out logic to allow for the possibility that one of its DDE partners is unable to respond to the WM_DDE_TERMINATE message as expected. The following routine illustrates how a server application terminates all DDE conversations:

```
void TerminateConversations(hwndServerDDE)
   HWND  hwndServerDDE;
{
   HWND  hwndClientDDE;
   LONG  lTimeOut;
   MSG   msg;


   /* Terminate each active conversation */
   hwndClientDDE = NULL;
   while (hwndClientDDE = GetNextLink(hwndClientDDE))
   {
       SendTerminate(hwndServerDDE, hwndClientDDE);
   }

   /* Wait for all conversations to terminate OR for time out */
   lTimeOut = GetTickCount() + (LONG)nAckTimeOut;
   while (PeekMessage(&msg, NULL, WM_DDE_FIRST, WM_DDE_LAST, PM_REMOVE))
   {
         DispatchMessage (&msg);
         if (msg.message == WM_DDE_TERMINATE)
         {
             if (!AtLeastOneLinkActive())
             break;
         }
         if (GetTickCount() > lTimeOut)
             break;
    }

   return;
}
```

22.5 Sample DDE Client and Server Applications

The SDK Sample Source Code disk directory named DDE has two source code examples named Client and Server. These examples illustrate most of the DDE transactions discussed above.

The Server application contains a window with three edit controls, labeled "Item1", "Item2", and "Item3". These represent data items for which a permanent data link may be established.

Multiple instances of the Server application may be run. Each instance is associated with a distinct filename ("File1", "File2", and so forth), which serves as the topic name for a DDE conversation.

The Client application contains a menu with commands for issuing the following DDE transactions:

- Initiate
- Terminate
- Advise
- Unadvise
- Request
- Poke
- Execute

In addition, the Edit menus of the Client and Server applications support the Paste Link feature which initiates a hot link for a selected item.

The Client window displays all current conversations by indicating the client and server window handles, and the application and topic names. Below each displayed conversation, the Client window lists any data links that have been established using the Advise or Paste Link commands. The display of the data link includes the current value notified by the server.

The Client application supports conversations with multiple servers, multiple topics for a given server, and multiple data links for a given topic. Similarly, the Server application supports conversations with multiple clients, multiple topics for a given client, and multiple data links for a given topic.

The Client and Server applications are designed with parallel modular structures. Each application has three modules. The first module (CLIENT.C and SERVER.C) handles all user interface transactions, and therefore includes all window and dialog procedures. The second module (CLIDATA.C and SERVDATA.C) manages the data base of all active conversations and data links. The third module (CLIDDE.C and SERVDDE.C) isolates all logic specific to DDE transactions. Given this modular structure, these two source code examples can be more readily adapted to suit your particular application requirements.

22.6 Summary

This chapter explained how to use Windows Dynamic Data Exchange (DDE) to exchange data between two Windows applications. It introduced the core concepts of DDE and described how an application initiates a DDE conversation, requests data or responds to a request for data, and then terminates the conversation. It also explained how to establish "hot" or "warm" links between applications, and how one application can request another application to execute a command.

For more information on topics related to data exchange, see the following:

Topic	Reference
Exchanging data using the clipboard	*Guide to Programming:* Chapter 13, "The Clipboard"
Allocating and using memory blocks for exchanging data in a DDE conversation	*Guide to Programming:* Chapter 15, "Memory Management," and Chapter 16, "More Memory Management"
Sending messages to other applications	*Reference, Volume 1:* Chapter 1, "Window Manager Interface Functions," and Chapter 4, "Functions Directory"
A full description of the Windows DDE protocol	*Reference, Volume 2:* Chapter 15, "Windows DDE Protocol Definition"

Index

Special Characters

A

B

C

D

E

F

G

H

I

M

N

O

Y

Z

Other Titles from Microsoft Press

MICROSOFT® WINDOWS™ PROGRAMMER'S REFERENCE

Microsoft Corporation

If you are a Windows programmer, you need this up-to-date, comprehensive reference to each component in the Windows Application Programming Interface (API). Included is detailed information on every Windows version 3 function, message, data type, resource-compiler statement, assembly-language macro, and file format. This information is the foundation for any program that takes advantage of Windows' special capabilities: data interchange with other applications; device-independent graphics; multitasking; dynamic linking and shared display; and memory, keyboard, mouse, and system timer resources.

1136 pages, softcover 7 3/8 x 9 1/4 $39.95 Order Code WIPRRE

MICROSOFT® WINDOWS™ PROGRAMMING TOOLS

Microsoft Corporation

MICROSOFT WINDOWS PROGRAMMING TOOLS provides detailed information on using the C Compiler and the linker to compile and link source files and the Resource Compiler to compile application resources. In addition, you'll find details on debugging and on using the Resource Editors and optimizing tools (including CodeView) that come with the Microsoft Windows Software Development Kit. Of special importance is the section on the Windows Help system, its design, and its programming guidelines.

384 pages, softcover 7 3/8 x 9 1/4 $24.95 Order Code WIPRTO

WINDOWS™ 3 COMPANION

Lori L. Lorenz and R. Michael O'Mara

This up-to-date resource thoroughly covers Windows version 3—everything from installing and starting Windows to using all its built-in applications and desktop accessories. Novices will value the book for its step-by-step tutorials and great examples; more experienced users will turn to it again and again for its expert advice, tips, and information. The authors detail the features and use of Windows' Program Manager, File Manager, and Print Manager so that users will be able to expertly maneuver through Windows, control the environment, and easily manage files, disks, and printers. Includes a special 8-page section—printed in full color—that highlights Windows' exciting capabilities.

536 pages, softcover 7 1/2 x 9 1/4 $27.95 Order Code WI3CO

TOOLBOOK® COMPANION

Joseph R. Pierce

The first and definitive book on using and understanding ToolBook—the software construction set that makes it possible for users to "desktop program" in the Windows environment. This authoritative tutorial is for anyone—regardless of Windows programming experience—who wants to create Windows applications with ToolBook. Along with step-by-step instructions are dozens of practical examples that show how to create buttons, fields, and other elements in the typical Windows application. Most importantly, there is a special section on using OpenScript, ToolBook's built-in programming language.

720 pages, softcover 7 1/2 x 9 1/4 $27.95 Order Code TOCO

WORKING WITH WORD FOR WINDOWS™

Russell Borland

WORKING WITH WORD FOR WINDOWS is the most comprehensive book available for intermediate users of Microsoft Word for Windows. Written by a member of the Word for Windows development team, this example-packed book will be your primary reference to all the exciting document processing, desktop publishing, and WYSIWYG features of Microsoft Word for Windows. In-depth information, advice, and hands-on examples show you how to customize the user interface, use a variety of fonts and type sizes, insert graphics into documents, use macros to automate routine editing, position text and graphics, link text and graphics within documents, and more.

656 pages, softcover 7 3/8 x 9 1/4 $22.95 Order Code WOWOWI

MICROSOFT® WORD TECHNICAL REFERENCE
For Windows™ and OS/2 Presentation Manager

Microsoft Corporation

The extraordinary power of Microsoft Word for Windows and Word for OS/2 Presentation Manager places them far ahead of conventional word processors and document processors—even desktop-publishing software. They are an ideal platform for developing sophisticated business applications for individual, work-group, or companywide needs. MICROSOFT WORD TECHNICAL REFERENCE is the single source of detailed, authoritative information for advanced users and corporate developers creating applications and document-processing systems with Microsoft Word in the PC environment. This guide includes in-depth coverage on macros and fields, WordBASIC, external file converters, Rich Text Format (RTF), Dynamic Data Exchange (DDE), and Dynamic Link Libraries (DLL).

450 pages, softcover 7 3/8 x 9 1/4 $22.95 Order Code WOTERE

RUNNING MICROSOFT® EXCEL
The Complete Reference to Microsoft Excel on the IBM® PC, PS/2,® and Compatibles

The Cobb Group: Douglas Cobb and Judy Mynhier

Here is the most complete and authoritative guide to Microsoft Excel available anywhere. No matter what your level of expertise—seasoned spreadsheet user, beginning or occasional Microsoft Excel user, or longtime Lotus 1-2-3 user—RUNNING MICROSOFT EXCEL will be your primary source of information, advice, and tutorials. It's packed with step-by-step instructions, scores of examples and tips, and dozens of illustrations, and it covers every significant function and command of the spreadsheet, database, and charting environments. The easy-to-follow tutorial will help you quickly learn both the basics and most advanced features of Microsoft Excel.

736 pages, softcover 7 3/8 x 9 1/4 $24.95 Order Code RUEX

Microsoft Press® books are available wherever quality computer books are sold.
Or call **1-800-MSPRESS** *for ordering information or placing credit card orders.*
Please refer to **BBK** *when placing your order.*